Dear Valued Customer,

We realize you're a busy professional with deadlines to hit. Whether your goal is to learn a new technology or solve a critical problem, we want to be there to lend you a hand. Our primary objective is to provide you with the insight and knowledge you need to stay atop the highly competitive and ever-changing technology industry.

Wiley Publishing, Inc., offers books on a wide variety of technical categories, including security, data warehousing, software development tools, and networking — everything you need to reach your peak. Regardless of your level of expertise, the Wiley family of books has you covered.

- For Dummies – The ***fun*** and ***easy*** way to learn
- The Weekend Crash Course –The ***fastest*** way to learn a new tool or technology
- Visual – For those who prefer to learn a new topic ***visually***
- The Bible – The ***100% comprehensive*** tutorial and reference
- The Wiley Professional list – ***Practical*** and ***reliable*** resources for IT professionals

The book you now hold, *Remoting with C# and .NET,* is your inside look at how Microsoft handles messaging within the .NET Framework. Written by an expert author who was a part of the .NET documentation team, this book helps to explain not just how, but also why remoting works as it does, offering valuable information not available from other books. The road from COM to COM+ to remoting has not always been clear and straight: this book is your roadmap to the new world of messaging for Web Services.

Our commitment to you does not end at the last page of this book. We'd want to open a dialog with you to see what other solutions we can provide. Please be sure to visit us at www.wiley.com/compbooks to review our complete title list and explore the other resources we offer. If you have a comment, suggestion, or any other inquiry, please locate the "contact us" link at www.wiley.com.

Finally, we encourage you to review the following page for a list of Wiley titles on related topics. Thank you for your support and we look forward to hearing from you and serving your needs again in the future.

Sincerely,

Richard K Swadley

Richard K. Swadley
Vice President & Executive Group Publisher
Wiley Technology Publishing

15 HOUR WEEKEND CRASH COURSE

FOR DUMMIES

Wiley Publishing, Inc.

A Note from Gearhead Press

Gearhead Press is dedicated to publishing technical books for experienced Information Technology professionals—network engineers, developers, system administrators, and others—who need to update their skills, learn how to use technology more effectively, or simply want a quality reference to the latest technology. Gearhead Press emerged from my experience with professional trainers of engineers and developers: people who truly understand first-hand the needs of working professionals. Gearhead Press authors are the crème de la crème of industry trainers, working at the companies that define the technology revolution. For this reason, Gearhead Press authors are regularly in the trenches with the developers and engineers that have changed the world through innovative products. Drawing from this experience in IT training, our books deliver superior technical content with a unique perspective that is based on real-world experience.

Now, as an imprint of Wiley Publishing, Inc., Gearhead Press will continue to bring you, the reader, the level of quality that Wiley has delivered consistently for nearly 200 years.

Thank you.

Donis Marshall
Founder, Gearhead Press
Consulting Editor, Wiley Publishing, Inc.

Gearhead Press Books in Print

(For complete information about current and upcoming titles, go to www.wiley.com/compbooks/)

Books in the Gearhead Press *Point to Point* Series

Migrating to Microsoft Exchange 2000 by Stan Reimer
ISBN: 0-471-06116-6

Installing and Configuring Web Servers Using Apache by Melanie Hoag
ISBN: 0-471-07155-2

VoiceXML: 10 Projects to Voice Enable Your Website by Mark Miller
ISBN: 0-471-20737-3

Books in the Gearhead Press *In the Trenches* Series

Mastering SQL Server 2000 Security by Mike Young and Curtis Young
ISBN: 0-471-21970-3

Windows 2000 Automated Deployment by Ted Malone and Rolly Perraux
ISBN: 0-471-06114-X

Robust Linux: Assuring High Availability by Iain Campbell
ISBN: 0-471-07040-8

Programming Directory Services for Windows 2000 by Donis Marshall
ISBN: 0-471-15216-1

Customizing and Upgrading Linux, Second Edition by Linda McKinnon and Al McKinnon
ISBN: 0-471-20885-X

Installing and Administering Linux, Second Edition by Linda McKinnon and Al McKinnon
ISBN: 0-471-20884-1

Programming ADO.NET by Richard Hundhausen and Steven Borg
ISBN: 0-471-20187-1

Making Win32 Applications Mobile by Nancy Nicolaisen
ISBN: 0-471-21618-6

Building Web Applications with ADO.NET and XML by Richard Hundhausen, Steven Borg, Cole Francis, and Kenneth Wilcox
ISBN: 0-471-20786-3

Deploying Solutions with .NET Enterprise Servers by Mike Young and Curtis Young
ISBN: 0-471-23594-6

Remoting with C# and .NET

Remote Objects for Distributed Applications

David Conger

Gearhead Press™

Wiley Publishing, Inc.

Publisher: Joe Wikert
Executive Editor: Ben Ryan
Editorial Manager: Kathryn A. Malm
Managing Editor: Pamela Hanley
New Media Editor: Brian Snapp
Text Design & Composition: Wiley Composition Services

This book is printed on acid-free paper. ∞

Published by Wiley Publishing, Inc., Indianapolis, Indiana
Published simultaneously in Canada

For general information on our other products and services please contact our Customer Care Department within the United States at (800) 762-2974, outside the United States at (317) 572-3993 or fax (317) 572-4002.

Wiley also publishes its books in a variety of electronic formats. Some content that appears in print may not be available in electronic books.

ISBN 0-471-27352-X

Printed in the United States of America

10 9 8 7 6 5 4 3 2 1

About the Author

David Conger has been programming professionally for 20 years. Formerly a Professor at Albuquerque Technical-Vocational Institute, David is currently a contract author and software engineer. He has developed software for military aircraft, games, a variety of small businesses, and interactive TV. For about 5 years, he wrote documentation for Microsoft Corporation. The projects he wrote for include DirectDraw and Direct3D (versions 5 and 6), OpenGL, Extensible Scene Graph (XSG), Image Color Management (ICM), Still Image (STI), Windows Image Acquisition (WIA), Remote Procedure Calls (RPC), the Microsoft Interface Definition Language Compiler (MIDL), and the Mobile Internet Toolkit (MIT). He has also written books on topics such as the fundamentals of microcomputers, and programming in C, C++, and C#.

About the Technical Reviewer

Manish Godse is a developer with bachelor's and master's degrees in Computer Science. He currently works as part of the .Net Remoting team at Microsoft Corporation. A noted expert in .NET Remoting, Manish has participated in several MSDN user chats on the subject.

CONTENTS

Introduction **xv**

Part One An Overview of .NET Remoting **1**

Chapter 1 Remoting, C#, and the .NET Framework **3**

What Is Remoting? 3

What Is the .NET Framework? 4

Why .NET? 5

The .NET Framework Class Library 8

.NET and Java 9

Debugging Support 11

.NET Remoting and Distributed Objects 11

Dynamic Link Libraries (DLLs) 12

COM 12

COM+ 13

Remote .NET Objects 14

Using COM, COM+, and .NET Remoting Together 14

Assemblies 15

Introducing Visual C# 16

What is C#? 16

A Brief Look at Visual Studio.NET 17

Solutions and Projects in Visual Studio 20

Summary 20

Chapter 2 Remote Objects and Remoting **23**

Why Use Remoting? 23

Multitiered Applications 24

Scalability 25

Extensibility 25

Security 27

Centralized Administration 29

Web Services 29

It's Easy 31

The Remoting Architecture 31
Object Activation 32
Server-Activated Objects 32
Client Activated Objects (CAOs) 33
Client/Server Communication Channels 34
The TCP Channel 35
The HTTP Channel 36
Summary 36

Part Two .NET Remoting in Action 39

Chapter 3 Building Applications that Use Remote Objects 41
The Basic Steps 41
A Simple Application 43
Writing the Server 44
Writing a Simple Remotable Object 45
Making the Object Available on the Network 47
Waiting for Connections 49
The Server Program 49
Writing the Client 51
Identifying the Remote Server Object to the Client 51
Connecting to the Server 51
Activating the Remote Object 52
Using the Remote Object 53
The Client Program 53
Using the Application 56
Improving the Application 57
Enhancing the Server 57
Enhancing the Client 61
Summary 65

Chapter 4 Using Remote Objects 67
Remote Object Activation 67
Passing Data 73
Communication Channels 73
Marshal by Value 77
Marshal by Reference 85
Formatters 88
.NET Remoting Rules 89
Summary 95

Chapter 5 Remoting, XML, and SOAP **97**

XML 97

Defining Data Structures in XML 98
The XML in the .NET Framework 101
Reading and Parsing XML Files 102
Writing XML Files 108

SOAP 110

SOAP Messages 112
Data Types in SOAP 114
SOAP and WSDL 115

Summary 116

Chapter 6 Providing Remote Objects for Clients **117**

Compiling Remote Objects into Client Programs 117
Sharing Interfaces 118
Sharing Abstract Base Classes 119
Describing Objects with Metadata 129

SOAPSUDS 129
Wrapped Proxies 130
Unwrapped Proxies 137

Direct Remoting 138
Summary 144

Chapter 7 Remote Object Lifetimes and Leases **145**

Controlling Lifetimes with Leases 145
Renewing Leases 147
Customizing Object Lifetimes 151

The LifetimeServices Class 151
The InitializeLifeTimeService Method 154

Sponsors 164

Server-Side Sponsors 165
Client-Side Sponsors 173

Summary 174

Chapter 8 Configuring Distributed Applications **177**

Essentials of Configuration Files 178
Elements of Configuration Files 180

<service> 181
<wellknown> 181
<activated> 182

<client> 183
<wellknown> 183
<activated> 184
<channels> 185
<lifetime> 187
Configuration Files for Remoting Applications 188
Configuration Files for SAOs 188
Configuration Files for CAOs 194
Configuration Files for Controlling Object Lifetimes 197
Summary 198

Chapter 9 Deploying Distributed Applications 199
Stong-Named Assemblies 200
Installing Distributed Applications 202
Deploying Server Objects as Windows Forms or Windows Console Applications 203
Deploying Server Objects as Windows Services 203
Deploying Server Objects in Internet Information Services (IIS) 214
Versioning Your Application 221
Version Information and Clients 222
Version Information and SAOs 222
Version Information and CAOs 225
Summary 226

Chapter 10 Remoting and Web Services 229
The Wider World of Web Services 229
UDDI, DISCO, and WSDL 231
UDDI Registries 233
UDDI Categories 233
UDDI Data Structures 234
Remoting, Web Services, and ASP.NET 235
FasterCharge: An Example Web Service 237
Designing the FasterCharge Web Service 237
Implementing the FasterCharge Web Service 244
Deploying the FasterCharge Web Service 261
Deploying FasterCharge as a Windows Service 262
Deploying FasterCharge in IIS 265
Summary 266

Part Three Advanced Topics in Remoting 269

Chapter 11 Asynchronous Remoting 271
Asynchronous Calls on Remote Objects 272
Using Delegates for Local Asynchronous Calls 276
Using Delegates for Remote Asynchronous Calls 280
Delegates and Callback Functions 286
One-Way Method Calls 290
The Gotchas of Asynchronous Calls 291
Synchronization Techniques 294
WaitHandle 295
Mutex 295
ManualResetEvent 296
AutoResetEvent 297
Interlocked 297
Summary 298

Chapter 12 Security 301
Secure Code 302
Starting with Strong Names 302
Signcode Signatures 303
Authenticode Signatures 303
Custom Certificates 306
Secure Application Use 306
Secure Channels 306
IPSec 307
PPTP 308
Secure HTTP 309
Encryption 310
Encryption Essentials 310
Custom Encryption in Distributed Applications 312
Encryption Through Custom Channel Sinks 336
User Authentication and Authorization 336
System-Level Authentication 337
Application-Level Authentication 338
Third Party Authentication 338
Summary 339

Chapter 13 Message Sinks and Message Chains 341
Proxies, Messages, and Message Sinks 342
A Detailed Look at Channels 343
Customizing Sink Chains 344
Sink Providers 346

Custom Message Sinks 347
Client-Side Sinks 348
Server-Side Sinks 362
Configuration Options for Channel Sinks 368
Selecting Non-Default Formatters 369
Creating Channel Templates for Custom Channels 370
Summary 372

Appendix 373
Glossary 375
Index 379

INTRODUCTION

People in ancient civilizations saw great value in the timelessness and changelessness of their ways of life. We're nothing like that. In fact, the single most overriding characteristic of modern civilization is change. We love it. We revel in it. We completely reinvent ourselves on almost a daily basis.

Software professionals must perform their labors in this environment of constant change. The software that we write must be easy (or at least inexpensive) to adapt, enhance, and extend. An application that can be readily changed is more likely to meet the needs and expectations of our clients, customers, and employers. To meet these needs and expectations, today's software professionals build often applications by writing multiple programs. Each of these programs performs a specific task or a specific group of tasks. The programs run on computers that are distributed around an organization's network. If the programs are well designed, they can be replaced, updated, and enhanced without disturbing the other programs in the application.

Applications created from a group of cooperating programs are called distributed applications. Developing distributed programs can be excruciatingly painful or relatively straightforward. Which it is primarily depends on how good our tools are. Many different companies and organizations have offered toolsets for writing distributed applications. If you've been around awhile, you may remember remote procedure calls (RPC). RPC enables programmers to invoke functions on remote computers. It was not a particularly straightforward technology to use. Just getting your program to connect to a remote computer was sometimes a challenge. RPC required developers to learn and use a special language, called Interface Definition Language (IDL) to describe the data that was passed to remote procedures. Using IDL can get very complicated very quickly. In addition, RPC forces you to worry about the way to remote computers stored data (for example, whether the computer was little endian or big endian). These and other considerations made RPC a struggle for many programmers.

Companies recognize the difficulties associated with RPC. To make distributed applications easier to develop, they came up with technologies such as Common Object Resource Broker Architecture (CORBA) and Distributed Component Object Model (DCOM). Both of these technologies were based on RPC. In fact, *all* distributed component technology is based on RPC. It's surprising how fundamental RPC is to modern operating systems and applications given the fact that not many programmers know how to use it.

CORBA and DCOM did not eliminate the need for Interface Definition Language. As a result, they do not eliminate all of the complexities of RPC. They did, however, simplify some aspects of writing distributed applications. Specifically, they allowed components written in different languages to interoperate. Nevertheless, debugging CORBA and DCOM components was no easy task. They also caused multiple versions of components to proliferate on users' computers. It soon became clear that better toolsets were required.

In response to that need, a new generation of toolsets and standards for building distributed applications emerged. For instance, the Simple Open Access Protocol (SOAP) toolkit (which is explained in detail in Chapter 5) and the extensible markup language RPC (XML-RPC) protocol define industry-standard methods of invoking procedures or functions on remote computers, passing, data to them, and receiving data from them. These technologies enable programs written in disparate languages on non-homogenous networks to communicate and interoperate in flexible and powerful ways. However, building distributed applications with these SOAP and XML-RPC alone is far too labor intensive to be practical in a large corporate environment.

Among the newest technologies for writing distributed applications is .NET Remoting by Microsoft Corporation. .NET Remoting takes a new and vastly simplified approach to writing distributed applications. Programs written with .NET Remoting can interoperate with components written in different languages. For example, you do not need to use an interface definition language to describe the data passed between programs and components. The .NET Remoting system does this for you. In addition, the class libraries supplied with the .NET Framework vastly simplify the task of getting programs to communicate with remote components. Unlike many Web-based technologies that have emerged for writing distributed applications, .NET Remoting enables you to build stateful objects. It also performs many of the management tasks associated with using stateful objects for you. It gives you an extensible framework that enables programs to communicate through encodings you choose (currently, HTTP or binary). .NET Remoting simplifies the complex issues associated with security and provides you with the ability to add custom security measures.

An Overview of this Book

Invariably, anyone who picks up a book in a bookstore asks the same question, "Why should I buy this book?" The answer is that this book gets you up and running with Microsoft's .NET Remoting very rapidly. It introduces you to the relevant terminology and helps you get past the initial learning curve associated with jumping into the complex world of distributed applications.

Unlike other books on .NET Remoting, I do not assume that you are a programming guru, an expert in building distributed applications, or .NET maven. The .NET Framework and the C# language are relatively new technologies. Many capable and talented software developers are only marginally familiar with them. Therefore, this book introduces .NET Remoting into comprehensible, step-by-step matter. The only assumption I make is that you are a programmer that is somewhat familiar with the C# language. If you have this knowledge, you have what it takes to begin developing distributed applications with .NET Remoting.

Part I reviews the history of the technologies developers have used to build distributed applications. It also presents the essentials of the .NET Framework. You'll learn what it's for and why it's worth bothering to learn to use. You'll see the similarities between solutions based on .NET and those based on Java.

In addition, Part I covers the tools you'll use to build applications with .NET Remoting. Specifically, it provides a look at Microsoft's Visual Studio .NET and the C# language. You'll see that Visual Studio .NET integrates a huge number of tools and technologies to supply you with a powerful and flexible development environment.

Next, Part I shows how .NET Remoting can be used to build multitiered applications, and why multitiered applications are so well suited to today's ever-changing business environment. You'll get an overview of making distributed applications from remote objects. You'll get a look at the architecture of the .NET Remoting system and learn the relevant .NET terminologies and technologies.

As you move into Part II, you begin building distributed applications with .NET Remoting. You'll write client and server programs, and see how to connect them across networks. You'll start with simple, straightforward distributed applications that demonstrate only the most essential techniques to get going with .NET Remoting fast.

Once you've got client programs connected to remote objects, you'll learn the skills you need to get your clients and server objects to exchange data in industry standard formats. Part II explains how these formats enable your application to communicate with remote objects and other distributed systems.

Next, you'll see the different ways of sharing information about remote object with clients at compile time. Each method has its own advantages and disadvantages. Once you've had a look at each of them, you'll be able to select which are appropriate for your applications.

Part II also shows you how to configure objects to control whether they are stateful or stateless. You'll soon be able to manage the "lifetime" of remote objects, enabling you to keep them in memory or throw them away at appropriate times.

In addition, Part II explains how to deploy remote objects and client programs on networks. This can be a very daunting task. However, with the information you'll find here, you'll cut through many of the complexities of this task and quickly build applications that "play nice" in a heterogeneous network environment.

Remote objects can be used on the Internet as Web Services. Part II introduces the fundamentals of Web Services and demonstrates how you can deploy remote objects on your Web server. Using this information, you can provide controlled, secure access to the functionality of your corporate applications across the Web.

By the time you reach Part III of this book, you'll be working at the advanced level. Part III shows you how to execute asynchronous method calls across networks. It also provides a solid introduction to security in distributed applications. You'll see what you can do to build applications that ensure authorized users utilize authorized program code in an authorized manner.

Finally, Part III shows how you can extend and enhance the capabilities of the .NET Remoting system. You'll see the vast possibilities that extending .NET Remoting offers, and get some demonstrations of how it's done.

What You Need to Use This Book

To build .NET Remoting applications, you'll need to use Microsoft's development tools. Specifically, you should obtain Microsoft Visual Studio .NET (Visual Studio version 7). Visual Studio .NET provides you with the .NET Framework, which includes the .NET Remoting system.

All of the example source code in this book is in C#. I do not consider myself an expert in Visual Basic .NET. Therefore I have not provided VB source code. If you are a VB programmer that can read C# code, you'll find this book and its examples extremely helpful.

Obtaining the Source Code

You can download all of the source code for this book from the Wiley web site at wiley.com/compbooks/conger. See the Web Site Appendix for more details.

PART ONE

An Overview of .NET Remoting

Unless you're even more reclusive than I am (that's unlikely), you've undoubtedly heard about all of the new technology the Microsoft has been releasing as part of its new .NET initiative. The focus of most of the marketing blitz seems to be Microsoft's Web-based technologies. Almost unmentioned in the industry press and Microsoft press releases, Microsoft has also released a technology that, in my opinion, will have as profound an impact on programming as any of its Web software. That technology is .NET Remoting.

When I started programming 20 years ago, most computers were not connected to any other computers. The applications we wrote then were small and monolithic. That is, each program was a unit unto itself. It didn't need anything from any other computer.

My, how times have changed. Increasingly, we're using interconnected computers and distributed applications. This trend has been going on for years. Microsoft's .NET Remoting is a step forward in distributed object technology. And, again in my opinion, it's a *big* step forward.

Microsoft has taken a new direction in distributed object with .NET Remoting. As they always do, the developers in Redmond have not only invented a whole new way of doing things, they've invented a whole new vocabulary to go with it. Part One provides you with an overview of what .NET Remoting is, and what it does for you. It also introduces you to .NET Remoting terminology. Even if you're familiar with other distributed object technologies, I strongly recommend you read these chapters.

CHAPTER 1

Remoting, C#, and the .NET Framework

Microsoft has been sticking the .NET moniker on pretty much everything it produces (is Solitair.NET next?). Even though they're called .NET, not all of the technologies Microsoft is releasing are big changes. However, .NET Remoting is both a big change and a significant one. But before we get into that, it's best to talk about what Remoting is.

What Is Remoting?

Remoting, which in my opinion is one of the least descriptive names Microsoft has ever come up with, is a set of software libraries that enable developers to rapidly build distributed software objects. These distributed objects provide services to remote clients.

For example, suppose you work for a company that wants to create online games. One way you can do this is to provide a client program to your users. When they play your games, users would run the client program and connect to your game servers. These computers would provide software objects that implement the game.

.NET Remoting provides the infrastructure for client programs to connect to and use software objects on remote servers. The remote software objects provide the services consumed by the client program. A variety of technologies have been used to accomplish this same task. Before object-oriented programming existed, clients got services from remote programs using Remote Procedure Calls (RPC). With the advent of object-oriented languages, remote client/server technologies also moved toward an object-oriented interface. Microsoft offered the Component Object Model (COM) and later, the Distributed Component Object Model (DCOM). On top of this, it built Object Linking and Embedding (OLE), which it later renamed ActiveX.

Although for its own reasons Microsoft does not say so, .NET Remoting is the successor to DCOM, OLE, and ActiveX. As later chapters will demonstrate, it is much easier to use than those technologies. Part of the reason for this is that .NET Remoting is built on the .NET Framework.

What Is the .NET Framework?

Microsoft's .NET Framework is a new approach to building applications. In many ways, it resembles the Java environment. It is written according to the **Common Language Specification (CLS)**. The CLS defines **Intermediate Language (IL)**, which is roughly equivalent to the object code produced by a conventional compiler. In actuality, IL is very similar to Java's byte code. It is a binary language for a type of computer that doesn't really exist, called a **Virtual Machine (VM)**. Microsoft named this VM the **Common Language Runtime (CLR)**. Programs and components written in a variety of different source languages can be compiled to IL and linked together. Currently, Microsoft has implemented C# (pronounced See Sharp) and Visual Basic (VB) as IL-compatible languages.

NOTE

The CLR and .NET Framework has the potential to be as portable as Java's VM. To its credit, Microsoft has contracted with outside companies to produce versions of them for some commercial versions of Unix. However, its real commitment to portability remains to be seen. (There is an alternative implementation of the .NET Framework being built that is intended to be highly portable. For more information, see `www.go-mon.com`.)

Figure 1.1 shows a simplified diagram of the .NET environment.

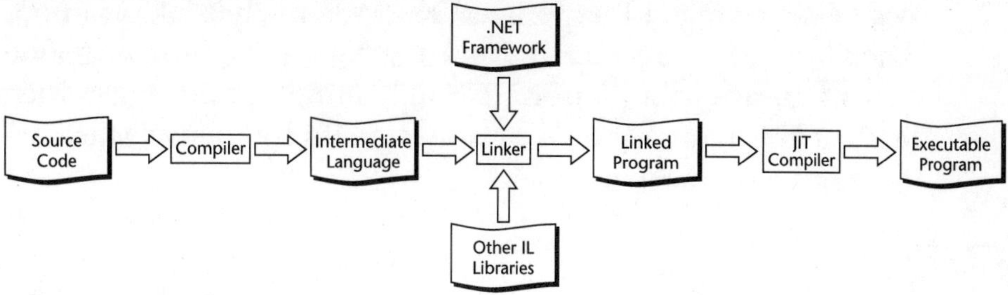

Figure 1.1 The Architecture of .NET

As the figure indicates, CLR-compatible compilers compile source code into IL. The linker combines the IL program with classes, types, constants, and other items from the .NET Framework. It can also link in IL libraries from other sources. These libraries can be written in any programming language that compiles to IL. Therefore, you can write some components of a program in C# and others in Visual Basic.NET.

The linker creates linked IL code, not an executable program. The program stays in this form on the disk until you are ready to run it. When the IL program runs, the CLR compiles it into a native executable binary using its **Just in Time (JIT) compiler**. The JIT compiler translates linked IL into an executable binary program. The linked program is then compiled by the .NET Framework's Just In Time (JIT) compiler, which translates the program from IL into native executable code. After a program has been compiled by the JIT, the CLR keeps it in this form. It does not recompile the program every time a user runs it.

Why .NET?

Microsoft introduced the .NET platform to counter industry trends that threatened its very existence. These were the advent of the World Wide Web, the introduction of sophisticated browser technology, the Open Source movement spearheaded by the people behind the Linux operating system, and the creation of Java.

Microsoft has, from its beginning, been a company centered around its operating systems. However, the growth in popularity of the World

Wide Web changed that forever. The Web really took off in popularity when browsers, specifically Netscape Navigator, became sophisticated enough to use as a platform for delivering applications. Microsoft at first tried to ignore the Web. However, its company leaders soon saw the writing on the wall.

RECOLLECTION

I was working at Microsoft as a contractor when it did a complete about-face and embraced the Web like no other company on earth. The magnitude of the change was startling.

What caused this change was that the entire industry was beginning to see a day when Windows would be irrelevant. Distributed applications delivered through a browser decreased the importance of the underlying operating system. Sun's invention of Java only made matters worse for Microsoft. Java is a portable language that provides a Virtual Machine (VM) that programmers can develop to. This level of portability had long been the Holy Grail of programming. Although programs for the Java VM were slower than programs written directly for Windows, it was only a matter of time before the increasing speed of microprocessors made that irrelevant. To top it all off, the release of Linux, a very powerful and stable and *free* operating system, made it clear that Windows would one day be obsolete.

Microsoft saw that it must embrace open standards to stay alive. It also had to offer something to compete with the interoperability provided by Java. In pursuit of these goals, Microsoft has provided developers with some distinct advantages for developing to the .NET platform. One of them is that the .NET platform provides multilanguage integration. Any programmer who has ever tried to get components written in one programming language to work with components written in other languages understands how difficult this task has been through the years. The .NET platform may just eliminate all of the problems associated with this task. Potentially, all or most all programming languages can be ported to .NET by producing IL-compatible compilers for them. As previously mentioned, Microsoft has already released C# and VB for .NET.

RUMOR MILL

As of this writing, C# and VB are the only IL-compatible languages. You can write managed C++ code, but it is not an IL-compatible language by default. Microsoft has also released a beta version of a language similar to Java called J#. Currently, the

talk around the computer industry is that many companies are working on creating IL-compatible compilers for other languages. Supposedly, there will be versions of Eiffel, Perl, Cobol, and even Java for the .NET platform.

In addition to multilanguge support, the .NET platform goes a long way toward solving one of the most common problems that has plagued developers over the years — memory management. Most professional programs must allocate and deallocate objects in programs as they run. All too often, complex programs do not accurately keep track of allocated memory as they should. This causes memory leaks. A memory leak occurs when a program allocates memory, but doesn't deallocate it.

The .NET platform eliminates memory leaks. Programs written to the CLR are written in **managed code**. When code is managed by the CLR, the CLR keeps track of all memory blocks the program allocates. It automatically deallocates the memory when it is no longer used. This technique is called **garbage collection**. The CLR's use of garbage collection vastly simplifies many aspects of program development.

WARNING

If you're a C++ programmer moving to .NET, be aware that garbage collection has a profound impact on how the CLR handles objects. In particular, destructor functions are not called when an object goes out of scope. The CLR calls destructors when it performs garbage collection. Therefore, you cannot predict when the CLR will call an object's destructor. The result of this is that the role of destructors is greatly diminished in IL-compatible languages such as C#.

Garbage collection and managed code make pointers far less important in IL-compatible languages. Instead, programs generally use references. However, there are times when you need your programs to use pointers and handle memory management themselves. You can do this by marking those sections of the program as **unsafe code**. Code that is marked as unsafe is managed by the CLR, but it sidesteps the normal type-checking and memory management mechanisms.

TIP

Because unsafe code can be a source of memory errors, it is best to avoid using it as much as possible.

In those times when using pointers and handling memory management yourself are important, you may need to write code that is not executed by the CLR. In .NET terminology, this type of code is called **unmanaged code**. Unmanaged code is native code that is not executed by the CLR.

The primary purpose of unmanaged code is backward compatibility with existing program components.

WARNING

Opponents of the .NET platform (particularly Java programmers) have pointed out that unmanaged .NET code can be a source of security problems. In this, they are correct. Therefore, it is wise to make sure you take appropriate security measures in your program whenever you use unmanaged code.

One additional advantage of the .NET platform is that it frees us from having to program directly to the Windows operating system. Prior to .NET, our programs had to call functions from the Win32 operating system application program interface (API). Anyone who has programmed to the Win32 API knows that it can be truly painful. The API was developed by many Microsoft programmers over many years. They were not always consistent about following Microsoft's own published standards. They often added new functions to the API that were similar to, but not the same as existing functions. For those of us outside of Microsoft, it was often confusing as to which functions we should use, and under what circumstances.

.NET programs do not directly access the Win32 API. This is particularly helpful for programmers who are developing distributed applications. You no longer have to worry about whether you're working within Win32, COM, or DCOM. The .NET class library handles that for you.

Because we no longer need to access the Win32 API directly, error handling is much simpler. Have you ever tried figuring out what Win32 errors to trap and how to trap them? Did you ever even try to find a list of all Win32 error codes in the Microsoft documentation? Forget it. Error handling is *much* easier under .NET. If you're familiar with handling exceptions from languages such as C++ or Java, you know how to handle errors under .NET.

NOTE

It is possible to access the Win32 API through the .NET Framework Class Library, which is presented next. The class libraries provide a namespace called Microsoft.Win32. You can use this namespace to call Win32 functions.

The .NET Framework Class Library

The .NET Framework comes with a huge collection (currently in excess of 9,000) of classes, enumerated types, and so forth, called the .NET

Framework Class Library. The class library is the view most programmers see of the .NET Framework. It is divided into namespaces. Each namespace is focused on a particular group of tasks or a particular Microsoft technology. The two namespaces we'll use for virtually every program in this book are System and System.Runtime.Remoting.

It is through the class library that Microsoft preserves platform independence. All of the functions of the operating system are abstracted through the class library. There are classes for threading, data I/O, generating and parsing XML, and much, much more. As programmers, it's wise for us to become familiar with the services offered in the .NET Framework Class Library. It provides us assistance with almost any programming task we do.

NOTE

The .NET Framework Class Library is similar to the Java class libraries. Both of them provide a layer that you and I can develop to that is independent of the underlying operating system.

Because the class library is object-oriented, you and I can use those objects as base classes for classes that we need to build. If you need an object that does just a little bit more than a particular object in the class library, you can use the existing object as a base class and add the new functionality in the new object.

LOOKING FORWARD

Hopefully, the partitioning of the class library into namespaces and the inheritance of objects will help Microsoft continue to keep the API for .NET Framework cleaner and less cluttered than the Win32 API. The class library's namespaces enable Microsoft's developers to replace old technologies with new ones by creating new namespaces. If we want to access the new functionality, we use the new namespace. If we need backward compatibility, we use the old namespace.

The same technique works for inheritance. Microsoft (or anyone else) can derive new objects from the old ones. We can just choose which one we want, the new or old functionality.

.NET and Java

Inevitably, everyone wants to know the difference between .NET and Java. People want to know which of these technologies they should use for their distributed applications. Simply put, .NET and Java are very much the same. They do many of the same things, and do them in much the same way. There are differences on a few key points. In my mind, the most important is security.

As previously mentioned, the .NET initiative preserves backward compatibility by allowing applications to contain unmanaged code. Managed code is (theoretically) always safe. No such guarantees can be made about unmanaged code. If you use unmanaged code to access legacy program components, you must ensure that these components do not contain security holes. This is not an issue if you write only managed code in your application.

Java, on the other hand, does not allow unmanaged code. Therefore, all code written in Java is safe (also theoretically). To attain this security, Java sacrifices backward compatibility. It doesn't work natively with components written in DCOM, for instance. You can get them to work together, but it's not as easy as using DCOM components with .NET.

Another important difference between Java and .NET is that .NET applications currently result in more efficient applications. In the early days of Java, some companies eagerly embraced it and began porting their large programs to it. One of the most notable examples was the WordPerfect Corporation. With rather a lot of fanfare, it began porting WordPerfect to Java. The intent was to create one word processor that would run on the Windows, Macintosh, and Linux operating systems. In the end, the effort was quietly abandoned. The primary reason was that Java turned out to be too slow.

.NET applications, on the other hand, are currently faster. I stress the word *currently* because efforts are under way to rectify the situation. By the time you read this book, there may be no speed difference between them. In addition, it may be that the speed difference won't matter. Every 18 months, microprocessor speeds double. In a very short time, microprocessors may be so fast that users won't notice whatever speed differences exist between Java and .NET.

An additional difference between the two development environments is that when you develop with Java, it provides a single language targeted at multiple operating systems. The .NET development environment provides multiple languages targeted primarily to a single operating system. Applications written with .NET execute almost exclusively on hardware executing a version of Windows.

NOTE

Although .NET applications run almost exclusively on Windows, they can be viewed on many different platforms. For example, the code for applications written with ASP.NET executes on servers running Windows. However, the resulting output can be viewed with virtually any browser running on nearly any operating system.

Debugging Support

The .NET Framework ships with a built-in debugging API. Through this API debugger programs can debug across all IL-compatible programming languages. It is actually possible to use the same debugger to debug components written in VB that make calls into remote objects written in C# that in turn call managed C++ code. Visual Studio .NET uses the debugging API to provide full cross-language debugging support in its IDE.

Microsoft also ships a command-line CLR debugging program, called CORDBG.EXE, with the .NET SDK. It even provides full source code of the CORDBG program so that you can see how to use the debugging API.

.NET Remoting and Distributed Objects

One of the major goals that all programmers strive for is code reuse. We want to be able to leverage our coding efforts across as many different programs as possible. This saves us time and helps ensure we're building programs with robust code. .NET Remoting improves on past methods in the area of code reuse.

Ideally, we want code libraries to be collections of **black box code**. When we use black box code, we don't have to know how it's implemented to be able to use it. For example, suppose you and I are on a project together. Imagine that I write a class called TextString that you will use in your portion of the program. If I write my code as a black box, you do not need to know how the TextString class is implemented in order to use it. All you need to know is how to call the methods in the TextString class.

In Microsoft terminology, objects created by clients from a compiled black box code library are called components. Over the years, Microsoft has advocated other strategies for creating components. As a result, it's easy to confuse .NET componentization with other Microsoft approaches. To help reduce this confusion, let's take a quick look at what's been done in the past.

Dynamic Link Libraries (DLLs)

In the days before object-oriented programming, libraries of functions were compiled together and statically linked with programs. The result was large, monolithic executable file. All programs that used a library contained a copy of it. All that was saved was the effort to write the library.

Later, some very bright people realized that libraries could be dynamically linked to programs. In other words, programs could link themselves to shared libraries each time they executed. All programs that used a library could share the same copy.

The result was smaller executable files. There was also another unintended result that programmers often called "DLL Hell." The problem with shared libraries is that they are shared. That sounds funny, but it's true. Let's say program A needs library X version 1.1. Two years later, the user installs program B, which also uses library X. However, it uses version 2.3. The install program for program B faithfully replaces library X version 1.1 with version 2.3. Now program A no longer works because of version differences in library X. Welcome to DLL Hell.

COM

One limitation of DLLs was that they had to be written in the same language as the rest of the program. It was not possible to combine a program written in Visual C++ with a DLL written in Borland's Delphi. Because it produced multiple programming languages, Microsoft wanted that interoperability. Therefore, it created the COM initiative. COM defines a binary standard to which interoperable components could be compiled. All components compiled to this binary standard could be used together in the same program. The language that the source code was written in did not matter.

COM components were able to interoperate because they communicated through interfaces mediated by COM Services. To successfully recognize each other, they used **globally unique identifiers (GUIDs)** that were stored in the system registry. This created a new version of DLL Hell. It was called Registry Hell. The clash of multiple versions of the same components listed in the registry caused essentially the same problems as DLL Hell. The new twist was that, all too often, programs and components using the registry corrupted it. The most common way to fix it was to reformat the hard drive, reinstall the operating system, and reinstall all of the programs.

A byproduct of requiring registry entries were complicated installation procedures. Your program had to go to great lengths to ensure that it did not create DLL Hell and Registry Hell for your users. If your program caused all of their other applications to stop working, it was generally your program that users got rid of.

NOTE

I've actually had personal experience with this. I installed a desktop publishing program that I bought for about $100. I was happy to get it because it had all the features I needed, and it did not cost $500 (the going rate for desktop publishing programs at the time). Unfortunately, I did not know when I bought it that it had a very simple-minded install program. It replaced some COM components and registry entries on my computer, causing many of my other applications to stop working. When I called the company for help in getting my programs to work with its application, I was told that I needed to update all of my other applications. If I had done that, it would have cost me about $3000. I took the cheap desktop publishing program back and bought one for $500.

Eventually, COM was extended to enable the production of remote components. This new version of COM was named Distributed COM (DCOM). As time passed, COM and DCOM became the basis for OLE and then ActiveX.

COM+

The increasing popularity of distributed components quickly demonstrated that DCOM needed additional services to meet the needs of large corporate applications. To meet this need, Microsoft combined services provided by its Microsoft Transaction Server (MTS) with DCOM. MTS served the same sort of managerial role that .NET now serves.

Microsoft also added message queuing, which originated in MS Message Queuing (MSMQ). In addition, it built in Event Service, which provides a publisher-subscriber method of asynchronous client/server communication, and Load Balancing Service. Microsoft calls this combined package COM+ Services.

Remote .NET Objects

.NET components are objects stored in **assemblies**. Assemblies are very similar to DLLs. As such, they are a complete departure from COM and COM+. For example, .NET objects do not have a GUID in the registry. This vastly simplifies the task of providing remote objects to applications. It also eliminates DLL and Registry Hell and simplifies installation.

Creating a remote object in C# or VB is easy, especially by comparison to creating COM/COM+ objects. As Chapter 3 demonstrates, you can write a simple remote object and its client in half an hour or less. The .NET Framework does most of the work for you. It takes care of creating the underlying plumbing needed to get the client and the server connected. You don't have to worry about GUIDs, ATL macros, using the IUnknown interface, or maintaining reference counts. Your client and server programs simply state the method they will use to communicate and create the communication channel. .NET handles most of the rest.

Using COM, COM+, and .NET Remoting Together

With the advent of .NET Remoting, the fate of COM+ is unsure. Microsoft invested significant resources in the development of COM+. The huge number of COM and COM+ components that are currently in use means that these technologies will be with us for some time. Fortunately, the .NET Framework provides ways to access COM and COM+ components.

First, Microsoft provides a tool called Type Library Importer (TLBIMP.EXE). This tool creates .NET wrappers for COM and COM+ components, enabling them to be called from your .NET programs. In addition, Microsoft ships a program called Type Library Exporter (TLBEXP.EXE). With this utility, you can generate COM components that wrap .NET assemblies, enabling COM components to call remote .NET objects. The purpose of these tools is to enable you to gradually replace old components with remote .NET objects one at a time. This helps keep large distributed systems up and running while they are gradually being upgraded.

NOTE

The Microsoft .NET documentation uses the term "COM Interop" for the topic of using COM/COM+/DCOM objects in the same program with .NET objects. It presents an extensive discussion with examples on how this is done.

Assemblies

As previously mentioned, assemblies contain .NET objects. The objects can be local or remote. Programs can link to local assemblies at compile time. They can also connect to assemblies containing remote objects.

NOTE

In saying that an object is remote, we are saying that it resides outside the application space of the current program. The object may be in another application on the same computer. It can also be located on another computer connected via a network.

Assemblies are, in many respects, more like DLLs than COM components. You might think of them as DLLs on steroids. Unlike DLLs, which usually contain only code, assemblies can hold other information as well. In fact, they can contain up to four different types of data. These are

- **The assembly manifest**. Every assembly carries with it a manifest that describes the assembly's public contents. In particular, it holds the assembly's version requirements and strong name. It also describes the objects and resources in the assembly. In addition, it provides locale information and indicates what assemblies the current assembly references.
- **Type metadata**. Metadata is a language-independent way of describing classes and methods. Type metadata describes all of the objects that an assembly provides for use by classes outside the assembly.
- **Program code in IL**. The assemblies IL code provides the implementation of the objects the assembly offers.
- **Resources**. The resources in an assembly are the standard resources that Windows programmers have been using for years. This includes bitmaps, strings, and so forth.

Although you can write remote .NET objects without really knowing what an assembly contains, there are a couple of reasons why you should take the time to learn what these items are. Among the most important is that the metadata in an assembly helps provide support for multiple programming languages. Also, Chapter 6 will demonstrate that one of ways remote objects can describe themselves to client programs is through sharing metadata. Although there are other techniques for doing this, sharing metadata is one of the most desirable. Knowing, at least, what metadata is helps when it comes time to generate and share metadata between clients and servers.

Programs can uniquely identify each assembly using its **strong name**. A strong name uniquely identifies an assembly anywhere on a network, similar to the way GUIDs identified COM/COM+ components. Strong names consist of the assembly's text name, version, and culture information (if any is provided). It also holds a public key and a digital signature. You can generate strong names for your assemblies with Visual Studio.

I strongly recommend that you assign a strong name to all assemblies that you deploy on your network. The public key and digital signature in the strong name helps ensure that a malicious attacker has not replaced your assembly with one of his own.

Introducing Visual C#

In this book, we'll be using the C# programming language for all of the code examples. If you are familiar with C and C++, the transition to C# should not be difficult at all.

What is C#?

Along with the .NET Framework, Microsoft introduced the C# programming language as a counter offering to Sun's Java. Like Java, C# is derived from the C and C++ programming languages. Languages derived from C have always been favorites with many programmers. That's because the philosophy behind C was to create a language that let you do pretty much what you wanted to, even if it was really off the wall. In fact, it's often been said that C gives you enough rope to hang yourself with great speed and efficiency.

C was created at Bell Labs in the 1970s by Ken Thompson, Dennis Ritchie, and some of their colleagues. In the 1980s, Bjarne Stroustrup, also working at Bell Labs, extended C to include the object-oriented programming techniques that first appeared in a language called Smalltalk. The C++ programming language became very popular because it provided an easy way for C programmers to move to an object-oriented programming language.

C has a very compact syntax. Unfortunately, the same is not true for C++. Like every programming language, C++ has its strengths and weaknesses. One of its weaknesses is that it adds many new keywords and operators. C++ is not always an easy language to learn to program well with. It can surprise even experienced C++ programmers from time to time.

C# extends the object-oriented features of C++. However, it is more like C in that its syntax is more compact. It has fewer keywords than C++. Like Java, C# is designed to be an excellent programming language for the World Wide Web. C# programs can be attached to Web pages via server controls and executed on Web servers when the user's computer loads a Web page. This is actually one way to access remote objects. However, Web pages are stateless. A request to a Web page cannot be connected to any other request. .NET Remoting overcomes this limitation, and enables you to extend the functionality of Web services in ways that server-side controls cannot.

NOTE

At present, Microsoft Visual Studio .NET is the only compiler for C#. Microsoft is submitting the C# language specification to a standards organization so that anyone who wants to can create a C# compiler.

A Brief Look at Visual Studio.NET

Microsoft introduced numerous changes to the development environment of Visual Studio.NET when compared to Visual Studio 6.0. Because many readers may be familiar with VS 6.0 rather than VS.NET, let's take a quick look at VS.NET before developing any .NET Remoting applications.

After you install Visual Studio .NET and set your profile information, you'll see an opening screen is similar to the one shown in Figure 1.2. This opening screen enables you to start a new project or open an existing one.

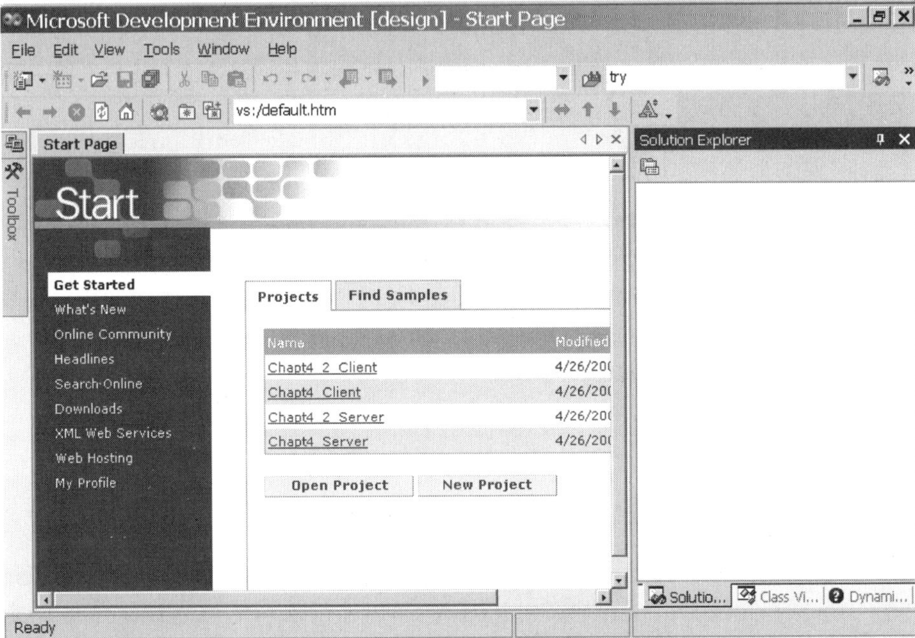

Figure 1.2 Visual Studio's Opening Screen

If you create or open a project, Visual Studio displays its IDE window, which is shown in Figure 1.3. Visual Studio divides its IDE window into multiple subwindows. Each one contains one or more tabbed panels. The panels enable you to examine and edit source files or use IDE tools.

NOTE

Unfortunately, the Microsoft documentation is rather loose in how it uses the term "window." It calls Visual Studio's main window a window. It also says that collection of tabbed panels inside that window is a window. When it speaks of individual tabbed panels that contain C# source code, it calls them edit windows.

While it may be true that these are all various types of windows, using the term "windows" this loosely makes it hard on those writing and reading documentation about Visual Studio. It's hard to specify exactly what you're talking about without showing a picture of it.

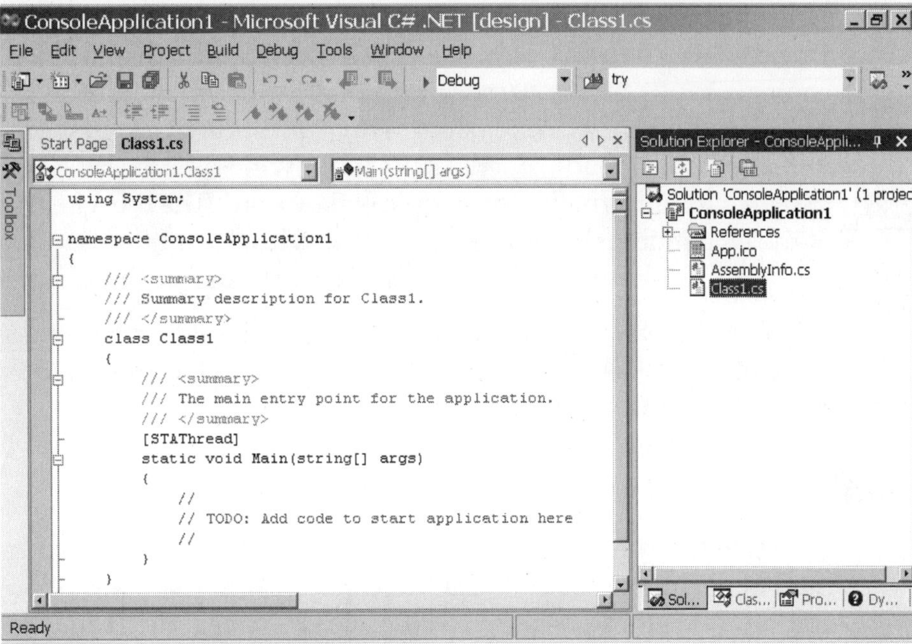

Figure 1.3 Visual Studio's IDE Window

The left pane of the Visual Studio window shows a work area. This collection of tabbed panels can contain a variety of file items. First, and most important, the individual panels can contain source code. When they do, they are called edit windows in the Microsoft documentation. If they contain the rendering of Windows Forms, they are called design palettes, or just designers. They can also display online help text. You view an individual file by clicking on its tab.

Visual Studio's upper right subwindow, or pane, displays the current solution and project. Microsoft calls this the Solution Explorer. Like the left pane, the right pane is a tabbed window. Among the tabs along the bottom of the pane, you'll see the Class View. If you use your mouse to select it, the Class View shows you all of the classes in your program. In the lower right pane , you'll find the Dynamic Help and the Properties window.

Near the top of the Dynamic Help window you'll see three small icons. One resembles a book. If you click it, Visual Studio displays the table of contents for its online help. The second icon at the top of the Dynamic Help window is a piece of paper with a question mark on it. If you click that icon, Visual Studio opens up its Index window. You can use the index to search for information on a topic by keyword. The third icon at the top of the Dynamic Help window brings up Visual Studio's Search window. With it, you can search through the extensive online documentation.

When you compile and link programs, Visual Studio prints messages in the Output window. By default, it displays the Output window across the bottom of its main program window.

Solutions and Projects in Visual Studio

To create the client or server programs you will need for your distributed application, you will first need to create a new solution. Solutions contain everything needed to compile programs. Programmers generally build professional C# programs from many source files. They also combine their source files with components from assemblies. To combine all of the source files and assemblies into one program, you create a project. Projects can be either programs or class libraries. You can create more than one project in a solution. In software released to the professional market, it's not unusual to have several projects in one solution. Typically, some of them are components. At least one of them must be a program.

The Solution Explorer shows a list of all of the projects, source files, and assemblies in the current solution. If you accidentally close a design or edit window you want to work in, the Solution Explorer provides a quick way to open it back up. Just double-click the file's name in the Solution Explorer's list. Visual Studio pops it up in an edit or design pane on the left.

Summary

.NET Remoting is a new technology from Microsoft that enables programs to provided distributed objects over networks. The distributed objects provide services to client programs. .NET Remoting is built on the .NET Framework.

The .NET Framework provides a virtual machine to which programmers can develop applications. The VM is a generic computing environment that is independent of programming languages and operating systems. Programs written to t he .NET Framework automatically have multilanguage support. In addition, the Framework manages memory for us, so it prevents accidental memory leaks. As developers, we can bypass those memory management features by marking code as unsafe. The Framework also provides backward compatibility with existing distributed components through unmanaged code and a technique Microsoft calls **COM Interop.**

We gain access to the services of the .NET Framework and to the underlying operating system through the .NET Framework Class Library. The class library is partitioned into namespaces. When creating distributed objects through .NET's Remoting services, the most important namespace is System.Runtime.Remoting.

There is a distinct difference between .NET Remoting and Microsoft's past efforts to provide distributed objects. It is far less complicated to use than DCOM or COM+.

The basic unit of a .NET component is the assembly. An assembly contains a manifest. It can also contain metadata, IL program code, and resources. Any assembly can be assigned a strong name. Assemblies containing distributed objects should always have a strong name for security purposes.

When it released the .NET Framework, Microsoft also released a programming language called C#. The C# language is derived from C and shares many of the features of Java. Like Java and C++, C# is object oriented. However, its syntax is more compact than that of C++.

CHAPTER 2

Remote Objects and Remoting

Chapter 1 answered the question, "What is .NET Remoting?" This chapter discusses why we use remote objects and explains what types of remote objects are provided by .NET Remoting.

Why Use Remoting?

When a program runs on a computer, it has its own **application space**. The application space is the memory in which the program runs. It contains the application's **program context**. The context is the current state of the program. It includes the program's code, variables, and any data the program allocated from the heap.

Remote objects enable programs to access objects outside their application space. The object can be in the application space of another program on the same computer. It can also be in the application space of a program on another computer. With .NET Remoting, it doesn't matter as long as the two computers are connected by some type of network. If a program uses remote objects, it is said to use objects outside its context boundary. Getting objects to work together across context boundaries is not an easy task. Chapter 3 presents some of the issues involved, as well as how .NET Remoting solves these problems.

As mentioned in Chapter 1, distributed objects have been used in business applications for some years now. There are several important reasons why businesses develop and deploy remote objects.

Multitiered Applications

One of the primary reasons for using remoting and remote objects is that they enable developers to create **multitiered applications**. Applications that contain multiple tiers separate the functions they perform into components that can be distributed across a network. Figure 2.1 illustrates a typical 3-tier application.

The lowest tier in the application in Figure 2.1, which is often called the data tier, offers the services of the company's database. The middle tier implements the company's rules and policies. The top tier is the presentation tier. It provides the user's view of the company's data.

Each tier in this application performs a specific function. The interfaces between the tiers are well defined. The programs in any tier do not have to "know" anything about the internal operation of the programs in other tiers. As long as the interface between the tiers stays the same, a company can completely change the implementation of any one layer. So, for instance, it could switch to a new database program without affecting the other tiers.

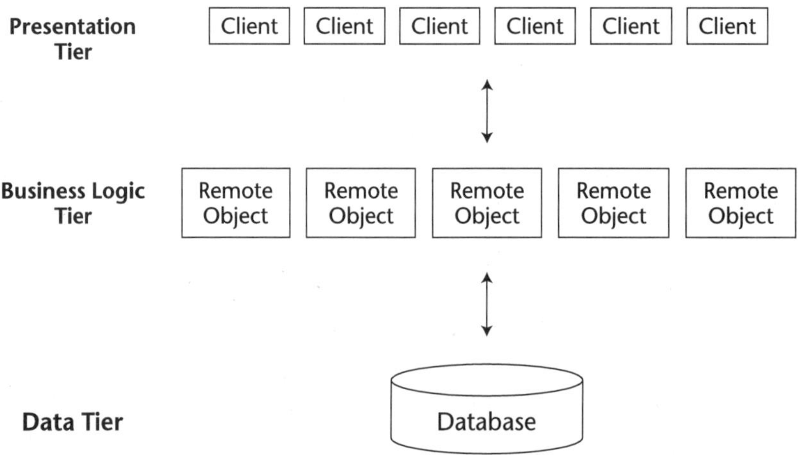

Figure 2.1 A 3-Tier Application

Scalability

Using a 3-tiered approach increases the scalability of the application. This is important to growing companies. For example, the database tier can consist of multiple computers each offering access to the database. As the need for access increases, new database servers can be added without disrupting the operation of current servers (in theory, at least). The programs in the other tiers have no knowledge of which database server they are using or how many of them there are. It doesn't matter. They can access any computer in the cluster of database servers and get the same functionality.

Programs in a particular tier gain access to programs in another tier across the company's network. Therefore, the programs in any given tier can be anywhere in the world. As long as they are accessible across the network, their physical location does not matter. This enables companies to rapidly expand into new markets and move to new locations. The application easily scales as the company grows.

Extensibility

Multitiered applications can be adapted to new technologies as they appear. For example, when the Web became an important technology, multitiered applications were adapted to integrate with it. Two approaches were typically used to accomplish this. The first uses the company's Web site as the presentation layer, as shown in Figure 2.2. The second inserts a client program between the server object and the Web site. This is depicted in Figure 2.3.

Using a Web site as the presentation tier means that there are fewer pieces of software to write and maintain. However, using a special client to provide Web access means that the remote objects do not have to be changed when a new technology appears. When the World Wide Web became important, companies with multitiered applications often provided Web access by writing a new client that "talked" to the Web site and to the business tier. It converted input from the Web site into a format recognized by programs in the middle tier. When it received output from the middle tier, the client converted it into a format recognized by Web browsers. As far as the program in the middle tier could tell, they were dealing with the same kind of client it always dealt with. Simply adding a specialized piece of client software was often all it took to enable Web access to many existing applications.

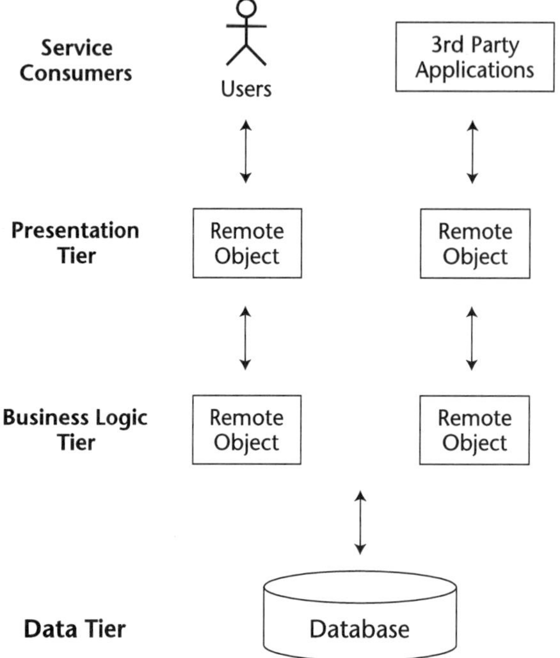

Figure 2.2 Using a Web Site as the Presentation Tier

Being able to rapidly integrate the Web into existing applications was a tremendous boon to many companies. With the current rapid pace of software development, it is likely that new technologies will appear in the near future whose importance will rival that of the World Wide Web. Distributed applications using remote objects provide businesses with the flexibility needed to integrate new technologies into their existing software infrastructure.

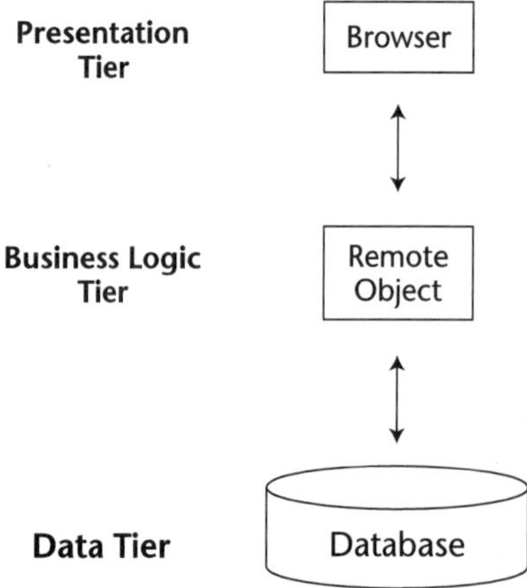

Figure 2.3 Connecting a Client Program to the Web Site

Security

Another strong motivation for using remoting and remote objects is security. Suppose that you are asked to create a Web site for a company that provides information from the company's database to potential customers. There are a few different ways to build such a site. The first method is shown in Figure 2.1.

The Web site in Figure 2.4 generates SQL queries, which it sends to the company's database; the database responds by sending the data back to the Web site. Now let's ask ourselves, what would happen if a malicious attacker got control of the Web site? Potentially, he could send *any* SQL query to the database. Even if he can't gain the ability to change data, he can get access to *all* of the data in the database. This is a serious security breach. The firewall shown in Figure 2.4 may prevent the attacker from gaining direct control of the database server. However, it does little to protect the actual information the database contains.

The illustration in Figure 2.5 offers a solution to this problem through the use of a remote object.

The application in Figure 2.5 is distinctly more secure than that shown in Figure 2.1. This version of the application uses a multitiered approach. The Web page still generates requests for information. The requests may or may not be in SQL (probably not). The request goes to a client program on the Web server. The client program calls a remote object on a server. The remote object searches the database for information and sends it back to the client, which in turn sends it to the Web page. There is a firewall between the Web page and the client program, and another between the client and the server.

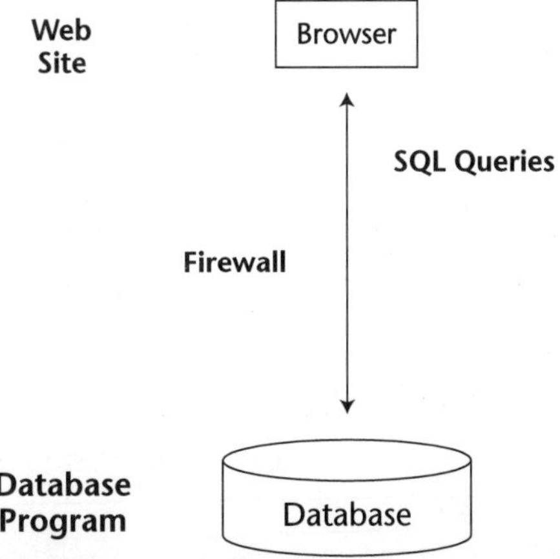

Figure 2.4 A Web Site that Queries a Database

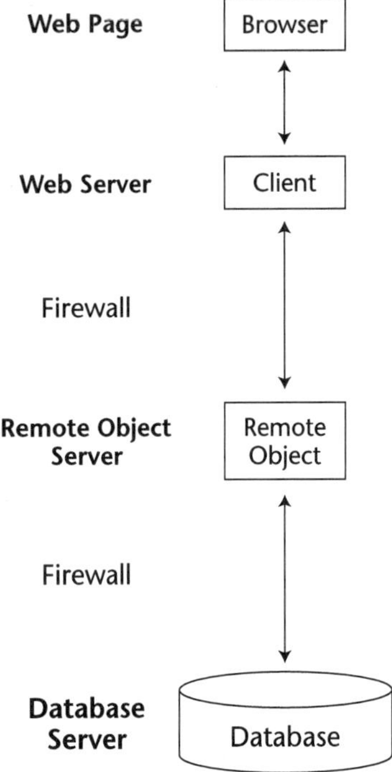

Figure 2.5 Querying the Database Through a Remote Object

In this scenario, access to the database is strictly controlled. The client program is written in such a way that it recognizes requests only for the information that the company wants made public. Even if a malicious attacker gains control of the Web server and uses it to send queries for confidential information, the client program rejects all such requests. The use of two firewalls in the application makes it difficult, if not impossible, for attackers to gain access to the corporate database. Both the computer on which the database resides and the information in the database are highly protected from unauthorized attack.

Remoting also enables companies to enforce their security policies through **role-based security**. Companies that use role-based security provide client programs targeted toward particular types of users. Each type of user is granted very focused access to company information by the client.

For instance, imagine that you are writing a client/server program for a bank. The server program for this application must authorize access to data according to the role of each user. As the system developer, you would give bank executives a client program that is able to perform all types of transactions allowed by the bank's security policies. Bank tellers would receive a different client program because they have a different role in the organization. You would create yet another client program for automatic teller machines, which provide database access directly to customers. The type of transactions each client could perform would depend on the role of the person using the software. Executives, tellers, and customers each have different levels of security clearances. These are enforced by the software.

Centralized Administration

Building distributed applications from remote objects eases the burden of maintaining software. The majority of the application's program logic resides on the server, not the client. As a result, updating the application often means updating just the servers rather than client programs on thousands of PCs spread across the world. The administration of the application is centralized on one server or a centralized group of servers that the company's information technology staff has direct access to.

In addition to making deployment simpler, centralized administration makes it easier to provide redundant servers. In the event of one server failing, backup servers can handle the load until the problem is handled. In fact, using remote objects, even an entire data center can be made redundant. Companies can use multiple data centers located in distant parts of the world. If a disaster, such as an earthquake or flood, destroys one data center, the other handles the load until repairs are made.

Web Services

Microsoft is currently promoting a technology it calls **Web services**. If a Web site provides a Web service, it exposes some or all of the functionality of the company's multitiered application. External developers can use that functionality in applications of their own. Web services are generally not for end users. They are for developers. Figure 2.6 contrasts Web services and Web pages.

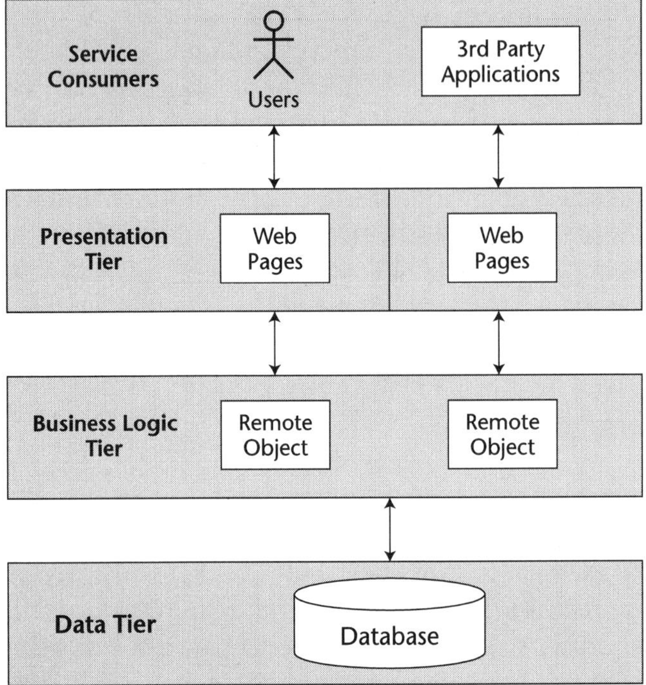

Figure 2.6 Web Services and Web Pages

To illustrate the type of service that Figure 2.6 depicts, suppose that you work for a credit card company called FasterCharge. Credit card verification companies need a way to validate your customers' FasterCharge cards whenever your customers charge something. Your company has an internal distributed application that does this. If you create a Web service, you can provide that functionality to credit card verification companies. Other credit card companies can provide the same functionality for their cards on their Web sites. Credit card verification companies can build their own application that uses the verification functionality exposed by all of the credit card companies. They can then provide their verification service to merchants.

Web services are becoming increasingly important in business today. Microsoft's .NET Remoting is one way to implement them.

NOTE
Web services are covered in greater detail in Chapter 10.

It's Easy

Most of the preceding discussion consists of reasons for using remote objects, rather than .NET Remoting. Simply put, .NET Remoting is easier to build and integrate remote applications with than anything else out there. Others come close, particularly Java's J2EE. However, to my knowledge, no other remote object technology makes it as easy to create distributed objects. Nothing else "plays nice" with existing distributed technologies as well as .NET Remoting. Microsoft has done an excellent job of building a first-class, distributed application infrastructure.

The Remoting Architecture

.NET Remoting enables client programs to call methods of remote objects. When the client creates a connection to the server object, the .NET Framework creates a proxy object on the client. The proxy object provides the client with the same view of the server object that it would have if the server object were in its application space. It can call the server object's methods through the proxy object. Figure 2.7 depicts this process.

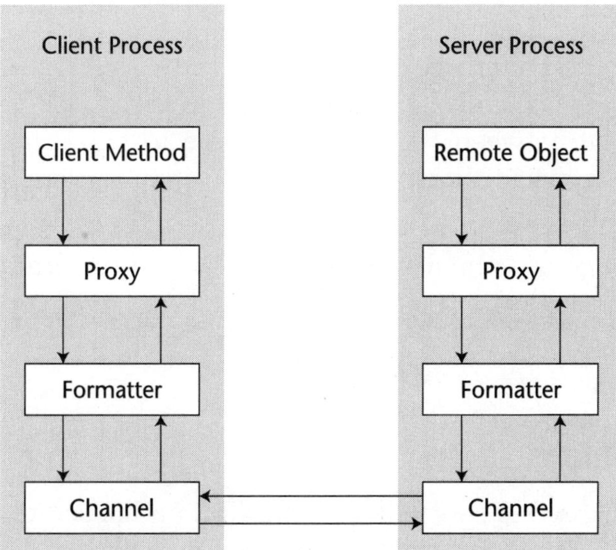

Figure 2.7 How Remoting Works

The figure shows a client method that calls a method on the remote object through the proxy object created by CLR at runtime. Any data passed by the client method to the proxy is packaged by a formatter so that it can be sent across the network. The process of packaging the data for transmission is called **marshaling**.

NOTE

Chapter 4 presents more information on marshaling.

After the data is marshaled by the formatter, the CLR sends it through the channel, out across the network to the server. A formatter on the server unmarshals the data and calls the appropriate method on the server. It passes the data to the method. When the server object's method finishes its processing, it sends any data it might need to return back to the formatter, and the entire process is reversed.

Object Activation

Remote objects come in two flavors, objects that are marshaled by value and objects that are marshaled by reference. Objects that are marshaled by value are copied between the client and the server. Objects that are marshaled by reference reside only on the server. This type of object is often called a **reference object**.

Within the category of reference objects, there are two subtypes, server-activated objects (SAOs) and client-activated objects (CAOs). To understand the different between the two, you have to know that every remote object has a specific **lifetime**. An object's lifetime is the length of time it resides in memory.

NOTE

Chapter 7 presents a detailed discussion of object lifetimes and how they are controlled.

Server-Activated Objects

The lifetime of an SAO is controlled by the CLR on the server. Server-activated objects do not keep state information between calls from the client. Because SAOs do not keep their state between uses by clients, they are called stateless objects.

An SAO can be either a **single-call object** or a **singleton object**. The CLR creates single-call objects each time a client invokes one of its methods. Therefore, it is probable that multiple copies of a single-call object could be in the server's memory at any given moment.

If an object is defined as a singleton object, the CLR creates only one instance of it. That one instance services all client requests. Because of the way object lifetimes operate, it is possible for the lifetime of a singleton object to expire while the program runs. If it does, the CLR creates a new copy of the singleton object when the next client request arrives. Therefore, the client will be dealing with a new instance of the remote object. The new instance generally does not contain the information the old instance had. You cannot assume that just because all client requests are serviced by the same singleton object that it still contains information given to it previously. Like single-call objects, singleton objects are considered stateless.

WARNING

A singleton object is said to be recycled if its lifetime expires, it is deleted, and the CLR creates a new instance of it. Singleton objects may be recycled even if a client holds a reference to it. This is very different from the way that COM operates.

When a client creates a remote object that is defined as an SAO, it only creates the SAO's proxy object. The CLR on the server does not create the SAO until the client invokes one of the object's methods. As a result, clients may only use an SAO's default constructors to create it.

It is possible for your server program to create singleton objects with indefinite lifetimes. You might want to do this if, for instance, you are creating an object that implements a multiplayer network game in which all clients in the game log into a central server object. If the game's server object is a singleton with an indefinite lifetime, it will continue to service all of the clients for as long as the game continues.

Client Activated Objects (CAOs)

Client activated objects provide functionality that is similar to a COM component. However, you do not have to worry about maintaining object references with .NET Remoting as you do with COM. When the client creates a CAO, the CLR on the client's computer creates the proxy. It also sends a message to the server to cause the CLR on the server to create the remote object. The server returns a reference to the remote object to the client. From then on, that instance of the remote object will only service requests made through the reference it sent to the client. The client can create other instances of the same type of remote object. Each will have a unique reference.

NOTE

CAOs keep their state between uses by clients. Therefore, they are called stateful objects.

The lifetime of a CAO is determined by several factors, many of them set by the client. However, the CLR has mechanisms for recycling the CAO if the client becomes disconnected from the network. Specifically, if the server does not receive calls on the object from the client for a while, the CLR checks to see if a special type of object called a sponsor has been registered for the CAO. If it has, the CLR pings the sponsor to see if the server object should be marked for deletion. If sponsor does not extend the CAO's lifetime, it does not answer, or there is no sponsor, the CLR marks the server object for deletion the next time it does garbage collection. Chapter 7 presents a detailed discussion of sponsors.

JARGON

The term ping comes from an program that was widely used on Unix to test whether computers were active on networks. When you used the ping program to send a signal to a remote computer, it would return a reply if it was active. More recently, the term has been expanded to cover the same concept in a wider variety of situations.

Client/Server Communication Channels

For remote objects to communicate, both the client and the server programs must be connected to the same communication channel. Channels connect via server ports. The .NET Framework requires your application to register the channels you use. When you do, you must select the port the channel connects through. If you are unsure about what port is available on your client, you can register the channel with a port number of zero. When you do, the .NET Framework assigns the first available port to the channel.

Remote server objects can communicate with clients through more than one channel. However, remote objects do not "own" individual channels.

When your server program registers a channel, the CLR creates a channel object that listens to the port. If your server program is able to create multiple types of remote objects, requests for any of those objects can come over the registered channel. So if your server offers two remote objects, called A and B, it can process requests to execute A's methods and B's methods over the same channel.

It is possible for you to run multiple instances of a program on the same computer. If you run multiple instances of your server program, be careful. If the first instance assigns a particular channel to a particular port, other instances of the program cannot assign the same channel to the same port. Channels objects are essentially global to the CLR. Therefore, additional instances of the program must use a different port or a different channel.

The .NET Framework currently supports two kinds of channels for remoting, TCP and HTTP. Because .NET Remoting is highly extensible, you can add additional channels. Chapter 14 shows an example of how to do this by implementing a channel using the POP3 mail protocol.

The TCP Channel

Throughout the years, many networking protocols have come and gone. However, the most lasting and popular is also one of the first ever invented, Transmission Control Protocol/Internet Protocol (TCP/IP). TCP/IP is not a network operating system. Rather, it is a set of protocols that operating systems can use to communicate over a network.

NOTE

A protocol is like a language. When we connect computers into a network, the operating systems of each computer must speak the same "language" (use the same protocol) to communicate with each other. TCP/IP is the protocol used for the Internet.

The TCP portion of the TCP/IP protocol is connection oriented. This means that it provides a point-to-point, guaranteed-delivery service between two computers on a network. This generally implies that the computers are on the same network with no firewalls between them. As a result, the TCP channel is most appropriate for use on corporate LANs and WANs, rather than the Internet.

NOTE

The TCP channel connects the client and the server using a technology called sockets. You do not have to be familiar with sockets to use the TCP channel.

Distributed applications that use the TCP channel transmit their data in binary. This usually ends up being faster and more compact than using the HTTP channel (which is discussed next).

The HTTP Channel

TCP/IP is considered a mid-level network protocol. Low-level protocols define the meaning of the electrical signals that pieces of networking hardware exchange with each other. Mid-level protocols define the meaning of the data that the hardware transmits across the network. There are high-level protocols as well. One of them is Hypertext Transfer Protocol (HTTP).

HTTP is typically used over TCP/IP, but it can work on top of any mid-level networking protocol. The advantage of HTTP is that it is able to pass information through firewalls. This makes it ideal for use across the Internet. The HTTP channel transmits data in Extensible Markup Language (XML). Data in XML format is implemented as text strings. The strings describe data using a set of industry-standard terms. This set of terms is called Simple Object Access Protocol (SOAP).

NOTE

SOAP describes data in a way that is independent of any company, programming language, or transmission method. It is finding extremely wide use in the software industry today.

The HTTP protocol defines a set of **request messages** that clients transmit to servers. Servers send back **response messages**. HTTP messages contain an envelope, a header, and a message body. Applications that use the HTTP channel transmit SOAP strings in the message's body.

OPINION

You do not have to know the details of how HTTP, XML, and SOAP are implemented to use the HTTP channel. However, as Chapter 13 shows, knowing these details can help when you implement your security policies. Security is important for remote objects you make available over the Internet.

Summary

.NET Remoting enables rapid construction of multitiered applications. It provides a scalable architecture that can be used for enterprises of virtually any size. It is extensible, customizable, and provides a number of security features. Creating distributed object through .NET Remoting enables companies to centrally administrate the servers that provide the core code they use to run their businesses. In addition, .NET Remoting offers organizations the ability to provide Web services for their business partners and customers.

Remoting is based on two types of objects, those that are marshaled by value and those that are marshaled by reference. Objects that are marshaled by reference can be server-activated objects or client-activated objects. Server-activated objects can be either singleton objects or single-call objects. Server-activated objects are stateless.

Clients and servers communicate through channels. The .NET Framework currently provides two types of channels, TCP and HTTP. The TCP channel is more appropriate for the internal network of a company. The HTTP channel is well-suited for applications used across the Internet.

PART TWO

.NET Remoting in Action

With the knowledge of .NET Remoting concepts that you gained from Part 1, you are now ready to start building your own distributed applications. This part of the book provides you with a step-by-step guide for building applications with .NET Remoting.

First, you'll learn how to write client and server programs and get them talking to each other. This involves writing remote objects, server programs to host them, and client programs that access them. In addition, it involves sharing both compile-time and run-time information about remote objects between clients and servers. There are various methods for accomplishing these tasks. Each of the different methods requires you to build your program in a slightly different way. They also influence how the program operates.

This part also delves into the details of the communication channels that distributed applications use to connect clients to servers. It describes and demonstrates how the .NET Remoting system packages and unpackages information when it is transmitted across networks.

Remote objects have definite limits on the time spans when they are active in memory. Part Two explains and illustrates how you can customize and control those time spans. It also demonstrates how to configure your distributed application for a variety of environments and how to deploy it to those environments.

Finally, this part of the book explains the essentials of Web Services and how you can use .NET Remoting to implement them.

CHAPTER 3

Building Applications That Use Remote Objects

The previous chapters provided an overview of .NET Remoting and its uses. Beginning with this chapter, you'll get some hands-on experience with writing programs that use remote objects. This chapter is an overview of remote application implementation. The program developed in this chapter demonstrates the simplest way to create a distributed program using .NET Remoting. The techniques shown here are not the best way to create a production-quality application. However, they will get you up and running with the basics right away. Later chapters show how to enhance these basic steps to create distributed applications that you can release for professional use.

The Basic Steps

When you write a distributed application, you must write both the client and the server programs. The server implements the remote objects. The client consumes the services offered by the remote objects on the server.

To write a server program, you must do the following:

1. *Write the remote object.* This includes implementing all of the object's methods, properties, and so forth.

2. *Create or select a method of hosting the object on the server.* The server makes the remote object available to the network so that clients can connect to it. You must either write a program to host the object or use Internet Information Server (IIS) to host it. Chapter 9 covers both of these techniques in detail. In this chapter, you'll write a program that hosts a remote object.
3. *Prepare for client connections.* The program that hosts the remote object must perform the setup necessary for the object to receive client connections. There are ways of moving these setup tasks into configuration files. For more information, see Chapters 8 and 9.
4. *Wait for client connections.* The object must wait for clients to connect and consume its services.

When writing a client program, use these steps:

1. *Identify the remote server object to the client.* The client program must be able to "see" the remote object on the server. There are multiple ways of accomplishing this, each with its own advantages and disadvantages. See Chapter 6 for details.
2. *Connect to the server.* The client must create a communication channel and connect to the server.
3. *Activate the remote object.* The client program needs to activate the remote object and create a reference to it.
4. *Use the remote object.* Once the preparation is complete, the client program can use remote objects very much the same way they do local objects.

The remainder of this chapter demonstrates straightforward methods of accomplishing these tasks. As you can see, they are considerably simpler than those required by previous remote technologies such as remote procedure calls (RPC) and Microsoft's distributed common object model (DCOM). You do not have to worry about managing object reference counts. Nor do you need to learn a data definition language such as Microsoft Interface Definition Language (MIDL). The simplicity of .NET Remoting when compared to previous technologies is nothing less than amazing, at least to me. It is a major step forward in distributed object technology.

However, just because .NET Remoting is easier to use doesn't mean that it is less powerful or flexible than previous technologies. In fact, my opinion is that quite the opposite is true.

A Simple Application

The first remoting application you'll create in this book simulates how client programs might access a database through a remote object. In this example, the client connects to an object of type `InformationManager`. It calls the object's methods to obtain data from the server. In this case, the data items it receives are strings.

Before you can begin developing the application, you need to create the client and server projects in Visual Studio. Use the following steps to create your projects.

1. Start an instance of Visual Studio for the client program.
2. In the main menu of Visual Studio, select **New**, and then choose **Project**.
3. In the **Project Types** box, select **Visual C# Projects**. In the **Templates** box, choose **Console Application**.
4. Use **Chapt3Client** as the name of the project. Enter the path where you want the solution to be created on your hard drive, or just use the default path provided by Visual Studio. Click OK.
5. The client project has a file called Class1.cs. Delete it from the Solution Explorer.
6. The Solution Explorer also shows that the client project contains an item called **References**. Right-click this item and select **Add Reference**.
7. In the dialog box that appears, scroll the list labeled **Component Name** until you see System.Runtime.Remoting. Double-click that item.
8. Start another instance of Visual Studio for the server program.
9. In the main menu of Visual Studio, select **New**, and then choose **Project**. Like the client, this project should also be a C# console application.
10. Use **Chapt3Server** as the name of the project. Enter the path where you want the solution to be created on your hard drive, or just use the default path provided by Visual Studio. Click OK.
11. The server project has a file called Class1.cs. Delete it from the Solution Explorer.

12. The server project contains an item called **References**. Right-click this item in the Solution Explorer and select **Add Reference**.
13. In the dialog box that appears, scroll the list labeled **Component Name** until you see System.Runtime.Remoting. Double-click that item.

You're now ready to begin developing the application. Let's start with the server program.

Writing the Server

The server program for our database simulator application only requires two source files. One of them will contain the application class with a method called `Main()`. The other contains a class that implements the remote object. Although it is true that these could be kept in the same file, it is better to separate them into two files. The reasons for this will become clear in later chapters as we look at the various ways remote objects can be shared.

It's generally best to put the source code for the remote object into a source file by itself. The reasons for this will become clear soon.

To simulate a database, the `InformationManager` class will contain an array of strings. It will allocate the array when it is instantiated. The `InformationManager` class must provide at least one method that enables the client to access strings in the array. The client will pass the array index of a string to the method. The method will return the requested string.

This process is similar to the one clients use to query databases through a remote object. They generally pass an identifier or a search key to the server object. In many implementations, the server object would formulate an SQL query to get the requested information from a database. After it retrieves the data, the server object would return the requested data to the client. As mentioned in Chapter 2, this process is more secure than providing direct access to the database from a Web page.

When you create client and server programs, you must think about the namespaces they use. For simplicity, the `InformationManager` object will be in the same namespace as the server program's application class.

In general, this is not the best practice. Better methods, and the reasons for using them, will be demonstrated later.

Writing a Simple Remotable Object

.NET Remoting provides multiple ways of making an object remotable. These are discussed in detail in Chapter 4. The essence of that discussion is that remote objects are like local objects. They can be passed by value or by reference. After an object is passed by value, a copy of it exists in the program domains of both the client and the server.

On the other hand, if an object is passed by reference to the client program, it exists only on the server. Clients must access its methods through the reference. This is the technique we'll use in this sample program. To do this, we must derive the `InformationManager` class from the `MarshalByRefObject` class in the System namespace.

Listing 3.1 shows the implementation of the remotable `InformationManager` object. Note that I've added line numbers to the listing to make it easy to discuss individual lines of code. The line numbers do not appear in the actual code that you obtain from the Web site.

NOTE

See Obtaining the Source Code in the Introduction for more information on downloading the source code from the Web.

```
using System;
using System.Runtime.Remoting;



namespace Chapt3_Server
{
    public class InformationManager : MarshalByRefObject
    {
        //
        // Private Data.
        //

        private string [] theData = new string [ARRAY_SIZE];

        public const int ARRAY_SIZE = 13;

        //
```

Listing 3.1 The InformationManagerObject *(continues)*

```
19            // Public Methods
20            //
21
22            public InformationManager()
23            {
24                // Initialize the array.
25                theData[0] = "In a village of La Mancha, ";
26                theData[1] = "the name of which I have no desire ";
27                theData[2] = "to call to mind, there lived ";
28                theData[3] = "not long since one of those ";
29                theData[4] = "gentlemen that keep a lance in the ";
30                theData[5] = "lance-rack, an old buckler, a lean ";
31                theData[6] = "hack, and a greyhound for coursing. ";
32                theData[7] = "An olla of rather more beef than ";
33                theData[8] = "mutton, a salad on most nights, ";
34                theData[9] = "scraps on Saturdays, lentils on ";
35                theData[10] = "Fridays, and a pigeon or so extra ";
36                theData[11] = "on Sundays, made away with ";
37                theData[12] = "three-quarters of his income.";
38            }
39
40            public String DataItem(int whichItem)
41            {
42                string theItem = null;
43
44                // If the item number is valid...
45                if ((whichItem >= 0) && (whichItem < ARRAY_SIZE))
46                {
47                    // Get the item.
48                    theItem = theData[whichItem];
49                }
50
51                // Return the item to the client.
52                return (theItem);
53            }
54        }
55    }
```

Listing 3.1 The InformationManagerObject *(continued)*

Listing 3.1 begins by declaring the namespaces that the `InformationManager` needs to access. The declarations appear on lines 1 and 2. The `System.Runtime.Remoting` namespace is available because of the reference you added to the project in the Solution Explorer. Without this reference, Visual Studio will not be able to find the `System.Runtime.Remoting` namespace when you compile your program.

Next, on lines 6-8, the listing states that the `InformationManager` object is in the `Chapt3_Server` namespace. As mentioned previously, the `InformationManager` class inherits from `System.MarshalByRefObject`.

On line 14, the object declares a private array of strings that it uses to contain the information that it passes to the client. Line 16 shows the declaration of a public constant used with this class. Although this is allowed, it is not the best practice. Later chapters show that there are distinct advantages to separating the interface of a remote object from its implementation. This makes it rather unfeasible to declare constants in the remote class.

In addition, the size of the data collection should generally not be a constant. Real-world data collections are seldom a fixed size. It's much more likely that the size of the collection will vary over time. Rather than hard-coding the size of the data collection into the program, the `InformationManager` class should provide a public method that enables clients to query the size of the data collection.

Listing 3.1 next declares the `InformationManager` class's constructor (lines 22-38). The constructor loads the data collection with strings of data.

The only other item offered by the `InformationManager` class is the `DataItem()` method. This method takes one integer parameter, which identifies the string to be returned to the client. If the parameter contains an integer in the valid range, the method returns the specified string. Otherwise, it returns null.

Making the Object Available on the Network

The server makes the remotable `InformationManager` object available on the network. There are several techniques for accomplishing this task. One of the easiest is to programmatically declare its availability. To do so, the server program must create a communication channel on a port. As mentioned in Chapter 2, .NET Remoting currently supports two channels, HTTP and TCP. In this sample program, we'll use a TCP channel.

Accessing channels requires the statement:

```
using System.Runtime.Remoting.Channels;
```

near the beginning of the server program. Using a TCP channel also requires the server to contain the statement:

```
using System.Runtime.Remoting.Channels.Tcp;
```

This provides the server with access to the types it requires to create and open the channel it uses. To actually create the channel, the server uses the C# new keyword, as in the following example.

```
TcpChannel theChannel = new TcpChannel(8085);
```

This statement invokes the `TcpChannel` class's constructor. The constructor takes a port number as its parameter. The client and the server communicate through this port. Coding the port number into the program in this manner fixes the port that the remote object uses. It is not possible for the client or the server to use a different port. Objects developed this way are said to be **well-known objects** or **well-known services**. The World Wide Web is an example of a well-known service. Web servers and browsers always communicate with each other through port 80.

NOTE

It is possible to specify the port number in a configuration file, rather than hard code it into the program. This provides greater flexibility for your distributed applications. Chapter 8 presents the details of deploying applications in this manner.

After the server creates a channel, it must register the channel with a call to the `RegisterChannel()` method from the `ChannelServices` class. A call to this method looks similar to the following:

```
ChannelServices.RegisterChannel(theChannel);
```

The server can now register the service on the channel. It does so with calls like these.

```
RemotingConfiguration.ApplicationName = "InfoMan";
RemotingConfiguration.RegisterWellKnownServiceType(
    typeof(InformationManager),
    "InfoMan",
    WellKnownObjectMode.SingleCall);
```

The RemotingConfiguration class's `ApplicationName` property stores the name of the remoting application. It can only be set once. The method `RegisterWellKnownServiceType()` registers the object as a well-known service. Its first parameter is the object that provides the service. The second parameter to the `RegisterWellKnownServiceType()` method is the uniform resource identifier (URI) of the service. The .NET Framework uses the URI to route the client's remote requests.

The final parameter to the `RegisterWellKnownServiceType()` method is a constant from the `WellKnownObjectMode` enumeration. If the value is `WellKnownObjectMode.SingleCall`, each client request is serviced by a new instance of the remote object. If it is `WellKnownObjectMode`.Singleton, the requests are all serviced by a single object.

Waiting for Connections

The server program must continue to execute while it waits for clients to connect. The worst way to get it to do that is by having it enter a loop. Continuous looping eats up huge amounts of microprocessor time while doing nothing. It is better to have the sever "go to sleep" by blocking. When a program blocks, it does not use any microprocessor time. Instead, it waits for a signal to reactivate itself. In this chapter, we'll implement the client and the server as console programs. An easy way to get a console program to block is to call the method `System.Console.Read()`. That's exactly what's done in all of the programs in this chapter.

TIP

Do not use a loop to get your server program to wait for client connections. Instead, make the server "go to sleep" by blocking. Blocked programs use little or no microprocessor time while they wait for a signal to wake them back up.

Implementing servers as console programs has definite advantages. One of them is that it's quick to implement. Another is that it enables you to easily debug the server program in Visual Studio. However, it's usually not the optimal solution. It does not provide as easy a means of implementing features such as encryption and authentication as other types of server programs.

The Server Program

Now it's time to put it all together and build the server program. Listing 3.2 shows its source code.

```
using System;
using System.Runtime.Remoting;
using System.Runtime.Remoting.Channels;
using System.Runtime.Remoting.Channels.Tcp;

namespace Chapt3_Server
{
    /// <summary>
    /// Summary description for ApplicationClass.
```

Listing 3.2 ServerAppClass.cs *(continues)*

```
    /// </summary>
    public class ApplicationClass
    {
        /// <summary>
        /// The main entry point for the application.
        /// </summary>
        [STAThread]
        static void Main(string[] args)
        {
            // Create a TCP channel.
            TcpChannel theChannel = new TcpChannel(8085);

            /* Register the channel so that clients can
               connect to the server. */
            ChannelServices.RegisterChannel(theChannel);

            // Register the service on the channel.
            RemotingConfiguration.ApplicationName = "InfoMan";
            RemotingConfiguration.RegisterWellKnownServiceType(
                typeof(InformationManager),
                "InfoMan",
                WellKnownObjectMode.SingleCall);

            /* Keep the server running so that clients
               can connect to it. */
            System.Console.WriteLine(
                "Press Enter to end this server.");
            System.Console.Read();
        }
    }
}
```

Listing 3.2 ServerAppClass.cs *(continued)*

Earlier in this chapter, you created a Visual Studio project for the server program that contained no source code. At this point, you should add two C# source files to the project and type the code from Listings 3.1 and 3.2 into them. Alternatively, if you used the Web to download the code, you can add the files InfoManager.cs and ServerAppClass.cs to your empty project.

Writing the Client Program

The client for the sample application must obtain a reference to the remote object on the server. It uses this reference to gain access to the data offered by the server object. Because the client in this sample application is so simple, the only thing it does with the data is display it in a console window.

Identifying the Remote Server Object to the Client

The client program retrieves data from the server. To do so, it must have a description of the remote object. The simplest is to compile the source code for the remote object into the client application. Doing this requires that the object be implemented in a different file than the rest of the server program. This is one of the reasons that the `InformationManager` class is in the file InfoManager.cs.

Using this technique is the least secure way to implement a distributed client. Anyone with a disassembler can see exactly how your remote object operates. This can lead to serious breaches of security. It should not be used in a production environment. Later in this chapter, we'll look at a straightforward way of identifying a remote object to clients without sharing its implementation.

WARNING

Compiling the source code for the remote object into the client is an easy way to describe the remote object to the client program. However, it is not secure and should not be used in a production environment. If you do use this technique in your programs, it should be for sample or test purposes only.

Connecting to the Server

The client program must connect to the server program to access the services of the remote object. Like the server, the client creates and registers a communication channel. It uses nearly the same code as the server, as shown here.

```
TcpChannel theChannel = new TcpChannel();
ChannelServices.RegisterChannel(theChannel);
```

The primary difference between the calls on the client and the corresponding calls on the server is that the client doesn't have to specify the server's port number until it activates the remote object. Therefore, the client doesn't pass a port number to the TcpChannel() constructor like the server does.

NOTE

Strictly speaking, the .NET Remoting system does not require you to register a channel on the client. It will automatically load client channels when needed. If your client program uses a special communication technique called callbacks, then your client *must* register a channel. I recommend, however, that should include the statements to register a channel in your client program. I find this makes debugging much easier. It enables me to verify that the channel has been created when I am debugging a program.

Activating the Remote Object

When a client activates a remote object, it also obtains a reference to the object. For applications built in the manner that the sample application for this chapter is, clients call the `GetObject()` method in the `Activator` class. The `Activator` object is provided by the .NET Framework in the `System` namespace.

The call to `GetObject()` would resemble the following:

```
InformationManager infoMan =
    (InformationManager)Activator.GetObject(
        typeof(Chapt3_Server.InformationManager),
        "tcp://localhost:8085/InfoMan");
```

The first parameter to `GetObject()` is the type of the object to be created. The second is the URI of the object on the server. This URI specifies the channel (tcp), the host's name (localhost), the port, and the application URI that the server uses to advertise its remote object. Using localhost for the name of the server indicates that the client and the server programs are running on the same computer. If that is not the case, you must substitute the server's name or IP address instead. For example, if sample application's server programming were running on a server called ourserver on the current network, the call to `GetObject()` would look like this:

```
InformationManager infoMan =
    (InformationManager)Activator.GetObject(
        typeof(Chapt3_Server.InformationManager),
        "tcp://ourserver:8085/InfoMan");
```

Calling `Activator.GetObject()` creates a reference to the remote object and stores it in the variable `infoMan`. It is possible that the activation may fail. When `Activator.GetObject()` is called, it allocates a proxy object. Therefore, the `Activator.GetObject()` method would fail for all of the same reasons as a call to the C# `new` statement.

NOTE

The Activator.GetObject() method never actually makes a remote call. As a result, it can succeed even if the URI is misspelled, if the server is down, or if the network is not responding.

Using the Remote Object

After the client obtains a reference to the remote object, it can call the object's methods just as if the object was local to the program. When it does, the server instantiates the object and processes the call. For example, a call to the `DataItem()` method in the `InformationManager` class might look like the following.

```
string aString = infoMan.DataItem(i);
```

As you can see, it looks no different than calling a local object. This example call also demonstrates that passing data to and receiving data from a remote object is accomplished using the normal mechanisms of C#. That is, clients can pass data to the remote object through the parameter lists of its methods. It can receive data through the methods' return values.

There are, however, some limitations on what data can and cannot be transferred between the client and server programs. Data that you pass to and receive from remote objects must be **serializable**. Data that is serializable can be packaged into a data stream and sent over the network. It can be represented completely independently of the application space in which it resides. Classes that you write are serializable if they implement the `ISerializable` interface or if they are decorated with the `[Serializable]` attribute.

The Client Program

Near the beginning of this chapter, you created an project for the client that contained no source files. You can build the client now by creating a file called ClientAppClass.cs and adding it to the project. Type the source code shown in Listing 3.3 into ClientAppClass.cs. If you've downloaded ClientAppClass.cs from the Web, you can just add it to your client project.

In addition to ClientAppClass.cs, you'll need to add the file InfoManager.cs to the client project. This provides the client with access to the `InformationManager` type.

```
using System;
using System.Runtime.Remoting;
using System.Runtime.Remoting.Channels;
using System.Runtime.Remoting.Channels.Tcp;
using Chapt3_Server;

namespace Chapt3_Client
{
    /// <summary>
    /// Summary description for ApplicationClass.
    /// </summary>
    class ApplicationClass
    {
        /// <summary>
        /// The main entry point for the application.
        /// </summary>
        [STAThread]
        static void Main(string[] args)
        {
            // Create a TCP channel.
            TcpChannel theChannel = new TcpChannel();

            /* Register the channel so that this client can
               connect to the server. */
            ChannelServices.RegisterChannel(theChannel);

            // Activate the server object.
            InformationManager infoMan =
                (InformationManager)Activator.GetObject(
                    typeof(Chapt3_Server.InformationManager),
                    "tcp://localhost:8085/InfoMan");

            // If the remote object was activated...
            if (infoMan != null)
            {
                string tempString;

                // For each item in the "database"
                for (int i=0;
                     i<InformationManager.ARRAY_SIZE;
                     i++)
```

Listing 3.3 ClientAppClass.cs

```
42                      {
43                          tempString = null;
44
45                          // Get the item.
46                          tempString = infoMan.DataItem(i);
47
48                          // Print it to the console.
49                          System.Console.WriteLine(tempString);
50                      }
51                  }
52                  // Else the remote object was not activated...
53                  else
54                  {
55                      // Print an error message.
56                      System.Console.WriteLine(
57                          "Remote object could not be activated");
58                  }
59
60                  System.Console.WriteLine(
61                      "\nPaused. Press Enter to continue...");
62                  System.Console.Read();
63              }
64          }
65      }
```

Listing 3.3 ClientAppClass.cs *(continued)*

Listing 3.3 begins by declaring the namespaces it uses. Notice that it states on line 5 that it uses the `Chapt3_Server` namespaces. This is the namespace in which the remote object resides.

The client program follows the steps discussed previously. It creates and registers a TCP channel on lines 20-25. It then activates the server object and obtains a reference to it. The program stores the reference in the variable infoMan. Line 31 states that the server offering the `InformationManager` object is on the same computer as the client.

If the client program is not able to activate the `InformationManager` object, the variable `infoMan` contains null. In that case, the program jumps to the else statement beginning on line 53. It handles the error by outputting a message to the console.

On the other hand, if the program can activate the remote `InformationManager` object, it enters a for loop beginning on line 39. Inside the loop, it calls the `DataItem()` method to successively get each string contained in the InformationManager object. The program prints each string it retrieves to the console.

When the loop completes, program execution continues on line 60. The client program prints a prompt to the user and then calls the System.Console.Read() method to wait. This gives the user time to read the output before the program finishes. When the user presses Enter, the program ends.

Using the Application

After you've compiled the client and server programs, you can run them from Windows Explorer. Navigate to the executable files and double-click their file names. Start the server first. When your screen looks like Figure 3.1, you can start the client.

The server prompts the user and waits for client connections. As soon as the user presses Enter, the server ends. When it does, the .NET Framework automatically unregisters the service provided by the remote object, unregisters the channel, and closes the channel down.

If the server is up and running, you can start the client program. Figure 3.2 shows its output.

Figure 3.2 demonstrates that, with very little code, the client is able to establish a connection to the server. It utilizes that connection to access the service provided by the remote InformationManager object.

Figure 3.1 Output from the Server

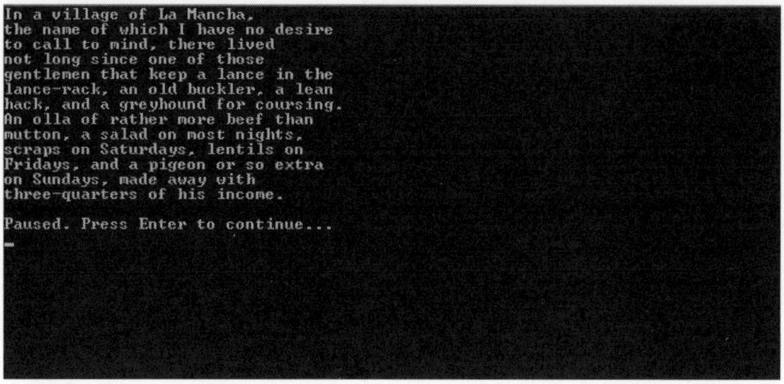

```
In a village of La Mancha,
the name of which I have no desire
to call to mind, there lived
not long since one of those
gentlemen that keep a lance in the
lance-rack, an old buckler, a lean
hack, and a greyhound for coursing.
An olla of rather more beef than
mutton, a salad on most nights,
scraps on Saturdays, lentils on
Fridays, and a pigeon or so extra
on Sundays, made away with
three-quarters of his income.

Paused. Press Enter to continue...
```

Figure 3.2 The Client's Output

Improving the Application

When you run the sample application, it operates just as you would expect. However, it only does so *if* the network is running properly and *if* the computer hosting the server program is running properly and *if* you start the server program before you run the client. That's a lot of ifs.

In the real world, your distributed applications must gracefully handle all runtime errors that can occur. Should any of the conditions in the preceding paragraph fail to be met, the client program will throw an exception. Your program must catch the exception. At the very least, it should inform the user that there's a problem before shutting the client down.

There are other problems with this version of the program. As mentioned previously, the server program shares the implementation of the remote object with the client. This is a serious security risk. In addition, the remote object should be in a namespace by itself. Also, `InformationManager` class contains a public constant that really should be eliminated.

Enhancing the Server

To create a version of the sample application that fixes these problems, we first need to separate the implementation of the remote object from its interface. One way to do that is to define an interface that describes the remote object and to share the interface between the client and the server. Listing 3.4 shows such an interface.

```
using System;
using System.Runtime.Remoting;

namespace InfoMan
{
    public interface IInformationManager
    {
        String DataItem(int whichItem);
        int DataCollectionLength();
    }
}
```

Listing 3.4 IInfoMan.cs

The interface presented in Listing 3.4 describes the remote object. It contains two methods. The first, DataItem(), was presented in the sample application. It retrieves a string from the remote object. The second method, DataCollectionLength(), gets the number of strings in the data collection.

The InformationManager class must inherit from the IInformationManager interface. It provides the server with implementations of both of the interface's methods. Listing 3.5 gives the new version of the `InformationManager` class. The changes are shown in bold.

```
using System;
using System.Runtime.Remoting;



namespace InfoMan
{
    public class InformationManager :
        MarshalByRefObject, IInformationManager
    {
        //
        // Private Data.
```

Listing 3.5 The New Version of InfoManager.cs

```
        //

        private string [] theData = new string [ARRAY_SIZE];
        private const int ARRAY_SIZE = 13;

        //
        // Public Methods
        //

        public InformationManager()
        {
            // Initialize the array.
            theData[0] = "In a village of La Mancha, ";
            theData[1] = "the name of which I have no desire ";
            theData[2] = "to call to mind, there lived ";
            theData[3] = "not long since one of those ";
            theData[4] = "gentlemen that keep a lance in the ";
            theData[5] = "lance-rack, an old buckler, a lean ";
            theData[6] = "hack, and a greyhound for coursing. ";
            theData[7] = "An olla of rather more beef than ";
            theData[8] = "mutton, a salad on most nights, ";
            theData[9] = "scraps on Saturdays, lentils on ";
            theData[10] = "Fridays, and a pigeon or so extra ";
            theData[11] = "on Sundays, made away with ";
            theData[12] = "three-quarters of his income.";
        }

        public String DataItem(int whichItem)
        {
            string theItem = null;

            // If the item number is valid...
            if ((whichItem >= 0) && (whichItem < ARRAY_SIZE))
            {
                // Get the item.
                theItem = theData[whichItem];
            }

            // Return the item to the client.
            return (theItem);
        }

        public int DataCollectionLength()
        {
            return (ARRAY_SIZE);
        }
    }
}
```

Listing 3.5 The New Version of InfoManager.cs *(continued)*

Line 9 of Listing 3.5 shows that in addition to inheriting from `MarshalByRefObject`, this version of the `InformationManager` class also inherits from the `IInformationManager` interface. The constant `ARRAY_SIZE`, which appears on line 16, is now private rather than public. It is no longer shared directly with clients.

As with the previous version, this version of the `InformationManager` class's constructor initializes the private array of strings with data. There are no changes to the `DataItem()` method. The new `InformationManager` class implements the `DataCollectionLength()` method, which returns the value of the constant `ARRAY_SIZE`.

Implementing the `InformationManager` class in this way requires little change to the server program. Listing 3.6 contains the updated version.

```
using System;
using System.Runtime.Remoting;
using System.Runtime.Remoting.Channels;
using System.Runtime.Remoting.Channels.Tcp;
using InfoMan;

namespace Chapt3_Server
{
    /// <summary>
    /// Summary description for ApplicationClass.
    /// </summary>
    public class ApplicationClass
    {
        /// <summary>
        /// The main entry point for the application.
        /// </summary>
        [STAThread]
        static void Main(string[] args)
        {
            // Create a TCP channel.
            TcpChannel theChannel = new TcpChannel(8085);

            /* Register the channel so that clients can
               connect to the server. */
            ChannelServices.RegisterChannel(theChannel);

            // Register the service on the channel.
            RemotingConfiguration.ApplicationName = "InfoMan";
            RemotingConfiguration.RegisterWellKnownServiceType(
                typeof(InformationManager),
                "InfoMan",
```

Listing 3.6 The New Version of ServerAppClass.cs

```
32                          WellKnownObjectMode.SingleCall);
33
34                      /* Keep the server running so that clients
35                         can connect to it. */
36                      System.Console.WriteLine(
37                          "Press Enter to end this server.");
38                      System.Console.Read();
39                  }
40          }
41      }
```

Listing 3.6 The New Version of ServerAppClass.cs *(continued)*

The only change to the server is on line 5. This using statement is new. It gives the server program access to the `InformationManager` class's namespace. Other than that, no changes were needed. If you've never worked with RPC or DCOM, you may not appreciate how significant this is. Even minor changes to remote objects or services, especially when using RPC, could require significant amounts of recoding in both the client and the server programs. The fact that so little change is required to the server program shows the great convenience of .NET Remoting.

To build the new version of the server program, you need to create a console application project in Visual Studio. Add the IInfoMan.cs to the project. Also add the new versions of InfoManager.cs and ServerAppClass.cs.

Enhancing the Client

The new version of the client does not use the file InfoManager.cs. Instead of compiling the remote object's source code into the client program, we'll add the file IInfoMan.cs into the client. This file contains a complete description of the remote object, but it does not contain the implementation. It provides the application with greater security.

Like the server program, the client program requires very little change. Even though it now uses an interface rather than an object, the code for accessing the remote object is largely the same. Listing 3.7 contains the updated version of ClientAppClass.cs. As before, the changes are shown in bold.

```
using System;
using System.Runtime.Remoting;
using System.Runtime.Remoting.Channels;
using System.Runtime.Remoting.Channels.Tcp;
using InfoMan;

namespace Chapt3_Client
{
    /// <summary>
    /// Summary description for ApplicationClass.
    /// </summary>
    class ApplicationClass
    {
        /// <summary>
        /// The main entry point for the application.
        /// </summary>
        [STAThread]
        static void Main(string[] args)
        {
            // Create a TCP channel.
            TcpChannel theChannel = new TcpChannel();

            /* Register the channel so that this client can
               connect to the server. */
            ChannelServices.RegisterChannel(theChannel);

            // Activate the server object.
            IInformationManager infoMan =
                (IInformationManager)Activator.GetObject(
                    typeof(IInformationManager),
                    "tcp://localhost:8085/InfoMan");

            // If the remote object was activated...
            if (infoMan != null)
            {
                string tempString;
                int dataCollectionLength;

                try
                {
                    dataCollectionLength =
                        infoMan.DataCollectionLength();
                }
                catch (Exception)
                {
                    ServerAccessError();
                    dataCollectionLength = 0;
```

Listing 3.7 The New Version of ClientAppClass.cs

```
                }

                bool errorOccurred = false;
                // For each item in the "database"
                for (int i=0;
                     (i<dataCollectionLength) &&
                        (!errorOccurred);
                     i++)
                {
                    tempString = null;

                    try
                    {
                        // Get the item.
                        tempString = infoMan.DataItem(i);

                        // Print it to the console.
                        System.Console.WriteLine(tempString);
                    }
                    catch (Exception)
                    {
                        ServerAccessError();
                        errorOccurred = true;
                    }
                }
            }
            // Else the remote object was not activated...
            else
            {
                // Print an error message.
                System.Console.WriteLine(
                    "Remote object could not be activated");
            }

            System.Console.WriteLine(
                "\nPaused. Press Enter to continue...");
            System.Console.Read();
        }

        static void ServerAccessError()
        {
            System.Console.WriteLine(
                "Error: Could not access the server");
        }
    }
}
```

Listing 3.7 The New Version of ClientAppClass.cs *(continued)*

The first change to ClientAppClass.cs appears on line 5 of Listing 3.7. Because the `IInformationManager` interface is now in its own namespace, the client requires the statement:

```
using InfoMan;
```

to access the interface.

Lines 28-31 also show minor changes. Instead of declaring a variable of type `InformationManager`, line 28 declares a variable of type `IInformationManager`. The type cast on line 29 and the typeof statement on line 30 also use the type `IInformationManager` type rather than type `InformationManager`. These declarations provide the client with access to all of the services offered by `InformationManager` without packaging the `InformationManager` class into the client program.

In addition, the client now uses some error detection. I've added try-catch statements wherever the program tries to access the remote object. For example, the client program attempts to retrieve the length of the data collection on line 40. If an error occurs, the .NET Framework throws an exception. The statement on line 44 catches that exception and prints an error message by calling the new `ServerAccessError()` method. The `ServerAccessError()` method appears on lines 87-91. The program also sets `dataCollectionLength` to 0 so that the client program does nothing significant from that point until it ends.

On line 50, the program declares a variable called `errorOccurred` and initializes it to false. The loop beginning on line 52 uses this variable in its condition on lines 53-54. The try-catch statement beginning on line 59 contains a statement that retrieves a data item from the server object. If it succeeds, the loop continues. Otherwise, the catch statement on line 67 catches the exception thrown by the .NET Framework. It calls `ServerAccessError()` on line 69 to print a message for the user. Next, it sets the variable `errorOccurred` to true. This terminates the loop.

TIP

Enclose all accesses to remote objects in try-catch statements. This prevents the client program from crashing should the access to the remote object fail.

To test the ability of the new client to handle an error condition, start it up without running the server program. If you do, you'll see the output that appears in Figure 3.3.

```
Error: Could not access the server
Paused. Press Enter to continue...
```

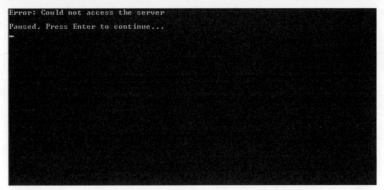

Figure 3.3 Screenshot of client handling an error condition

The figure shows that the client is able to handle the problem in a reasonable manner.

Summary

This chapter demonstrated straightforward techniques for implementing remote objects. It showed basic methods of connecting clients to remote objects offered by server programs. The client also passed some data to and from the remote object. However, transmitting data between components of distributed applications can be more complex than the techniques in this chapter have demonstrated. The next chapter presents this subject in greater detail.

CHAPTER 4

Using Remote Objects

Previous chapters provided an introduction to Remoting, and demonstrated how to build some simple Remoting applications. At this point, it's a good idea to take a more detailed look at how .NET Remoting works.

Remote Object Activation

Chapter 2 described the two methods of object activation provided by .NET Remoting, server-activated objects and client-activated objects. Sever-activated objects can be singletons or single-call objects. Chapter 3 demonstrated how to write a single-call object. Creating a singleton object, rather than a single-call object, is just a matter of using the constant `WellKnownObjectMode.Singleton` rather than `WellKnownObjectMode.SingleCall` in the invocation of the method `RemotingConfiguration.RegisterWellKnownServiceType()`, like this:

```
RemotingConfiguration.RegisterWellKnownServiceType(
    typeof(MyObject),
    "MyApp",
    WellKnownObjectMode.Singleton);
```

where MyObject is the name of the remote object and `MyApp` is its URI.

The process of writing and using client-activated objects, however, is somewhat different. The CLR does not activate a CAO until it receives a client request for the object. Instead, it creates an SAO that listens to the CAO's channel. When a request for the CAO arrives, the SAO notifies the CLR, which creates the CAO. The CAO can then service the request of the client program.

To demonstrate the differences between SAOs and CAOs, we'll rewrite the first program from Chapter 3 so that it publishes the server object as a CAO. The code for the object itself will not change. The only changes are in the application classes of the client and server programs. Therefore, that's all that will be presented here. If you want to see the code for the remote object, please refer to Listing 3.1 in Chapter 3.

Let's start with the server program's application class, which is given in Listing 4.1. The listing shows in bold type the changes needed to make the object a CAO.

```
using System;
using System.Runtime.Remoting;
using System.Runtime.Remoting.Channels;
using System.Runtime.Remoting.Channels.Tcp;

namespace Chapt4_Server
{
    /// <summary>
    /// Summary description for ApplicationClass.
    /// </summary>
    public class ApplicationClass
    {
        /// <summary>
        /// The main entry point for the application.
        /// </summary>
        [STAThread]
        static void Main(string[] args)
        {
            // Create a TCP channel.
            TcpChannel theChannel = new TcpChannel(8085);

            /* Register the channel so that clients can
               connect to the server. */
            ChannelServices.RegisterChannel(theChannel);

            // Register the service on the channel.
            RemotingConfiguration.ApplicationName = "InfoMan";
```

Listing 4.1 The Server for a Client-Activated Object

```
28                RemotingConfiguration.RegisterActivatedServiceType(
29                    typeof(InformationManager));
30
31                /* Keep the server running so that clients
32                   can connect to it. */
33                System.Console.WriteLine(
34                    "Press Enter to end this server.");
35                System.Console.Read();
36            }
37        }
38    }
```

Listing 4.1 The Server for a Client-Activated Object *(continued)*

The only change to the server program occurs on lines 28-29 of Listing 4.1. A CAO is not a well-known service. You cannot provide a single URI for each instance of the object. As a result, the server program does not call the method `RemotingConfiguration.RegisterWellKnownServiceType()` as it did in Chapter 3. Instead, it calls `RemotingConfiguration.RegisterActivatedServiceType()`. This method registers the remote object and creates a URI for it. The URI takes the form:

```
http://<host name>:<port>/<application name>
```

where <host name> is the name of the computer hosting the object, <port> is the number of the port that the CAO uses to communicate with clients, and <application name> is the name of the application that was set with the call to `RemotingConfiguration.ApplicationName`.

To make the client use a CAO, only minimal modifications are necessary. Listing 4.2 gives the client program's application class.

```
using System;
using System.Runtime.Remoting;
using System.Runtime.Remoting.Channels;
using System.Runtime.Remoting.Channels.Tcp;
using Chapt4_Server;

namespace Chapt4_Client
{
    /// <summary>
```

Listing 4.2 A Client that Uses the Client-Activated Object *(continues)*

```
10         /// Summary description for ApplicationClass.
11         /// </summary>
12         class ApplicationClass
13         {
14             /// <summary>
15             /// The main entry point for the application.
16             /// </summary>
17             [STAThread]
18             static void Main(string[] args)
19             {
20                 // Create a TCP channel.
21                 TcpChannel theChannel = new TcpChannel();
22 
23                 /* Register the channel so that this client can
24                    connect to the server. */
25                 ChannelServices.RegisterChannel(theChannel);
26 
27                 // Activate the server object.
28                 RemotingConfiguration.RegisterActivatedClientType(
29                     typeof(Chapt4_Server.InformationManager),
30                     "tcp://localhost:8085/InfoMan");
31 
32                 // Allocate the CAO as if it were local.
33                 Chapt4_Server.InformationManager infoMan =
34                     new Chapt4_Server.InformationManager();
35 
36                 // If the remote object was allocated...
37                 if (infoMan != null)
38                 {
39                     // See Listing 3.3 for the rest of the code.
```

Listing 4.2 A Client that Uses the Client-Activated Object *(continued)*

I've omitted the code after line 39 in Listing 4.2 because it is unchanged from Listing 3.3. On lines 28-30 of Listing 4.2, the client's application class calls `RemotingConfiguration.RegisterActivatedClientType()` rather than `Activator.GetObject()` to activate the CAO. After it does, it can allocate instances of the CAO just as if they were local objects. If it allocates more than one instance, each instance has its own state.

If you make the modifications shown in Listings 4.1 and 4.2 to the first program you created in Chapter 3, you'll find that that it compiles without any errors. However, when you run the program, you'll get an exception. The client is not able to find the server. The exception is not caused by an error in the code. This problem is caused by the way the application in Chapter 3 was originally compiled.

When you create an application using a remote object, the client must have information describing the remote object. In this program, we communicate that information by sharing the code for the remote object itself. As noted in Chapter 3, this is a simple approach, but not the best.

There are two ways you can share the code for the remote object with the client program. The first is to do what we did in Chapter 3, compile the file InfoMan.cs into both the client and the server programs. It actually works for simple programs. However, CAOs will not work properly if you build your program this way.

The other way to include the InfoMan.cs into the client program is to compile it into an assembly by itself when you build the server program. You then include a reference to the assembly in your client program. If you use this approach, the client and server programs communicate properly. If you're unfamiliar with how to do this, use the steps defined in Procedure 4.1.

WARNING

In all but the simplest Remoting situations, you cannot include the source code for the remote object in both the client and the server programs. If you do, they will not be able to communicate.

During compilation, Visual Studio generates a unique identifier for assemblies. If you compile the file InfoMan.cs into both the client and the server, it has a different identifier on the client than it does on the server. The CLR checks those identifiers. If they do not match, your client and server can't communicate. The error that you get is shown in Figure 4.1.

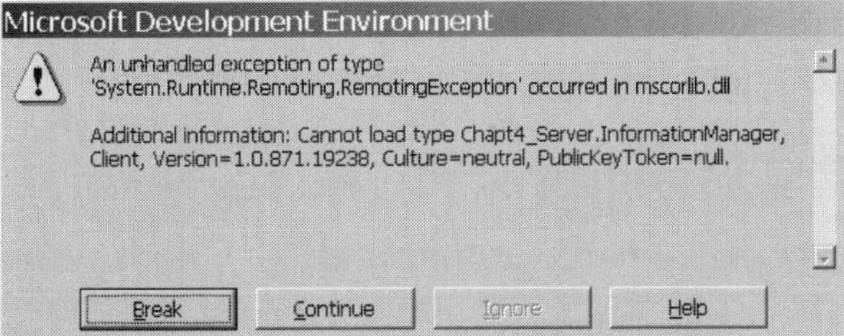

Figure 4.1 The Error from Improper Compilation

Procedure 4.1 Compiling Remote Applications Properly

1. From Visual Studio's **File** menu, select **New**. In the menu that appears, choose **Blank Solution**. Visual Studio displays the **New Project** dialog box.
2. Specify the name of the solution and the directory in which you want to store the solution's files. Click **OK**.
3. In the Solution Explorer, right-click the name of the solution. Choose **Add**, and then **New Project**. Visual Studio displays the **Add New Project** dialog box.
4. In the **Project Types** list, select **Visual C# Projects**. In the **Templates** list, click **Console Application**.
5. Type **Server** as the name of the project and specify the directory in which it should reside. Click **OK**.
6. Visual Studio automatically opens the file Class1.cs. Close Class1.cs and go back to the Solution Explorer. Delete Class1.cs from the Solution Explorer's list of files in the project.
7. Right-click the name of the server project in the Solution Explorer. From the menu that appears, choose **Add**, and then click **Add Existing Item**. Visual Studio displays a dialog box that you can use to navigate to and select the file ServerAppClass.cs.
8. In the Solution Explorer, right-click the name of the solution. Choose **Add**, and then **New Project**. Visual Studio displays the **Add New Project** dialog box.
9. In the **Project Types** list, select **Visual C# Projects**. In the **Templates** list, click **Class Library**.
10. Type **InfoMan** as the name of the project and specify the directory in which it should reside. Click **OK**.
11. Visual Studio automatically opens the file Class1.cs. Close Class1.cs and go back to the Solution Explorer. Delete Class1.cs from the Solution Explorer's list of files in the project.
12. Right-click the name of the InfoMan project in the Solution Explorer. From the menu that appears, choose **Add**, and then click **Add Existing Item**. Visual Studio displays a dialog box that you can use to navigate to and select the file InfoManager.cs.
13. Once more, right-click the name of the solution. Choose **Add**, and then **New Project**. Visual Studio displays the **Add New Project** dialog box.

14. In the **Project Types** list, select **Visual C# Projects**. In the **Templates** list, click **Console Application**.
15. Type **Client** as the name of the project and specify the directory in which it should reside. Click **OK**.
16. Visual Studio automatically opens the file Class1.cs. Close Class1.cs and go back to the Solution Explorer. Delete Class1.cs from the Solution Explorer's list of files in the project.
17. Right-click the name of the server project in the Solution Explorer. From the menu that appears, choose **Add**, and then click **Add Existing Item**. Visual Studio displays a dialog box that you can use to navigate to and select the file ClientAppClass.cs.
18. Add references to the System.Runtime.Remoting namespace to both the client and the server projects as described in Chapter 3.
19. Also add a reference to InfoMan.dll to both the client and the server projects.
20. In the Solution Explorer, right-click the Server project. In the menu that appears, click **Debug**, and then choose **Start New Instance**. Visual Studio compiles and runs the project.
21. In the Solution Explorer, right-click the Client project. In the menu that appears, click **Debug**, and then choose **Start New Instance**. Visual Studio compiles and runs the project.

Passing Data

Previous chapters stated that clients invoke methods on remote objects using communication channels established between the client and the server. Data can be marshaled by value or marshaled by reference. Prior to being sent through communication channels, data is serialized using formatters. This section gives some details on how all of this is done.

Communication Channels

Chapter 2 introduced the two types of channels that .NET Remoting supplies, the TCP channel and the HTTP channel. Chapter 3 demonstrated how to use the TCP channel. Applications typically use TCP channels when communicating over a company's **intranet** (internal network). For applications that use the Internet, it's usually best to use an HTTP channel. As stated previously, HTTP channels are able to pass data through firewalls.

From a programming point of view, communicating over an HTTP channel is extremely similar to using a TCP channel. The primary difference is that, when the data is transmitted, the .NET Framework creates a SOAP file that it sends over the network. To demonstrate how this works, let's rewrite the second program from Chapter 3 so that it uses an HTTP channel rather than a TCP channel.

Recall that the final version of the program from Chapter 3 contains the files IInfoMan.cs, InfoManager.cs, ServerAppClass.cs, and ClientAppClass.cs. To modify the program to use an HTTP channel, only the files ServerAppClass.cs and ClientAppClass.cs need to be changed. Listing 4.3 shows the new version of ServerAppClass.cs.

```
using System;
using System.Runtime.Remoting;
using System.Runtime.Remoting.Channels;
using System.Runtime.Remoting.Channels.Http;
using InfoMan;

namespace Chapt4_Server
{
    /// <summary>
    /// Summary description for ApplicationClass.
    /// </summary>
    public class ApplicationClass
    {
        /// <summary>
        /// The main entry point for the application.
        /// </summary>
        [STAThread]
        static void Main(string[] args)
        {
            // Create an HTTP channel.
            HttpChannel theChannel = new HttpChannel(8085);

            /* Register the channel so that clients can
               connect to the server. */
            ChannelServices.RegisterChannel(theChannel);

            // Register the service on the channel.
            RemotingConfiguration.ApplicationName = "InfoMan";
            RemotingConfiguration.RegisterWellKnownServiceType(
                typeof(InformationManager),
                "InfoMan.soap",
                WellKnownObjectMode.SingleCall);

            /* Keep the server running so that clients
```

Listing 4.3 A Server that Uses an HTTP Channel

```
35                 can connect to it. */
36              System.Console.WriteLine(
37                  "Press Enter to end this server.");
38              System.Console.Read();
39          }
40      }
41  }
```

Listing 4.3 A Server that Uses an HTTP Channel *(continued)*

Most of this code is identical to the code shown in Listing 3.6, in Chapter 3. The changes are shown in boldface text. The first difference occurs on line 4 of Listing 4.3. It specifies that this program uses the namespace containing the `HttpChannel` class. Lines 20-21 create the HTTP channel. On line 31, the server's URI is now InfoMan.soap, rather than just InfoMan.

NOTE

You can use any extension that you want for the name of the SOAP file generated by an HTTP channel. You can even omit it altogether. However, if you decide to host your remote object in IIS (which is discussed in Chapter 9), you must either use the extension .soap or .rem. In my opinion, it's best to get in the habit of using just one of these extensions every time you create a remote object that uses the HTTP channel.

Like the server code, the code for the client program changes very little when we modify it to use an HTTP channel. Listing 4.4 gives the code for the client program's application class.

```
using System;
using System.Runtime.Remoting;
using System.Runtime.Remoting.Channels;
using System.Runtime.Remoting.Channels.Http;
using InfoMan;

namespace Chapt4_Client
{
    /// <summary>
    /// Summary description for ApplicationClass.
    /// </summary>
    class ApplicationClass
    {
```

Listing 4.4 A Client that Uses an HTTP Channel *(continues)*

```
14          /// <summary>
15          /// The main entry point for the application.
16          /// </summary>
17          [STAThread]
18          static void Main(string[] args)
19          {
20              // Create an HTTP channel.
21              HttpChannel theChannel = new HttpChannel();
22
23              /* Register the channel so that this client can
24                 connect to the server. */
25              ChannelServices.RegisterChannel(theChannel);
26
27              // Activate the server object.
28              IInformationManager infoMan =
29                  (IInformationManager)Activator.GetObject(
30                      typeof(IInformationManager),
31                      "http://localhost:8085/InfoMan.soap");
32
```

Listing 4.4 A Client that Uses an HTTP Channel *(continued)*

Because it does not change, I omitted all of the code after line 32 in Listing 4.4. If you want to see the rest of the code for the file, please look back to Listing 3.3 in Chapter 3.

Like the server program, the client program specifies the namespace containing the `HttpChannel` class on line 4. It creates the HTTP channel on lines 20-21. On line 31, the client specifies the URI using the full file name, InfoMan.soap. As with the program in Chapter 3, we're assuming that the client and the server programs are running on the same computer. If you want to run them on different computers, you must delete the word "localhost" and modify the URI on line 31 to use the name of the computer on which the server program runs.

This program must be compiled properly to get it to run. It uses an interface to describe the remote object. That interface must be compiled into its own assembly, called IInfoMan.dll. Both the client and server projects must contain a reference to IInfoMan.dll. If you try to compile the file IInfoMan.cs into both the client and the server, the client will not be able to find the server object. Your program will throw an exception claiming that you are attempting an invalid SOAP operation.

Marshal by Value

Programs that use marshal by value (MBV) objects copy the objects between the client and the server. If, for example, a client requests an MBV object from a server (they can also go from client to server), the object exists on both the client and the server after the request is fulfilled. This is an important point. Changes to the copy on the client do not affect the copy on the server, and vice versa.

All MBV objects must be serializable. The .NET Framework provides two ways to make objects serializable. The first, and by far the most common, is to decorate the class of the MBV object with the `[Serializable]` attribute. This will be demonstrated shortly.

The second way to make objects serializable is to make them implement the `ISerializable` interface. This is typically done only if you want to implement your own serialization techniques.

Because MBV objects are copied across networks, you need to be selective about which objects your applications transmits between the client and the server. Copying large objects across networks, especially across the Internet, can be a serious performance bottleneck in your application. Marshaling complex objects by value can limit the scalability of your application. If a hundred people are using your application around the world, marshaling large data objects by value may be just fine. The same may not be true when there are thousands, tens of thousands, or even millions of people worldwide using your applications at the same time.

Avoid marshaling large, complex object by value. In a distributed application with many users, transmitting large amounts of data across the network can seriously degrade performance.

To increase the efficiency of marshaling by value, you can make your application retrieve several objects per request, rather than one at a time. Although this increases the time it takes to fill a request for data, it decreases the total number of requests. In a large-scale corporate environment, simple techniques such as this make a big difference in network performance.

TIP

You can decrease the number of network requests your application performs by getting several MBV objects at once, rather than retrieving them one at a time. Programmers call this technique retrieving "chunky data" or making "chunky calls."

Implementing MBV objects is relatively straightforward. To demonstrate how it's done, we'll write a program that simulates a small portion of a networked multiplayer game. As a first step, let's define the MBV object and the interface for the server. Listing 4.5 shows the code for them.

```
using System;

namespace Game
{
    // This is the data item.
    [Serializable]
    public class GameState
    {
        private int currentPlayerID;
        private string currentPlayerName;

        public GameState()
        {
            currentPlayerID = 0;
            currentPlayerName = null;
        }

        public int WhoseTurn()
        {
            return (currentPlayerID);
        }

        public void WhoseTurn(int playerNumber)
        {
            currentPlayerID = playerNumber;
        }

        public string PlayerName()
        {
            return (currentPlayerName);
        }

        public void PlayerName(string playerName)
        {
            currentPlayerName = playerName;
        }
    }
```

Listing 4.5 IGame.cs

```
38
39        // Interface for the server object.
40        public interface IGame
41        {
42            GameState GetGameState();
43        }
44    }
```

Listing 4.5 IGame.cs *(continued)*

The file IGame.cs in Listing 4.5 contains an object called GameState that the game uses to transmit its current state to its clients. Objects similar to this would be use in turn-based games, such as online board or card games. With each turn, the current state of the server must be transmitted to all of the client programs. The `GameState` object encapsulates that information.

The definition of the GameState object looks like any other. It contains methods for getting and setting its data. The only difference is the appearance of the `[Serializable]` attribute on line 6.

Listing 4.5 also defines the game object's interface on lines 40-43. The only method in the interface is `GetGameState()` which clients call to obtain the game state from the server.

This game will use the HTTP channel, so the file IGame.cs needs to be compiled into its own assembly.

REMINDER

If you are using the HTTP channel and you are sharing an interface to the remote object between the client and the server, you need to compile the interface file into its own assembly. Add a reference to that assembly in projects for both the client and the server.

Listing 4.6 shows the source code for the game object that resides on the server. Notice that it is marshaled by reference. It uses the `GetGameState()` method to transmit a the MBV `GameState` object to the client.

```
using System;
using Game;

```

Listing 4.6 Game.cs *(continues)*

```
4
5    namespace Game
6    {
7        public class NetGame :
8            MarshalByRefObject, IGame
9        {
10           private const int TOTAL_PLAYERS = 4;
11           private string [] allPlayers;
12           private int currentPlayer;
13
14           public NetGame()
15           {
16               allPlayers = new string [TOTAL_PLAYERS];
17               allPlayers[0] = "Fred";
18               allPlayers[1] = "Noel";
19               allPlayers[2] = "Abdul";
20               allPlayers[3] = "Hannah";
21               currentPlayer = 0;
22           }
23
24           public GameState GetGameState()
25           {
26               GameState currentGameState = new GameState();
27
28               currentGameState.WhoseTurn(currentPlayer+1);
29               currentGameState.PlayerName(
30                   allPlayers[currentPlayer]);
31
32               currentPlayer++;
33
34               if (currentPlayer >= TOTAL_PLAYERS)
35               {
36                   currentPlayer = 0;
37               }
38
39               return (currentGameState);
40           }
41       }
42   }
```

Listing 4.6 Game.cs *(continued)*

The NetGame object simulates a multiplayer game by declaring an array of strings on line 11. In the NetGame() constructor, it initializes each of the strings to the name of a player. The NetGame class also contains an integer identifier that indicates whose turn it is. It uses this identifier as a zero-based index number into the array of player names.

Each time the client calls the `GetGameState()` method, the server creates a GameState object called `currentGameState`. It copies the name of the current player into `currentGameState`. It also sets the players ID number. The ID numbers that the user sees begin with 1 rather than 0. Therefore, the `GetGameState()` method always adds 1 to the current player number before it sends the game state. Next, it increments the current player number. If the current player number is greater than the total number of players, `GetGameState()` sets the current player number to 0. This indicates that everyone has had a turn and it's time to start through the list of players again. The `GetGameState()` method ends by returning the current game state to the client.

To make things easy, we'll modify the file ServerAppClass.cs from Listing 4.3. The changes are shown in bold type in Listing 4.7.

```
using System;
using System.Runtime.Remoting;
using System.Runtime.Remoting.Channels;
using System.Runtime.Remoting.Channels.Http;
using Game;

namespace Chapt4_Server
{
    /// <summary>
    /// Summary description for ApplicationClass.
    /// </summary>
    public class ApplicationClass
    {
        /// <summary>
        /// The main entry point for the application.
        /// </summary>
        [STAThread]
        static void Main(string[] args)
        {
            // Create an HTTP channel.
            HttpChannel theChannel = new HttpChannel(8085);

            /* Register the channel so that clients can
               connect to the server. */
            ChannelServices.RegisterChannel(theChannel);

            // Register the service on the channel.
            RemotingConfiguration.ApplicationName = "NetGame";
            RemotingConfiguration.RegisterWellKnownServiceType(
                typeof(NetGame),
                "NetGame.soap",
```

Listing 4.7 The File ServerAppClass.cs for the Game *(continues)*

```
32                        WellKnownObjectMode.Singleton);
33
34                    /* Keep the server running so that clients
35                       can connect to it. */
36                    System.Console.WriteLine(
37                        "Press Enter to end this server.");
38                    System.Console.Read();
39            }
40        }
41    }
```

Listing 4.7 The File ServerAppClass.cs for the Game *(continued)*

As you can see, this version of ServerAppClass.cs was modified to use the appropriate namespace on line 5. On lines 28 and 31 it uses the name `"NetGame"` for the application name and `"NetGame.soap"` for name of the SOAP file that gets transmitted between the client and the server. Notice also that the server application class declares the `NetGame` object as a singleton, rather than a single-call object. This enables the `NetGame` object to preserve its state from client call to client call.

WARNING

It is important to remember that singletons have a default lifetime that is specified by the CLR. If there are no client requests for a while (for instance, someone takes a really long turn in the game), the CLR may recycle the singleton game object. The result would be that the game would "forget" what state it was in. The solution to this is to give the game object an indefinite lifetime so that it exists for as long as the game runs. Chapter 7 demonstrates how this is done.

The client for the game connects to the server through an HTTP channel. This generally means that it can work across the Internet, even through firewalls. The client queries the game state 10 times and prints the result each time.

REMINDER

You should not compile the file IGame.cs into the client program. Create a separate assembly from IGame.cs. Next, use Visual Studio's Solution Explorer to set a reference to the file IGame.dll in the project files for the client and server programs.

The code for the game is shown in Listing 4.8.

```
using System;
using System.Runtime.Remoting;
using System.Runtime.Remoting.Channels;
using System.Runtime.Remoting.Channels.Http;
using System.Threading;
using Game;

namespace Chapt4_Client
{
    /// <summary>
    /// Summary description for ApplicationClass.
    /// </summary>
    class ApplicationClass
    {
        /// <summary>
        /// The main entry point for the application.
        /// </summary>
        [STAThread]
        static void Main(string[] args)
        {
            // Create an HTTP channel.
            HttpChannel theChannel = new HttpChannel();

            /* Register the channel so that this client can
               connect to the server. */
            ChannelServices.RegisterChannel(theChannel);

            // Activate the server object.
            IGame theGame =
                (IGame)Activator.GetObject(
                    typeof(IGame),
                    "http://localhost:8085/NetGame.soap");

            // If the remote object was activated...
            if (theGame != null)
            {
                for (int i=0; i<10; i++)
                {
                    try
                    {
                        // Get the current game state.
                        GameState currentState =
                            theGame.GetGameState();

                        System.Console.WriteLine(
                            "It is your turn.");
                        System.Console.WriteLine(
```

Listing 4.8 The File ClientAppClass.cs for the Game *(continues)*

```
48                                 "Player Number: {0}",
49                                 currentState.WhoseTurn());
50                             System.Console.WriteLine(
51                                 currentState.PlayerName());
52                             System.Console.Write("\n");
53                         }
54                         catch (Exception)
55                         {
56                             ServerAccessError();
57                         }
58
59                         Thread.Sleep(1000);
60                     }
61                 }
62                 // Else the remote object was not activated...
63                 else
64                 {
65                     ServerAccessError();
66                 }
67
68                 System.Console.WriteLine(
69                     "\nPaused. Press Enter to continue...");
70                 System.Console.Read();
71             }
72
73             static void ServerAccessError()
74             {
75                 System.Console.WriteLine(
76                     "Error: Could not access the server");
77             }
78         }
79     }
```

Listing 4.8 The File ClientAppClass.cs for the Game *(continued)*

The output of this program is given in Figure 4.2.

This program establishes an HTTP channel and then enters a for loop on lines 37-60 of Listing 4.8. Inside the loop, it calls `GetGameState()`. This sends a call through the .NET Remoting system to the server. A look back at Listing 4.6 shows that the `NetGame` object sends back the current player's name as an ID number in a `GameState` object. It also increments the current player to indicate that it is the next person's turn.

```
E:\Visual Studio Projects\Remoting\Chapter04\Program02\Client\...
Fred

It is your turn.
Player Number: 2
Noel

It is your turn.
Player Number: 3
Abdul

It is your turn.
Player Number: 4
Hannah

It is your turn.
Player Number: 1
Fred

It is your turn.
Player Number: 2
Noel

Paused. Press Enter to continue...
```

Figure 4.2 The Output of the Game Program

When the call to `GetGameState()` returns to line 42 of Listing 4.8, the program copies the game state information that it received from the server into the variable `currentState`. Because the `GameState` object is marshaled by value, this information has been copied from the server to the client. You can alter the information in any way that your program requires, and it will not affect the information on the server.

The loop in Listing 4.8 continues by printing the game state information to the console. Notice that on each pass through the loop, the program calls the `Thread.Sleep()` method, and passes it a value of 1,000. This makes the program pause for 1,000 milliseconds (1 second) so that the user can see the output. Because it uses the `Thread.Sleep()` method, the client program contains the statement:

```
using System.Threading;
```

on line 5. This makes the threading methods available to the program.

When the for loop finishes, the program prints a prompt for the user and pauses for a response. It ends when the user presses Enter.

Marshal by Reference

As stated previously, marshal by reference objects do not get copied between the client and the server. Instead, they access they services of the remote object through the reference. All of the programs presented so far have used at least one MBR object.

When it marshals an MBR object, the .NET Framework uses the method `RemotingServices.Marshal()`. The `RemotingServices.Marshal()` method returns an object of type `ObjRef`. All `ObjRef` objects are serializable, so they can be marshaled by value. An `ObjRef` object contains information on how to locate the remote object. Specifically, it holds the remote object's host computer name, the port number the object listens to, and the name of the object. In addition, it contains a description of the object itself. The description includes a unique object identifier and the object's class hierarchy.

Chapter 2 stated that the client uses a proxy object to call methods on the server object. You may wonder why the client needs an `ObjRef` if it uses the proxy. Figure 4.3 shows the relationship between them.

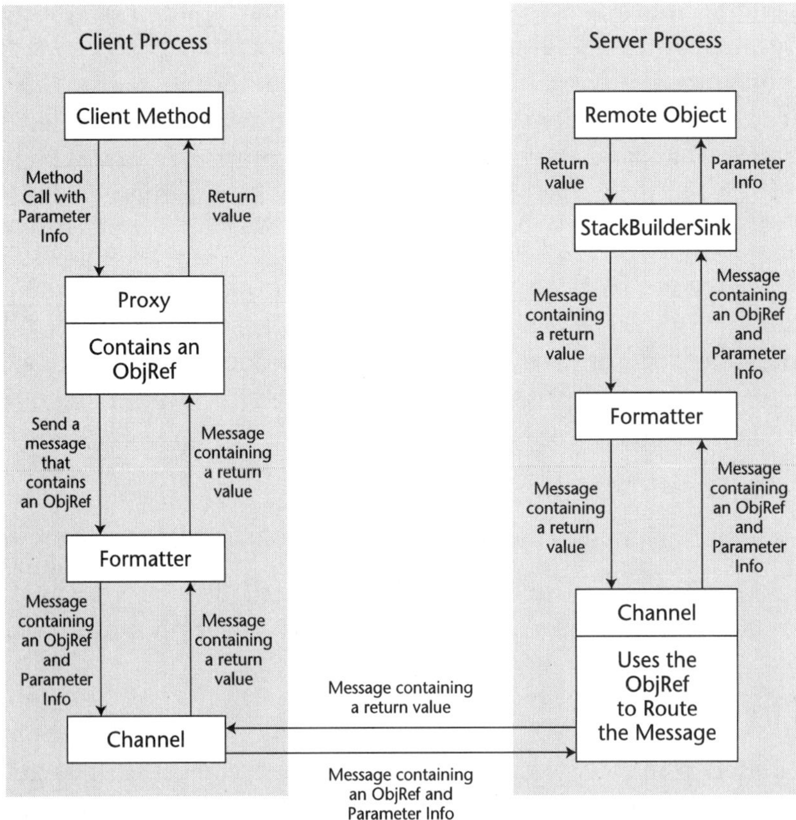

Figure 4.3 Proxies, Object References, and Remoting Messages

When a client calls a method on a proxy, the proxy uses the `ObjRef` to access the remote object on the server. As Figure 4.3 illustrates, the proxy creates a **remoting message** that it sends to the server. Remoting messages are messages used by the Framework to get remote methods executed. A remoting message is derived from the `IMessage` interface and contains the object reference it got from the proxy. This enables the message to get to the correct destination. A remoting message also contains the parameter information that the client needs to transmit to the server.

NOTE

The server does not use a proxy. Instead, it uses an object called a stack builder sink. Stack builder sinks are explained in greater detail in Chapter 12.

After a remote method finishes, it must transmit its return value back to the client. It uses a remoting message to accomplish the task. The remoting message contains, among other things, the server method's return value.

NOTE

When clients pass data, such as parameter values, to remote methods the parameter values must be packaged into the remoting message for transmission across the network. The Framework uses formatters to accomplish this. Likewise, when remote methods transmit return values to clients, they also use formatters. Formatters are presented later in this chapter.

Clients can pass object references to remote methods as parameters. When server methods receive object references as parameters, the CLR creates a proxy for the object reference within the server's application space. This enables clients to obtain a reference to an object on one server and pass the reference to a remote method on another server.

Remote methods can send object references back to clients as return values. When they do, the CLR on the client creates a proxy for the object reference in the client's application space.

Whenever the Framework creates a proxy, it creates an object called a real proxy. Real proxies are implemented by the Framework's `RealProxy` class. The real proxy, in turn, creates an instance of the `TransparentProxy` class. Transparent proxies do the initial remote method call interception. They then use real proxies to do the rest of the work.

This combination of real proxy and transparent proxy enables the Framework to provide clients with a view of remote objects. The real proxy does the actual proxy work, but its "appearance" never changes. A transparent proxy looks just like the remote object to the client application. It doesn't do much besides intercept remote calls. Basically, it's a facade that makes the real proxy look like any remote object.

If you need to, you can create custom real proxies in your application. The techniques for doing this are presented in Chapter 14. Because the real proxy generates the transparent proxy, you cannot create custom transparent proxies. Applications can implement custom object references by deriving classes from ObjRef.

Formatters

.NET Remoting serializes data for transmission across the network using formatter objects. By default, the Framework provides two formatters. One serializes data into a binary format. The other serializes it into a SOAP file, which can then be transmitted across the network to any program that understands SOAP. This enables you to integrate many different types of programs into your Remoting applications.

It is possible to create your own custom formatters. You may want to do this to enhance the efficiency of data transfer. Another reason to create a custom formatter is to package data into an encrypted format that is customized for your needs. Alternatively, you might want to create a formatter than inserts error-correcting codes, such as Hamming codes, into your data when you know it will be transmitted across high-speed wireless links. This helps ensure that accurate data moves between the client and the server no matter what the weather conditions.

To create your own formatters, your custom formatter class must implement the `IRemotingFormatter` interface. You will need to write your own versions of the `Serialize()` and `Deserialize()` methods. Chapter 14 shows the implementation of a custom formatter.

After your formatter is built, you select it by associating it with a channel. You can do this in your application's configuration files. For more information on using configuration files to select formatters, please see Chapter 8.

.NET Remoting Rules

Here's another example program. The server offers a singleton object. It communicates with clients using an HTTP channel. Listing 4.9 contains the code for the remote object.

```
using System;

namespace Test
{
    public class TestProg : MarshalByRefObject
    {
        private static int anInt;

        TestProg()
        {
            anInt = 5;
        }

        public static void StaticSetAnInt(int newValue)
        {
            anInt = newValue;
        }

        public void SetAnInt(int newValue)
        {
            anInt = newValue;
        }

        public static int StaticGetAnInt()
        {
            return (anInt);
        }

        public int GetAnInt()
        {
            return (anInt);
        }
    }
}
```

Listing 4.9 A Remote Object that Demonstrates Some Remoting Features

The purpose of the remote object in Listing 4.9 is to demonstrate some of the behaviors of .NET Remoting. The object contains a private data member called `anInt`. In its constructor, it initializes `anInt` to the value 5. The class provides four additional methods. Two of them are `static`, and two of them are not. These methods set or get the value of `anInt`.

Listing 4.10 shows the server program that offers the remote object from Listing 4.9.

```
using System;
using System.Runtime.Remoting;
using System.Runtime.Remoting.Channels;
using System.Runtime.Remoting.Channels.Http;
using Test;

namespace Server
{
    /// <summary>
    /// Summary description for ServerAppClass.
    /// </summary>
    class ServerAppClass
    {
        /// <summary>
        /// The main entry point for the application.
        /// </summary>
        [STAThread]
        static void Main(string[] args)
        {
            // Create an HTTP channel.
            HttpChannel theChannel = new HttpChannel(8085);

            /* Register the channel so that clients can
               connect to the server. */
            ChannelServices.RegisterChannel(theChannel);

            // Register the service on the channel.
            RemotingConfiguration.ApplicationName = "TestProg";
            RemotingConfiguration.RegisterWellKnownServiceType(
                typeof(TestProg),
                "TestProg.soap",
                WellKnownObjectMode.Singleton);

            /* Keep the server running so that clients
               can connect to it. */
            System.Console.WriteLine(
```

Listing 4.10 A Server for the TestProg Object

```
                    "Press Enter to end this server.");
                System.Console.Read();
            }
        }
    }
```

Listing 4.10 A Server for the TestProg Object *(continued)*

As you can see, this server program is very much like others shown in this chapter. At this point, there appears to be nothing special about either the remote object or its server. However, let's press on by presenting the code for this application's client in Listing 4.11.

```
using System;
using System.Runtime.Remoting;
using System.Runtime.Remoting.Channels;
using System.Runtime.Remoting.Channels.Http;
using Test;

namespace Client
{
    /// <summary>
    /// Summary description for ClientAppClass.
    /// </summary>
    class ClientAppClass
    {
        /// <summary>
        /// The main entry point for the application.
        /// </summary>
        [STAThread]
        static void Main(string[] args)
        {
            // Create an HTTP channel.
            HttpChannel theChannel = new HttpChannel();

            /* Register the channel so that this client can
               connect to the server. */
            ChannelServices.RegisterChannel(theChannel);

            // Activate the server object.
            TestProg theTest =
```

Listing 4.11 The Client for the TestProg Object *(continues)*

```
29                  (TestProg)Activator.GetObject(
30                  typeof(TestProg),
31                  "http://localhost:8085/TestProg.soap");
32
33              System.Console.WriteLine(
34                  "Setting the remote object's value to 10.");
35              TestProg.StaticSetAnInt(10);
36              System.Console.WriteLine(
37                  "The remote object's value is:{0}",
38                  theTest.GetAnInt());
39              System.Console.WriteLine(
40                  "The remote object's value is:{0}",
41                  TestProg.StaticGetAnInt());
42
43              System.Console.WriteLine(
44                  "Setting the remote object's value to 20.");
45              theTest.SetAnInt(20);
46              System.Console.WriteLine(
47                  "The remote object's value is:{0}",
48                  theTest.GetAnInt());
49              System.Console.WriteLine(
50                  "The remote object's value is:{0}",
51                  TestProg.StaticGetAnInt());
52
53              // Pause so the user can see the output.
54              System.Console.WriteLine(
55                  "\nPress Enter to end this client.");
56              System.Console.Read();
57          }
58      }
59  }
```

Listing 4.11 The Client for the TestProg Object *(continued)*

Now here's where things get interesting. If we compile the application, run the server, and run the client, we get the output shown in Figure 4.4.

If you compare the output in Figure 4.4 to the code in Listing 4.11, you may seem some things that raise a few questions. For instance, the client program states on lines 33-34 of Listing 4.11 that it is setting the value of the remote object to 10. It sets the value on line 35. On lines 36-38, the client prints the value contained in the `TestProg` object. It calls the function `GetAnInt()` to retrieve the value, which it then passes to the `WriteLine()` method. However, looking at the output in Figure 4.4 shows that the value of the remote object is still 5. To make matters worse, the client calls `WriteLine()` again on lines 39-41 to print the current value of the remote object. This time it uses `StaticGetAnInt()` to retrieve the remote object's value. It faithfully reports that the object's value is, in fact, 10.

What's going on here?

There is actually no problem here. We're just seeing an example of how .NET Remoting operates. When servers share remote objects, the CLR creates local copies of the remote objects whenever it can. Accessing the remote object through a static method makes the CLR route the call to the local copy. If it calls non-static methods, the CLR sends the calls to the remote object. This explains the behavior of the `TestProg` object.

Because the `TestProg` object's `StaticSetAnInt()` method is declared with the `static` keyword, the CLR creates and calls the method on a local object. Therefore, line 35 of Listing 4.11 sets the anInt member of the local `TestProg` object to 10. Even after the statement on line 35 executes, the remote object is unchanged. It still contains 5 in its private anInt member. Calling `GetAnInt()` on line 38 retrieves the value in the remote copy of the object, while the invocation of `StaticGetAnInt()` on line 41 fetches the value in the local copy.

If we continue the program, we see this behavior exhibited again. Line 45 uses the `SetAnInt()` method to set the value of `anInt` to 20. This call sets the value of the remote object because `SetAnInt()` is not static. Using the non-static `GetAnInt()` method on line 48 shows that the value of the remote copy of the object was changed. Calling `StaticGetAnInt()` demonstrates that the value in the local copy of the object is unchanged.

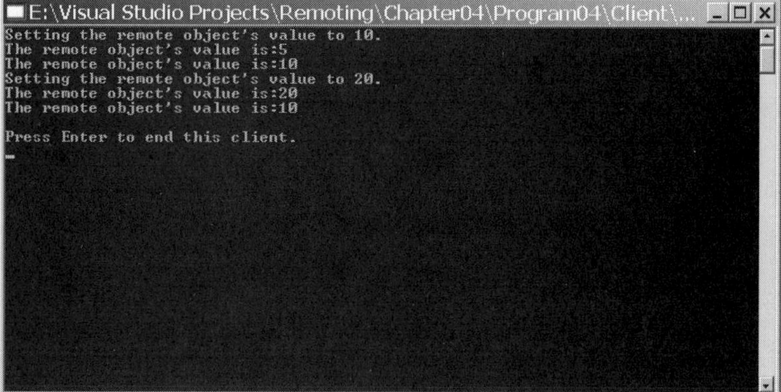

Figure 4.4 The Output of the TestProg Client

So what are the rules that .NET Remoting uses to decide when to access a local copy of an object and when to use a remote copy? Table 4.1 gives a summary of these rules. The Microsoft .NET Remoting documentation calls them the scope of object publication.

The table shows that some types of class members provide access to local copies of remote objects. Others access the remote object itself. In addition to the rules given in Table 4.1, the .NET documentation provides directives for overriding methods from the `Object` class, from which all other C# types are derived. Because all objects are ultimately derived from the `Object` class, programs can execute its methods using almost any type of object. Certain methods, such as `ToString()` and `Equals()` are used in many C# programs. Therefore, it's important to know how they work when your program calls them on a remote object.

In general, the methods from the `Object` class execute on a local copy of the remote object. However, the `Equals()` and `ToString()` methods will execute remotely if you override them in your remote object's class. All other methods from the `Object` class execute on local objects.

WARNING

Although the virtual method Object.Equals() executes remotely if your remote object overrides it, the static version of this method always executes on a local object. Be sure you know which one you're calling.

Table 4.1 The .NET Remoting Scope of Publication

OBJECT ATTRIBUTE	PUBLICATION SCOPE
Data Members	Uses the remote object, if a proxy exists. Uses a local copy if no proxy exists.
Properties (Accessors)	Uses the remote object, if a proxy exists. Uses a local copy if no proxy exists.
Private Methods	Private static methods invoked by public static methods used a local copy. All others use the remote object.
Static Methods	Uses a local copy.
Static Data Members	Uses a local copy.
Delegates	Always marshaled by value. Can use MBV or MBR the object within the delegate.

Summary

Objects can be activated by either the client or the server. To pass data between the client and the server, applications establish a communication channel. Currently, .NET Remoting supplies the TCP and HTTP channels. Before data can be passed across communication channels, it must be marshaled, packaged into a message by the remote object's proxy, and serialized by a formatter. The CLR uses the object reference supplied by the proxy on the client to route the message to the correct destination.

Remoting applications can marshal objects by reference or by value. MBR objects must be derived from `MarshalByRefObject`. Serializable objects must be decorated with the `[Serializable]` attribute.

Usually, the .NET Framework creates a local copy of remote objects. When using remote objects, it's important to understand when your program is using a local copy and when it is using a remote copy. The Microsoft Remoting documentation calls the rules the object's scope of publication.

CHAPTER 5

Remoting, XML, and SOAP

The chapters you've read so far provided an overview of what .NET Remoting is and why it's used. You've seen the basics of building Remoting applications and looked at some of the specifics of how remote objects work. This chapter provides some details on Extensible Markup Language (XML) and Simple Object Access Protocol (SOAP).

XML and SOAP are rapidly becoming industry-standard methods of defining and exchanging data. They are both fundamental to the .NET Framework. For example, all .NET Remoting configuration files are defined using XML. Also, SOAP provides a way to access remote methods when applications use the HTTP channel. An understanding of the basics of XML and SOAP is usually required when building commercial-grade distributed applications.

XML

Extensible Markup Language is a subset of Standard Generalized Markup Language (SGML), a system for organizing and tagging elements of a document. SGML was developed and standardized by the International Organization for Standards (ISO) in 1986. SGML itself does not specify any particular formatting. Instead, it specifies a set of rules for tagging elements in documents. The tags are interpreted by the software rendering the document. Different rendering software can interpret the tags in different ways. This capability gives the rendering software the freedom to render the document in the way that looks best for the particular hardware and operating system.

Many subsets of SGML have been defined. The World Wide Web is based on one such subset, called HyperText Markup Language (HTML). HTML describes the elements of a Web page. It's for *displaying* data.

As the popularity of the Web increased, it quickly became apparent that a subset of SGML was needed to provide a standardized way of *describing* or *defining* data (as opposed to displaying it). The World Wide Web Consortium (W3C), an international consortium of companies involved with the Internet and the Web, created XML for exactly this purpose. The W3C was founded in 1994 by Tim Berners-Lee, the original architect of the World Wide Web. The organization's purpose is to develop open standards so that the Web evolves in a single direction rather than being splintered among competing factions.

By providing a standard method of describing data, XML provides distributed applications with a number of powerful features. It enables applications to serialize and exchange data in a universal format. For example, remote objects that can output information in XML can "talk" to Web sites. They can also communicate with database programs that recognize XML.

Being able to easily exchange data through XML means that we can use components together in a distributed application that are built using widely different technologies. Remote objects written in many different programming languages can interoperate, even though their binary format is extremely different. The individual programs, Web pages, remote objects, and so forth, form a cohesive application even though the parts are very loosely coupled. Their only real connection is the capability to exchange XML data over a common communication channel, such as HTTP. And, as previously noted, exchanging data over HTTP means that the data can go virtually anywhere.

Defining Data Structures in XML

To encode data into XML, you must first create an XML document. Listing 5.1 contains an XML document that describes a very small customer database.

```
1     <?xml version='1.0'?>
2     <!-- This file is a fragment of a customer database -->
3     <customer-list>
4         <customer>
5             <ID>7890</ID>
6             <name>
7                 <first>John</first>
8                 <middle>Queue</middle>
9                 <last>Public</last>
10            </name>
11            <address>
12                <street-address lines="1">
13                    <street>1234 5th St. NW</street>
14                </street-address>
15                <city>Somewhere</city>
16                <area name="state">WA</area>
17                <mail-code>98765</mail-code>
18                <country>USA</country>
19            </address>
20            <phone-number>321-654-0987</phone-number>
21        </customer>
22        <customer>
23            <ID>3456</ID>
24            <name>
25                <first>Taro</first>
26                <last>Tanaka</last>
27            </name>
28            <address>
29                <street-address lines="4">
30                    <street>Green Heights</street>
31                    <street>#404</street>
32                    <street>1 Chome 15-3</street>
33                    <street>Ishikawa Cho</street>
34                </street-address>
35                <city>Haneda</city>
36                <area name="prefecture">Gifu</area>
37                <mail-code>312</mail-code>
38                <country>Japan</country>
39            </address>
40            <phone-number>321-654-0987</phone-number>
41        </customer>
42    </customer-list>
```

Listing 5.1 A Customer Database in an XML File

All XML files should begin with a header. The header for the example XML file is on line 1 of Listing 5.1. It specifies that this file is compatible with version 1.0 of XML. Line 2 demonstrates how to insert comments into your XML files. Any program that parses this XML file will ignore the comment on line 2.

You describe each data item in an XML with a tag. The individual data item is called an element. Elements are enclosed in tags. XML does not define what the tags are. You make them up yourself. That's why XML is so useful. You can use it to describe data in the way that is most suited to your application. When a program or component in a distributed application exchanges XML data with another program or component, they must use a common set of XML tags. That's the only limitation on the format of the data.

The first tag in Listing 5.1 that describes data is on line 3. It states that it defines a list of customers and marks the beginning of the list. The tag on line 42 marks the end of the customer list. If you needed to, you could include other types of lists in the same document. The flexibility of XML allows this. It only requires that each list be marked with its own beginning and ending tags. For example, the customer list could be followed by a parts list that used the tags `<parts-list>` and `</parts-list>`.

NOTE

There must be an opening and closing tag for most elements in an XML file. Opening and closing tags are nearly identical. The only difference is that closing tags contain a / before the tag name, for example <customer-list> and </customer-list>.

The element inside a pair of tags can contain data and other tags. For example, the tags `<customer>` and `</customer>` occur inside the `<customer-list>` and `</customer-list>` tags. The customer list itself is an element. It contains records with information about customers. Each record, marked by `<customer>` and `</customer>`, is one element. The list can contain as many of them as needed. The individual customer record elements also contain multiple elements. You can nest elements as deeply as you need to. Some elements in an XML document contain other elements; others do not. Notice, for instance, that city name on line 15 of Listing 5.1 just contains the name of the city.

The tags in an XML file describe the structure of data. In addition to the data itself, tags can contain attributes. The `<street-address>` tag on line 12, for instance, contains an attribute called `lines`. This describes the data by specifying the number of lines in the street address. The street address on lines 12-14 has only one line of text. However, it can have as many as is needed. This is demonstrated on lines 29-34. This street address for an apartment building in Japan has four lines of text. The fact that street addresses can contain any number of text lines makes it extremely easy to accommodate international addresses in an application. Attributes make the `<street-address>` tag very flexible.

Whenever you assign a value to an attribute, the value must be contained inside quote marks. You can assign virtually any type of value to an attribute. They are not limited to numbers. An attribute's value can be any string of characters. This doesn't mean that we can assign the string "`green`" to the `lines` attribute in Listing 5.1. It only makes sense to allow integers that are greater than or equal to zero to be assigned to `lines`. What it means is that you can make up any attribute and assign any appropriate string to it.

An example of this is shown in lines 16 and 36. They both contain an `<area>` tag. In the United States, the value of the `<area>` tag is the state in which the customer lives. In Japan, the area is called a prefecture. The <area> tag's `name` attribute reflects this. It is a string containing the name used to describe the area. In Canada, the `name` attribute would be set to "`province`" rather than "`state`" or "`prefecture`".

Although not demonstrated in this example, some XML elements only use one tag. This is generally done when the element's data is contained entirely within its attributes. When an element has only one tag, the tag takes the form `<tagname/>`.

The combination of tags, attributes, and elements means that you can describe your data in just about any way that's required for your application. Again, when you exchange data between remote objects, Web pages, or programs, the only limitation that XML places on you is that both ends of the data transfer must recognize the same set of tags and attributes.

The XML in the .NET Framework

Microsoft's .NET Framework makes heavy use of XML for data exchange. Not only that, but its configuration files are also in XML. If you use .NET Remoting, you will use XML. As a result of this dependence on XML, the .NET Framework provides an extensive set of classes to help your programs read, parse, and write XML data.

NOTE

.NET Remoting does not *force* you to use XML. It is possible to write programs using .NET Remoting that contain no XML. This means, however, that your program must do everything programmatically and avoid the use of custom configuration files. In some situations, this can reduce the flexibility of your program and severely limit your deployment options. Therefore, an understanding of XML is important for all but the most trivial Remoting applications.

The highest-level XML class it provides is called `XmlDocument`. It represents the document as a whole. When the Framework parses XML documents, it creates tree structure. The root of the tree is an `XmlDocument` object. For each element in the document, it adds a node to the tree. Nodes are represented with the `XmlNode` class. Individual nodes can have attributes, which are contained in `XmlAttribute` objects. If a program uses the .NET Framework to parse the XML file in Listing 5.1, it gets the tree shown in Figure 5.1. Note that part of the tree is omitted to save space.

As the tree in Figure 5.1 illustrates, some nodes represent element tags. Those that do can also have attribute objects. Nodes that represent tags and attributes make up the nodes in the inner part of the tree. Nodes in the tree that hold the data for the individual elements reside at the ends of the tree's branches.

Your programs use the XML classes in the .NET Framework to build trees such as this. After a program builds an XML tree, it can traverse the tree and process tree items as it goes. When it is done, it can alter the contents of the tree, write it back to a disk, send it over the Internet, or whatever else you need to do with it.

Reading and Parsing XML Files

Programs read XML files using an `XmlTextReader` object. When your program calls the object's constructor, it can pass the `XmlTextReader` the name of the file you want it to read. If there are any errors when reading the file, the `XmlTextReader` object throws an exception. One source of errors is incorrectly formed XML tags. For instance, if you accidentally type the tags for the customer list in Listing 5.1 as `<customerlist>` and `</customerlist>`, the `XmlTextReader` object throws an exception because the tag names do not match.

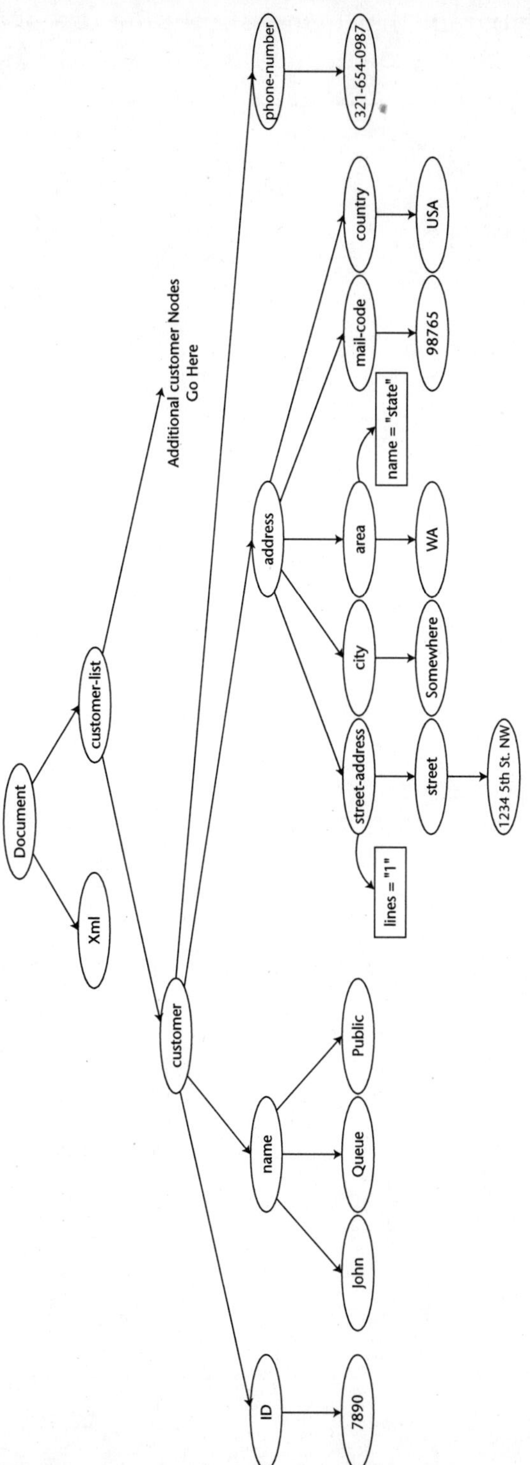

Figure 5.1 The .NET Framework's Tree Representation of an XML File

Listing 5.2 contains a program that demonstrates the use of the the `XmlTextReader` object. It's my own simplified implementation of a sample that comes with the .NET SDK.

```
using System;
using System.Xml;


namespace ReadXML
{
    class ReadXML
    {
        private const string FILE_NAME = "customers.xml";

        [STAThread]
        static void Main()
        {
            XmlTextReader xmlReader = null;

            try
            {
                Console.WriteLine("Reading file...");
                xmlReader = new XmlTextReader(FILE_NAME);
                Console.WriteLine("Done.");

                Console.WriteLine("Processing...");
                Console.WriteLine();
                ProcessFile(xmlReader);
            }
            catch (Exception e)
            {
                Console.WriteLine("\nFile read error.");
                Console.WriteLine(
                    "Exception: {0}",
                    e.ToString());
            }

            System.Console.WriteLine("\nFile processed.\n");
            System.Console.WriteLine(
                "Press Enter to end the program...");
            System.Console.Read();

            if (xmlReader != null)
                xmlReader.Close();
        }

        private static void ProcessFile(
            XmlReader theReader)
```

Listing 5.2 Parsing an XML File

```
        {
            while (theReader.Read())
            {
                switch (theReader.NodeType)
                {
                    case XmlNodeType.XmlDeclaration:
                        DisplayOutput(theReader, "XmlDeclara-
tion");
                    break;
                    case XmlNodeType.Comment:
                        DisplayOutput(theReader, "Comment");
                    break;
                    case XmlNodeType.Element:
                        DisplayOutput(theReader, "Element");
                    break;
                    case XmlNodeType.Text:
                        DisplayOutput(theReader, "Text");
                    break;
                }
            }
        }

        private static void DisplayOutput(
            XmlReader theReader,
            string nodeType)
        {
            for (int i=0; i < theReader.Depth; i++)
            {
                Console.Write('\t');
            }

            string outputString;

            outputString = theReader.Prefix +  nodeType + ": ";

            if (theReader.Name != "")
            {
                outputString += theReader.Name;
            }

            if (theReader.Value != "")
            {
                outputString += theReader.Value;
            }

            System.Console.Write(outputString);

            if (theReader.HasAttributes)
```

Listing 5.2 Parsing an XML File *(continues)*

```
92                  {
93                      System.Console.Write(" Attributes:");
94
95                      for (int j=0; j < theReader.AttributeCount; j++)
96                      {
97                          System.Console.Write(
98                              " [{0}] " + theReader[j], j);
99                      }
100                 }
101                 System.Console.WriteLine();
102             }
103
104         }
105     }
```

Listing 5.2 Parsing an XML File *(continued)*

This program produces a report about the XML file that it reads. Note that it specifies the use of the `System.Xml` namespace on line 2. This statement gives the program access to the Framework's XML classes.

Line 14 of the program in Listing 5.2 declares a reference to an `XmlTextReader` object. The program allocates the object on line 19. The constructor reads the file into memory and builds the tree representation of the XML statements.

On line 24, the program calls the `ProcessFile()` method. This method produces the report about the XML file and prints it to the screen. Figure 5.2 displays part of the report that it produces.

As you can see from the figure, the program parses the XML file and describes the type of each element it contains. The section of the code that does the processing begins on line 46 of Listing 5.2. The `while` statement loops for as long as the `XmlTextReader` is able to read information from the file. It uses a `switch` statement that begins on line 48. The `switch` statement uses the `XmlTextReader` object's `NodeType` property to determine what type of element the `XmlTextReader` read in and parsed. There is a `case` statement for each of the major types of XML elements. Note that there are some other elements that are not as frequently used that are ignored by this program for simplicity.

```
Reading file...
Done.
Processing...

XmlDeclaration: xmlversion='1.0' Attributes: [0] 1.0
Comment:  This file is a fragment of a customer database
Element: customer-list
        Element: customer
                Element: ID
                        Text: 7890
                Element: name
                        Element: first
                                Text: John
                        Element: middle
                                Text: Queue
                        Element: last
                                Text: Public
                Element: address
                        Element: street-address Attributes: [0] 1
                                Element: street
                                        Text: 1234 5th St. NW
                        Element: city
                                Text: Somewhere
                        Element: area Attributes: [0] state
                                Text: WA
                        Element: mail-code
                                Text: 98765
                        Element: country
                                Text: USA
                Element: phone-number
                        Text: 321-654-0987
```

Figure 5.2 Partial Output from the Program in Listing 5.2

The individual lines of the report are printed to the screen by the `DisplayOutput()` method. When the `XmlTextReader` object reads and parses an element in the XML file, the `XmlTextReader` object provides access to the elements attributes. For example, the `DisplayOutput()` method accesses each elements, name, type, and value with the `XmlTextReader` object's `Name`, `NodeType`, and `Value` properties. Your program can also use the `HasAttributes` and `AttributeCount` properties to determine whether an element has attributes, and, if so, how many there are.

This program demonstrates just a few of the classes that the .NET Framework provides for reading and parsing XML files. It's wise to become familiar with as many of them as possible.

Writing XML Files

The program in Listing 5.2 demonstrates one way to read and parse an XML file. However, if your program handles complex or large XML files, a more efficient way to process it is to use the `XmlDocument` class to build the type of tree demonstrated previously. Using the `XmlDocument` class makes the .NET Framework do most of the work for you. It loads the XML file, parses it, and builds the tree with one method call. Your program can then traverse the tree and perform custom processing on it.

Listing 5.3 shows a program that uses the `XmlDocument` class to load and process the XML file from Listing 5.1.

```
using System;
using System.Xml;

namespace WriteXML
{
    class WriteXML
    {
        private const string INPUT_FILE = "customers.xml";
        private const string OUTPUT_FILE = "customers.v2.xml";

        [STAThread]
        static void Main(string[] args)
        {
            try
            {
                XmlDocument theDoc = new XmlDocument();
                System.Console.WriteLine ("Loading document...");
                theDoc.Load(new XmlTextReader(INPUT_FILE));
                System.Console.WriteLine ("Done.");
                System.Console.WriteLine("\nProcessing XML
file...");

                TraverseTree(theDoc.DocumentElement);
                theDoc.Save(OUTPUT_FILE);

                System.Console.WriteLine("\nFile processed.\n");
                System.Console.WriteLine(
                    "Press Enter to end the program...");
```

Listing 5.3 Processing an XML File with an XmlDocument Object

```
                System.Console.Read();
            }
            catch (Exception e)
            {
                System.Console.WriteLine(
                    "Exception: {0}",
                    e.ToString());
            }
        }

        public static void TraverseTree(XmlNode theNode)
        {
            if (theNode.Name == "area")
            {
                for (int i=0;
                     i<theNode.Attributes.Count;
                     i++)
                {
                    if (theNode.Attributes.Item(i).Name == "name")
                    {
                        switch (theNode.Attributes.Item(i).Value)
                        {
                            case "state":
                                theNode.Attributes.Item(i).Value =
                                    "State";
                            break;

                            case "prefecture":
                                theNode.Attributes.Item(i).Value =
                                    "Prefecture";
                            break;

                            case "province":
                                theNode.Attributes.Item(i).Value =
                                    "Province";
                            break;
                        }
                    }
                }
            }

            for (theNode = theNode.FirstChild;
                 theNode != null;
                 theNode = theNode.NextSibling)
            {
                TraverseTree(theNode);
            }
        }
    }
}
```

Listing 5.3 Processing an XML File with an XmlDocument Object *(continued)*

This program creates an `XmlDocument` object on line 16 of Listing 5.3. On line 18, it uses an `XmlTextReader` to load the XML file into the `XmlDocument` object. The `XmlDocument` object automatically parses the file and builds an XML tree in memory. On line 22, the program calls the `TraverseTree()` method and passes it the first element in the XML tree.

The `TraverseTree()` method, which begins on line 38, recursively traverses the XML tree. It uses an `if` statement (lines 40-67) to test whether the name property of the current node is the string "`area`". If it is, the method enters a `for` loop to iterate through the `<area>` node's list of attributes. In our example, an `<area>` node only has one attribute. However, the loop demonstrates how easy it is to move through a list of several attributes and select one of them for processing. In this case, the `if` statement beginning on line 46 selects the `name` attribute. It uses a `switch` statement to test the `name` attribute's value. If the value is "`state`", it substitutes the string "`State`" instead. The method performs the similar processing for the values "`prefecture`" and "`province`" by substituting the strings "`prefecture`" and "`province`", respectively, into the attribute's `Value` property.

On line 69 of Listing 5.3, the `TraverseTree()` method enters a `for` loop. In the loop, it moves through the current node's list of children and recursively calls itself for each child node in the list. When the `TraverseTree()` method finishes its recursive processing, program execution jumps back to line 22. On line 23, the program calls the `XmlDocument.Save()` method to write the XML tree back out to a file.

SOAP

XML defines or describes data. It can also be used to describe services provided by remote objects. SOAP, or Simple Object Access Protocol, is a standard that specifies how to use XML to create messages that call methods on remote objects. The messages can state which methods the client wants to call. They also describe the data that the clients pass to the remote objects as parameters. When a remote method finishes, it sends a SOAP message containing the return value back to the client.

.NET Remoting makes heavy use of SOAP in a way that is very transparent to developers. However, the use of SOAP is not limited to the .NET Framework. SOAP is an industry-wide standard and is independent of any one company. Several companies are working on implementations of SOAP-based toolkits and SDKs. For example, at the Web site

```
http://xml.apache.org/soap/
```

you'll find an open source implementation of SOAP that includes both binaries and source code.

The SOAP specification contains a set of rules for serializing data. It does not say how a remote object's methods are implemented, nor does it specify how client programs must be implemented. As a result, you can create both remote objects and clients with any technology you see fit. This gives objects built with .NET Remoting on Windows the ability to work with Linux clients written in Java. The reverse is also true. Objects written in Java that understand SOAP can provide services to clients written with the .NET Framework.

This high degree of interoperability means that you can build your distributed applications in nearly any way you see fit. As long as all of the pieces understand XML and SOAP, they should be able to work together.

By default, SOAP uses the HTTP transport. However, the SOAP standard explicitly states that other transport methods can be used to exchange SOAP messages. Most distributed applications use HTTP because it is so widely available and because it enables services to be accessed across firewalls.

NOTE

The biggest limitation with using SOAP is performance. Because it involves transmitting messages as text, requesting services and moving data can be slow. This is not usually a problem when you make remote objects available in the Internet because everyone understands that the Internet has built-in performance problems by its very nature. Even remote objects not offered on the Internet may have compelling reasons to make use of SOAP because of its ability to provide interoperability with COM, Java, and other types of components. In these cases, it may be worthwhile to live with the SOAP's performance limitations.

Because the .NET Remoting classes make the use of SOAP so transparent, it isn't absolutely necessary to understand how SOAP works to use it. However, if you plan to write remote applications that involve objects made with COM, Java, or other distributed technologies, you'll need to at least know the basics of SOAP.

SOAP Messages

The SOAP specification defines three types of messages. They are:

- Method calls
- Response messages
- Error Messages

Method call messages invoke methods provided by remote objects. They contain name of the method to execute and the parameters sent by the client. When a remote object's method finishes, it generates a response message containing the return value. If there was an error, the remote object's method sends an error message to the client. Error messages are also called fault messages. Only remote objects can generate SOAP error messages. If some other type of error occurs, the appropriate software component generates the error condition. For example, if an HTTP error occurs, the client receives an HTTP error rather than a SOAP error.

The format of all three types of messages is very similar. Each message type contains an envelope, an optional header, and a message body. Figure 5.3 demonstrates a sample SOAP message.

```
<SOAP-ENV:Envelope
   xmlns:SOAP-ENV=
      "http://schemas.xmlsoap.org/soap/envelope/"
   SOAP-ENV:encodingStyle=
      "http://schemas.xmlsoap.org/soap/encoding/">
   <SOAP-ENV:Header>
      <t:Customer-Update-Type
         xmlns:t="some-URI" SOAP-ENV:mustUnderstand="1">
            5
      </t: Customer-Update-Type>
   </SOAP-ENV:Header>
   <SOAP-ENV:Body>
      <m:GetCustomerName
         xmlns:m="Some-URI">
            <customerID>12345</customerID>
      </m:GetCustomerName>
   </SOAP-ENV:Body>
</SOAP-ENV:Envelope>
```

Figure 5.3 A SOAP Message

The message in Figure 5.3 begins with the SOAP <Envelope> tag. The tag is prefixed with the namespace `SOAP-ENV`. This namespace contains the definitions of the standard SOAP tags such as <Envelope> and <Body>. XML allows you to define your own custom tags for your application. Using the `SOAP-ENV` namespace ensures that the application does not confuse the SOAP tags with application-specific tags. The `SOAP-ENV` namespace is defined at the URI `http://schemas.xmlsoap.org/soap/envelope/`.

WARNING

By default, SOAP messages generated the .NET Framework use the SOAP-ENV namespace on all standard SOAP elements in the message. If you integrate remote objects into your application that are not created with the .NET Remoting classes (a Java object, for instance), it is up to you to ensure that all of the SOAP messages it generates use the SOAP-ENV namespace.

This message has an optional header. The header contains the element `Customer-Update-Type`, which is an application-specific message element. It has nothing to do with SOAP. Therefore, it is not prefixed by the namespace `SOAP-ENV`. It's up to the application to determine what this element means and how to process it. However, the `Customer-Update-Type` element has the SOAP attribute `mustUnderstand` on it. The `mustUnderstand` attribute is set to 1, which means true. Therefore, the remote object must recognize the `Customer-Update-Type` element to be able to process the message. If the remote object does not understand this element, it must not process the message. It also needs to send the client an message indicating the failure.

The body of the SOAP message in Figure 5.3 invokes a method called `GetCustomerName()`. It passes the number 12345 as the value of a parameter called `customerID`. The `GetCustomerName()` method retrieves the name of the customer whose ID is 12345. The body of the message specifies that the `GetCustomerName()` method is located at the URI specified by the name `Some-URI`.

To send the requested information back to the client, the remote object must generate a reply similar to the message given in Figure 5.4.

```
<SOAP-ENV:Envelope
   xmlns:SOAP-ENV=
      "http://schemas.xmlsoap.org/soap/envelope/"
   SOAP-ENV:encodingStyle=
      "http://schemas.xmlsoap.org/soap/encoding/">
   <SOAP-ENV:Header>
      <t:Customer-Update-Type
         xmlns:t="some-URI" SOAP-ENV:mustUnderstand="1">
            5
      </t: Customer-Update-Type>
   </SOAP-ENV:Header>
   <SOAP-ENV:Body>
      <m:GetCustomerNameResponse
         xmlns:m="Some-URI">
            <return>John Queue Public</return>
      </m:GetCustomerNameResponse>
   </SOAP-ENV:Body>
</SOAP-ENV:Envelope>
```

Figure 5.4 Remote Object Reply

The response is often nearly identical to the original message. The differences typically occur in the body of the message, as in Figure 5.4. The word Response has been appended to the name of the remote method. The `<customerID>` element in Figure 5.3 is replaced by the element `<return>`. This element contains the return value from the remote method.

Data Types in SOAP

Because all of the clients and servers in a distributed application must agree on how data is serialized, the SOAP specification states the serialization rules explicitly. Messages that conform to the SOAP standard should use the types specified in the namespace:

```
http://www.w3.org/2001/XMLSchema-instance/
```

Each parameter or return value in a message has the `xsi:type` attribute associated with it. This attribute specifies the parameter or return value's data type from the set of data types available in the XML Schema. If the `xsi:type` attribute is not present, the data is assumed to be a string. Figure 5.5 demonstrates how a SOAP message's `<Body>` element might look.

```
<SOAP-ENV:Body>
   <m:SomeMethod
      xmlns:m="Some-URI">
         <thisParam xsi:type = "int">12345</thisParam>
         <thatParam xsi:type = "float">12.345</thatParam>
         <anotherParam xsi:type = "boolean">false</anotherParam>
   </m: >
</SOAP-ENV:Body>
```

Figure 5.5 Specifying Data Types

This message body passes three parameters to a method called `SomeMethod()`. The first parameter, which is named `thisParam`, is an integer. The second, `thatParam`, is a floating point number whose value is 12.345. The final parameter is of type `boolean`. It is set to the value `false`.

You'll find the complete specification for all of the standard XML data types at:

```
http://www.w3.org/TR/xmlschema-2/
```

SOAP and WSDL

XML and SOAP provide developers with a method of describing data, exchanging it across a network, and invoking remote methods. However, neither of them state how a client program discovers what objects are available on a server and what methods the object supports. Neither do they enable the discovery of what parameters and return values are required by a remote object's methods.

To solve this problem, we use Web Service Description Language (WSDL). Like SOAP, WSDL is based on XML. WSDL documents contain all of the methods, parameters, and return values offered by remote objects available on the server. Applications can ask a Web server for its WSDL document and then use that document to control the format of the SOAP messages it sends to the Web server.

REMINDER

A Web Service is the use of one or more remote objects to offer the functionality of a company's proprietary multitiered network application on the Web.

In fact, the .NET Framework uses the published WSDL files on servers to create the proxy for remote objects. The .NET SDK includes a tool called wsdl.exe that you can use to create a proxy object from a given WSDL document. If you use Visual Studio, however, you do not need to use this tool. Visual Studio provides this capability in its integrated development environment (IDE).

You'll find the complete WSDL specification at:

```
http://www.w3.org/TR/wsdl
```

Summary

XML is an industry-standard language for defining the structure of information. Remote applications often use XML to define the structure of data. SOAP, which is a set of standard protocols for defining data in XML, provides distributed applications with a standard format for invoking methods provided by remote objects, passing data to those methods, and receiving data back from them. Microsoft's .NET Framework provides an extensive set of classes for reading, parsing, and writing files in XML and SOAP.

XML and SOAP provides standard formats for applications to communicate across networks. Data in XML or soap format is always text. It can pass across Internet firewalls. However, because it is text it impacts the performance of distributed applications. In particular, transmitting data as text generally consumes more network bandwidth than transmitting equivalent data in binary format.

There are three types of SOAP messages. These include method calls, response messages, and error messages. When SOAP messages contain data they also specify the types of the data.

Applications can discover a remote object's methods using WSDL. This XML-based language provides a standard method of describing what methods an object provides, what parameters they require, and what values they return.

CHAPTER 6

Providing Remote Objects for Clients

The various example programs shown so far demonstrated that server objects must provide a description of their remote objects to client programs. The description must be available when we compile the client programs so that they can treat the remote objects very much as if they were local to the clients.

There are multiple techniques for providing a compile-time description of a remote object. This chapter presents each technique and discusses its advantages and disadvantages.

Compiling Remote Objects into Client Programs

The first, and simplest, method of providing clients with a compile-time description of a remote object is to compile the object's source code into the client. Chapter 3 demonstrated this technique. However, this technique is highly problematic in all but the simplest of applications. There are many circumstances under which it does not work. Also this technique is a serious security risk for a real-world application. It can cause maintenance problems if the object's source code on the server gets out of sync with the object's code on the client.

Because of the many problems with sharing the object's source code, it should be avoided in commercial-grade applications. The only possible exception that I can think of for using this technique is when you are creating an application that can operate either connected or disconnected and you want it to use the same objects and code either way. To make this work, you must compile the remote object in its own assembly and put a reference to it into both the client and server projects. Your application must have specific logic in it that distinguishes between remote and local versions of the object so that it can dynamically change from one to the other. If the user works with local objects while disconnected from the network, your application must provide a means of synchronizing the local and remote objects.

WARNING

If your application shares the source code for an object between the client and the server, be sure that it is not an object that will compromise the application's security.

Sharing Interfaces

A far better approach than sharing an object's source code is to share an interface between the client and the server. Chapters 3 and 4 demonstrated this technique as well. We saw that sharing compile-time information this way enables clients to have a complete description of and access to the remote object's public methods. However, it does not pass private implementation information to clients. Recall that, for this technique to succeed, you must compile the interface into its own assembly. Both the client and server project files must contain a reference to this assembly.

In the previous section, I mentioned that it is possible that you might want to share source code between the client and server programs if your application can be used when disconnected from the network. Sharing interfaces between the client and the server can provide you with a better way to accomplish the same thing. To help increase security, you may find it advantageous to define an interface for the object instead of providing the object itself. You can then write a version of the object that will be used only in disconnected mode on the client. Another version, one that is used when the application is connected to network, is used on the server. If your application is disconnected, it uses the local object that implements the shared interface. When it is connected, it uses the remote object on the server.

Using this approach ensures that the server's implementation is not compromised. Because both the local and remote versions of the object implement the same interface, most of your application's code will be usable with either object.

Unfortunately, there are some circumstances in which sharing an interface will not work. In particular, if a client passes a reference to a `MarshalByRef` object to another process on the server computer (or to a process on different server), the `ObjRef` is serialized and deserialized. When it is received by the second server process, the .NET Framework generates a proxy from the `ObjRef`. It then attempts to downcast the `ObjRef` to the type of the object. However, it cannot perform the downcast if all it has is an interface. A solution to this problem is to share an abstract base class instead. This technique is presented next.

Sharing Abstract Base Classes

Sharing an abstract base class between servers and clients provides many of the same advantages as sharing interfaces. Like interfaces, they contain no implementation information because the base classes are abstract. This helps keep distributed applications secure.

Unlike interfaces, abstract base classes can be downcast when a client passes the `ObjRef` it obtained for a remote object to another process on the same server, or to a process on another server. To demonstrate how this is done, let's create a version of the `InformationManager` object, shown in previous chapters, that uses an abstract base class. The client for this object will send its reference to an `InformationProcessor` object in another server program. The `InformationProcessor` object will also share information about itself using an abstract base class.

Listing 6.1 shows the abstract base class for the `InformationManager` object.

```
using System;

namespace InfoMan
{
    public abstract class InfoManBase : MarshalByRefObject
    {
```

Listing 6.1 The Abstract Base Class for the Information Manager *(continues)*

```
        public abstract string DataItem(int whichItem);
        public abstract void DataItem(
            int whichItem,
            string newValue);

        public abstract int DataCollectionLength();
    }
}
```

Listing 6.1 The Abstract Base Class for the Information Manager *(continued)*

This version of the information manager is similar to previous implementations. However, instead of being defined as an interface, it is an abstract class that inherits from `MarshalByRefObject`. It provides an additional overloaded method over previous versions that enables clients to set a data item. As with interfaces, you must compile abstract base classes into their own assemblies.

The `InformationManager` object is presented in Listing 6.2.

```
using System;

namespace InfoMan
{
    public class InformationManager : InfoManBase
    {
        private const int ARRAY_SIZE = 12;
        private string [] theData = new string [ARRAY_SIZE];

        public InformationManager()
        {
            // Initialize the array.
            theData[0] = "\"Just the place for a Snark!\"";
            theData[1] =  "the Bellman cried,";
            theData[2] = "As he landed his crew with care;";
            theData[3] = "Supporting each man on the top of";
            theData[4] = "the tide";
            theData[5] = "By a finger entwined in his hair.";
            theData[6] = "\"Just the place for a Snark!";
            theData[7] = "I have said it twice:";
            theData[8] = "That alone should encourage the crew.";
            theData[9] = "Just the place for a Snark!";
            theData[10] = "I have said it thrice:";
```

Listing 6.2 The Information Manager

```
            theData[11] = "What i tell you three times is true.\"";
        }

        public override string DataItem(int whichItem)
        {
            string theItem = null;

            // If the item number is valid...
            if ((whichItem >= 0) && (whichItem < ARRAY_SIZE))
            {
                // Get the item.
                theItem = theData[whichItem];
            }

            // Return the item to the client.
            return (theItem);
        }

        public override void DataItem(
            int whichItem,
            string newValue)
        {
            // If the item number is valid...
            if ((whichItem >= 0) && (whichItem < ARRAY_SIZE))
            {
                // Set the item.
                theData[whichItem] = newValue;
            }
        }

        public override int DataCollectionLength()
        {
            return (ARRAY_SIZE);
        }
    }
}
```

Listing 6.2 The Information Manager *(continued)*

The `InformationManager` object inherits from the `InfoManBase` object. Because `InfoManBase` derives from `MarshalByRefObject`, the `InformationManager` object also inherits from it as well. This enables applications to pass an `InformationManager` object to client programs by reference.

This version of the InformationManager class uses the same method, called DataItem(), to retrieve data as previous implementations. It also implements the additional overload of the DataItem() method that enables clients to set data items.

NOTE

When you use abstract base classes in C#, all methods in the derived class that override methods in the base class must contain the keyword override in their definitions.

The InformationManager object is offered to remote clients by the server program in Listing 6.3.

```
using System;
using System.Runtime.Remoting;
using System.Runtime.Remoting.Channels;
using System.Runtime.Remoting.Channels.Http;
using InfoMan;

namespace Server01
{
    class Server01AppClass
    {
        [STAThread]
        static void Main(string[] args)
        {
            HttpChannel theChannel = new HttpChannel(8085);
            ChannelServices.RegisterChannel(theChannel);

            RemotingConfiguration.ApplicationName = "InfoMan";
            RemotingConfiguration.RegisterWellKnownServiceType(
                typeof(InformationManager),
                "InfoMan.soap",
                WellKnownObjectMode.Singleton);

            System.Console.WriteLine(
                "Press Enter to end the InformationManager.");
            System.Console.Read();
        }
    }
}
```

Listing 6.3 The Information Manager Server

As you can see, this implementation of the server program is nearly identical to previous versions. Like the others, this program offers the

InformationManager object over an HTTP channel on port 8085. This time, the InformationManager object is a singleton object, so it keeps its state between method calls.

Remember that, when you compile the InformationManager object into this server program, you must include a reference to the System .Runtime.Remoting namespace in the server's project file. The project file also needs a reference to the DLL containing the InfoManBase class.

The client for this application passes a reference for the Information-Manager object to another server. The abstract base class for the second remote server object is shown in Listing 6.4.

```
using System;
using InfoMan;

namespace InfoProc
{
    public abstract class InfoProcBase : MarshalByRefObject
    {
        public abstract void SortData(InfoManBase dataSource);
    }
}
```

Listing 6.4 The Abstract Base Class for the Information Processor

Like the InfoManBase class in Listing 6.1, the InfoProcBase class in Listing 6.4 inherits from the MarshalByRefObject class. Of course, the InfoProcBase class must also be compiled into its own assembly.

The information processor offers a method that sorts the data in the order defined by the ASCII set of characters. It takes a reference to the information manager as its only parameter.

The implementation of the information processor is given in Listing 6.5.

```
using System;
using System.Runtime.Remoting;
using InfoMan;


namespace InfoProc
{
```

Listing 6.5 The Information Processor *(continues)*

```
8        public class InformationProcessor : InfoProcBase
9        {
10           InformationProcessor()
11           {
12           }
13
14           public override void SortData(InfoManBase dataSource)
15           {
16               int collectionLength =
17                   dataSource.DataCollectionLength();
18
19               // Sort with a simple Bubble Sort.
20               for (int i=1; i<collectionLength; i++)
21               {
22                   for (int j=0; j<i; j++)
23                   {
24                       string string1 = dataSource.DataItem(i);
25                       string string2 = dataSource.DataItem(j);
26
27                       if (string1.CompareTo(string2)<0)
28                       {
29                           dataSource.DataItem(i,string2);
30                           dataSource.DataItem(j,string1);
31                       }
32                   }
33               }
34           }
35       }
36   }
```

Listing 6.5 The Information Processor *(continued)*

The `InformationProcessor` class, which inherits from `Info-ProcBase`, is an object that can be marshaled by reference. Its `SortData()` method, shown on lines 14-34, receives a reference to the `InformationManager` object from the client through its `dataSource` parameter. On lines 16-17, it retrieves the length of the data collection. It then enters a for loop beginning on line 20.

The loop implements a Bubble Sort to sort the data. Each time through its inner loop, it retrieves two strings to sort. If the string in the variable `string2` is less than the string in `string1`, the `SortData()` method switches them on lines 29-30.

Its important to note that when the client passes its reference to the `InformationManager` object to the `InformationProcessor` object, the CLR on the computer on which the `InformationProcessor` object runs creates a proxy for the `InformationManager` object. As a result, both the client and the information processor have proxies for the `InformationManager`. Having its own reference to the `InformationManager` object enables the `InformationProcessor` to communicate directly with the `InformationManager`.

Listing 6.6 gives the code for the server program that makes the `InformationProcessor` object available on the network.

```
using System;
using System.Runtime.Remoting;
using System.Runtime.Remoting.Channels;
using System.Runtime.Remoting.Channels.Http;
using InfoProc;

namespace Server02
{
    class Server02AppClass
    {
        [STAThread]
        static void Main(string[] args)
        {
            HttpChannel theChannel = new HttpChannel(8080);
            ChannelServices.RegisterChannel(theChannel);

            RemotingConfiguration.ApplicationName = "InfoProc";
            RemotingConfiguration.RegisterWellKnownServiceType(
                typeof(InformationProcessor),
                "InfoProc.soap",
                WellKnownObjectMode.SingleCall);

            System.Console.WriteLine(
                "Press Enter to end the InformationProcessor.");
            System.Console.Read();
        }
    }
}
```

Listing 6.6 The Information Processor Server

Of course, when you compile this server program with the `InformationManager` class, you must include a reference to `System.Runtime.Remoting` in the project file. You'll also need a reference to the DLL that contains `InfoProcBase`.

If the server programs in Listings 6.3 and 6.6 are running on the same computer, they must be listening to different ports. That's why the information manager is on port 8085, and the information processor is on port 8080. If they are running off of different computers, the port assignment doesn't matter.

The information processor is available on an HTTP channel. The server program could offer it on a TCP channel. However, if it did, the client would need to open two channels, an HTTP channel to communicate with the information manager, and a TCP channel to communicate with the information processor. Because both servers offer their objects on HTTP channels, the client only needs to open one HTTP channel to communicate with both objects. Listing 6.7 gives the code for the client program.

```
using System;
using System.Runtime.Remoting;
using System.Runtime.Remoting.Channels;
using System.Runtime.Remoting.Channels.Http;
using InfoMan;
using InfoProc;

namespace Chapt4_Client
{
    /// <summary>
    /// Summary description for ApplicationClass.
    /// </summary>
    class ApplicationClass
    {
        /// <summary>
        /// The main entry point for the application.
        /// </summary>
        [STAThread]
        static void Main(string[] args)
        {
            // Create an HTTP channel.
            HttpChannel theChannel = new HttpChannel();

            /* Register the channel so that this client can
               connect to the server. */
            ChannelServices.RegisterChannel(theChannel);

            // Activate the server object.
            InfoManBase infoManager =
                (InfoManBase)Activator.GetObject(
                    typeof(InfoManBase),
```

Listing 6.7 The Client Program

```
                "http://localhost:8085/InfoMan.soap");

            // Activate the server object.
            InfoProcBase infoProcessor =
                (InfoProcBase)Activator.GetObject(
                typeof(InfoProcBase),
                "http://localhost:8080/InfoProc.soap");

            // If the remote objects were activated...
            if ((infoManager != null) &&
                (infoProcessor != null))
            {
                string tempString;
                int dataCollectionLength;

                try
                {
                    dataCollectionLength =
                        infoManager.DataCollectionLength();

                    // Print the unsorted list.
                    System.Console.WriteLine("Unsorted
Data...\n");
                    for (int i=0; i<dataCollectionLength; i++)
                    {
                        tempString = null;

                            // Get the item.
                            tempString = infoManager.DataItem(i);

                            // Print it to the console.
                            System.Console.WriteLine(tempString);
                    }

                    infoProcessor.SortData(infoManager);

                    // Print the sorted list.
                    System.Console.WriteLine("\nSorted
Data...\n");
                    for (int i=0; i<dataCollectionLength; i++)
                    {
                        tempString = null;

                        // Get the item.
                        tempString = infoManager.DataItem(i);

                        // Print it to the console.
                        System.Console.WriteLine(tempString);
                    }
```

Listing 6.7 The Client Program *(continues)*

```
79              }
80              catch (Exception)
81              {
82                  ServerAccessError();
83              }
84          }
85          // Else the remote object was not activated...
86          else
87          {
88              // Print an error message.
89              System.Console.WriteLine(
90                  "Remote object could not be activated");
91          }
92
93          System.Console.WriteLine(
94              "\nPaused. Press Enter to continue...");
95          System.Console.Read();
96      }
97
98      static void ServerAccessError()
99      {
100         System.Console.WriteLine(
101             "Error: Could not access the server");
102     }
103   }
104 }
```

Listing 6.7 The Client Program *(continued)*

The client program for the two-server application needs references to `System.Runtime.Remoting`, the DLL that contains `InfoManBase`, and the DLL that contains `InfoProcBase` in its project file.

First, the client opens and registers a single HTTP channel to communicate with both server objects. On lines 29-32 of Listing 6.7, it obtains a reference to the information manager object. It retrieves a reference to the information processor on lines 34-38. If it successfully obtains the references, it gets the length of the data collection on lines 49-50. It then uses a `for` loop to print the unsorted information.

Next, the client program uses the reference to the information processor to call the `SortData()` method on line 65. After the `SortData()` method returns, the data contained in the information manager object will be in sorted order. The client program demonstrates this by entering another `for` loop on line 69. Inside the `for` loop, the client program prints the sorted strings to the console.

Previously, it was mentioned that once the information processor has a reference to the information manager, the two remote objects communicate directly with each other. This saves us from having to put code in the client program to pass data between the two objects, thus saving us work and increasing the application's efficiency.

Describing Objects with Metadata

Probably the best way of sharing compile-time information about remote server objects with clients is through sharing metadata. Metadata is a language-independent way of describing classes and methods. Like interfaces and abstract base classes, metadata provides a description of a type. It does not communicate the type's implementation. Therefore, it improves the security of your distributed applications.

A great advantage of metadata is that it describes the specific type of the remote object. This enables you to instantiate an instance of the remote type with the C# new keyword. Using new in your program code makes the remote type look much more like a local object. This can't be done with interfaces and abstract base classes.

NOTE

To use the new keyword in client programs to instantiate remote objects, you generally need to create a configuration file for your application. Chapter 8 presents the techniques for creating configuration files.

The only real drawback to using metadata that I can see is that you cannot call non-default constructors when you create a remote object. If you want your object to contain non-default values, you can set them immediately after creating the object or you can use direct remoting, which is presented later in this chapter.

SOAPSUDS

Microsoft provides a command-line tool for generating metadata called SOAPSUDS.EXE. The best way to access SOAPSUDS is to open a command window from the Visual Studio group in your Start menu. If you do, all of the environment variables are set correctly to enable you to execute the command-line tools that Visual Studio provides. To access the command window from the Visual Studio group in your Start menu, select **Start** and then **Programs** (choose **All Programs** if you are using Windows XP). Next, click **Microsoft Visual Studio.Net**. In the menu that appears, choose **Visual Studio.NET Tools**, and then select **Visual Studio.NET Command Prompt**.

Soapsuds generates a proxy that you can compile into your application. Actually, it generates two types of proxies. By default, you get a wrapped proxy (also called a simple proxy). You can also make SOAPSUDS generate an unwrapped proxy. One difference between the two is that a wrapped proxy contains the URI of the remote object. An unwrapped proxy does not.

You can generate proxies from URLs or from assemblies. Either way, you get a DLL containing metadata. To generate a wrapped proxy from a URL, use a command line similar to Command 6.1.

In Command 6.1, the source URL is specified by the -url command-line switch. The symbol `<URL>` represents the URL address of the the remote object. The `-oa` switch specifies the name of the output file, which is an assembly. The filename itself is represented in Command 6.1 by the symbol `<FileName>`.

It's important to note that you probably need to append the string ?wsdl to the URL you specify for the symbol <URL> in Command 6.1. When you generate a proxy from a URL, it's often because you want to create a distributed application that uses a remote object on someone else's Web site. Recall from Chapter 5 that Web sites offering remote objects offer a WSDL file to describe their remote objects. SOAPSUDS can use the WSDL file to create a proxy for your application. In this way, you can make someone else's remote objects look like part of your program.

Wrapped Proxies

Metadata proxies eliminate the need for DLLs containing interfaces or abstract base classes. When you generate a wrapped proxy from a DLL, you use the command line given in Command 6.2.

```
soapsuds -url:<URL> -oa:<FileName>.dll
```

Command 6.1 The Command for Generating a Wrapped Proxy from a URL

```
soapsuds -ia:<InputFileName> -oa:<OutputFileName>.dll
```

Command 6.2 The Command for Generating a Wrapped Proxy from an Assembly

The command in Command 6.2 uses the `-ia` switch to specify the name of the input file. When you use this command, be sure you do not specify the extension .dll in the input file name.

To see how they work, let's create a version of the information manager program that uses a wrapped proxy. Listing 6.8 provides the code for the remote object.

```
using System;

namespace InfoMan
{
    public class InformationManager : MarshalByRefObject
    {
        private const int ARRAY_SIZE = 12;
        private string [] theData = new string [ARRAY_SIZE];

        public InformationManager()
        {
            // Initialize the array.
            theData[0] = "\"Just the place for a Snark!\"";
            theData[1] =  "the Bellman cried,";
            theData[2] = "As he landed his crew with care;";
            theData[3] = "Supporting each man on the top of";
            theData[4] = "the tide";
            theData[5] = "By a finger entwined in his hair.";
            theData[6] = "\"Just the place for a Snark!";
            theData[7] = "I have said it twice:";
            theData[8] = "That alone should encourage the crew.";
            theData[9] = "Just the place for a Snark!";
            theData[10] = "I have said it thrice:";
            theData[11] = "What i tell you three times is
true.\"";
        }

        public string DataItem(int whichItem)
        {
            string theItem = null;
```

Listing 6.8 The Remote Object for the Wrapped Proxy Program *(continues)*

```

            // If the item number is valid...
            if ((whichItem >= 0) && (whichItem < ARRAY_SIZE))
            {
                // Get the item.
                theItem = theData[whichItem];
            }

            // Return the item to the client.
            return (theItem);
        }

        public void DataItem(
            int whichItem,
            string newValue)
        {
            // If the item number is valid...
            if ((whichItem >= 0) && (whichItem < ARRAY_SIZE))
            {
                // Set the item.
                theData[whichItem] = newValue;
            }
        }

        public int DataCollectionLength()
        {
            return (ARRAY_SIZE);
        }
    }
}
```

Listing 6.8 The Remote Object for the Wrapped Proxy Program *(continued)*

This remote object derives directly from the `MarshalByRefObject` type. Like the information manager in Listing 6.1, this class implements both versions of the overloaded `DataItem()` method. The client for this application only calls the `DataItem()` method that retrieves information. However, the second overload of the function is included so that we can get a look at its metadata later in this chapter.

The `InformationManager` object can be compiled into its own assembly. If it is, the project file for the server program needs a reference to the DLL that contains the `InformationManager object`. You can, however, compile the `InformationManager` object into the server program and create an executable program (EXE file). SOAPSUDS can extract metadata from EXE files.

Listing 6.9 shows the server program for the `InformationManager` object.

```
using System;
using System.Runtime.Remoting;
using System.Runtime.Remoting.Channels;
using System.Runtime.Remoting.Channels.Http;
using InfoMan;

namespace Server
{
    class ServerAppClass
    {
        [STAThread]
        static void Main(string[] args)
        {
            HttpChannel theChannel = new HttpChannel(8085);
            ChannelServices.RegisterChannel(theChannel);

            RemotingConfiguration.ApplicationName = "InfoMan";
            RemotingConfiguration.RegisterWellKnownServiceType(
                typeof(InformationManager),
                "InfoMan.soap",
                WellKnownObjectMode.Singleton);

            System.Console.WriteLine(
                "Press Enter to end the InformationManager.");
            System.Console.Read();
        }
    }
}

```

Listing 6.9 The Server for the Wrapped Proxy Program

This code demonstrates that, as far as the server program is concerned, the process of offering a remote object by sharing metadata is virtually identical to sharing it through interfaces and abstract base classes. As Listing 6.10 shows, the real changes are on the client side.

```
using System;
using System.Runtime.Remoting;
using System.Runtime.Remoting.Channels;
using System.Runtime.Remoting.Channels.Http;
using InfoMan;

namespace Client
{
    class ClientAppClass
    {
        [STAThread]
        static void Main(string[] args)
        {
            HttpChannel theChannel = new HttpChannel();
            ChannelServices.RegisterChannel(theChannel);

            InfoMan.InformationManager infoManager =
                (InfoMan.InformationManager)Activator.GetObject(
                typeof(InfoMan.InformationManager),
                "http://localhost:8085/InfoMan.soap");

            // If the remote object was activated...
            if (infoManager != null)
            {
                string tempString;
                int dataCollectionLength;

                try
                {
                    dataCollectionLength =
                        infoManager.DataCollectionLength();

                    // Print the data.
                    for (int i=0; i<dataCollectionLength; i++)
                    {
                        tempString = null;

                        // Get the item.
                        tempString = infoManager.DataItem(i);

                        // Print it to the console.
                        System.Console.WriteLine(tempString);
                    }
                }
                catch (Exception)
                {
                    ServerAccessError();
```

Listing 6.10 The Client for the Wrapped Proxy Program

```
48                  }
49              }
50                  // Else the remote object was not activated...
51              else
52              {
53                  // Print an error message.
54                  System.Console.WriteLine(
55                      "Remote object could not be activated");
56              }
57
58              System.Console.WriteLine(
59                  "\nPaused. Press Enter to continue...");
60              System.Console.Read();
61          }
62
63          static void ServerAccessError()
64          {
65              System.Console.WriteLine(
66                  "Error: Could not access the server");
67          }
68      }
69  }
```

Listing 6.10 The Client for the Wrapped Proxy Program *(continued)*

Lines 14-20 of Listing 6.10 demonstrate that, although the process of establishing a communication channel and getting a reference to an object is similar to doing it through interfaces and abstract base classes, it is not the same. Sharing a metadata assembly enables clients to instantiate remote objects. Because they are not using interfaces or abstract base classes, complications such as downcasts do not crop up.

It's instructive to examine the proxy that SOAPSUDS creates. To do so, use the command in Command 6.3.

The command in Command 6.3 makes the SOAPSUDS program generate the source code for the proxy, rather than a DLL. If you want to, you can compile this source code into your program.

```
soapsuds -ia:<InputFileName> -gc
```

Command 6.3 The Command for Generating Wrapped Proxy Source Code

When I generated the proxy's source code for the wrapped proxy program, I got the results shown in Listing 6.11.

```
using System;
using System.Runtime.Remoting.Messaging;
using System.Runtime.Remoting.Metadata;
using System.Runtime.Remoting.Metadata.W3cXsd2001;

namespace InfoMan {

    public class InformationManager :
        System.Runtime.Remoting.Services.RemotingClientProxy
    {
        // Constructor
        public InformationManager()
        {
        }

        public Object RemotingReference
        {
            get{return(_tp);}
        }

        public String DataItem(Int32 whichItem)
        {
            return ((InformationManager) _tp).DataItem(whichItem);
        }

        public void DataItem(Int32 whichItem, String newValue)
        {
            ((InformationManager) _tp).DataItem(whichItem, newValue);
        }

        public Int32 DataCollectionLength()
        {
            return ((InformationManager) _tp).DataCollectionLength();
        }

    }
}
```

Listing 6.11 The Source Code for the Proxy in the Wrapped Proxy Program

If you generate the proxy's source code for the wrapped proxy program, your output will look a bit different from Listing 6.11. I've removed some attribute information from the listing because it was quite lengthy. Also, that information is not particularly readable to humans.

Line 4 of Listing 6.11 shows that SOAPSUDS adds a `using` directive to provide access to the `W3cXsd2001` namespace in the .NET Framework. This namespace contains some standards-based information used in distributed applications.

In addition, SOAPSUDS adds a method called `RemotingReference()`, that returns a reference to the remote object. Applications should not call this method. The proxy provides it for use by the .NET Remoting classes. Lines 21-29 contain wrappers for the overloaded `DataItem()` methods offered by the remote `InformationManager` object. On lines 31-34, you'll find a wrapper for the `DataCollectionLength()` method.

TRY THIS

I mentioned earlier that you cannot use non-default constructors when using metadata. That's because SOAPSUDS does not generate proxy information for non-default constructors. You can verify this by creating a remote object with a non-default constructor. Use Command 6.3 to generate the source code for your object's wrapped proxy. If you examine the source code, you'll find that it does not contain the non-default constructor.

Unwrapped Proxies

Using an unwrapped proxy is almost identical to the preceding example. You use all of the same code. The difference comes in the way you use SOAPSUDS. To generate an unwrapped proxy, you use Command 6.4.

```
soapsuds -ia:infoman -oa:InfoManMetaData.dll -nowp
```

Command 6.4 Command to Generate an Unwrapped Proxy with SOAPSUDS

The primary differences between wrapped and unwrapped proxies are evident when you are creating a proxy from a URL. A wrapped proxy contains both the metadata and the remote object's URL. An unwrapped proxy contains no URL. If you use a wrapped proxy, you must deploy an updated client program whenever the object's URL changes.

With an unwrapped proxy, you can specify the remote object's URL in a configuration file. Chapter 8 shows how to do this. Because the remote object's URL is not hard-coded into the client program, using an unwrapped proxy is more flexible.

NOTE

Some technical literature about .NET Remoting refers to unwrapped proxies as non-wrapped proxies. However, the Microsoft documentation does not use the term "non-wrapped proxy."

Direct Remoting

The .NET Remoting classes provide applications with a way to publish an object directly to an endpoint (a URI). This technique is called direct remoting. Among other things, direct remoting enables applications to use object factories.

Object factories are objects whose sole purpose is to create other objects. Many uses exist for object factories. For instance, suppose a remote object receives a data file over the network. Imagine that the file contains several different types of data items. Using an object factory, the remote object can parse the data and create an object to represent each type of data item. The factory would create the various types of objects and initialize them with data from the file.

Another use of object factories is to enable programs to instantiate remote objects with non-default constructors. In this scenario, your server program offers an object factory as an MBR singleton object. The client calls a method provided by the factory object that instantiates other remote objects. It can do so with non-default values. After it instantiates an object, the method uses direct remoting techniques to make the object available to the client. The client creates a reference to the remote object with the C# `new` keyword, just as if it were allocating a local object.

Let's get a look at direct remoting and object factories by writing an example program. Listing 6.12 shows the code for a remote object and the object factory that creates it.

```
using System;
using System.Runtime.Remoting;

namespace WidgetSpace
{
    public class WidgetFactory : MarshalByRefObject
    {
        public WidgetFactory()
        {
        }

        public void BuildWidget()
        {
            Widget tempWidget = new Widget();
            RemotingServices.Marshal(
                tempWidget,
                "Widget.soap",
                typeof(Widget));
        }

        public void BuildWidget(int initialValue)
        {
            Widget tempWidget = new Widget(initialValue);
            RemotingServices.Marshal(
                tempWidget,
                "Widget.soap",
                typeof(Widget));
        }
    }

    public class Widget : MarshalByRefObject
    {
        private int currentValue;

        public Widget()
        {
            currentValue = 0;
        }

        public Widget(int initialValue)
        {
            currentValue = initialValue;
```

Listing 6.12 An Object and Its Object Factory *(continues)*

```
43          }
44
45          public int CurrentValue()
46          {
47              return (currentValue);
48          }
49      }
50  }
```

Listing 6.12 An Object and Its Object Factory *(continued)*

In this program, we'll use the SOAPSUDS utility to generate metadata for the `WidgetFactory` and `Widget` objects. Therefore, we don't need to define any interfaces or abstract base classes. When I created the program, I compiled the file in Listing 6.12 into an assembly of its own. The project file for the server used a reference to access the assembly. Before I went any further, I generated a wrapped proxy from the assembly for the client.

If you want to, you can compile the `WidgetFactory` and `Widget` objects into the same program as the server's application class rather than into their own assembly. If you do, you must generate the wrapped proxy from the resulting EXE file.

Listing 6.12 contains the definition of two objects. The first, which is the object factory, appears on lines 4-29. The `WidgetFactory` object provides two overloaded versions of its `BuildWidget()` method. The first version uses `new` to instantiate a `Widget` object by invoking the default constructor. It then calls the `RemotingServices.Marshal()` method to make the Widget available to clients. This version of the `RemotingServices.Marshal()` method (there are other overloaded versions) takes three parameters. The first is the object to be published on the endpoint. The second parameter is the object's URI. The last parameter is its type.

The second version of the `BuildWidget()` method performs exactly the same steps. However, when it allocates the `Widget`, it uses the `Widget` class's non-default constructor to pass the object an initial value that it receives from the client program. It can do this because it is in the same application space as the `Widget` class. It is not trying to call the Widget constructor through a proxy. The object factory allocates

`Widget` objects locally. It then passes them to the `RemotingServices.Marshal()` method to make them available remotely.

NOTE

The object factory in this applications establishes the Widget object on the same channel and port number that the server creates for the object factory. They are differentiated by their URIs.

The server program for the `Widget` object is given in Listing 6.13.

```
using System;
using System.Runtime.Remoting;
using System.Runtime.Remoting.Channels;
using System.Runtime.Remoting.Channels.Http;
using WidgetSpace;

namespace Server
{
    class ServerAppClass
    {
        [STAThread]
        static void Main(string[] args)
        {
            HttpChannel theChannel = new HttpChannel(8085);
            ChannelServices.RegisterChannel(theChannel);

            RemotingConfiguration.ApplicationName = "Widget";
            RemotingConfiguration.RegisterWellKnownServiceType(
                typeof(WidgetFactory),
                "WidgetFactory.soap",
                WellKnownObjectMode.Singleton);

            System.Console.WriteLine(
                "Press Enter to end the server.");
            System.Console.Read();
        }
    }
}
```

Listing 6.13 The Server for the Object Factory Program

After the server program for the `Widget` object allocates and registers a channel, it creates an instance of the `WidgetFactory` class as a singleton object. The `WidgetFactory` object listens for calls to either of its `BuildWidget()` methods, and then instantiates the object as explained previously.

The client program for the object factory application appears in Listing 6.14.

```
using System;
using System.Runtime.Remoting;
using System.Runtime.Remoting.Channels;
using System.Runtime.Remoting.Channels.Http;
using WidgetSpace;

namespace Client
{
    class ClientAppClass
    {
        [STAThread]
        static void Main(string[] args)
        {
            HttpChannel theChannel = new HttpChannel();
            ChannelServices.RegisterChannel(theChannel);

            WidgetFactory widgetFactory =
                (WidgetFactory)Activator.GetObject(
                typeof(WidgetFactory),
                "http://localhost:8085/WidgetFactory.soap");

            // If the remote object was activated...
            if (widgetFactory != null)
            {
                try
                {
                    widgetFactory.BuildWidget(1000);
                    RemotingConfiguration.RegisterWellKnownClientType(
                        typeof(Widget),
                        "http://localhost:8085/Widget.soap"
                        );
                    Widget remoteWidget = new Widget();

                    System.Console.WriteLine(
                        "The widget's value is {0}",
                        remoteWidget.CurrentValue());
                }
                catch (Exception theException)
                {
                    ServerAccessError(theException.ToString());
                }
            }
                // Else the remote object was not activated...
            else
```

Listing 6.14 The Client for the Object Factory Program

```
45                  {
46                      ServerAccessError(
47                          "Error: Could not access the server");
48                  }
49
50                  System.Console.WriteLine(
51                      "\nPaused. Press Enter to continue...");
52                  System.Console.Read();
53              }
54
55              static void ServerAccessError(string errorMessage)
56              {
57                  System.Console.WriteLine(errorMessage);
58              }
59          }
60      }
```

Listing 6.14 The Client for the Object Factory Program *(continued)*

The client in Listing 6.14 begins by allocating and registering its communication channel. It uses the `Activator.GetObject()` method to activate the object factory on the server. On line 27, the client calls the object factory's `BuildWidget()` method and passes it an initial value. Provided that there was no error, the `Widget` object is instantiated and ready for use on the server when the `BuildWidget()` method returns. The client calls `RemotingConfiguration.RegisterWellKnownClientType()` and passes it the Widget object's URI. It can then obtain a reference to the `Widget` using `new`. Because it's actually creating a reference, and not the object itself, the client does not need to pass the non-default values to the constructor in the `new` statement.

If you use direct remoting and object factories to publish well-known objects as shown in this example program, the objects are essentially singletons. They continue to exist for as long as the server program runs. If the client program uses the object factory to build another server object, it will get an error. This is due to the fact that an object already exists at the URI.

There are a few ways to handle this problem. The first is to offer a method in the object factory that disconnects the server object. In the preceding example program, we could do this by adding a method called `DisconnectWidget()` to the `WidgetFactory` class. The `DisconnectWidget()` method would call the `RemotingServices.Disconnect()`

method, which disconnects objects published with direct remoting from the communication channel. Adding the `DisconnectWidget()` method to the `WidgetFactory` class enables client programs to disconnect a `Widget` object anytime it needs to.

NOTE

The `RemotingServices.Disconnect()` method does not mark the disconnected object for garbage collection. Your server program or object factory could republish it.

Another way to handle the problem of multiple objects being published at the same URI is to have the object factory published each instance at a slightly different URI. However, you must have the object factory return the URI of the object that it creates each time it creates an object. That way, the client knows where to look for the object that the object factory creates.

Summary

To share compile-time information about remote objects with clients, you can share the object's source code with the client. However, there are many drawbacks to this method. The most important is that it can compromise security.

Another way to accomplish the same thing is to share interfaces between the client and the server. If you use this method, you cannot pass the client's reference to a server object to another remote object. If you are writing an application in which clients pass references to remote objects to other remote objects, shared abstract base classes provide a better approach.

In addition, you can provide compile-time information about remote objects to clients by using Microsoft's SOAPSUDS utility to generate a metadata proxy. With a metadata proxy, clients can instantiate the remote type, rather than an interface it implements or a base class from which it derives.

SOAPSUDS can generate wrapped or unwrapped proxies. Wrapped proxies contain the remote object's URI in addition to the proxy metadata. Unwrapped proxies do not contain the URL.

The .NET Remoting classes can be used to publish an object at an endpoint. This technique is called direct remoting. It enables programmers to have the most control possible over remote object instantiation.

CHAPTER 7

Remote Object Lifetimes and Leases

Programs keep local objects in memory for specific periods of time. For instance, unless we put some sort of modifier on it, a local variable in a method is allocated from the program's stack. The variable exists while the method executes. When the method finishes, the program gives the memory allocated to the local variable back to the stack. In this case, the variable's lifetime is the length of time it takes to execute the method.

Like local variables and objects, remote objects have definite lifetimes. In particular, the length of time that the CLR keeps MBR objects in memory depends both on what type of objects they are and how often clients access them. This chapter describes the rules and techniques for managing the lifetimes of the remote objects your applications use.

Controlling Lifetimes with Leases

Before the Internet became such a strong factor in the software industry, DCOM was one of the most common methods of developing remote objects. Under DCOM, programs had to manage reference counts. Each time they instantiated an object, they had to increment the object's reference count. When they stopped using the object, they decremented the reference count. In a perfect networked world, this scheme alone works very well. It enables you to know exactly when a remote server object should and should not be deallocated.

Unfortunately, we do not live in a perfect networked world. Servers crash and entire networks sometimes go down. Events such as these can leave objects allocated on servers that are no longer used. DCOM kept track of how recently objects were accessed by clients. After a certain length of time, they would ping the client to see if it still needed the remote object.

The advent of the Internet made these techniques difficult for some important reasons. First, a server cannot ping a client that communicates with it through HTTP and SOAP. Second, sending a ping to a client that resides behind a firewall is a formidable (and sometimes impossible) task. Finally, pinging a client program does not scale to the Internet. If you provide remote objects publicly on the Internet, literally millions of clients may be using the object at any given moment. If the server needed to ping all available clients, it would spend all of its time just sending the ping signals.

To overcome these limitations, the .NET CLR uses a very different scheme for controlling the lifetimes of remote objects. In particular, it employs the concept of a **lease** on the object. An object's lease is essentially a counter that specifies its lifetime. When the lease expires, the CLR begins the process of deleting the object and reclaiming the memory it uses. Leases are controlled by the server's lease manager object, which is created in the server's application domain.

By default, the CLR gives CAO and singleton objects a lease of five minutes. It decrements the lease at certain intervals. Each time a client access the object, the lease manager increases the lease by two minutes. If clients do not access an object for several minutes, it is likely that the lease will expire.

NOTE

Even though single-call objects are marshaled by reference, they do not have leases. They exist until the call completes. The CLR then performs garbage collection on them.

There are a few different approaches that you can use to prevent the leases of remote objects expiring. One technique is to write your clients so that they access the object fairly frequently. This often isn't practical, and it is seldom the most efficient way of keeping remote objects alive. A better way is for the client to periodically renew the object's lease. Alternatively, you can customize the lease itself. Lastly, you can create a sponsor for the object.

Renewing Leases

Any client that has a reference to a remote object can renew the lease of that remote object. It requires no changes in the remote object or its server program. Client programs renew object leases by calling the lease's `Renew()` method and pass it an object of type `TimeSpan`.

The program in Listing 7.1 illustrates how to renew a lease. This example reuses code from Chapter 6. In particular, it uses the server program from Listing 6.9, and the `InformationManager` object from Listing 6.8. Because these two files are unchanged from Chapter 6, the code for them is not repeated here. Only the new client program is shown in Listing 7.1.

```
using System;
using System.Runtime.Remoting;
using System.Runtime.Remoting.Channels;
using System.Runtime.Remoting.Channels.Http;
using System.Runtime.Remoting.Lifetime;
using System.Threading;
using InfoMan;

namespace Client
{
    class ClientAppClass
    {
        [STAThread]
        static void Main(string[] args)
        {
            HttpChannel theChannel = new HttpChannel();
            ChannelServices.RegisterChannel(theChannel);

            InfoMan.InformationManager infoManager =
                (InfoMan.InformationManager)Activator.GetObject(
                typeof(InfoMan.InformationManager),
                "http://localhost:8085/InfoMan.soap");

            // If the remote object was activated...
            if (infoManager != null)
            {
                int dataCollectionLength;

                try
                {
```

Listing 7.1 A Client that Renews a Remote Object *(continues)*

```
dataCollectionLength =
    infoManager.DataCollectionLength();

int i;

// Sort with a simple Bubble Sort.
for (i=1; i<dataCollectionLength; i++)
{
    for (int j=0; j<i; j++)
    {
        string string1 =
infoManager.DataItem(i);
        string string2 =
infoManager.DataItem(j);

        if (string1.CompareTo(string2)<0)
        {
            infoManager.DataItem(i,string2);
            infoManager.DataItem(j,string1);
        }
    }
}

System.Console.WriteLine(
    "Printing the data...");
for (i=0; i<dataCollectionLength; i++)
{
    System.Console.WriteLine(
        infoManager.DataItem(i));
}

ILease theLease =
    (ILease)RemotingServices.GetLifetimeSer-
vice(
        infoManager);
System.Console.WriteLine(
    "\nThe lease has {0} minutes left.",
    theLease.CurrentLeaseTime.Minutes);

System.Console.WriteLine(
    "Time for a snooze...");
const int ONE_SECOND = 1000;
const int ONE_MINUTE = ONE_SECOND * 60;
Thread.Sleep(ONE_MINUTE * 3);

System.Console.WriteLine(
    "The lease has {0} minutes left.",
```

Listing 7.1 A Client that Renews a Remote Object

```
75                          theLease.CurrentLeaseTime.Minutes);
76
77                      theLease.Renew(TimeSpan.FromMinutes(10.0));
78
79                      System.Console.WriteLine(
80                          "\nThe lease has {0} minutes left.",
81                          theLease.CurrentLeaseTime.Minutes);
82
83                      System.Console.WriteLine(
84                          "Printing the data...");
85                      for (i=0; i<dataCollectionLength; i++)
86                      {
87                          System.Console.WriteLine(
88                              infoManager.DataItem(i));
89                      }
90                  }
91                  catch (Exception)
92                  {
93                      ServerAccessError();
94                  }
95              }
96                  // Else the remote object was not activated...
97              else
98              {
99                  // Print an error message.
100                 ServerAccessError();
101             }
102
103             System.Console.WriteLine(
104                 "\nPaused. Press Enter to continue...");
105             System.Console.Read();
106         }
107
108         static void ServerAccessError()
109         {
110             System.Console.WriteLine(
111                 "Error: Could not access the server");
112         }
113     }
114 }
```

Listing 7.1 A Client that Renews a Remote Object *(continued)*

The client program begins by declaring the namespaces it uses. To gain access to the lifetime management objects offered by .NET Remoting, the program states that it is using the `System.Runtime.Remoting.Lifetime` namespace on line 5. Also, this version of the client program calls the `Sleep()` method from the `System.Threading` namespace. The `using` statement on line 6 provides access to that namespace.

After establishing the communication channel (lines 16-17) and retrieving a reference to the `InformationManager` object (lines 19-22), the client program gets the length of the data collection and stores it in a local variable (lines 30-31). It then enters a `for` loop that starts on line 37. The loop uses a Bubble Sort to sort the data in the collection. Next, it enters another `for` loop to print the sorted data.

The client program obtains a reference to the `InformationManager` object's lease on lines 60-62. To get the reference, it declares a variable of type `ILease` and calls the `RemotingServices.GetLifetime-Service()` method.

Once it has the lease, the client can query the object's remaining lifetime by accessing the lease's `CurrentLeaseTime` property. The return value of the `CurrentLeaseTime` property is an object of type TimeSpan. The `TimeSpan` object has a property called `Minutes`, which returns the integer number of minutes left in the lease. That does not take into account any additional seconds. In other words, if the lease has 3 minutes and 6 seconds left, calling the `TimeSpan` object's `Minutes` property gives exactly 3. If you want the seconds, you can get them by calling the `TimeSpan` object's `Seconds` property. Figure 7.1 shows the program's output to this point.

After the program prints the lease's remaining time, it calls the `Threading.Sleep` method to go to sleep for three minutes. When three minutes have passed, the program awakens and prints the time remaining on the lease (lines 73-75).

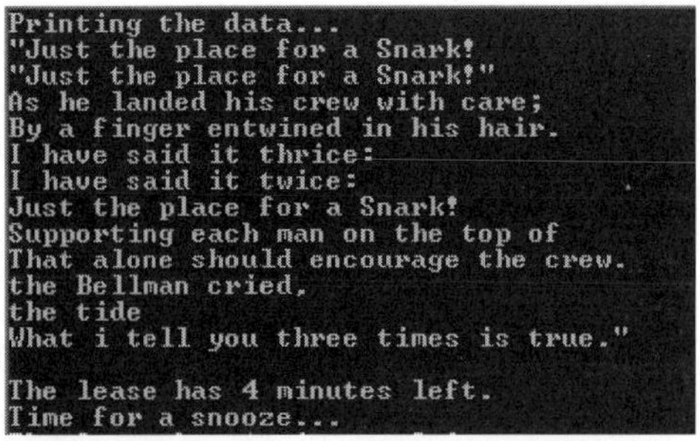

```
Printing the data...
"Just the place for a Snark!
"Just the place for a Snark!"
As he landed his crew with care;
By a finger entwined in his hair.
I have said it thrice:
I have said it twice:
Just the place for a Snark!
Supporting each man on the top of
That alone should encourage the crew.
the Bellman cried,
the tide
What i tell you three times is true."

The lease has 4 minutes left.
Time for a snooze...
```

Figure 7.1 The Sleeping Client Program

On line 77, the client program renews the lease on the remote `InformationManager` object. It sets the lease's time to 10 minutes. The program prints the lease's remaining time on lines 79-81. On lines 83-89, it prints the sorted data from the `InformationManager` object. This demonstrates that the program is still working with the same instance of the remote object. The `InformationManager` object has not been recycled. Figure 7.2 shows the output the program produces after it wakes up.

Customizing Object Lifetimes

Another way to control the lifetime of remote objects is to customize the objects' leases. You can do this for all objects in a server program by setting properties of the `LifetimeServices` class. If you need to manage object lifetimes on a class-by-class basis, you can override the `InitializeLifeTimeService()` method provided to each class by the `MarshalByRefObject` class.

The LifetimeServices Class

The properties of the `LifetimeServices` class enable server programs to customize the leases of all of the objects that they offer. Changes to these properties in a server program affect every remote object the server program offers. You cannot manage the lifetimes of individual objects through the properties of the `LifetimeServices` class.

```
That alone should encourage the crew.
the Bellman cried,
the tide
What i tell you three times is true."

The lease has 4 minutes left.
Time for a snooze...
The lease has 1 minutes left.

The lease has 9 minutes left.
Printing the data...
"Just the place for a Snark!
"Just the place for a Snark!"
As he landed his crew with care;
By a finger entwined in his hair.
I have said it thrice:
I have said it twice:
Just the place for a Snark!
Supporting each man on the top of
That alone should encourage the crew.
the Bellman cried,
the tide
What i tell you three times is true."

Paused. Press Enter to continue...
```

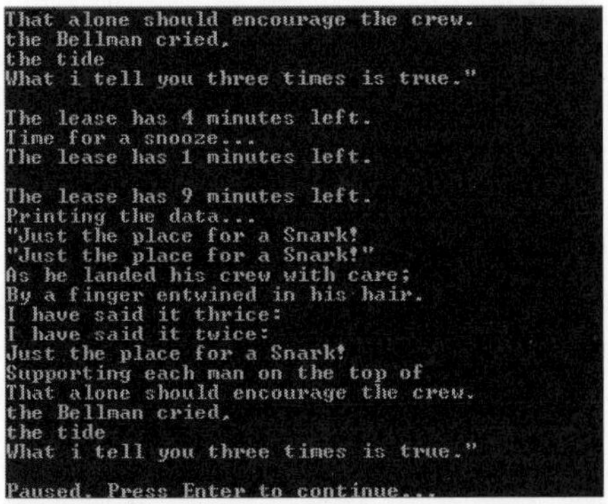

Figure 7.2 The Client Program's Final Output

WARNING

Changing the property values of a server program's `LifetimeServices` class changes the leases of *all* of the remote objects that the server offers in a particular application domain. Because the server's process can contain multiple application domains, it is possible to set different lifetimes in different application domains.

Changing the properties of a server program's `LifetimeServices` class alters the behavior of the server program's lease manger. Because the properties of the `LifetimeServices` class are static, you do not need to create an instance of the `LifetimeServices` class to set its properties.

It is possible for a server program to set the properties of the `LifetimeServices` class after it registers its remote objects. However, it is not wise to do so. You generally cannot guarantee that no server objects will be created before the changes are made. It is far better to make changes to the properties of the `LifetimeServices` class before you register any remote objects.

The properties of the `LifetimeServices` class control the behavior of the server program's lease manager. By default, the lease manager checks every 10 seconds for remote objects that need to be cleaned up. After it polls the leases of all of its remote objects, the lease manager goes to sleep until 10 seconds have passed. It then awakens and polls the leases again.

You can increase that time span by setting the `LeaseManagerPollTime` property. Example 7.1 shows a code fragment that demonstrates how a server program might set the lease manager's poll time to 50 seconds.

Changing the poll time may or may not affect the lifetime of a remote server object. If the lifetime is shorter than the poll time and the object's lease expires, the object stays in memory until the next time the lease manager wakes up. If the poll time is shorter than the lifetime, changing the poll time does not affect the lifetime of the object.

If your server program offers objects that you know have long lifetimes, garbage collection can be performed less frequently. Therefore, setting the `LeaseManagerPollTime` property to a larger number can increase the efficiency of your server program.

```
LifetimeServices.LeaseManagerPollTime = System.TimeSpan.FromSeconds(50);
```

Example 7.1 Setting the Lease Manager's Poll Time to 50 Seconds

```
LifetimeServices.LeaseTime = System.TimeSpan.FromMinutes(20);
```

Example 7.2 Setting the Initial Lease Time

Server programs have a greater impact on object lifetime when they set the `LifetimeServices` class's `LeaseTime` property. This property controls the initial lease time span for a program. When the server creates singletons or CAOs, it assigns the time span in the `LeaseTime` property to their leases. The code fragment in Example 7.2 shows the use of the `LeaseTime` property.

It is possible to set the initial lease time to 0. If you do, you essentially make your singletons and CAOs into single-call objects. Attempting this makes no real sense, but the .NET Remoting classes do not prevent you from doing so.

WARNING

Think carefully before you use the `LifetimeServices.LeaseTime` property. Remember that, when you use it, you are setting the initial lease times of *all* objects the server program offers. If a server program offers many object instances and gives them all long lifetimes, it may run out of memory.

The `LeaseTime` property only controls the *initial* amount of time on the lease. Whenever a client calls a method on one of the server program's remote objects, the lease manager adds some time to the object's lease. However, it does so only conditionally. If the amount of time in the lease's `CurrentleaseTime` property plus the amount of time in the lease's `RenewOnCallTime` property is greater than the amount of time in the `LeaseTime` property, the lease manager adds the amount of time in the `RenewOnCallTime` property to the lease.

By default, the amount of time that the lease manager adds when a client calls an object's method is 2 minutes. Your server programs can increase or decrease that time by setting the `RenewOnCallTime` property. Example 7.3 shows how it might be used in a server program.

```
LifetimeServices.RenewOnCallTime = System.TimeSpan.FromMinutes(5);
```

Example 7.3 Increasing the Lease Renewal Time

The call in Example 7.3 tells the lease manager to add 5 minutes to every object's lease whenever a client calls one of its methods. As with initial lease times, you should be cautious when increasing the lease renewal time of every object offered by a server program. If the program offers a lot of objects, it could rapidly run out of memory.

The `LifetimeServices` class also contains a property called `SponsorshipTimeout`. Its use is explained later in this chapter.

The InitializeLifeTimeService Method

The `LifetimeServices` class enables server programs to manage leases of their objects. However, it does not enable them to manage leases on a class-by-class basis. You can achieve this functionality by overriding the `MarshalByRefObject.InitializeLifetimeService()` method, which all MBR objects inherit.

The CLR calls the `InitializeLifetimeService()` method when it instantiates MBR objects. It is possible that the object could already have a lease when this method is called. The lease's properties can only be set when the lease is first created. Therefore, your version of the `InitializeLifetimeService()` method must check to be sure that the current state of the lease equals the constant `LeaseState.Initial` before it attempts to set the lease's properties.

NOTE

If a lease's current state is no longer equal to `LeaseState.Initial`, only its `CurrentLeaseTime` property can be altered. This is done by renewing the lease.

Let's demonstrate how this works by writing a program. We'll create a new version of the information manager program from Chapter 6. Specifically, this program reuses the server program from Listing 6.9 without modification. It also reuses the client program from Listing 6.10 with no changes. For the `InformationManager` object, the program uses the code given in Listing 7.2.

```
using System;
using System.Runtime.Remoting.Lifetime;

namespace InfoMan
{
    public class InformationManager : MarshalByRefObject
```

Listing 7.2 A Remote Object that Manages its Lease

```
    {
        private const int ARRAY_SIZE = 12;
        private string [] theData = new string [ARRAY_SIZE];

        public InformationManager()
        {
            // Initialize the array.
            theData[0] = "\"Just the place for a Snark!\"";
            theData[1] =  "the Bellman cried,";
            theData[2] = "As he landed his crew with care;";
            theData[3] = "Supporting each man on the top of";
            theData[4] = "the tide";
            theData[5] = "By a finger entwined in his hair.";
            theData[6] = "\"Just the place for a Snark!";
            theData[7] = "I have said it twice:";
            theData[8] = "That alone should encourage the crew.";
            theData[9] = "Just the place for a Snark!";
            theData[10] = "I have said it thrice:";
            theData[11] = "What i tell you three times is
true.\"";
        }

        public override object InitializeLifetimeService()
        {
            ILease myLease =
                (ILease)base.InitializeLifetimeService();

            if (myLease.CurrentState == LeaseState.Initial)
            {
                myLease.InitialLeaseTime =
                    TimeSpan.FromMinutes(10);
                myLease.RenewOnCallTime =
                    TimeSpan.FromMinutes(5);
            }
            return (myLease);
        }

        public string DataItem(int whichItem)
        {
            string theItem = null;

            // If the item number is valid...
            if ((whichItem >= 0) && (whichItem < ARRAY_SIZE))
            {
                // Get the item.
                theItem = theData[whichItem];
            }

            // Return the item to the client.
```

Listing 7.2 A Remote Object that Manages its Lease *(continues)*

```
55                  return (theItem);
56              }
57
58              public void DataItem(
59                  int whichItem,
60                  string newValue)
61              {
62                  // If the item number is valid...
63                  if ((whichItem >= 0) && (whichItem < ARRAY_SIZE))
64                  {
65                      // Set the item.
66                      theData[whichItem] = newValue;
67                  }
68              }
69
70              public int DataCollectionLength()
71              {
72                  return (ARRAY_SIZE);
73              }
74          }
75      }
```

Listing 7.2 A Remote Object that Manages its Lease *(continued)*

As in Chapter 6, I used SOAPSUDS to create a wrapped proxy for this class. I put a reference to the wrapped proxy into the client's project file. The server program's project file contained a reference to the DLL containing the `InformationManager` class.

The new method in the `InformationManager` class appears on lines 28-41 of Listing 7.2. Once again, the file containing the `InformationManager` class must contain a `using` statement that provides access to the `System.Runtime.Remoting.Lifetime` namespace. This is shown on line 2 of Listing 7.2.

The `InitializeLifetimeService()` method begins by calling the method that it overrides in the base class. The base implementation of `InitializeLifetimeService()` returns the object's lease. The `InformationManager` class's implementation of `InitializeLifetimeService()` saves a reference to that lease in the variable `myLease`. It tests the lease's `CurrentState` property to determine if this lease was just created. If so, the method sets the lease's `InitialLeaseTime` and `RenewOnCallTime` properties. It ends by returning the reference to the lease on line 40.

NOTE

If the `InitializeLifetimeService()` method returns `null`, the object has an indefinite lease.

If you create objects with custom lifetimes very often, you can save yourself from having to rewrite code for the `InitializeLifetimeService()` method. You can do this by deriving some classes from the `MarshalByRefObject` class that implements specialized leases. You then derive your remote objects from these specialized classes.

For example, Listing 7.3 illustrates this technique by creating a class called `ImmortalMBRObject`. All objects derived from the `ImmortalMBRObject` are marshaled by reference and have indefinite leases.

```
public class ImmortalMBRObject : MarshalByRefObject
{
    public override object InitializeLifetimeService()
    {
        return (null);
    }
}
```

Listing 7.3 The **`ImmortalMBRObject`** Class

Another variation of this technique is to derive a class from `MarshalByRefObject` that enables programs to pass values for the lease properties to a non-default constructor. Objects derived from such a class would be able to specify their lease properties when they were constructed. However, because it would require the uses of non-default constructors, this implementation would also necessitate the use of a factory to create the remote object. Let's write an application to see how this works.

To build this program, we'll need a class derived from `MarshalByRefObject` that overrides the `InitializeLifetimeService()` method. We'll call this class `ControlledLeaseMBRObject`. The CLR invokes `InitializeLifetimeService()` after it calls the constructor for the `ControlledLeaseMBRObject` class. This enables us to pass lease management parame- ters to a constructor. The constructor will save the information in the `ControlledLeaseMBRObject` class's private data members. The `InitializeLifetimeService()` method will read the lease information from the private data members.

The remote object will be derived from the `ControlledLeaseMBR-Object` class. It will need at least one constructor that accepts the lease management information. As already mentioned, the use of a non-default constructor will require that the object be built by an object factory.

We'll implement this scheme by modifying the object factory application from Chapter 6. The server program won't change from how it appeared in Listing 6.13. Therefore, it will not be repeated here. Listing 7.4 presents the code for the remote object, its factory, and the `ControlledLease-MBRObject` class.

```
using System;
using System.Runtime.Remoting;
using System.Runtime.Remoting.Lifetime;

namespace WidgetSpace
{
    public class ControlledLeaseMBRObject : MarshalByRefObject
    {
        private bool useDefaultLease;
        private TimeSpan initLeaseTime;
        private TimeSpan renewLeaseTime;

        public ControlledLeaseMBRObject()
        {
            useDefaultLease = true;
        }

        public ControlledLeaseMBRObject(
            TimeSpan initialLeaseTime,
            TimeSpan renewOnCallTime)
        {
            initLeaseTime = initialLeaseTime;
            renewLeaseTime = renewOnCallTime;
            useDefaultLease = false;
        }

        public override object InitializeLifetimeService()
        {
            ILease myLease =
                (ILease)base.InitializeLifetimeService();

            if ((useDefaultLease == false) &&
                (myLease.CurrentState == LeaseState.Initial))
            {
                myLease.InitialLeaseTime = initLeaseTime;
```

Listing 7.4 A Remote Object with a Managed Lease

```
                myLease.RenewOnCallTime = renewLeaseTime;
            }
            return (myLease);
        }
    }

    public class WidgetFactory : MarshalByRefObject
    {
        public void BuildWidget()
        {
            Widget tempWidget = new Widget();
            RemotingServices.Marshal(
                tempWidget,
                "Widget.soap",
                typeof(Widget));
        }

        public void BuildWidget(int initialValue)
        {
            Widget tempWidget = new Widget(initialValue);
            RemotingServices.Marshal(
                tempWidget,
                "Widget.soap",
                typeof(Widget));
        }

        public void BuildWidget(
            int initialValue,
            TimeSpan initialLeaseTime,
            TimeSpan renewOnCallTime)
        {
            Widget tempWidget = new Widget(initialValue,
                                           initialLeaseTime,
                                           renewOnCallTime);
            RemotingServices.Marshal(
                tempWidget,
                "Widget.soap",
                typeof(Widget));
        }

    }

    public class Widget : ControlledLeaseMBRObject
    {
        private int currentValue;

        public Widget() : base()
        {
```

Listing 7.4 A Remote Object with a Managed Lease *(continues)*

```
84                  currentValue = 0;
85              }
86
87              public Widget(int initialValue)  : base()
88              {
89                  currentValue = initialValue;
90              }
91
92              public Widget(
93                  int initialValue,
94                  TimeSpan initialLeaseTime,
95                  TimeSpan renewOnCallTime)  :
96                  base(initialLeaseTime,
97                       renewOnCallTime)
98              {
99                  currentValue = initialValue;
100             }
101
102             public int CurrentValue()
103             {
104                 return (currentValue);
105             }
106         }
107     }
```

Listing 7.4 A Remote Object with a Managed Lease *(continued)*

Clients use these three objects by first creating an object factory. The `WidgetFactory` class begins on line 42 of Listing 7.4. To build a `Widget` object, clients call one of the overloaded `BuildWidget()` methods. The first version of the `BuildWidget()` method enables clients to pass no initialization information. It uses the default constructor. The second implementation of `BuildWidget()` provides a means for clients to pass the initial value for the `Widget` object.

If clients want to manage a `Widget` object's lease when they create one, they call the third version of `BuildWidget()`. This version, which starts on line 62, enables clients to pass an initial value, an initial lease time, and a time span that will be added to the lease each time it receives a client call.

`BuildWidget()` calls a three-argument constructor in the `Widget` class, which starts on line 92. The three-argument constructor calls a constructor from its base class. If you look on line 78, you'll see that the `Widget` class inherits from `ControlledLeaseMBRObject`. The

ControlledLeaseMBRObject class, in turn, inherits from MarshalByRefObject (see line 7).

When the three-argument Widget constructor calls the constructor from the ControlledLeaseMBRObject, program execution jumps to line 18 of Listing 7.4. This constructor stores the times it receives into two private data members. It also sets the useDefaultLease member to false.

Whenever client creates an object derived from the ControlledLeaseMBRObject class, and does so without passing lease information, the no-argument constructor starting on line 13 gets called instead. This sets the useDefaultLease member to true.

The value of the useDefaultLease member is important. It enables clients to chose whether objects will be created with managed leases. In the current example, when the two-argument constructor for the ControlledLeaseMBRObject class finishes, the program jumps back to the three-argument Widget constructor. On line 99, the Widget constructor sets the initial value of its private data member. It then returns to the overloaded BuildWidget() method. It executes the RemotingServices.Marshal() method to publish the Widget at an endpoint.

REMINDER

Programs that invoke the RemotingServices.Marshal() method are using a technique called direct remoting.

When the CLR turns the Widget into a remote object, it attempts to call the Widget class's InitializeLifetimeService() method. However, because the Widget class does not have a InitializeLifetimeService() method, it uses the version of InitializeLifetimeService() that it finds in the Controlled-LeaseMBRObject class. This method is shown on lines 27-39 of Listing 7.4.

The InitializeLifetimeService() method first obtains the lease of the current object. It saves the lease in the myLease variable. If the client passed lease management information when it created the current object, the useDafaultLease member is false. If it is false and the lease is new, The InitializeLifetimeService() method uses the lease management information in the private data members initLeaseTime and renewLeaseTime to set the lease's InitialLeaseTime and RenewOnCallTime properties. If the useDafaultLease member is true, the InitializeLifetimeService() method does not alter the default lease. It ends by returning the lease.

Now we're ready to write the client for this program. It's shown in Listing 7.5.

```
using System;
using System.Runtime.Remoting;
using System.Runtime.Remoting.Channels;
using System.Runtime.Remoting.Channels.Http;
using System.Runtime.Remoting.Lifetime;
using WidgetSpace;

namespace Client
{
    class ClientAppClass
    {
        [STAThread]
        static void Main(string[] args)
        {
            HttpChannel theChannel = new HttpChannel();
            ChannelServices.RegisterChannel(theChannel);

            WidgetFactory widgetFactory =
                (WidgetFactory)Activator.GetObject(
                typeof(WidgetFactory),
                "http://localhost:8085/WidgetFactory.soap");

            // If the remote object was activated...
            if (widgetFactory != null)
            {
                try
                {
                    widgetFactory.BuildWidget(
                        1000,
                        TimeSpan.FromMinutes(15),
                        TimeSpan.FromMinutes(3));
                    RemotingConfiguration.RegisterWellKnownClient-
Type(
                        typeof(Widget),
                        "http://localhost:8085/Widget.soap");
                    Widget remoteWidget = new Widget();

                    System.Console.WriteLine(
                        "The widget's value is {0}",
                        remoteWidget.CurrentValue());

                    ILease theLease =
                        (ILease)RemotingServices.GetLifetimeSer-
vice(
                            remoteWidget);
```

Listing 7.5 The Client for a Remote Object with a Managed Lease

```
44                          System.Console.WriteLine(
45                              "\nThe lease has {0} minutes left.",
46                              theLease.CurrentLeaseTime.Minutes);
47
48                      }
49                      catch (Exception theException)
50                      {
51                          ServerAccessError(theException.ToString());
52                      }
53                  }
54                      // Else the remote object was not activated...
55                  else
56                  {
57                      ServerAccessError(
58                          "Error: Could not access the server");
59                  }
60
61                  System.Console.WriteLine(
62                      "\nPaused. Press Enter to continue...");
63                  System.Console.Read();
64              }
65
66              static void ServerAccessError(string errorMessage)
67              {
68                  System.Console.WriteLine(errorMessage);
69              }
70          }
71      }
```

Listing 7.5 The Client for a Remote Object with a Managed Lease *(continued)*

The client program for this application functions very much as the client program in Chapter 6 did. Like the program in Listing 6.14, the program in Listing 7.5 starts by creating and registering its communication channel. On lines 18-21 of Listing 7.5, the program gets a reference to the `WidgetFactory` object offered by the server program.

NOTE

When I built this application, I used a wrapped proxy to describe the remote objects to the client program. As with most of the programs in this book, I ran both the client and the server programs on the same computer.

On line 28, the client program calls the factory's `BuildWidget()` method, and passes three values. The first is an initial value for the

Widget object's private data member. The other two are time spans for the Widget object's lease. After building the Widget, the client program uses the C# new statement to create a reference to it. Next, the client prints the Widget object's current value. It retrieves the Widget object's lease on lines 41-43. On lines 44-46, it also prints the number of minutes remaining on the lease. The client program's output appears in Figure 7.3.

The client program's output clearly demonstrates that the remote Widget object does not contain the default times in its lease.

Sponsors

Sponsor objects provide .NET Remoting applications with a powerful and flexible technique of managing object lifetimes. A sponsor is an object that is responsible for determining whether a remote object's lease should be renewed, and if so, setting the lease's new values.

When the lease expires on a remote object, the .NET Remoting system checks to see whether it has any registered sponsors. If it does, the Remoting system sends a signal to the sponsor object to ask whether the remote object's lease should be renewed. This implies that the sponsor must be easily accessible to the remote object.

Remote objects can have multiple sponsors. If an object has more than one sponsor registered, the Remoting system calls the first one in the list. If the sponsor doesn't respond within the time specified in the lease's SponsorshipTimeout property, the .NET Remoting system calls the next sponsor in the list. It stops calling sponsors when it gets a reply that renews the lease or when it runs out of sponsors to call.

The widget's value is 1000
The lease has 14 minutes left.
Paused. Press Enter to continue...

Figure 7.3 The Output of the Managed Lease Client

Sponsor objects can sponsor multiple remote objects. They can also determine programmatically whether to renew an object's lease. This capability lets your application renew leases under some conditions and lets them expire under others.

All sponsor objects must implement the `ISponsor` interface, which is provided by the .NET Framework. When your application creates remote objects, it can register a sponsor to manage the object's lifetime. This can be done by either the client or the server program. In fact, sponsors do not have to reside on either the client or the server. They can be on a different computer altogether.

WARNING

Sponsors can reside on clients, servers, or any other computer. When you are choosing where your sponsors should go, it is important to remember that they must be easily accessible to the server.

Wherever the sponsor resides, the application implementing it obtains the remote object's lease by calling the `RemotingServices.GetLifetimeService()` method and passing in a reference to the remote object. Next, the program calls the lease's `Register()` method and passes in the sponsor object.

If the sponsor is not running in the application space of the program that is registering it, it can be implemented as a remote MBR object. The program that is registering the sponsor must obtain a reference to the sponsor object. It passes the reference to the lease's `Register()` method. If, on the other hand, the sponsor is in the same application space as the registering program, the program can pass the sponsor object to the lease's `Register()` method.

Sponsors do not have to be MBR objects. You can make them serializable instead. Recall that serializable objects are copied between the clients and the servers. When your program registers a serializable sponsor, the sponsor gets copied into the server object's application space. From that time forward, it executes on the server.

Server-Side Sponsors

Server-side sponsors generally run in the same application space as the server program. If you want, you can create a separate program on the server computer for the sponsor. However, this means that you will have to manage the sponsor's lifetime somehow. Therefore, I recommend you put the sponsor in the same server program as the remote object. If you do, the sponsor is a local object that can be kept in memory for as long as the server runs.

Listing 7.6 gives the code for a remote object whose lifetime is managed by a server-side sponsor.

```
using System;
using System.Runtime.Remoting.Lifetime;
using InfoManSponspor;

namespace InfoMan
{
    public class InformationManager : MarshalByRefObject
    {
        private const int ARRAY_SIZE = 13;
        private string [] theData = new string [ARRAY_SIZE];
        private InformationManagerSponsor mySponsor;

        public InformationManager(
            InformationManagerSponsor theSponsor)
        {
            mySponsor = theSponsor;

            // Initialize the array.
            theData[0] = "\"I am afraid, Watson, ";
            theData[1] =  "that I shall have to go,\" ";
            theData[2] = "said  Holmes, as we sat down ";
            theData[3] = "together to our breakfast one";
            theData[4] = "morning.";
            theData[5] = "\"Go! Where to?\"";
            theData[6] = "\"To Dartmoor; to King's Pyland.\"";
            theData[7] = "I was not surprised.  Indeed, my";
            theData[8] = "only wonder was that he had not ";
            theData[9] = "already been mixed upon this ";
            theData[10] = "extraordinary case, which was the ";
            theData[11] = "one topic of conversation through ";
            theData[12] = "the length and breadth of England.";
        }

        public override object InitializeLifetimeService()
        {
            ILease myLease =
                (ILease)base.InitializeLifetimeService();
```

Listing 7.6 A Remote Object with a Managed Lease

```

                if (myLease.CurrentState == LeaseState.Initial)
                {
                    myLease.InitialLeaseTime =
                        TimeSpan.FromMinutes(1);
                    myLease.RenewOnCallTime =
                        TimeSpan.FromSeconds(5);

                    myLease.Register(mySponsor);
                }
                return (myLease);
            }

            public string DataItem(int whichItem)
            {
                string theItem = null;

                // If the item number is valid...
                if ((whichItem >= 0) && (whichItem < ARRAY_SIZE))
                {
                    // Get the item.
                    theItem = theData[whichItem];
                }

                // Return the item to the client.
                return (theItem);
            }

            public void DataItem(
                int whichItem,
                string newValue)
            {
                // If the item number is valid...
                if ((whichItem >= 0) && (whichItem < ARRAY_SIZE))
                {
                    // Set the item.
                    theData[whichItem] = newValue;
                }
            }

            public int DataCollectionLength()
            {
                return (ARRAY_SIZE);
            }
        }
    }

```

Listing 7.6 A Remote Object with a Managed Lease *(continued)*

The remote object in Listing 7.6 is very similar to those used throughout this book. Unlike other versions, this object contains a private data member that saves a reference to its sponsor. When the server program allocates the `InformationManager` object, it must pass the constructor a reference to the sponsor. The constructor saves the reference for when the .NET Remoting classes call the object's `InitializeLifetimeService()` method.

I've overridden the object's `InitializeLifetimeService()` method on lines 34-49. It obtains a copy of the `InformationManager` object's lease on lines 36-37. If the lease is in its initial state, the `InitializeLifetimeService()` method sets its initial lease time to one minute and its `RenewOnCall` time to 5 seconds. Typically, you'll use longer values than these. However, these short times make the sponsor program easier to demonstrate.

On line 46 of Listing 7.6 the `InitializeLifetimeService()` method calls its lease's `Register()` method. It passes the reference to the sponsor that the constructor stored in the private data member mySponsor. The `InitializeLifetimeService()` method finishes by returning the modified lease to the .NET REmoting classes.

The sponsor for the object in Listing 7.6 appears in Listing 7.7.

```
using System;
using System.Runtime.Remoting.Lifetime;

namespace InfoManSponspor
{
    public class InformationManagerSponsor : ISponsor
    {
        private int totalTimesCalled;

        public InformationManagerSponsor()
        {
            totalTimesCalled = 0;
        }

        public TimeSpan Renewal(ILease theLease)
        {
            if (totalTimesCalled < 5)
            {
                return (TimeSpan.FromMinutes(5));
            }
```

Listing 7.7 A Server-Side Sponsor

```
21                 else
22                 {
23                     return (TimeSpan.Zero);
24                 }
25             }
26         }
27     }
```

Listing 7.7 A Server-Side Sponsor *(continued)*

The sponsor object in Listing 7.7 contains only two methods. The first, on lines 10-13, is its constructor. The constructor initializes the sponsor's `totalTimesCalled` data member to zero. The second is the `Renewal()` method, which appears on lines 15-25. It uses the `totalTimesCalled` data member to determine when the sponsor should stop renewing the `InformationManager` object's lease. If the lease has been renewed less than five times, the `Renewal()` method renews the lease for five more minutes. Otherwise, it declines to renew the lease by returning `TimeSpan.Zero`.

The server program that uses the `InformationManager` and `InformationManagerSponsor` objects is given in Listing 7.8.

```
using System;
using System.Runtime.Remoting;
using System.Runtime.Remoting.Channels;
using System.Runtime.Remoting.Channels.Http;
using InfoMan;
using InfoManSponspor;

namespace Server
{
    class ServerAppClass
    {
        [STAThread]
        static void Main(string[] args)
        {
            HttpChannel theChannel = new HttpChannel(8085);
            ChannelServices.RegisterChannel(theChannel);

            InformationManagerSponsor infoManSponsor =
```

Listing 7.8 A Server that Uses a Sponsor *(continues)*

```
19                     new InformationManagerSponsor();
20
21                 InformationManager infoMan =
22                     new InformationManager(infoManSponsor);
23
24                 RemotingServices.Marshal(
25                     infoMan,
26                     "InfoMan.soap",
27                     typeof(InformationManager));
28
29                 System.Console.WriteLine(
30                     "Press Enter to end the InformationManager.");
31                 System.Console.Read();
32             }
33         }
34     }
```

Listing 7.8 A Server that Uses a Sponsor *(continued)*

After the server program creates and registers its communication channel (lines 15-16), it allocates an `InformationManagerSponsor` object. Next, it allocates an `InformationManager` object. When it does, it passes a local reference to the `InformationManagerSponsor` object into the constructor for the `InformationManager`. Because it allocates the `InformationManager` and `InformationManagerSponsor` objects locally, the server program uses direct remoting on lines 24-27 to make the `InformationManager` available on the network.

When I created the server program, I put the `InformationManager` and `InformationManagerSponsor` objects into their own projects and compiled them as class libraries. I then put references to the DLLs containing the `InformationManager` and `InformationManager-Sponsor` objects into the server program's project. You do not have to do this for your applications. I just find things easier to manage if I use this technique. Both the remote object and its sponsor could be compiled into the server program.

The client program that uses the `InformationManager` object is shown in Listing 7.9.

```
using System;
using System.Runtime.Remoting;
using System.Runtime.Remoting.Channels;
using System.Runtime.Remoting.Channels.Http;
using System.Threading;
using System.Runtime.Remoting.Lifetime;
using InfoMan;

namespace Client
{
    class ClientAppClass
    {
        [STAThread]
        static void Main(string[] args)
        {
            HttpChannel theChannel = new HttpChannel();
            ChannelServices.RegisterChannel(theChannel);

            InfoMan.InformationManager infoManager =
                (InfoMan.InformationManager)Activator.GetObject(
                typeof(InfoMan.InformationManager),
                "http://localhost:8085/InfoMan.soap");

            if (infoManager != null)
            {
                int dataCollectionLength;

                try
                {
                    ILease serverLease =
                        (ILease)infoManager.GetLifetimeService();

                    System.Console.WriteLine(
                        "Server lease time = {0}\n",
                        serverLease.CurrentLeaseTime);

                    dataCollectionLength =
                        infoManager.DataCollectionLength();

                    for (int i=0; i<dataCollectionLength; i++)
                    {
                        System.Console.WriteLine(
                            infoManager.DataItem(i));
                    }

                    System.Console.WriteLine(
```

Listing 7.9 The Client for the Server-Side Sponsor Application *(continues)*

```
47                          "\nServer lease time = {0}\n",
48                          serverLease.CurrentLeaseTime);
49
50                      Thread.Sleep(TimeSpan.FromMinutes(2));
51
52                      System.Console.WriteLine(
53                          "Server lease time = {0}",
54                          serverLease.CurrentLeaseTime);
55                  }
56                  catch (Exception theError)
57                  {
58                      ServerAccessError(theError.ToString());
59                  }
60              }
61              else
62              {
63                  ServerAccessError(
64                      "Remote object could not be activated");
65              }
66
67              System.Console.WriteLine(
68                  "\nPaused. Press Enter to continue...");
69              System.Console.Read();
70          }
71
72          static void ServerAccessError(string errorMessage)
73          {
74              System.Console.WriteLine(
75                  "{0}",
76                  errorMessage);
77          }
78      }
79  }
```

Listing 7.9 The Client for the Server-Side Sponsor Application *(continued)*

To demonstrate that the remote object's lease is being managed, this client program repeatedly accesses the lease and prints its remaining time. The client's output appears in Figure 7.4.

After establishing its communication channel and obtaining a reference to the remote object, the program in Listing 7.9 gets a reference to the server object's lease (lines 30-31). It then prints the time remaining on the lease. When the lease was created on the server, it began with one minute on it. Figure 7.4 shows that by the time I ran the client, it had just over 39 seconds left.

```
Server lease time = 00:00:39.4704800

"I am afraid, Watson,
that I shall have to go,"
said Holmes, as we sat down
together to our breakfast one
morning.
"Go? Where to?"
"To Dartmoor; to King's Pyland."
I was not surprised. Indeed, my
only wonder was that he had not
already been mixed upon this
extraordinary case, which was the
one topic of conversation through
the length and breadth of England.

Server lease time = 00:00:37.9182480

Server lease time = 00:03:38.5528848

Paused. Press Enter to continue...
```

Figure 7.4 The Output of the Client for the Server-Side Sponsor Application

On lines 40-44, the client prints data from the remote `InformationManager` object. As the output in Figure 7.4 demonstrates, that took a bit less than two seconds. To enable the lease to be renewed by the sponsor, the client program calls the `Thread.Sleep()` method on line 50. This blocks the program for two minutes. When it wakes back up, it prints the lease's remaining time. Figure 7.4 shows that the sponsor renewed the lease. By the time the program awoke, the lease had about three and one half minutes left on it.

Client-Side Sponsors

Client s-side sponsors are used with CAOs. I generally recommend against using a client-side sponsor unless you have an extremely good reason to do so. The safest approach to sponsor implementation is to have the sponsor object available on the same computer as the server object. If a network error occurs, the server object may be unable to reach the sponsor. As a result, the server object may be recycled at an inconvenient time.

The most common justification for having client-side sponsor objects is that the sponsor must determine when it is time to shut down the server object based on conditions on the client. You can achieve this same effect by including a method or property on the server object that enables the client to tell it not to renew its lease any more. When the client determines that it is time for the server object to stop renewing its lease, it calls the remote method or property to inform the server.

Also, because client-side sponsors are used with CAOs, the client typically shuts down the server object anyway. In light of that, I can't see a strong justification for having a special object on the client for managing the server's lease that might become inaccessible to the server.

However, if you do create a client-side sponsor, the procedure is essentially the same as creating it on the server. You obtain the server object's lease, then call the lease's `Register()` method to register the sponsor. Using a client-side sponsor essentially turns the client into both a client and a server. It offers the sponsor as a remote object on the client for the server. This makes your client code more complex.

One way to avoid additional complexity on your client and still use a client-side implementation, is to make the sponsor object serializable. Calling the lease's `Register()` method copies the sponsor from the client to the server. This enables the server to always have access to it.

Summary

The .NET remoting classes enable applications to control the lifetimes of remote objects through the use of object leases. The leases that remote objects use enable the applications to determine how long objects should exist in memory. Using leases, server programs can avoid pinging clients to determine whether the client still needs specific object instances.

Client programs can prevent server objects from being recycled by renewing the object's lease. To renew a server object's lease, a client first obtains a reference to the lease. It then calls the `ILease.Renew()` method.

Through the use of the the `LifetimeServices` class, server programs can customize the lifetimes of all of the remote objects that they offer.

MBR server objects can customize their individual lifetimes by overriding the `InitializeLifetimeService()` method, which they inherit from the MarshalByRefObject class. The `InitializeLifetimeService()` method can be used to set the initial time span of an object's lease. It can also set the amount of time that gets added to the lease each time a client accesses the MBR server object. To give a remote object an indefinite lifetime, the overridden `InitializeLifetimeService()` method should return null.

Applications can also use sponsor objects to control lease renewals. The sponsor objects can reside on the client, the server, or on a different computer altogether. Wherever the sponsor exists, it must be easily accessible to the computer that hosts the remote object. Ideally, the sponsor should be in the same program as the remote server object whenever possible.

CHAPTER 8

Configuring Distributed Applications

In .NET Remoting applications, some tasks can be done either programmatically or in configuration files. For example, you can use configuration files to specify the channels your applications use, to state the type of object activation they provide (SAO or CAO), and to control object lifetimes.

The primary advantage of using configuration files is that they enable you to change an application's operational parameters without recompiling the application. One byproduct of this is that you can install your client programs to a wider variety of computer configurations. Your install program can determine what channels to use based on conditions on the client computer at the time of the install. If, for instance, your install program detects that the user dials up to the Internet to access your application, it can install a configuration file that has your application use an HTTP channel. If, on the other hand, the install program detects that the client computer is on your corporate network, it can install a configuration file that tells your application to use a TCP channel.

The kind of flexibility that configuration files provide is both desirable and necessary in modern, diverse computing environments. Therefore, those developing applications for .NET Remoting should familiarize themselves with the mechanics of configuration files. This chapter presents information that will help you achieve that goal.

Essentials of Configuration Files

Configuration files for .NET applications are defined in XML. Distributed applications can have any number of configuration files and name them anything. However, Microsoft advises that every distributed application have access to at least two configuration files. The first is the file machine.config. This file controls settings for an entire computer.

WARNING

Be extremely cautious about having your application or install program change the settings in a machine.config file. It is extremely easy to cause unintended problems by altering information in this file. You should avoid modifying machine.config unless you are absolutely sure you need to.

Every program can have its own optional configuration file. By convention, this file is called <appname>.config, where <appname> is the name of your program including its file extension. So if your program is named MyServer.exe, its configuration file should be named MyServer.exe.config. Both client and server programs can have their own configuration files.

JARGON

The configuration file for individual programs is often referred to by developers as the app.config (pronounced "app dot config") file, or the appconfig file.

Configuration files for applications follow a basic format. Listing 8.1 demonstrates this format.

```
<configuration>
    <system.runtime.remoting>
        <application>
        </application>
    </system.runtime.remoting>
</configuration>
```

Listing 8.1 The Basic Format for Application Configuration Files

Like the C# source code presented in this book, I've added line numbers to the listing of the configuration file. Of course, your XML configuration files won't have them.

The Pitfalls of Configuration Files

The Ability of any .NET program to have any number of configuration files carries with it profound implications. For example, you can define configuration files that do nothing but specify what channel a server uses. This configuration file, along with any others required, can be deployed to many servers. In effect, you're using a single configuration file as a template.

Because programmers know they can create whatever configuration files they need, they tend to create them in a rather offhand fashion. If, for instance, a programmer on a large project is assigned to work on a particular remote object, she can define any configuration files she decides to use. There can be any number of them. They can be called anything she decides. In addition to the standard .NET Remoting elements, her configuration files can contain any elements she decides to define. Every other programmer on the project has the same ability. This can be a serious problem.

If each programmer decides upon his own configuration file formats and names, your project can end up with literally hundreds (or even thousands!) of configuration files. Chances are, many of them will contain similar but slightly different tags that do the same things.

The resolution to this problem is simple, but it takes planning and communication. Before the project starts, you must decide what the conventions will be for your configuration files. You should define a standardized naming scheme for the file names. The same must be done for the XML elements in the files. Periodically, you must review the configuration files that all of the programmers on the project are requiring for your application. Look for elements that everyone is defining and come up with standardized templates that they can all use.

If you've been programming distributed applications for a while, you may remember the days of DLL Hell and Registry Hell. A moderate amount of planning and review in a large project can help you avoid the potential for a "Config File Hell."

The .NET Remoting configuration information must occur between the `<configuration>` and `</configuration>` tags. Just as with any XML file, this pair of tags specifies one element. As a result, you'll hear programmers refer to the `<configuration>` and `</configuration>` tags, or the `<configuration>` element. Either way, they're talking about the same thing.

The `<configuration>` element can contain information specifically intended to configure the .NET Remoting system. All such information must be within the `<system.runtime.remoting>` and `</system.`

runtime.remoting> tags. Within this pair of tags, you can specify the <application> and </application> tags.

The <application> tag can have a name attribute, like this

```
<application name = "AppName">
```

The name attribute specifies the application's name. This replaces the statement

```
RemotingConfiguration.ApplicationName = "AppName";
```

in the source code of your programs.

Elements of Configuration Files

Most of the business of a .NET Remoting configuration file occurs inside the <application> element. It can contain any or all the elements shown in Table 8.1.

It is possible, and even common, to use combinations of these tags. For example, it may not seem intuitive for a program to be both a client and a server, but it is perfectly possible. In such cases, a program's configuration file can have both the <service> and <client> elements. It uses the <service> element for the remote objects that it offers, and the <client> element for the remote objects it uses.

The <service> element can appear one or more times inside the <application> element. Specifically, it occurs once for each type of object the application offers. Likewise, the <client> element appears once for each type of object that the program uses. The <channels> element, however, only occurs once. It specifies one or more channels that the program uses. The <lifetime> element occurs once within the <application> element. Its settings apply to all of the CAOs the program offers.

Table 8.1 The Primary Elements for Configuring .NET Remoting Applications

ELEMENT	DESCRIPTION
<service>	Specifies a remote server object that is available on the server computer.
<client>	Configures a client for a remote application.
<channels>	Stipulates the channels the remote application uses.
<lifetime>	Controls the lifetimes of all CAOs offered in the application.

<service>

A configuration file for a program contains the `<service>` element when it offers remote objects. Because servers can offer both SAOs and CAOs, the `<service>` element can contain the elements `<wellknown>` and `<activated>`. As you might expect, `<wellknown>` is used for SAOs and `<activated>` indicates CAOs.

<wellknown>

When used within the `<service>` element, the `<wellknown>` element has four attributes. One of its attributes, called `displayName`, is optional. It is only used by Microsoft's .NET Framework Configuration Tool. The other three attributes (`mode`, `type`, and `objectUri`) are required.

The `mode` attribute states whether the server offers a singleton or a single-call object. Its value can be either `"Singleton"` or `"SingleCall"`.

You use the `type` attribute to state the name of the type being offered, and the assembly or program in which it exists. The type name must be fully scoped. You must include its namespace name. The name of the assembly should not include file extensions such as dll or exe.

It is possible to install objects in a **global assembly cache**. The global assembly cache is a group of directories that contains objects. All objects within the global assembly cache are visible to every program on the computer. If you install your remote object in the global assembly cache, you must include the version, culture, and public key information in the `<wellknown>` element's `type` attribute.

The last required attribute for the `<wellknown>` element is `objectUri`. This attribute specifies the URI endpoint where the remote object is to be published.

Listing 8.2 demonstrates how app.config files describe SAOs.

```
<service>
    <wellknown
        mode="Singleton"
        type="InfoMan.InformationManager, InfoMan"
        objectUri = "InfoMan.soap" />
</service>
```

Listing 8.2 Using the `<wellknown>` Element in a Server's Configuration File

This fragment from a configuration file uses the <wellknown> element to describe a singleton object. Its type name includes the namespace in which the object is defined (InfoMan) and the name of the object (InfomationManager). It states that the object resides in an assembly called InfoMan, and that it is not in the global assembly cache. It directs the .NET Remoting system to publish the object at the URI InfoMan.soap. The fact that the URI name contains the extension .soap implies that the application is using an HTTP channel. Specifying channels and port numbers is presented later in this chapter in the section for the <channels> element.

If you were publishing the singleton object described in Listing 8.2 and decided that you wanted to change it to a single-call object, you would only need to change the mode attribute to "SingleCall".

<activated>

Servers use the <activated> element to publish CAOs. Because programs do not publish CAOs at specific endpoints, you do not need to specify an endpoint in the server program's configuration file. Instead, you use the <activated> element's type attribute to specify the full type name (including its namespace) and the assembly or program that contains it. Listing 8.3 demonstrates its use.

```
<service>
    <activated
        type="InfoMan.InformationManager, InfoMan" />
</service>
```

Listing 8.3 Using the <activated> Element in a Server's Configuration File

If the object your server program publishes is in the global assembly cache, the <activated> element's type attribute must also contain the assembly's version, culture, and public key information.

Like the <wellknown> element, the <activated> element contains no information about the channel the object uses to communicate. Instead, it specifies channels and port numbers through the <channels> element, which is presented later in this chapter.

<client>

If a program uses a remote object, it is considered a client of that object. Client programs use the `<client>` element in their configuration files to specify the remote objects whose services they use.

JARGON

In programmer terminology client programs are said to "consume the services" of remote objects. For this reason, you'll sometimes hear programmers talking about clients "consuming" objects.

The `<client>` element has two attributes. The first is the optional `displayName` attribute, which is only used by Microsoft's configuration tool. The second attribute, `url`, is optional if the client only consumes the services of SAOs. If it uses any CAOs, you must specify the `url` attribute so that the client knows where to find the object.

Like the `<service>` element, the `<client>` element can contain the `<wellknown>` and `<activated>` elements.

<wellknown>

When used inside the `<client>` element, the `<wellknown>` element tells the .NET Remoting system where to find an SAO. On clients, the `<wellknown>` element has three attributes: displayName, type, and `objectUri`. As on servers, the `displayName` attribute is optional. The `type` and `url` state the full type name and URL, respectively, of the object on the server. Listing 8.4 illustrates the use of the `<wellknown>` element on clients.

```
1     <client>
2         <wellknown
3             type="InfoMan.InformationManager, Client"
4             url="http://localhost:8085/InfoMan.soap" />
5     </client>
```

Listing 8.4 Using the `<wellknown>` Element in a Client's Configuration File

The differences between the usage of the `<wellknown>` element on clients and servers are important to note. For example, the `type` attribute on line 3 of Listing 8.4 contains the fully scoped name of the object, just as it does on the server. However, the assembly name is different on the client than the server. In many of the example programs presented so far, the name of the client program is Client.exe. The configuration file fragment shown in Listing 8.4 is written with that assumption. Because I compiled the wrapped proxy into the program Client.exe, the .NET Remoting system on the client computer can look for the information about the remote type in Client.exe. Therefore, the `type` attribute on line 3 specifies Client as the name of the program in which the type information exists.

Another difference to note is the use of the `url` attribute rather than `objectUri`. The `url` attribute must state the full path to the server, including the transport type, the host name, the object's port number on the server, and the object's URI. The specification of the HTTP transport in Listing 8.4 tells the .NET Remoting system to communicate with the server over an HTTP channel.

<activated>

Configuration files for client programs use the `<activated>` element to specify the types of the remote objects. As with server programs, the `<activated>` element can only be used for CAOs. The `<activated>` element specifies the type of a remote object with its `type` attribute.

Like the `<wellknown>` element, clients using the `<activated>` element must specify the object's complete type name and the assembly or program on the client side that contains information about it. Listing 8.5 illustrates the use of the `<activated>` element.

```
<client url="http://localhost:8085/InfoMan">
    <activated
        type = "InfoMan.InformationManager,Client" />
</client>
```

Listing 8.5 Using the `<activated>` Element in a Client's Configuration File

Listing 8.5 demonstrates that the `<activated>` element must be used in conjunction with the `<client>` element's url attribute. As previously mentioned, the `<activated>` element's `type` attribute states the type of the remote object and the assembly or program that contains information about it. The `<client>` element's `url` attribute tells the client program where to go to connect to the server and activate the remote object.

<channels>

In .NET Remoting configuration files, the <channels> element contains a list that designates what channel (or channels) the client or server program uses. As such, the <channels> element appears in configuration files for both clients and servers. There can only be one <channels> element in an <application> element.

A <channels> element contains one or more <channel> elements. Each <channel> element defines one channel that the client or server uses for communication. An application can use as many channels as it needs. However, each channel must have a different name. For instance, an application can contain <channel> elements for both HTTP and TCP channels in the same configuration file. However, it cannot contain two different <channel> elements, each containing the name of the same HTTP channel.

Both clients and servers use the <channel> element's ref attribute to select the type of the communication channel. Servers use the <channel> element's port attribute to state the number of the port on which they offer objects. Listing 8.6 shows how the <channels> and <channel> elements can be used on a server.

```
<channels>
    <channel ref="http" port="8085"/>
</channels>
```

Listing 8.6 Using the <channels> and <channel> Elements on a Server

The example in Listing 8.6 states that the server offers a remote object on an HTTP channel using port 8085.

Clients can use the port attribute to state specific communication ports they want to use. In general, however, this is not necessary. Typically, clients can communicate through any port that is available when the program runs. Therefore, they often use a value of zero for the port attribute. This tells the .NET Remoting system to assign the client the first available port. Listing 8.7 demonstrates this usage.

```
<channels>
    <channel ref="http" port="0" />
</channels>
```

Listing 8.7 Using the <channels> and <channel> Elements on a Client

The configuration file fragment in Listing 8.7 stipulates that the client communicates with a remote object on an HTTP channel using whatever port is available on the client computer.

Within the <channel> element, you can insert another element to select the formatter the communication channel uses. Formatters were discussed in Chapter 4. The <channel> element can contain the <clientProviders> or <serverProviders> elements, depending on whether the configuration file is for a client or server, repectively. Inside the <clientProviders> and <serverProviders> elements, you can insert the <formatter> element. Setting the ref property of the <formatter> element selects the formatter the channel uses. Listing 8.8 demonstrates the use of the <formatter> element.

```
<channels>
    <channel ref="http" port="0" />
         <clientProviders>
              <formatter ref="binary"/>
         </clientProviders>
      </channel>
   </channels>
```

Listing 8.8 Selecting the Formatter on a Client

The configuration file fragment in Listing 8.8 enables a client application using the HTTP channel to use a binary formatter. Because binary data tends to be more compact than SOAP data, using a binary formatter may lead to increased communication speeds. Listing 8.9 demonstrates how to select a binary formatter for a server object.

```
<channels>
    <channel ref="http" port="0" />
         <serverProviders>
              <formatter ref="binary"/>
         </serverProviders>
      </channel>
   </channels>
```

Listing 8.9 Selecting the Binary Formatter on a Client

The only difference between Listing 8.8 and Listing 8.9 is that Listing 8.9 uses the `<serverProviders>` element rather than the `<clientProviders>` element.

NOTE

Recall that it is possible for a program to be both a client and a server. In that case, the program can use both the `<clientProviders>` and `<serverProviders>` elements in the same configuration file.

<lifetime>

Servers can manage the lifetimes of the CAOs they offer with the `<lifetime>` element. Setting the `<lifetime>` element in a server's configuration file alters the leases of *all* of the CAOs the server program offers. Because the `<lifetime>` element occurs in the server's app.config file, other objects offered by other server programs on the same computer are not affected.

The `<lifetime>` element has four attributes, all of which are optional. These attributes are time values that are assigned to the leases of the CAOs that the server program publishes. The time values that configuration files assign to these attributes are composed of an integer time and a letter indicating the time unit. Table 8.2 shows time units available.

According to the rules of XML, attribute values in configuration files can only be numbers or strings. When you're assigning times to the attributes of the <lifetime> element, you assign them all as strings. The strings are composed of integers combined with time unit specifiers. Example 8.1 uses the time units in Table 8.2.

Table 8.2 Time Units for the Attributes of the `<lifetime>` Element

UNIT	DESCRIPTION
D	Days
H	Hours
M	Minutes
S	Seconds
MS	Milliseconds

```
"1D"
"2H"
"35M"
"10S"
"550MS"
```

Example 8.1 Specifying Lease Times in Application Configuration Files

The time spans in Example 8.1 specify 1 day, 2 hours, 35 minutes, 10 seconds, and 555 milliseconds, respectively. Time spans defined this way cannot be combined. In other words, you cannot assign values such as "2H5M" to any of the attributes of the `<lifetime>` element.

The `<lifetime>` element's four attributes are called `leaseTime`, `renewOnCallTime`, `leaseManagerPollTime`, and `sponsorshipTimeout`. These correspond to the lease properties presented in Chapter 7. As you might expect, the `leaseTime` attribute designates the initial lease time. The amount of time added to a lease when a client invokes an object's method is specified in the `renewOnCallTime` attribute. The `leaseManagerPollTime` attribute sets the amount of time the application's lease manager goes to sleep after it checks the leases of all of the application's objects. The `leaseManagerPollTime` attribute controls the amount of time that the lease manager waits for an individual object sponsor to respond to its request.

Configuration Files for Remoting Applications

To see how the various configuration file elements presented so far work together, we need to build some sample programs. These samples also demonstrate the impact that configuration files have on our source code.

Configuration Files for SAOs

The first example program offers a simple singleton object. In fact, it reuses the `InformationManager` that appeared in Listing 6.2 in Chapter 6. To save space, it won't be repeated here. Instead, we'll start by writing the configuration file for the server program. This is shown in Listing 8.10.

```
1     <configuration>
2         <system.runtime.remoting>
3             <application>
4                 <channels>
5                     <channel ref="http" port="8085"/>
6                 </channels>
7                 <service>
8                     <wellknown
9                         mode="Singleton"
10                        type="InfoMan.InformationManager, InfoMan"
11                        objectUri = "InfoMan.soap" />
12                </service>
13            </application>
14        </system.runtime.remoting>
15    </configuration>
```

Listing 8.10 The Server Configuration File for the SAO Program

The use of the `<service>` element in Listing 8.10 tells the .NET Remoting system to publish an object. Lines 4-6 of the server configuration file state that the object is to be published on port 8085. They also state that the object uses an HTTP channel to communicate with its clients. Lines 7-12 define the object as well-known. Specifically, line 9 says that it is a singleton. Its type name, given on line 10, is `InfoMan.InformationManager`. The server program can find the object in an assembly called InfoMan. The object's URI on the server is to be InfoMan.soap.

This simple little configuration file does quite a bit. It also has a big impact on the way we write our server program. Listing 8.11 shows the server program that goes with the configuration file in Listing 8.10.

```
using System;
using System.Runtime.Remoting;
using System.Runtime.Remoting.Channels;
using System.Runtime.Remoting.Channels.Http;
using InfoMan;

namespace Server
{
    class ServerAppClass
    {
        [STAThread]
```

Listing 8.11 The Server for the SAO Program *(continues)*

```
        static void Main(string[] args)
        {
            RemotingConfiguration.Configure("Server.exe.config");
            System.Console.WriteLine(
                "Press Enter to end the InformationManager.");
            System.Console.Read();
        }
    }
}
```

Listing 8.11 The Server for the SAO Program *(continued)*

When you look at this server program, you may think, "Where did all the code go?" The server now requires very little code to get the object published. The channel, port number, object type, and URI are all defined in the configuration file. All of the code that did that programmatically is no longer necessary. However, to use the configuration file, the server program must contain a call to `RemotingConfiguration.Configure()`. This method loads the configuration file into the .NET Remoting system and applies the information the file contains to the current program.

Your program can call `RemotingConfiguration.Configure()` multiple times. Each time it does, the `RemotingConfiguration.Configure()` method loads another configuration file. The capability enables you to define configuration files for specific tasks. For example, when you ship your program on a CD, you can put configuration files onto the CD that do nothing but state the channel that the application uses. During the installation, your install program can detect (or ask) whether the user connects to your remote object over the Internet. If so, your install program can copy a configuration file onto the user's computer that selects an HTTP channel. If the user is connected directly to your corporate network, your install program can copy a configuration file onto the user's computer that selects a TCP channel.

You can even use this capability to select which remote object to use. If your program uses several remote objects and all of the `<service>` statements are in separate configuration files, your install program can copy configuration files for some of the objects and not others. Your application can detect which objects to use by the presence of a configuration file for that object. This gives you an incredible amount of flexibility in the way you build and deploy your applications.

The Arcane Arts of Configuration Files

The .NET Framework makes it easy to load and parse any XML file, especially configuration files. However, if there are errors in your configuration file, it will throw exceptions. The file may have errors in it if the user decides to edit it manually, or if it becomes corrupted. Your program should use the C# `try-catch` statement to trap and handle these errors.

When an error occurs in a configuration file, it may or may not be easy to figure out what the problem is. If, for example, the configuration file is not in the same directory as the program, the .NET Framework throws an exception with a very clear error message that states that it can't find the file.

However, when I was developing my first program that used configuration files, I was writing a program nearly identical to this SAO example. In fact, the configuration file in Listing 8.10 is based on the one I used for that program. Whenever I ran the program, I kept getting an error message stating that there was a problem in the file near the `</channel>` tag. As you can see from Listing 8.10, there is no `</channel>` tag. It took me over an hour to figure out that the .NET Framework could not read the file, even though it could find it. The reason was that I foolishly thought I could leave the configuration file up in an edit window just like I did my source code. However, when I did, Visual Studio locked the file as being in use. The XML classes .NET Framework could not read it until that lock was released. The message the Framework generated said nothing about this.

This and similar experiences taught me that debugging XML files is something of an art in itself.

At this point, we're ready to look at the client side of the SAO sample program. Like the server program, the client program has its own configuration file. It's provided in Listing 8.12.

```
<configuration>
    <system.runtime.remoting>
        <application>
            <client>
                <wellknown
                    type="InfoMan.InformationManager, Client"
                    url="http://localhost:8085/InfoMan.soap" />
            </client>
        </application>
    </system.runtime.remoting>
</configuration>
```

Listing 8.12 The Client Configuration File for the SAO Program

Through the use of the `<client>` element, the configuration file in Listing 8.12 says that it consumes the services of a remote object. It states that the object is published at a well-known endpoint. The object's type is `InfoMan.InformationManager`, and metadata about that type can be found in the program called Client. The object is published on the current computer on port 8085. Its endpoint name is InfoMan.soap.

As with server programs, using configuration files on clients can simplify the code for the client. Listing 8.13 shows the client's source code.

```
using System;
using System.Runtime.Remoting;
using System.Runtime.Remoting.Channels;
using System.Runtime.Remoting.Channels.Http;
using InfoMan;

namespace Client
{
    class ClientAppClass
    {
        [STAThread]
        static void Main(string[] args)
        {
            RemotingConfiguration.Configure("client.exe.config");

            InformationManager infoManager =
                new InformationManager();

            // If the remote object was activated...
            if (infoManager != null)
            {
                string tempString;
                int dataCollectionLength;

                try
                {
                    dataCollectionLength =
                        infoManager.DataCollectionLength();

                    // Print the data.
                    for (int i=0; i<dataCollectionLength; i++)
                    {
                        tempString = null;

                        // Get the item.
                        tempString = infoManager.DataItem(i);
```

Listing 8.13 The Client for the SAO Program

```
37
38                          // Print it to the console.
39                          System.Console.WriteLine(tempString);
40                      }
41                  }
42                  catch (Exception)
43                  {
44                      ServerAccessError();
45                  }
46              }
47                  // Else the remote object was not activated...
48              else
49              {
50                  // Print an error message.
51                  System.Console.WriteLine(
52                      "Remote object could not be activated");
53              }
54
55              System.Console.WriteLine(
56                  "\nPaused. Press Enter to continue...");
57              System.Console.Read();
58          }
59
60          static void ServerAccessError()
61          {
62              System.Console.WriteLine(
63                  "Error: Could not access the server");
64          }
65      }
66  }
```

Listing 8.13 The Client for the SAO Program *(continued)*

With a few important exceptions, this client program is very much like those presented earlier in this book. The differences are on lines 14-17. Like the server, the client does not need to create or register a channel. It doesn't have special code to acquire a reference to the object. It simply loads the configuration file on line 14. After that, it can use the `InformationManager` type just as if the type were local. As with any local type, the client program can allocate an instance of the `InformationManager` type with the C# new statement. The information in the configuration file told the .NET Remoting system to intercept all allocations of objects of type `InformationManager`. Instead of attempting to allocate them locally, the .NET Remoting system allocates a proxy for the object.

Configuration Files for CAOs

My experience with creating configuration files for publishing CAOs has been that they're a little trickier than SAOs for beginners. I think that's true of CAOs in general. I found when I first started writing .NET Remoting applications that it was easier for me to get CAOs working programmatically than with configuration files. Other programmers I've talked with have had just the opposite experience.

Because doing things programmatically seemed to be easier for me, I got my first CAO up and running programmatically. I wrote a very simple client that didn't do much more than the sample programs presented so far. Next, I modified the server to use a configuration file. When that was up and working properly, I modified the client so that it used a configuration file as well. I then started adding the functionality I needed to the client. If you're new to building distributed applications, I suggest you use small steps such as these. You'll find it much easier to isolate errors.

In the end, I think you'll discover the same thing that I did. CAOs are not that hard after all. To prove it, let's build one. We'll use the `InformationManager` object shown in Listing 8.14.

```
using System;
using System.Runtime.Remoting.Lifetime;
using InfoManSponspor;

namespace InfoMan
{
    public class InformationManager : MarshalByRefObject
    {
        private const int ARRAY_SIZE = 13;
        private string [] theData = new string [ARRAY_SIZE];
        private InformationManagerSponsor mySponsor;

        public InformationManager(
            InformationManagerSponsor theSponsor)
        {
            mySponsor = theSponsor;

            // Initialize the array.
            theData[0] = "\"I am afraid, Watson, ";
            theData[1] =  "that I shall have to go,\" ";
            theData[2] = "said  Holmes, as we sat down ";
```

Listing 8.14 The Remote Object for the CAO Program

```
            theData[3] = "together to our breakfast one";
            theData[4] = "morning.";
            theData[5] = "\"Go! Where to?\"";
            theData[6] = "\"To Dartmoor; to King's Pyland.\"";
            theData[7] = "I was not surprised.  Indeed, my";
            theData[8] = "only wonder was that he had not ";
            theData[9] = "already been mixed upon this ";
            theData[10] = "extraordinary case, which was the ";
            theData[11] = "one topic of conversation through ";
            theData[12] = "the length and breadth of England.";
        }

        public override object InitializeLifetimeService()
        {
            ILease myLease =
                (ILease)base.InitializeLifetimeService();

            if (myLease.CurrentState == LeaseState.Initial)
            {
                myLease.InitialLeaseTime =
                    TimeSpan.FromMinutes(1);
                myLease.RenewOnCallTime =
                    TimeSpan.FromSeconds(5);

                myLease.Register(mySponsor);
            }
            return (myLease);
        }

        public string DataItem(int whichItem)
        {
            string theItem = null;

            // If the item number is valid...
            if ((whichItem >= 0) && (whichItem < ARRAY_SIZE))
            {
                // Get the item.
                theItem = theData[whichItem];
            }

            // Return the item to the client.
            return (theItem);
        }

        public void DataItem(
            int whichItem,
            string newValue)
        {
```

Listing 8.14 The Remote Object for the CAO Program *(continues)*

```
            // If the item number is valid...
            if ((whichItem >= 0) && (whichItem < ARRAY_SIZE))
            {
                // Set the item.
                theData[whichItem] = newValue;
            }
        }

        public int DataCollectionLength()
        {
            return (ARRAY_SIZE);
        }
    }
}
```

Listing 8.14 The Remote Object for the CAO Program *(continued)*

This object is based on one we used in Chapter 7. To publish this object as a CAO, we need the server configuration file that appears in Listing 8.15.

```
1   <configuration>
2       <system.runtime.remoting>
3           <application>
4               <channels>
5                   <channel ref="http" port="8085"/>
6               </channels>
7               <service>
8                   <activated
9                       type="InfoMan.InformationManager, InfoMan" />
10              </service>
11          </application>
12      </system.runtime.remoting>
13  </configuration>
```

Listing 8.15 The Server Configuration File for the CAO Program

Lines 4-6 of the server's configuration file for the CAO stipulate that the CAO is to be published on port 8085 using an HTTP channel. The fact that it is a CAO is specified by the `<activated>` element on lines 8-9.

Amazingly, the server code for this program is exactly the same as the server code that appeared in Listing 8.8. The fact that the server is now publishing a CAO instead of a singleton makes no difference. The CAO server program just needs to load the configuration file; the.NET Remoting system handles the rest.

On the client side, the configuration file is nearly as straightforward as the server's. This is demonstrated in Listing 8.16.

```
1     <configuration>
2         <system.runtime.remoting>
3             <application>
4                 <client url="http://localhost:8085/InfoMan">
5                     <activated
6                         type = "InfoMan.InformationManager,Client" />
7                 </client>
8                 <channels>
9                     <channel ref="http" port="0" />
10                </channels>
11            </application>
12        </system.runtime.remoting>
13    </configuration>
```

Listing 8.16 The Client Configuration File for the CAO Program

On line 4 of Listing 8.16, the client's configuration file tells the .NET Remoting system that the client uses a remote object published on port 8085 of the current computer. The type of the object is specified on line 6, along with the name of the program that contains a description of the `InfoMan.InformationManager` type. Lines 8-10 tell the .NET Remoting system that the client uses an HTTP channel and whatever port is available.

The source code for the client program is the same as the code in Listing 8.13. As with SAOs, the client just needs to load the configuration file. After that, it can allocate the CAO with a new statement just as if it were a local object. Of course, what it's really allocating is the CAO's proxy.

Configuration Files for Controlling Object Lifetimes

Once you get a program that uses a CAO up and running, controlling its lifetime through configuration files is easy. You simply modify the server's configuration file to use the <lifetime> element. For this example, we'll use exactly the same source code we used for the previous CAO example. The only thing that changes is the server's configuration file. This is shown in Listing 8.17.

```
<configuration>
    <system.runtime.remoting>
        <application>
            <channels>
                <channel ref="http" port="8085"/>
            </channels>
            <service>
                <activated
                    type="InfoMan.InformationManager, InfoMan" />
            <lifetime
               leaseTime="5M"
               renewOnCallTime="30S"
               leaseManagerPollTime="20S" />
            </service>
        </application>
    </system.runtime.remoting>
</configuration>
```

Listing 8.17 The Server Configuration File for a CAO with a Non-Default Lease

This configuration file states that the CAO has an initial lease time of 5 minutes. The amount of time that the program's lease manager might add to the lease when a client calls on one of the object's methods is 30 seconds. The lease manager polls the lease every 20 seconds.

REMINDER

The lease manager might or might not add time to the object's lease when one of its methods is called. For further information, see Chapter 7.

Summary

Configuration files enhance the flexibility of your distributed applications. They also simplify your applications' code. Configuration files for .NET Remoting applications are written in XML. They specify the remote objects that a program offers or uses. Configuration files also state the channel (or channels) and port numbers through which the program communicates. In addition, they enable you to set non-default values for the leases of objects a server program publishes.

CHAPTER 9

Deploying Distributed Applications

In the past, the average developer did not have to deal much with deployment issues. If you were on a team writing a word processor, for instance, someone on the team wrote an install program. That usually was the extent of developer involvement with application deployment.

Not so with distributed applications. In a networked world of remote objects, deployment must be planned before development can begin. Developers write their server programs differently, depending on how the servers publish their remote objects and how the server themselves are deployed. All programmers on the development team must understand deployment issues to write their server programs appropriately.

Deploying professional applications begins with strong-named assemblies. To maximize deployment options, every member of the development team must release remote objects in assemblies with strong names. Using strong-named assemblies, you can choose your deployment and versioning methods. You can publish your remote objects using server programs developed as console programs or Windows Forms programs. If you prefer, your server programs can be Windows Services. Also, you can host your remote objects in Internet Information Services (IIS).

Stong-Named Assemblies

Under COM, objects on a network have GUIDs that uniquely identify them. Installing a COM object on a computer generally meant working with the computer's registry. As a result of the complexities of this approach, the .NET Framework does not publish and identify objects in this way. Instead, it enables you to assign a strong name to any object you publish. Strong names uniquely identify assemblies, much as GUIDs did under COM. An assembly's strong name contains its simple text name, version number, culture information, a public key, and a digital signature.

TIP

Although a strong name's culture information is optional, experienced developers generally recommend that you include it.

Nothing in the .NET Framework forces you to assign a strong name to an assembly before you publish it. However, I highly recommend that you do so. There are many reasons for this. One reason, which is presented in detail later in this chapter, is that the .NET Framework enables multiple version of the same object to be published concurrently. This helps you keep backward compatibility with prior versions of your applications. Assemblies need strong names to help ensure that clients are accessing the correct versions of objects.

Also, strong names improve the security of your applications because they use a pair of keys to generate the signature. One is a public key that your clients can use to identify the correct assembly. The other is a private key that you generate and keep on your development computer. It should not be released publicly.

WARNING

An assembly's strong name identifies it and guarantees that it has not been tampered with. However, it does not guarantee that the assembly is published by a trusted source. To ensure the trust level of an assembly, you should also sign it using Microsoft's Authenticode technology. Chapter 13 discusses Authenticode signatures.

Microsoft provides a tool called SN.EXE that you can use to generate the pair of keys for any assembly. It stores the private key/public key pair in a file. You combine the information in that file with your assembly when you compile it in Visual Studio.

Suppose, for example, that you want to deploy the SAO presented as the first application in Chapter 8. If you look back to Chapter 8 in the section titled **Configuration Files for SAOs**, you'll see the listings needed for this application. It uses the `InformationManager` object presented in Listing 6.2 in Chapter 6.

To deploy the SAO application, you should use Visual Studio's configuration manager to compile the release version, rather than a debug version. Set up the solution (or solutions) with projects for the server, the `InformationManager` object, and the client. Be sure that the configuration files you're using (client.exe.config and server.exe.config) are in the directories containing the executable programs. The file containing the private key/public key pair must be in the same directory as the assembly containing the remote object.

When I built this application, I created it in a directory called Chapter09\Program01. The `InformationManager` object, client, and server were in the InfoMan, Client, and Server directories, respectively. I used the same three names for the names of the projects. If you do likewise, you can use the following steps to create the application.

1. Compile the InfoMan project, which creates the assembly containing the `InformationManager` object, to be sure everything is okay.
2. Open a Visual Studio command window.
3. In the command window, change the current directory to Chapter09\Program01\InfoMan\obj\Release.
4. In the Visual Studio command window, type:

   ```
   sn -k InfoMan.snk
   ```

   to generate the file containing the strong name keys.
5. Go back to Visual Studio and look at the Solution Explorer. Double-click the file name AssemblyInfo.cs. Visual Studio loads the file into an edit window.
6. Scroll AssemblyInfo.cs until you see the attribute `[assembly: AssemblyKeyFile("")]`. In the quote marks, insert the file name InfoMan.snk, so that it looks like this:

   ```
   [assembly: AssemblyKeyFile("InfoMan.snk")]
   ```
7. Build the InfoMan assembly.
8. Add a reference to the strong-named assembly to the server program's project file.
9. Generate metadata from the strong-named assembly.

10. Add a reference to the metadata to the client program's project file.
11. Build the server and client programs.

When you build your applications with strong-named assemblies, you'll use steps very similar to these.

WARNING

If you are programming in Visual Basic, rather than Visual C#, the .snk file must be in the same directory as the solution file, rather than in the same directory as the assembly.

The `AssemblyKeyFile` class used in step 6 of the preceding activity comes from the `System.Reflection` namespace. This namespace handles dynamic type management. Applications that apply attributes to classes make use of the capabilities provided in the `System.Reflection` namespace.

The `System.Reflection` namespace also contains a class called `AssemblyKeyName`. You'll see an entry for the `AssemblyKeyName` class in the AssemblyInfo.cs file that Visual Studio generates for every project. Applications can use the `AssemblyKeyName` class to generate a strong name for an assembly. However, using this technique involves installing private key/public key entries in a .NET Framework component called the Cryptographic Service Provider (CSP). This is usually done through the SN.EXE tool. Using the `AssemblyKeyName` class and the CSP is typically more suited to deploying local objects rather than remote objects.

Installing Distributed Applications

In contrast to past technologies such as COM and DCOM, .NET Remoting gives you multiple options for installing your server objects. The result of this flexibility is that you can deploy your objects in the way that best fits your existing installation.

As we've already seen, .NET Remoting lets you write your server programs as console applications. They can also be written as Windows Forms programs. From an installation and deployment point of view, there is really no difference between these two methods.

Alternatively, you can write your server program as a Windows Service. This has several advantages for commercial applications, including better security, event logging, and increased automation.

If you are already using Internet Information Server (IIS), you may want to install your remote objects within IIS under ASP.NET.

Deploying Server Objects as Windows Forms or Windows Console Applications

Windows Forms (WinForm) and Windows console applications are nice because they're simple to deal with. You can debug them easily, and it's convenient to be able to start and stop them from the Visual Studio IDE. If you want to do a small test deployment and keep these advantages, you should think about deploying your server program as a WinForm or console application.

For deploying large-scale applications, however, WinForm and console programs have definite disadvantages. First, you must log onto a Windows account to start your server objects. Although this process can be automated by using the Start menu's Startup group, it's still generally not feasible. When your server goes down at 3 a.m., do you really want to get out of bed and go down to your workplace just to log onto your server so the server objects can restart? It's much nicer if they start automatically when the server starts.

Also, you must implement the code for tasks such as error and event logging yourself when you write WinForm and console applications. That's not the case when you use other deployment methods. When you're deploying a large distributed applications, error and event logs are critical to both troubleshooting and performance tuning.

These limitations generally make deploying server objects as WinForm or console applications impractical for everything but limited-sized deployments for testing purposes.

Deploying Server Objects as Windows Services

Another method of deploying remote objects on server computers is as a Windows Service. A Windows Service is a program that does not have a user interface. Instead, it provides functionality to the operating system and to other programs. The Windows operating system uses Windows Services to provide much of its own functionality. For example, remote procedure calls (RPC) and the Windows DHCP server are implemented as Windows Services.

You can configure a Windows Service to start when its host computer starts and to run for as long as the computer remains up and running. The advantage of this is that, if the computer suffers a power outage, a Windows Service restarts automatically whenever the power comes back on.

A Windows Service can run in an account that you create for it. This enables you to apply very specific security settings to that service that are not applied to regular user accounts.

Windows provides a component called the Services Control Manager. You access it by selecting **Settings** from your Start menu, and then opening the Control Panel. From the control panel, open the **Administrative Tools** group. Next, choose **Services**. You can use the Services Control Manager to start or stop any of the services it lists.

NOTE

If you've never written a Windows Service, you may find it helpful to develop your server program as a console application first. When you're finished debugging the remote object, you can modify the server program to run as a Windows Service. The reason I like this approach is that it enables me to debug my object right in Visual Studio. It is possible to install a remote object as a service, and then attach a debugger to its process. However, I don't find that as easy or as convenient.

To see how easy it is to modify a server program from being a console application to being a Windows Service, we'll write an application similar to those presented previously. Listing 9.1 shows the code for a remote object that should be very familiar by now.

```
using System;

namespace InfoMan
{
    public class InformationManager : MarshalByRefObject
    {
        private const int ARRAY_SIZE = 13;
        private string [] theData = new string [ARRAY_SIZE];

        public InformationManager()
        {
            // Initialize the array.
            theData[0] = "\"Are you Doctor Dolittle?\"" ;
```

Listing 9.1 The Information Manager Object for the Windows Service

```
            theData[1] =  "I shouted as we sped up the short";
            theData[2] = "said  Holmes, as we sat down ";
            theData[3] = "garden-path to the house.";
            theData[4] = "\"Yes, I'm Doctor Dolittle,\"";
            theData[5] = "\"Go! Where to?\"";
            theData[6] = "said he, opening the front door ";
            theData[7] = "with the same bunch of keys.";
            theData[8] = "\"Get in!  Don't bother about ";
            theData[9] = "wiping your feet. Never mind the ";
            theData[10] = "mud. Get in out of the rain!\"";
            theData[11] = "I popped in, he and Jip following.";
            theData[12] = "Then he slammed the door behind us.";
        }

        public string DataItem(int whichItem)
        {
            string theItem = null;

            // If the item number is valid...
            if ((whichItem >= 0) && (whichItem < ARRAY_SIZE))
            {
                // Get the item.
                theItem = theData[whichItem];
            }

            // Return the item to the client.
            return (theItem);
        }

        public void DataItem(
            int whichItem,
            string newValue)
        {
            // If the item nmber is valid...
            if ((whichItem >= 0) && (whichItem < ARRAY_SIZE))
            {
                // Set the item.
                theData[whichItem] = newValue;
            }
        }

        public int DataCollectionLength()
        {
            return (ARRAY_SIZE);
        }
    }
}
```

Listing 9.1 The Information Manager Object for the Windows Service *(continued)*

Listing 9.1 shows that you do not have to modify a remote object in any way to install it as a Windows Service. There are significant differences, however, in the server program.

To create the server program as a Windows Service, begin with the following steps.

1. Start Visual Studio and create a new project from the **File** menu. When Visual Studio displays the New Project dialog box, select **Windows Service**. For this example, enter **InfoManService** in the **Name** box. Set the project's directory to wherever you want to store the project's files.
2. When you proceed, Visual Studio generates the source file for your server program. It then displays its designer interface, as shown in Figure 9.1.
3. Go to the Properties window and ensure that the application's `AutoLog` property is set to `true`. If you do not see the property page shown in Figure 9.1, click in the designer window.

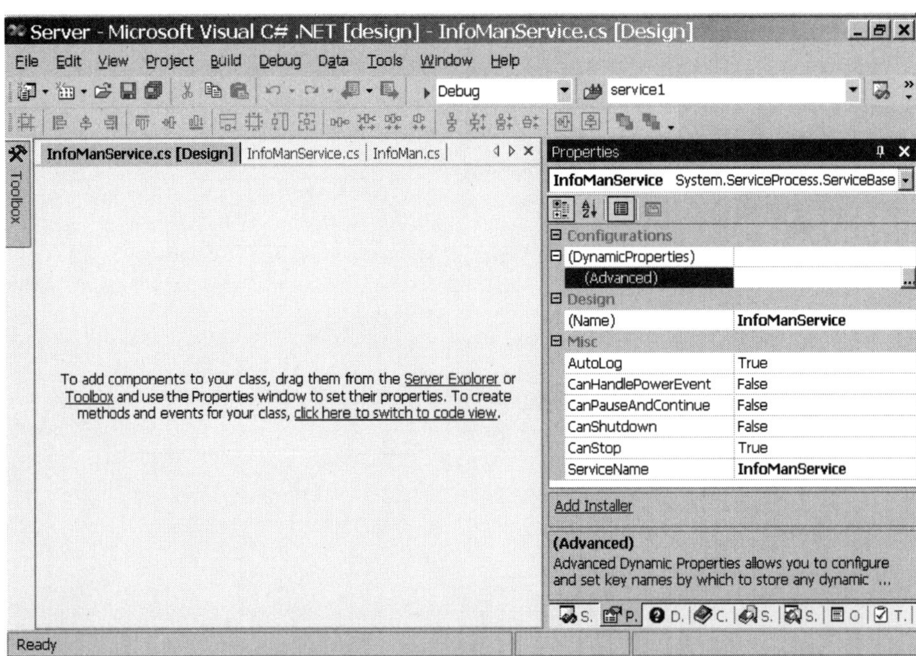

Figure 9.1 The Visual Studio Designer Interface for Creating Windows Services

4. To view the program's code, click on the link in the designer that says, "Click here to switch to code view." Visual Studio displays the server's code.
5. Make the modifications to the `InitializeComponent()`, `OnStart()`, and `OnStop()` methods, as shown in bold in Listing 9.2.

```
using System;
using System.Collections;
using System.ComponentModel;
using System.Data;
using System.Diagnostics;
using System.ServiceProcess;
using System.Runtime.Remoting;

namespace Server
{
    public class InfoManService :
        System.ServiceProcess.ServiceBase
    {
        private System.ComponentModel.Container components = null;

        public InfoManService()
        {
            InitializeComponent();
        }

        static void Main()
        {
            System.ServiceProcess.ServiceBase[] ServicesToRun;

            ServicesToRun =
                new System.ServiceProcess.ServiceBase[]
                {
                    new InfoManService()
                };

            System.ServiceProcess.ServiceBase.Run(ServicesToRun);
        }

        private void InitializeComponent()
        {
            components = new System.ComponentModel.Container();
            this.ServiceName = "InfoManService";
        }
```

Listing 9.2 The Windows Service Program *(continues)*

```
39
40            protected override void Dispose( bool disposing )
41            {
42                if( disposing )
43                {
44                    if (components != null)
45                    {
46                        components.Dispose();
47                    }
48                }
49                base.Dispose( disposing );
50            }
51
52            protected override void OnStart(string[] args)
53            {
54                EventLog.WriteEntry("InfoMan Service starting");
55                RemotingConfiguration.Configure(
56                    "Server.exe.config");
57            }
58
59            protected override void OnStop()
60            {
61                EventLog.WriteEntry("InfoMan Service ending");
62            }
63        }
64    }
```

Listing 9.2 The Windows Service Program *(continued)*

At this point, you have the code for offering a remote object as a Windows Service. Before we continue, let's examine the server code more closely.

When Visual Studio generates your code, it contains a number of explanatory comments. I deleted them from Listing 9.2. Lines 2-6 contain `using` statements that specify the namespaces required for a Windows Service. The server's application class is now called `InfoManService`. To be installed as a Windows Service, it must be derived from `System.ServiceProcess.ServiceBase`.

Visual Studio enables you to add components that it offers into your Windows Service. You can drag these from the ToolBox or from the Server Explorer. However, you do this in designer view, not in code view. If you do add components to your project, Visual Studio generates code to add them to the server application class's `components` member. In this example project, we're not adding any components. Therefore, the `components` member is initialized to `null` on line 14.

The constructor for the server's application class must call the `InitializeComponent()` method. You can add any other initialization code you need. However, it must come *after* the call to `InitializeComponent()`.

The `Main()` method begins by declaring an array variable called `ServicesToRun`. This refers the Windows Services that the program offers. It is possible for a single program to provide multiple services. That's why `ServicesToRun` is an array. It must contain one entry for each Windows Service. On lines 25-29, it allocates the application class of the server for the remote object. Because this is the only Windows Service this program offers, it is the only entry in the `ServicesToRun` array. On line 31, the program calls the static method `System.ServiceProcess.ServiceBase.Run()`. Doing this loads all of the services in the `ServicesToRun` array.

The code for the `InitializeComponent()` method appears on lines 34-38. When you create a Windows Service, you should have the `InitializeComponent()` method set the service name, as shown on line 37.

The `Dispose()` method performs much of the cleanup that is performed in C++ destructors. Because you cannot guarantee when a C# destructor is called, cleanup tasks are generally done in the `Dispose()` method in most classes in the .NET Framework. The Framework calls `Dispose()` at specific times, and so can your program.

Whenever a Windows Service is started, its `OnStart()` method is called. The `OnStart()` method shown on lines 52-57 writes an entry to the event log. In general, it's a good idea to make use of the event logs provided by Windows Services. The can help you with debugging, profiling, and performance tuning your server program.

Next, the `OnStart()` method calls `RemotingConfiguration.Configure()` to publish the `InformationManager` from Listing 9.1 as a remote object. The configuration file for this program appears in Listing 9.3.

```
<configuration>
    <system.runtime.remoting>
        <application>
            <channels>
                <channel ref="http" port="8085"/>
```

Listing 9.3 The Server Configuration File for the Windows Service *(continues)*

```
            </channels>
            <service>
                <wellknown
                    mode="Singleton"
                    type="InfoMan.InformationManager, InfoMan"
                    objectUri = "InfoMan.soap" />
            </service>
        </application>
    </system.runtime.remoting>
</configuration>
```

Listing 9.3 The Server Configuration File for the Windows Service *(continued)*

The startup directory for any Windows Service is:

```
<OS Drive>:<OS Dir>\system32
```

where <OS Drive> and <OS Dir> is the drive letter and directory where your operating system is installed. Usually, this is C:\WINNT. The configuration file for remote object servers must be placed in the startup directory for Windows Services. Therefore, on my computer, I had to put the InfoManService.exe.config file shown in Listing 9.3 in the C:\WINNT\system32 directory.

The program in Listing 9.2 ends with the `OnStop()` method. This is called whenever a Windows Service is halted. In this program, the `OnStop()` method writes an entry into the event log indicating that the service has stopped.

NOTE

There is an easy way to debug programs written as Windows Services. You add some of the conditional compilation statements that C# supports and modify `Main()` to call `OnStart()`. The conditional compilation statements should only allow this modification to be compiled when you are creating a debug build. When you're ready for a release build, the conditional compilation statements should direct Visual Studio to compile your program as a Windows Service.

Now that you have the code for the remote object, code for the server program, and the server's configuration file, you're almost ready to build this program. However, Windows Services require an installer class. Happily, you can add one without writing a line of code. To do so, use the following steps:

1. Return to the Visual Studio designer view shown in Figure 9.1. Click the mouse's secondary button[1] anywhere on the designer page that is not hyperlinked.
2. In the menu that appears, select **Add Installer**. Visual Studio displays the designer view shown in Figure 9.2.
3. If the item called serviceInstaller1 is not selected, click it.
4. Display the Properties window. It should resemble the Properties window in Figure 9.2.
5. In the Properties window, set the StartType property to Automatic.
6. In the designer window, click on serviceProcessInstaller1. If the Properties windows is not displayed, go to it now. Set the Account property to LocalSystem.
7. Save all files.

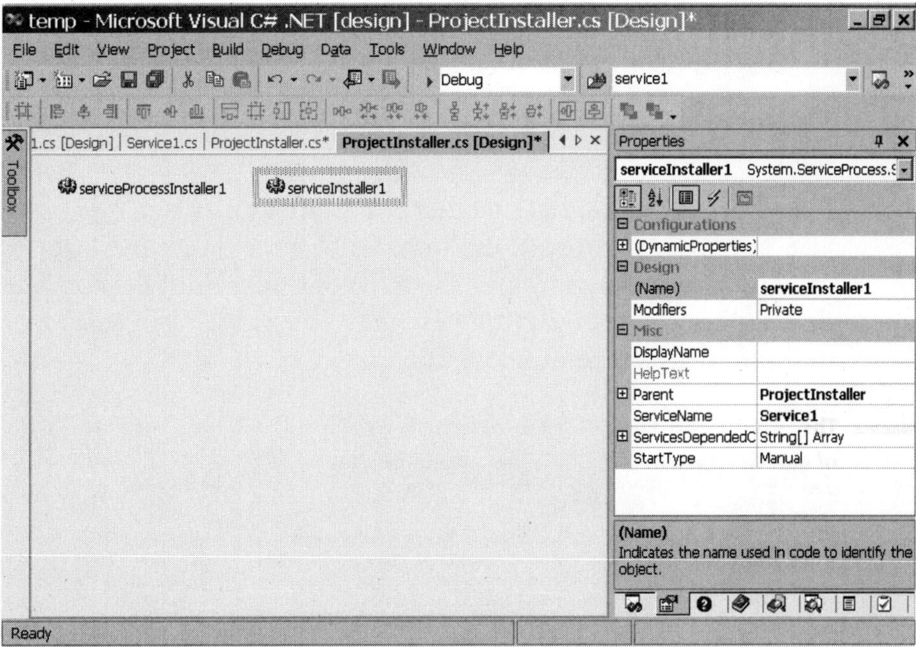

Figure 9.2 The Server Program with Its Installers (Designer View)

[1] When the mouse is configured for right-handed use, the left button is the primary button. The secondary button is the right button. When it's configured for left-handed use, the primary and secondary buttons are the right and left buttons, respectively. Most computer literature tell you to right-click or left-click items on the screen. This assumes right-handed use. I don't like to make that assumption.

8. In the Solution Explorer, ensure that you have the references that you need. Specifically, you must have a reference to InfoMan.dll or a proxy DLL, if you are using one. You also need a reference to System.Runtime.Remoting. If they are not present, add these two references.
9. Build the server program.

What you've got now is an executable that you can run as a Windows Service. The Services Control Manager displays the list of services currently installed on your computer. You can install your program into that list as a Windows Service using the INSTALLUTIL.EXE tool that comes with Visual Studio. To do so, start the Visual Studio Command Prompt and switch to the directory containing the InfoManService program. At the prompt, type the command:

```
installutil InfoMan.exe
```

INSTALLUTIL displays its output as it attempts to install the program. If it is successful, you will see InfoManService in the list of entries in your Services Control Manager. Start InfoManService by selecting **Start** from the Services Control Manager's **Action** menu. When it is started, the Services Control Manager will resemble Figure 9.3.

There are a number of important things to note about what you've just done.

First, you set the ServiceInstaller compoment's `StartType` property to `Automatic`. As a result, the InfoManService program starts automatically each time the computer starts. It continues until the computer shuts down. This is generally the behavior you want from server programs that publish your remote objects.

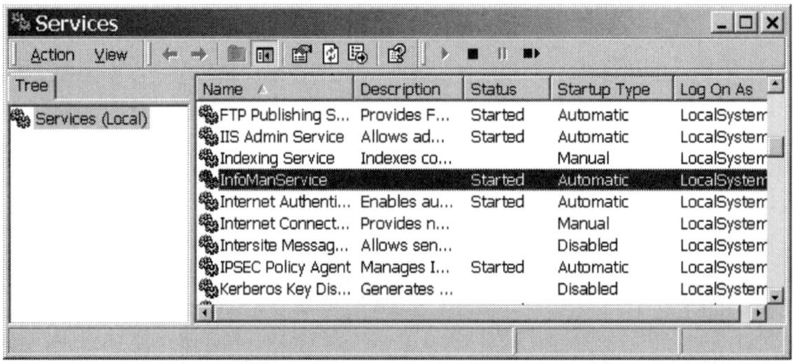

Services

Action View

Tree: Services (Local)

Name	Description	Status	Startup Type	Log On As
FTP Publishing S...	Provides F...	Started	Automatic	LocalSystem
IIS Admin Service	Allows ad...	Started	Automatic	LocalSystem
Indexing Service	Indexes co...		Manual	LocalSystem
InfoManService		Started	Automatic	LocalSystem
Internet Authenti...	Enables au...	Started	Automatic	LocalSystem
Internet Connect...	Provides n...		Manual	LocalSystem
Intersite Messag...	Allows sen...		Disabled	LocalSystem
IPSEC Policy Agent	Manages I...	Started	Automatic	LocalSystem
Kerberos Key Dis...	Generates ...		Disabled	LocalSystem

Figure 9.3 The Services Control Manager with the InfoManService Program Running

Second, you set the ServiceProcessInstaller component's `Account` property to `LocalSystem`. The `LocalSystem` account is defined for you by Windows. We used the `LocalSystem` account in this example because it's easy, not because it's the most appropriate account for your remote object.

This account has no password and does not have credentials. This means that it has limited access to network resources, such as shared directories and pipes. It must connect using a null session. This does not prevent it from accessing remote objects through .NET Remoting. The `LocalSystem` account has privileges on your server that the Microsoft documentation describes as "extensive," and that's a good description. In fact, it has enough privileges to bring down or possibly even corrupt the computer's operating system. It's actually very rare that your remote server object needs to run in the context of this account.

You can also set the ServiceProcessInstaller component's `Account` property to `LocalService`, `NetworkService`, and `User`. The `LocalService` account, which is also predefined by Windows, has minimal privileges on the server. It does not have a password and presents anonymous credentials on the network. Generally, it only has access to network resources that can be accessed by anyone in the groups Everyone and Authenticated users (both groups are defined by Windows).

The `LocalService` account is generally a good one to use for remote objects that you publish publicly. It helps prevent outside attackers from exploiting any weaknesses in the remote object that might enable them to get some measure of control over your server computer. If they do somehow get access, they have very minimal privileges.

Using the `NetworkService` account is also generally a better idea than using the `LocalSystem` account. Like the `LocalService` account, the `NetworkService` account has fewer privileges than the `LocalSystem` account. The `NetworkService` account presents itself to other computers on the network as if it were the computer on which it runs. It has the same privileges as its host computer. If you deploy a single type of object on a server, the NetworkService account enables you to configure the object's privileges by setting its host computer's privileges.

To get the most precise control over an object's privileges, set the `Account` property to `User`. This specifies that the Windows Service that publishes the remote object runs in a user account. You can create an account specifically for the Windows Service that publishes your remote object. You set the object's privileges by setting the account's privileges.

If you set the `Account` property to `User` and run INSTALLUTIL, it displays a dialog box asking you for the account's user name and password, as shown in Figure 9.4.

When this dialog box appears, enter the name and password of the account you created for the Windows Service. After you do so, INSTALLUTIL installs your server program as a Windows Service.

INSTALLUTIL is a great tool when you are developing your remote objects. However, if you are planning a large-scale deployment of your application, chances are good that installing the Windows Service program that publishes your remote objects using INSTALLUTIL will be too time consuming and tedious. For large deployments with many servers, I recommend that you create an install program like you would for any other Windows program. Visual Studio has a wizard to help you do this. Creating an install program enables you to burn your server program onto CD ROMs. It also enables you to install your remote objects over your corporate network.

Deploying Server Objects in Internet Information Services (IIS)

Internet Information Services (IIS) is an Internet content management tool that Microsoft includes with many editions of Visual Studio. If you're already familiar with IIS, using it to host your remote objects may be your easiest deployment option.

Hosting remote objects in IIS has several advantages. First, you don't have to write a server program. IIS *is* the server program. All you need to do is add a configuration file for IIS to use when it activates the object.

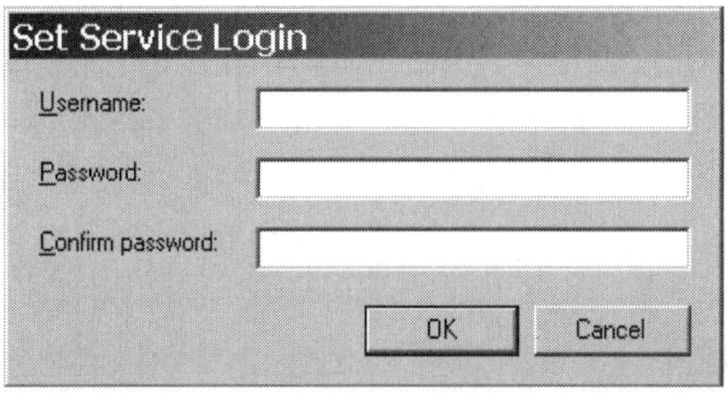

Set Service Login

Username:

Password:

Confirm password:

OK Cancel

Figure 9.4 INSTALLUTIL Asking for User Account Information

Second, your remote object can use the .NET Framework classes to access the features of ASP.NET. In the `System.Runtime.Remoting.Services` namespace, the Framework contains a class called `RemotingService`. The properties of this class provide access to ASP.NET state information.

WARNING

Don't confuse the class `System.Runtime.Remoting.Services.RemotingService` **with the** `System.Runtime.Remoting.RemotingServices` **class. They perform very different functions.**

In addition, IIS-hosted applications are able to access the user authentication capabilities of ASP.NET. By simply adding the authentication statements used in ASP.NET configuration to the configuration files for remote objects, you can get IIS to authenticate users for your remote objects.

Like objects hosted as Windows Services, IIS-hosted objects start automatically. Once they are installed, they require no manual intervention on your part.

The ease of deployment is probably the biggest advantage to hosting objects in IIS. If the release build of your object is up and running on a development or test server, all you need to do to deploy to your Internet server is create an IIS virtual directory on the Internet server. You can then copy the test deployment directly to a subdirectory of the virtual directory, called bin. If you use a configuration file, you'll need to name it web.config. That's all there is to it. In fact, you can automate most of this process with a command window batch file and the XCOPY command.

The primary disadvantage of using IIS to host your remote objects is that it won't host CAOs reliably. The reason for this has to do with ASP .NET application domain and process recycling. Because the internals of ASP .NET are not relevant to this book, I won't go into too much detail about the causes of this problem. For developers using .NET Remoting, the important thing to understand is that CAOs can't be reliably hosted in IIS.

WARNING

You cannot host CAOs reliably in IIS.

Another disadvantage of hosting remote objects in IIS (if, indeed, it is one) is that you *must* use the HTTP channel to access your remote object. You cannot use a TCP channel. In most cases, this is not a serious limitation.

NOTE

Although you must use the HTTP channel for IIS-hosted remote objects, you do not have to use the SOAP formatter. You can select a binary formatter in the object's configuration file.

Assuming IIS is already installed and running on your server, the steps for hosting a remote object in IIS are as follows:

1. Write your remote object as you normally would. No special coding is necessary.
2. Create a configuration file called web.config for the remote object.
3. Create an IIS virtual directory for the remote object on your server.
4. Create a directory called bin (it *must* be named bin) in the virtual directory.
5. Copy the remote object, and any other assemblies it needs, into the bin directory.
6. Copy the web.config file into the virtual directory.

That's it. You're done. Your object is hosted on your network. If you're deploying the object on an internal corporate network, clients access the remote object at the URL :

```
http://<servername>/<appname>/<URI.soap>
```

where <servername> is the name of the computer that hosts the object, <appname> is the name of the application (which is the same as the name of the virtual directory), and <URI.soap> is the URI that you specify in the object's web.config file.

Let's take a closer look at how this is done by creating an application. For the remote object, we'll use the code shown in Listing 9.1, which appeared near the beginning of this chapter. If you have not done so already, compile that code into a DLL.

Next, we need a web.config file for the remote object. This is shown in Listing 9.4.

```
1    <configuration>
2        <system.runtime.remoting>
3            <application>
4                <channels>
5                    <channel ref="http"/>
6                </channels>
7                <service>
8                    <wellknown
9                        mode="Singleton"
10                       type="InfoMan.InformationManager, InfoMan"
11                       objectUri = "InfoMan.soap" />
12               </service>
13           </application>
14       </system.runtime.remoting>
15   </configuration>
```

Listing 9.4 The web.config File for IIS

There are some important differences between this configuration file and those for other types of servers. First, and most significant, you cannot specify a port number in the `<channel>` element. The reason is that if there are a lot of clients trying to access the object, IIS may create multiple application domains for the object. Of course, this makes multiple instances of the object, and they all try to listen to the same port. However, the first instance of the object locks the port so that no other application domain can access it. As a result, additional object instances throw exceptions.

To avoid this problem, the `<channel>` element on line 5 of Listing 9.4 does not specify a port number. It only selects the channel type. Even this is not really needed. The only channel type you can use is HTTP. So if you wanted to, you could just omit lines 4-6 altogether. It would not make any difference.

WARNING

Do not specify a port number for an SAO in an IIS web.config file. IIS manages the ports on which remote objects are published.

Lines 7-12 of Listing 9.4 look like the `<service>` element you would find in any server configuration file. There are no changes required to this element. The only important thing to note here is that the filename in the `objectUri` attribute must have the extension .soap or .rem. IIS will not allow any other extension.

Now that we have a remote object and a web.config file, we're ready to create a virtual directory on the host computer. To do this, first go to your Inetpub directory. By default, IIS creates this directory to contain all of your Web sites, ftp sites, and other Internet offerings on the server computer. You can put your remote objects anywhere. However, I recommend that you use the Inetpub directory for them so that you can keep all of the Internet content your server offers together in one place.

The Inetpub directory is created on the C drive by default. In the following steps, I assume that's the way your computer is set up. If not, you'll have to make adjustments to the paths given:

1. In the Inetpub directory, create a directory called RemoteObjects.
2. Now create a directory called InfoMan in the RemoteObject directory.
3. In the Windows **Start** menu, select **Programs** and then **Administrative Tools**.
4. In the menu that appears, click **Internet Services Manager**.
5. The Internet Services Manager will resemble Figure 9.5. Instead of zaphod, it will display the name of the server computer on which you are currently working.

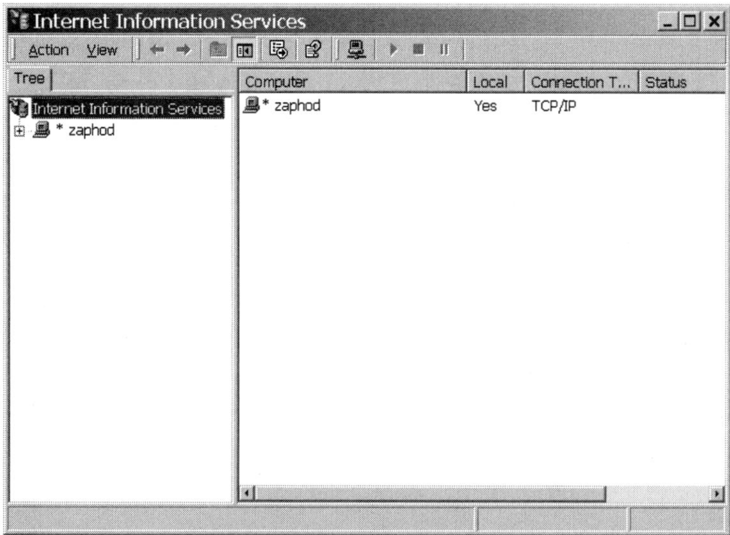

Figure 9.5 The Internet Services Manager

6. In the left-hand pane, click the + next to your server's name. A list appears
7. In the list, click on **Default Web Site**.
8. Click the mouse's secondary button (the right button if you are right-handed) on the **Default Web Site** entry in the list.
9. In the menu that appears, select **New**, and then **Virtual Directory**. This starts the Virtual Directory Creation Wizard.
10. Click **Next**. In the dialog box that appears, you are asked to type an alias for the virtual directory. This is the name of the virtual directory. IIS also uses it as the name of your server application.
11. Enter **InfoMan** for the alias. Click **Next**.
12. Click the **Browse** button and navigate to C:\Inetpub\RemoteObjects\InfoMan.
13. Click **OK**, and then click **Next**.
14. Again click **Next** to accept the default permissions.
15. Click **Finish**.

In this set of steps, you created a physical directory on your hard drive and made it into an IIS virtual directory. Let me emphasize that the physical directory does not *have* to be a subdirectory of Inetpub. You can put it anywhere on any of your server's hard drives.

By creating a virtual directory, what you've done is create a name for your service. It's similar to establishing a Web site. IIS automatically establishes a default Web site for your server. So, for instance, if the example server in the preceding steps is on an internal corporate network, typing:

```
http://zaphod
```

into a Web browser's **Address** or **Location** box (depending on which browser you use) displays the default Web page for your server. The URL on an internal corporate network for the `InformationManager` object offered on this example server would be:

```
http://zaphod/InfoMan/InfoMan.soap
```

IIS obtains the final part of the URL, InfoMan.soap, from the web.config file shown in Listing 9.4.

To finish getting your server object ready for publication, you must create a bin directory in C:\Inetput\RemoteObjects\InfoMan. Copy the remote object, and any other assemblies it needs, into the bin directory. Now copy the web.config file from Listing 9.4 into the C:\Inetput\ RemoteObjects\InfoMan directory. You do not have to restart IIS or reboot your computer. IIS automatically checks for the presence of the web.config file. When it finds the file, it performs the setup required to publish your remote object.

Before we move on, we should note another impact that using IIS has on a remote object's configuration file. Because IIS gets the name of the application from the name of the virtual directory, you cannot use the `name` attribute on the `<application>` element in the object's web.config file. If you look back at Listing 9.4, you'll see that the `<application>` element has no name attribute. It is not needed, and IIS will not like it if you put it on.

To finish this example, we need a client program. Publishing a remote object in IIS has only minor impact on the client. It does not change the client's code. However, it does require a small modification in the client's configuration file. For this example, I used the same client we've used in the other examples in this chapter. It's configuration file is given in Listing 9.5.

```
<configuration>
    <system.runtime.remoting>
        <application>
            <client>
                <wellknown
                    type="InfoMan.InformationManager,InfoManMeta-
Data"
                    url="http://localhost/InfoMan/InfoMan.soap" />
            </client>
        </application>
    </system.runtime.remoting>
</configuration>
```

Listing 9.5 The Configuration File of the Client of the IIS-Hosted Object

NOTE

For this example, I compiled the client with a wrapped proxy called InfoManMeta-Data. As a result, the configuration file needs to tell the .NET Remoting classes to look in that assembly for the information needed to create a proxy for the `Information-Manager` **object. If you would rather specify the name of the client program than**

`InfoManMetaData` on line 6, you can invoke SOAPSUDS with the -gc option to generate source code for the metadata. You can then compile the source code directly into your client program. Doing this builds the metadata directly into your client program, so you can specify its name on line 6 in the place of `InfoManMetaData`.

You have to look closely to spot the difference between this client configuration file and those used in past examples. Remember that, under IIS, you cannot publish an object at a specific port number. IIS assigns the port for the object. As a result, your client program cannot look for the remote object at a specific server port. If you examine line 7 of Listing 9.5, you'll see that the remote object's URL does not contain a port number as past examples did.

Versioning Your Application

Experience has shown that components in distributed applications often evolve separately. Changes to any server object can affect the functionality of many other objects in the system. They also have the potential of making some or all of the client programs inoperable.

It's not unusual for objects and clients to be written by different developers. The developers may even work for different companies. Component developers must be able to release new versions of existing components to add features or just fix problems. They have to be able to do this without affecting existing client applications. Client developers must be able to deploy new versions of client applications and expect them to work with existing component versions. Distributed object technologies of the past did not always provide clear solutions to these problems. Fortunately, .NET Remoting does. It forces a unique identity for every version of an assembly. This allows separate evolution paths for clients and servers. It also lets developers do side-by-side deployment of different versions of the same component.

Versioning under .NET works through assembly manifests and strong names. .NET relies on an assembly's manifest to describe the assembly's contents. As mentioned earlier in this chapter, it uses the assembly's strong name to uniquely identify its name and version number. When you install a program, .NET allows you to put each assembly in a subdirectory of the program's directory. Whenever the CLR needs to load a referenced assembly, it first searches the program's directory, then the program's subdirectories. Next, it looks in the global assembly cache.

This method of searching for assemblies enables you to install multiple versions of the same assembly, each in its own directory. Even though two or more versions of an assembly might have the same name, the differences in their version numbers lets the CLR see them as different.

Version Information and Clients

Let's assume that you've taken my earlier advice and attached a strong name to all of your remote objects. In that case, version information is sometimes communicated from remote MBR objects to clients. It depends on what kind of formatter you use. If you use a binary formatter, the MBR object sends version information. On the other hand, a SOAP formatter will not send version numbers.

REMINDER

By default, the TCP channel uses a binary formatter. The default for the HTTP channel is to use a SOAP formatter.

You can override this behavior by inserting the statement:

```
<formatter ref="soap" includeVersions="true" />
```

in the server program's configuration file. The `includeVersions` attribute tells the .NET Remoting system to transmit version numbers to clients.

If the version information is sent to the client, it is stored on the client when the client creates a proxy. Every proxy contains an `ObjRef` object. Proxies store version information in the `ObjRef` object's `TypeInfo` property. The version information a client receives is in the form <major version>.<minor version>.<build number>.<revision>.

Version Information and SAOs

When using SAOs, the server controls which version of an object gets created. The Microsoft documentation describes a rather complex set of rules that .NET Remoting uses to determine which version of an object to create under particular circumstances. I won't repeat all of those rules here. However, they can be summarized pretty easily. If a server program has access to multiple versions of an SAO, the default is for the server to create the latest version. If the client will not work with the latest version, you've got a problem.

One way to solve the problem is to use a configuration file to force the server to create a specific version of the object. Listing 9.6 shows a configuration file that makes a server program create version 1.0.0.0 of an object.

```
1    <configuration>
2        <system.runtime.remoting>
3            <application name="InfoMan">
4                <service>
5                    <wellknown
6                        mode="Singleton"
7   type="InfoMan.InformationManager,InfoMan,Version=1.0.0.0"
8                        objectUri="InfoMan.soap" />
9                </service>
10               <channels>
11                   <channel
12                       port="8085"
13                       ref="HTTP" >
14                   </channel>
15               </channels>
16           </application>
17       </system.runtime.remoting>
18   </configuration>
```

Listing 9.6 Forcing a Server to Create a Specific Version of an Object

In this example, I've altered the normal indentation for line 7 and put it in bold to emphasize it. As you can see, you use the `type` attribute to specify the object's version number. If you put the object in its host computer's global assembly cache, the `type` attribute must also include the culture information and the object's public key. I omitted it here for clarity.

Although forcing a server to create a specific version of an object can definitely help, it is not a complete solution by itself. Probably the best approach to versioning SAOs is to publish each version at a slightly different URI. In conjunction with that, you can deploy a server program for each type of object and force the server program to create only one specific object version.

The advantage of this approach is that it always keeps legacy clients working without modification. Current versions of object will not interfere with past versions because legacy clients do not see the current versions. If you want existing clients to use new versions of objects, you can send out an updated configuration file for the clients. You could even create a remote object that updates client configuration files automatically.

To publish each version of an SAO at a different URI, you need to make some slight modifications to the server's configuration file. These modifications are shown in Listing 9.7.

```
1     <configuration>
2         <system.runtime.remoting>
3             <application name="InfoMan">
4                 <service>
5                     <wellknown
6                         mode="Singleton"
7    type="InfoMan.InformationManager,InfoMan,Version=1.0.0.0"
8    objectUri="InfoMan_v1_0_0_0.soap" />
9                 </service>
10                <channels>
11                    <channel
12                        port="8085"
13                        ref="HTTP" >
14                    </channel>
15                </channels>
16            </application>
17        </system.runtime.remoting>
18    </configuration>
```

Listing 9.7 Connecting Version Numbers to Object URIs

Once again, I've emphasized particular lines in this listing by deviating from the normal indentation and using bold text. As with the previous example, this configuration file forces the server to create version 1.0.0.0 of the SAO. However, it includes the version information in the `objectURI` property on line 8. Using this technique, each successive version of the object would be published by its own server program at a slightly different URI.

To make this approach work, you must decide in advance how many versions of object you will support. My suggestion is to keep that number somewhere between 2 and 4. If you force your users to update their client programs every single time you modify an object, you may find that they see you as rather inflexible. In a real business environment, there are some situations when clients just should not be updated. If, on the other hand, you support too many versions of your remote objects, you're just creating extra work for yourself that probably isn't needed.

Ideally, you should deploy updated versions of your objects and the clients that use them while also running the old versions. You can keep the two versions running concurrently while one section of your organization after another goes through the update process. This enables you to deploy very methodically, and to test for problems thoroughly as you go. If a problem occurs, the department or section of your organization that is going through the update process can fall back on the old version of the software to keep them up and running. Critical business functions suffer only minor interruptions (if any) during the upgrade.

Developers must be kept in the loop when update strategies are being selected. At the very least, developers must be told that they need to write their server programs to use configuration files so that the deployment technique described here can be used.

Version Information and CAOs

There are multiple ways to compile a client program so that it has information about remote objects. You can include a reference in the client's project file to the remote object's assembly. You could include a reference to an assembly containing an abstract base class or an interface from which the remote object is derived. You can also include a reference to an assembly containing metadata about the remote object. Whichever method you choose, version information is included if you assign a strong name to the object. Therefore, the client program "knows" which version of its remote objects it needs to access.

If your client program accesses a CAO, the client controls which version of the object is created. It always creates the version of the object that it had when it was built. There is no way for a server to control which version of a CAO is created. No information in the server's program or configuration file will affect that. The server cannot publish different versions of CAOs at different URIs.

This behavior of CAOs makes versioning both easier and harder. It makes versioning easier by putting all of the control for selecting the object version in one place — the client. When you deploy new CAOs, you deploy new clients. The new clients select the new CAOs. Old clients can continue to use the old CAOs while deployment is in progress. Once all of yours users have received new clients, the old CAOs can be removed from the network. Sounds simple, right?

Sometimes it is that simple. Other times, it's not. Forcing users to update clients can mean that those clients no longer work with other objects that you didn't update. This can create an unintended ripple effect of updates throughout your organization.

In addition, large organizations often utilize many different clients targeted toward different types of users. Updating CAOs forces the update of *all* clients that use the objects. This also can increase the scale of your upgrade. Of course, you can have some clients using the new CAO and others using old versions. However, without careful planning, your organization may end up supporting many different versions of its CAOs. This can be very costly.

ONE MORE TIME

To avoid deployment problems such as these, developers must be involved in planning upgrades.

Summary

To enable the widest possible deployment and versioning options, all remote objects should be published in strong-named assemblies. Strong names uniquely identify an object and its version. You generally assign strong names to remote objects when you compile the release version of the object's assembly.

Although you can write your server programs as console or Windows Forms programs, it is generally not advisable to deploy them that way. Console and Windows Forms programs work well for debugging. However their disadvantages generally prevent their use in large-scale releases. Instead, most developers either create their server programs as Windows Services or they host their objects in IIS.

Hosting your remote objects in Windows Services gives you definite administrative and security advantages. You can assign specific accounts to specific objects and set their security privileges as needed.

Your server program can use the event logging capabilities offered by Windows Services. This can be critical to debugging and performance tuning applications.

Hosting remote objects in IIS saves you the effort of writing a server program. It relieves you from having to worry about port assignments for server objects. Deployment is fairly straightforward under this method of hosting remote objects. Although it does limit your using the HTTP channel, you can still use the binary formatter.

Through the use of strong-named assemblies, .NET Remoting enables you to publish multiple versions of an object. By default, servers create the latest version of an SAO. To get around this, you can force a server program to publish only one specific version of an object. Also you can publish different versions of the object at slightly different URIs.

Servers cannot control which version of a CAO gets created. The client specifies the object's version. Client programs always create the version of the object they were built against. You can still publish multiple versions of CAOs. New clients will create the new version of the object, and older clients will continue to use previous versions of the object.

Deployment and upgrading take careful planning and involvement from developers.

CHAPTER 10

Remoting and Web Services

Although the primary focus of this book is developing remote objects under .NET Remoting, it's useful to take a brief look at the context in which remote objects are used. This chapter provides an introduction to Web Services and describes the most important standards and technologies needed to deploy remote objects as Web Services. At the end of the chapter, you'll see a simplified example of a remote object intended for use as a Web Service.

Because this is a book on Remoting and not Web Services, not all of the technologies presented in this chapter's overview are demonstrated in the example at the end of the chapter. Nevertheless, the overview information is important for developers to know because you may need to branch out into these technologies to offer a successful Web Service.

The Wider World of Web Services

Remote objects provide an important step in the evolution of the Internet. If you've been around as long as I have, you can remember when using the Internet meant searching with tools like WAIS and using FTP to get files. If you don't know what WAIS and FTP are, don't worry. WAIS is long gone, and the role of FTP is greatly diminished (at least from a user's point of view) because it's been more or less assimilated into Web browsers.

When the World Wide Web appeared, it sparked a revolution in Internet use. Programs and information became instantly accessible to people with little or no background in computers. Web pages and Web browsers provide functionality to end users. More recently, the "new thing" is to provide Web functionality to programs. That's the essence of Web Services. Chapter 2 first introduced the idea of Web Services. A Web Service is one or more remote objects or procedures (or both) that an organization offers on its Web servers. Web Services are not browsed by end users. The are accessed by client programs.

Offering Web Services means more than companies providing services to their business partners or customers. It also enables them to provide controlled public access into their multitiered corporate computing environment. The same services, or a subset of them, that a company offers internally can be offered in a controlled way to other businesses. Remote objects essentially provide a portal into a corporation's internal network.

NOTE

The concept of Web Services has given rise to the term "the programmable Web." This is more than just marketing hype. Business-to-business services over the Web have the potential to create a very new type of Internet.

However, offering a Web Service involves more than just offering one or more remote objects on the Internet. It also requires that clients be able to interact with remote objects using standardized methods of communication. As we've seen in previous chapters, HTTP, XML, and SOAP fill that need. Because they define standard ways of exchanging data and invoking methods on remote objects, HTTP, XML, and SOAP enable clients and servers to be written on different types of computers using different operating systems and different programming languages. That's the ideal, anyway.

If that ideal is achieved, it's great. But it's still not enough for a successful Web Service. Think about the process of publishing a Web page for end users. You can have the greatest page on the Web and still have it be totally useless. For your page to see wide usage, people have to be able to find your Web page.

Web Services are the same. For it to be any use at all, companies must be able to search the Web and find your service. They need a search engine for Web Services just as you and I need search engines for finding Web pages. Companies looking for Web Services also require a description of all services offered at a given site. For each service, they need a definition of the API the service uses.

The cap ability to find sites offering Web Services, get descriptions of services, and retrieve a definition of the service's API form the necessary infrastructure for publishing Web Services.

UDDI, DISCO, and WSDL

The Universal Description, Discovery, and Integration (UDDI) specification defines a standard way of sharing information about the locations of Web Services. Using the UDDI standard, companies can create registries that list Web Services. These registries correspond to the search engines you and I use to find Web pages.

NOTE

The UDDI specification defines a non-proprietary standard that can be used by any company. It was created by a consortium of companies headed by Microsoft, IBM, and Ariba.

Entries in a UDDI registry contain information about businesses and the services they offer. Companies can publish Web pages that provide browser access to the contents UDDI registries. For example, you can view or search the registries at Hewlett-Packard, IBM, and Microsoft at the following URLs:

```
http://uddi.hp.com
http://www-3.ibm.com/services/uddi/find
http://uddi.microsoft.com
```

In addition to information about businesses and the services they offer, UDDI entries contain links to the discovery document associated with each Web Service. The discovery document is published in XML. However, the XML must conform to the Discovery Protocol (DISCO) specification. This specification defines a set of XML elements that anyone can publish to assist in the discovery of their Web Service.

By convention, all DISCO files have an extension of .disco. A site's .disco file typically resides on the same server as the Web Service itself, although that does not have to be the case. A DISCO file contains links to the files that, in turn, contain descriptions of individual services. Therefore, the DISCO file can reside on any server that is publicly available.

Each service is described by yet another file written in XML. The XML must conform to standard specified by the Web Service Description Language (WSDL). A WSDL file describes the interface to a Web Service. Specifically, it describes types a Web Services publishes, and the names, parameters, and return values of every method in a Web Service's API. In addition, it describes the message protocol that the Web Service uses to communicate. Because if its power, flexibility, and standardized format, most Web Services use SOAP as their message protocol. However, that does not have to be the case. For instance, the WSDL specification provides bindings for HTTP's GET and POST commands, among others.

NOTE

Companies and groups of companies have defined other service description languages besides WSDL. However, none of them are currently used as widely as WSDL.

A WSDL file contains six major sections, specified by the name of the elements that delimit them. They are:

- **<definitions>** — Contains all other WSDL elements in the document.
- **<types>** — Defines the custom data types used in the document.
- **<message>** — Specifies the format of the messages that the Web Services sends and receives. For most Web Services, this means the input and output parameters of the service's methods.
- **<portType>** — Contains a list of operations the service performs. This corresponds to a list of the Web Service's methods. This list also contains a description of the methods' parameters and return types.
- **<binding>** — Specifies the message format used by the service. Most Web Services use SOAP.
- **<service>** — Contains a list of endpoints or addresses clients use to communicate with the service.

You can use Microsoft's SOAPSUDS tool to generate a WSDL file for your Web Service by specifying the `-wsdl` option on the command line.

So programs can search for and find Web Services using a UDDI registry. The registry contains a link to the site's DISCO file. The DISCO file contains a description of the individual services a site offers. It also has a link to the WSDL file for each service being published. The WSDL file defines the remote objects that the service offers, as well as the remote objects' methods. This process is depicted in Figure 10.1.

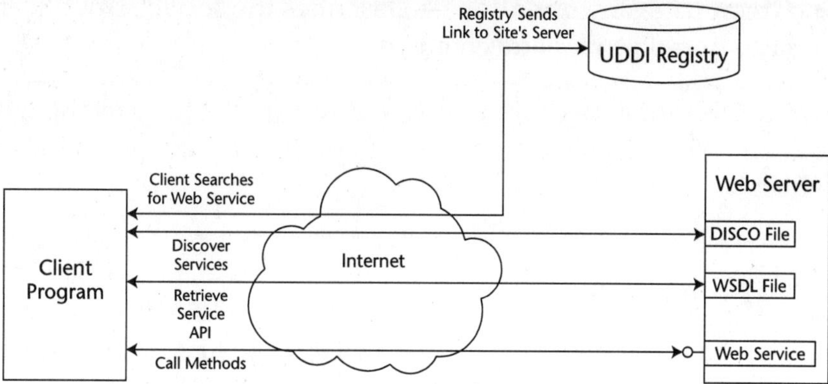

Figure 10.1 Finding a Web Service

Because information from the UDDI registry, DISCO files, and WSDL files are all in XML, virtually any type of client can use them. The client does not have to be written using .NET.

UDDI Registries

Your applications can query UDDI registries programmatically. The application just needs to send queries to a registry in XML. You can generate these queries from programs written in any language and running on any operating system. Microsoft publishes a downloadable UDDI SDK that helps you generate registry queries in Visual Basic or C# programs. With this SDK, or other similar SDKs published by other companies, you can set up your own UDDI to test your application.

UDDI Categories

When you query a UDDI registry, the Web Service information it sends back to you falls into three general categories. These are:

- **White pages information** — Contains a general description of the service and the company that publishes it. This typically includes contact information such as the company's name and address.
- **Yellow pages information** — Categorizes services by according to standard taxonomies defined by standards organizations. Example of standardized taxonomies are the North American Industrial Classification System (NAICS) and Universal Standard Products and Services Classification (UNSPSC).

- **Green pages information** — Describes the service's public interfaces and discovery mechanisms.

For applications, the core of a UDDI registry is the green pages information. With it, applications can obtain the location of the services for which they are searching.

UDDI Data Structures

Whenever you submit an entry to a UDDI registry, the registry program assigns the entry a unique identifier. This identifier is a GUID (also called a universally unique ID or UUID). The entries you submit and the information you get from the UDDI registry when you send a query are structured by predefined elements. The four most important elements are:

- `<businessEntity>` — Contains information such as company name, products and services, and the geographical locations that the company serves.
- `<businessService>` — Provides a technical description of the Web Services that the business offers. The descriptions include the URLs of child Web Services, prerequisite services that need to be run before the current service, and load balancing information.
- `<bindingTemplate>` — Specifies one or more technology models.
- `<tModel>` — Selects the technology model for the service. Technology models specify interfaces and abstract types that are particular to a kind of business, an industry, or a certain technology. Standards groups in particular industries can define technology models and specify a UUID for each one. Developers in that industry then develop their Web Services using that technology model by inserting its UUID into the `<tModel>` element.

Because developing programs that use these data structures is a topic that is not directly part of .NET Remoting, I'll refrain from discussing them any further at this point. However, you may need to deal with them, so I encourage you to learn more about them. These data structures are described in detail at `www.uddi.org`.

Remoting, Web Services, and ASP.NET

Microsoft provides another technology for building Web Services that I've previously mentioned in passing. This technology, called ASP.NET, is a set of components and services that are layered on top of the .NET Framework. ASP.NET is an extension of Microsoft's Active Server Pages (ASP).

ASP.NET can be used to build Web pages for end users as well as Web Services. Either way, ASP.NET applications are contained in one or more .aspx files. The individual .aspx files hold the application's code integrated with its Web pages. If you're creating an ASP.NET application that is meant to be viewed with a browser, you essentially create Web pages in a markup language, such as HTML, that reference Web controls. When a browser loads an ASP.NET page, it processes the HTML, which directs it to execute Web controls on the Web server. The controls emit markup language (usually HTML) to the browser that tell it how to render the control on the user's computer.

You can add your own custom code to controls by writing methods for them. All of the custom code for the control is executed on your server. The control emits HTML to the browser so that the browser can display the results of running the custom code.

So, for instance, you can use a customized calendar control on a Web page. The calendar control is one of the standard controls that comes with Visual Studio. Suppose your Web page uses the calendar control to reserve lanes at a bowling alley. Imagine further that lanes can only be reserved on Tuesdays, Thursdays, and Saturdays. You can add your own code to the calendar control to make it allow users to select only Tuesdays, Thursdays, and Saturdays. Being unable to select any other days of the week, they are not able to make reservations on any days but Tuesdays, Thursdays, and Saturdays.

When a user's browser loads your Web page with this customized calendar control, both the control's default code and the custom code you added to it are executed on your Web server. The control emits HTML to the user's browser that renders the calendar control with the behavior you added in the custom code.

ASP.NET Web Services are an extension of this idea. Instead of Web Forms server controls, you create a file with the .aspx extension that contains markup language statements. The markup language describes the objects that the Web Service offers, as well as the object's methods. You then write the objects and their methods. It all uses XML, SOAP, WSDL, UDDI, and DISCO.

This sounds a lot like .NET Remoting. So what's the difference between the two?

First, ASP.NET is basically a Web-oriented technology. As a result, it is stateless. This scales well to publishing services on the Internet where there may be thousands or even millions of users at any given moment. However, it imposes some important limitations on the applications you build.

.NET Remoting, on the other hand, enables you to develop objects that are either stateless or not. You choose which is best for your application.

NOTE

There are ways of making ASP.NET applications keep state information. Most notably, ASP.NET Web Services can access the Application and Session state objects provided by IIS. However, it's not as straightforward as using CAOs or creating remote singleton objects with an infinite lifetime.

Another difference between ASP.NET and .NET Remoting is that ASP. NET is a proprietary Microsoft technology. You need Microsoft products such as IIS to make it work. In contrast, .NET Remoting is a Microsoft implementation of industry-standard techniques. All you need to make it work is Visual Studio. No other Microsoft products are required.

Also, .NET Remoting is, in my opinion, the more powerful and flexible of the two technologies. Features such as its cap ability to host objects in a variety of ways, its object lifetime management capabilities, and its extreme configurability make .NET Remoting my choice for high-end Web Services.

Using .NET Remoting doesn't preclude you from accessing the features of ASP.NET. If you host your remote objects in IIS, they can access ASP.NET features. The reverse is also true. ASP.NET-based Web Services can use a variety of techniques to interact with remote objects developed with .NET Remoting. Your Web Service can be a mixture of the two technologies, as you see fit.

FasterCharge: An Example Web Service

The example Web Service presented back in Chapter 2 used an imaginary credit card company called FasterCharge. FasterCharge Corporation can offer a Web Service that enables credit card verification companies to verify purchases on a FasterCharge card. It deploys this on its Web server so that all of the card verification companies can use the Web Service.

Note that, in the real world, FasterCharge Corporation would build some security into the application so that only authorized verification companies could perform verification on its cards. To keep things clear and straightforward, we'll put off discussions of security until Chapter 13.

We'll pretend that we work for FasterCharge Corporation. Our task is to implement the company's credit card verification Web Service. We'll do that by pulling together everything presented so far.

Designing the FasterCharge Web Service

The FasterCharge credit card charge verification service must take card information from clients. In a real application, the client programs could take many forms. For example, the client might be a Windows Forms program used by a customer service representative on a desktop computer. The client could also be a card reader that is part of a point-of-sale terminal. These types of devices are very popular nowadays. They enable shoppers to use their credit cards at virtually any cashier's check-out stand.

No matter what form the client takes, our service should verify the charge as long as the data is in the right format. There are many formats we could use. The format of the data has a definite impact on the design of the software. In particular, it affects how we share compile-time information between the server and the client.

For example, if we just pass the card information as strings, we can implement the Web Service by writing an object, generating metadata for it, and including a reference to the metadata DLL in the client. If, on the other hand, we decide to package the data into a serializable object, we cannot share metadata between the client and the server.

When you write a serializable object, information about it must be available to both the remote object and the client. Ok, you say, I'll put the definition of the serializable object into the same DLL as the remote object. Then I'll generate metadata for the both of them and put a reference to it into the client.

Sounds good, but it doesn't work. At least, not the way you expect it to.

When SOAPSUDS generates metadata about a serializable object, it does not include information about the object's methods or properties. It makes all private data public. Want proof? Listing 10.1 shows a serializable object that we'll use in our FasterCharge program. Clients put charge information into it, and then send it over an HTTP channel to the server.

```
using System;

namespace ChargeVerifier
{
    [Serializable]
    public class VerificationRequest
    {
        private long cardNumber;
        private string nameOnCard;
        private DateTime expirationDate;
        private double amount;

        public VerificationRequest()
        {
            cardNumber = 0;
            nameOnCard = null;
            amount = 0.0;
        }

        public VerificationRequest(
            int cardIDNumber,
            string cardHolderName,
            DateTime cardExpirationDate,
            double amount)
        {
            cardNumber = cardIDNumber;
            nameOnCard = cardHolderName;
            expirationDate = cardExpirationDate;
        }

        public long CardIDNumber
```

Listing 10.1 A Serializable Object for the FasterCharge Application

```
        {
            get
            {
                return (cardNumber);
            }
            set
            {
                cardNumber = value;
            }
        }

        public string CardHolderName
        {
            get
            {
                return (nameOnCard);
            }
            set
            {
                nameOnCard = value;
            }
        }

        public DateTime CardExpirationDate
        {
            get
            {
                return (expirationDate);
            }
            set
            {
                expirationDate = value;
            }
        }

        public double ChargeAmount
        {
            get
            {
                return amount;
            }
            set
            {
                amount = value;
            }
        }
    }
}
```

Listing 10.1 A Serializable Object for the FasterCharge Application *(continued)*

The `VerificationRequest` object, which begins on line 6 of Listing 10.1, contains four private data members. It also has two constructors. The first begins on line 13, and the second starts on line 20. In addition, it has the properties `CardIDNumber`, `CardHolderName`, `CardExpirationDate`, and `ChargeAmount`. Programs use these properties to set or get the values of the private data members.

Everything looks good so far. But let's take a look at Listing 10.2 to see what SOAPSUDS does with this file.

```
using System;
using System.Runtime.Remoting.Messaging;
using System.Runtime.Remoting.Metadata;
using System.Runtime.Remoting.Metadata.W3cXsd2001;
namespace ChargeVerifier {
    public class VerificationRequest
    {
        // Class Fields
        public Int64 cardNumber;
        public String nameOnCard;
        public DateTime expirationDate;
        public Double amount;
    }
}
```

Listing 10.2 Metadata for the Serializable Object

I've stripped some irrelevant information out of this listing to make it easier to read. As you can see, the private members are now public. The constructors and the properties are gone. If you link this metadata into a client and try to access the constructors or properties, you'll get errors.

One way to try and get around this is to put serializable objects like this one into their own source files. You can then link those source files into both the client and server programs.

Sounds like a good plan, but it won't work. When you compile the remote object, the serializable object gets compiled into its DLL. If you then generate metadata for the DLL, you'll get the same metadata for the serializable object that you see in Listing 10.2. If you go ahead and link the metadata into the client *and* link in the source file containing the serializable object, the compiler will tell you that there are two definitions for the serializable object. It still lets you link and run the program, but the client throws exceptions when it tries to communicate with the server.

There are multiple ways of handling this situation.

First, you could make the serializable object a structure and make all of the data members public. That way, you don't need methods or properties. You just set the fields directly. The object's metadata reflects its actual design, so you can use the object as is on both the client and the server. However, you lose the functionality that methods and properties provide.

Alternatively, you could scrap the idea of using metadata all together. Instead of sharing metadata between the client and the server, you could share abstract base classes or interfaces for your MBR objects. You can put the serializable objects into the same file as the abstract base class or interface. You compile that file into a DLL and then put references to it in the project files for both the client and the server. We saw this technique demonstrated in earlier chapters.

The advantage of this second technique is that it lets us use the methods and properties of serializable objects. The disadvantage of sharing information about MBR objects by sharing interfaces and abstract base classes were discussed in Chapter 6.

So when you design your remote applications, you must pick an implementation for sending data that best fits your needs. Are you going to send objects across the network? Is it important that your serializable objects have methods and properties? Then you probably do not want to use metadata to share information about your remote objects. If you're not sending serializable objects across the network or the serializable objects you are sending don't need properties and methods, then you probably want to share information about remote MBR objects with metadata.

For our FasterCharge program, we'll provide data about a remote MBR object by sharing an interface. The DLL that contains the interface definition will also contain the definitions of the serializable objects the program needs. This hides implementation and enables us to use the methods and properties defined by the serializable objects.

Another design decision that needs to be made is whether to use configuration files on the client computers. When you're offering a Web Service, you may or may not have control over that decision. If you publish the client program yourself, then you can choose the implementation.

Why would the use of configuration files be important?

First, configuration files provide flexibility. They enable you to make changes to the channels, ports, and so forth that the client program uses without recompiling and redeploying the client program. This can be a great help in a large organization.

However, you must ask yourself who will be using your client program and on what operating system. Anyone can edit a text file on operating systems such as Windows 95/98 and Windows ME. One of the most dangerous things to a computer system is a user with a little knowledge and a lot of self-confidence. How likely is it that your users will edit or erase the configuration files? How likely are the files to become corrupted by user mistakes? Does the operating system you are deploying provide protection against such problems? Some do. On Unix, Linux, Macintosh OS X, Windows NT, Windows 2000, and Windows XP, you can install the configuration files with permissions that do not let regular users edit them.

Security is another consideration in the use of configuration files in client programs. Do you want users to be able to easily find the URL your client program connects to? Does it increase the security of your application to limit access to that information? If you programmatically register channels and connect to remote objects, most users will not be able to discover the URL of your Web Service. Sometimes that's what you want.

WARNING

If you want to limit the number of people who know the URL of your service, hard coding the information into your client can help, but it is not a completely secure solution. It does not prevent highly knowledgeable users from decompiling your program and finding the URL.

The example FasterCharge application will provide a client program. In particular, it will be a Windows Forms program that does not use configuration files.

As discussed previously, the FasterCharge Web Service must receive card and purchase information. It uses that information to determine whether the purchase can be completed. When it makes a determination, it must send a confirmation back to the client. If the card is declined, the service must send a reason for the rejection.

To meet these needs, the FasterCharge application will use two serializable objects. The first was already presented in Listing 10.1. It enables clients to programmatically build a charge verification request. Listing 10.1 shows that the verification request contains a card number, the name on the card, the card's expiration date, and the amount of the purchase. In a real application, the verification request might also contain a vendor or merchant number. The vendor number or merchant would enable the service to verify that the charge request comes from a vendor or merchant who is authorized to charge FasterCharge cards for its customers' purchases.

The client sends the validation request to the service and receives back a confirmation or rejection notice. The confirmation or rejection notice, which we'll just call a confirmation message, will be contained in the second serializable object the application uses. The confirmation message needs a data member to indicate whether the charge is accepted or not. It must also communicate a rejection reason when the transaction is rejected.

Verification is performed by an MBR object on the server. A real validation service would require a database of card holders, a database of their credit information, and possibly a database of authorized merchants. A system like that is far too complex to present in this sample program. Therefore, we'll implement an object that randomly accepts or rejects purchases (actually, it will only be *somewhat* random). When it sends a rejection to a client, it will also send a reason. A real verification system would probably also send a transaction ID, but we'll dispense with that for the sake of brevity.

The remote object that performs verification in the FasterCard Web Service would probably best be implemented as a single call object. In a real service, the information that persists would be stored in a database rather than in a remote object. The remote object would do little more than provide access to a particular subset of functionality offered by the database program. However, because our sample service will generate semi-random acceptances, it will need to keep some state information. Therefore, we'll publish it as a singleton with an indefinite lifetime.

The last decision that needs to be made is how to host the remote object. Will it be in a console program or a Windows Service? Or will it be hosted in IIS?

The answer for our example is yes. First, we'll develop a console program to host our service's remote object. Next, we'll show a version of it that runs as a Windows Service. Finally, we'll demonstrate how to host it in IIS.

Implementing the FasterCharge Web Service

We'll begin implementing the FasterCharge Web Service by developing the interface for the remote object that performs charge verification. We'll also write the verification request and confirmation objects. Listing 10.3 shows the code for them.

```
using System;

namespace ChargeVerifier
{
    [Serializable]
    public class VerificationRequest
    {
        private long cardNumber;
        private string nameOnCard;
        private DateTime expirationDate;
        private double amount;

        public VerificationRequest()
        {
            cardNumber = 0;
            nameOnCard = null;
            amount = 0.0;
        }

        public VerificationRequest(
            int cardIDNumber,
            string cardHolderName,
            DateTime cardExpirationDate,
            double amount)
        {
            cardNumber = cardIDNumber;
            nameOnCard = cardHolderName;
            expirationDate = cardExpirationDate;
        }

        public long CardIDNumber
        {
            get
            {
                return (cardNumber);
            }
            set
            {
                cardNumber = value;
```

Listing 10.3 The Interface and Serializable Objects

```
            }
        }

        public string CardHolderName
        {
            get
            {
                return (nameOnCard);
            }
            set
            {
                nameOnCard = value;
            }
        }

        public DateTime CardExpirationDate
        {
            get
            {
                return (expirationDate);
            }
            set
            {
                expirationDate = value;
            }
        }

        public double ChargeAmount
        {
            get
            {
                return amount;
            }
            set
            {
                amount = value;
            }
        }
    }

    [Serializable()]
    public class ChargeConfirmation
    {
        private Status confirmationStatus;
        private Reason rejectionReason;

        public enum Status
        {
```

Listing 10.3 The Interface and Serializable Objects *(continues)*

```
            ACCEPTED,
            REJECTED
        }

        public enum Reason
        {
            NONE,
            EXPIRED,
            CANCELED,
            STOLEN,
            LOST,
            OVER_LIMIT
        }

        public ChargeConfirmation()
        {
            confirmationStatus = Status.REJECTED;
            rejectionReason = Reason.NONE;
        }

        public ChargeConfirmation(
            Status status,
            Reason reasonForRejection)
        {
            confirmationStatus = status;
            rejectionReason = reasonForRejection;
        }

        public Status VerificationStatus
        {
            get
            {
                return (confirmationStatus);
            }
            set
            {
                confirmationStatus = value;
            }
        }

        public Reason ReasonForRejection
        {
            get
            {
                return (rejectionReason);
            }
            set
            {
                rejectionReason = value;
```

Listing 10.3 The Interface and Serializable Objects

```
            }
        }

        public string RejectionMessage
        {
            get
            {
                string theMessage = null;

                switch (rejectionReason)
                {
                    case Reason.NONE:
                        theMessage = "No reason.";
                    break;

                    case Reason.EXPIRED:
                        theMessage = "The card has expired.";
                    break;

                    case Reason.CANCELED:
                        theMessage = "The card was canceled.";
                    break;

                    case Reason.STOLEN:
                        theMessage = "The card is stolen.";
                    break;

                    case Reason.LOST:
                        theMessage = "The card was lost.";
                    break;

                    case Reason.OVER_LIMIT:
                        theMessage =
                            "The spending limit has been exceeded.";
                    break;
                }
                return (theMessage);
            }
        }
    }

    public interface IFasterChargeVerifier
    {
        ChargeConfirmation VerifyCharge(
            VerificationRequest cardInfo);
    }
}
```

Listing 10.3 The Interface and Serializable Objects *(continued)*

The namespace in which the charge verifier objects exist is called `ChargeVerifier`, as shown in line 3 of Listing 10.3. The namespace first declares the `VerificationRequest` object. As the attribute on line 5 states, this object is serializable.

Numbers on credit cards are four groups of four digits. Each digit requires four bits of storage. As a result, the data member in the `VerificationRequest` class that stores a card number must be at least 64 bits in length. The `VerificationRequest` class declares its `cardNumber` data member to be a `long` to meet this requirement.

The private data member that stores the name on the charge card is implemented as a string on line 9. The .NET Framework provides a class called `DateTime` for storing dates (and times, but we're not using that functionality). Line 10 declares a variable of type `DateTime` to store the card's expiration date. The amount of the charge is a data member of type `double`.

The `VerificationRequest` class provides two constructors, as well as property accessor methods for getting and setting the values of its private data members. Because this is an example program, these methods and properties are very simple. A real application would have some sanity checking on the data values that got executed whenever a program tried to set the private data members. For instance, the card number should be checked whenever it is set to ensure that it is in a valid form. Also, the card holder's name needs some validation. If nothing else, it should be checked to ensure that it is not being set to `null` or an empty string.

As it is, the implementation shown in Listing 10.3 forces the data validation to either be done by the server or client program. Because a company that provides a service may or may not write the client, it may not be a good idea to force the writer of the client program to write the code that does the data validation. They may not do it properly. This may simply be because they're not working at the same company that built the remote server object, and as a result, they're not very knowledgeable about the data checking that needs to done.

On the other hand, forcing the data validation to be done in the remote server object means that invalid data gets transmitted across the network. Putting some simple data validation into the `VerificationRequest` class would mean that the client program does consistent, reliable data validation no matter who writes it. It would also cut down on the amount of invalid data that gets sent across the network, providing more immediate feedback to the user when an error occurs.

The second serializable class that the sample program uses begins on line 80 of Listing 10.3. After the remote server object receives an instance of the `VerificationRequest` class, it either validates or rejects the charge. Either way, it sends an instance of the `ChargeConfirmation` class back to the client. The `ChargeConfirmation` class contains a private data member that holds a value from the enumerated type defined on lines 86-90. The values in the enumerated type specify whether the charge was accepted or rejected. The `ChargeConfirmation` class also defines an enumerated type that specifies the reason for rejection on lines 92-99. This type is used as the type of the `ChargeConfirmation` class's second private data member.

Like the `VerificationRequest` class, the constructors and property accessors of the `ChargeConfirmation` class contain no error checking. This is not as critical as it is for the `VerificationRequest` class because the values of the `ChargeConfirmation` class are always set by the server, never the client.

The last method in the `ChargeConfirmation` class is called `ReasonForRejection()`. This method is a nice convenience for the writer of the client program. It uses a switch statement (lines 146-172) to translate the rejection reason from an enumerated value to a printable string. This makes it easy for the developer of the client to display an error message for the user. These messages are set by you, the developer of the server object, so it does not matter whether or not you are also the developer of the client. The messages are always correct and consistent. Because these messages are coded into a method, they are not transmitted across the network. The client program obtains them when it is linked to the DLL containing the code in Listing 10.3. This gives you a simple way to provide error messages to clients without having to send the messages across the network.

WARNING

The downside of hard coding message strings into methods comes when you try to internationalize your program for multiple languages. You may have to make a version of the DLL for each language. There are some ways around that, but they involve providing an additional file with the DLL that contains the message strings.

The final item in Listing 10.3 is the interface for the remote server object. It appears on lines 178-183. It defines only one method, called `VerifyCharge()`. This is the method that client programs call to verify a purchase on a FasterCharge card. Its parameter is a value of type `VerificationRequest`, and its return value is of type `ChargeConfirmation`.

Listing 10.3 gives us everything we need to start building the remote server object. Its code is shown in Listing 10.4.

```
using System;

namespace ChargeVerifier
{
    public class FasterChargeVerifier :
        MarshalByRefObject,
        IFasterChargeVerifier
    {
        private bool accept;
        private int reason;


        public FasterChargeVerifier()
        {
            accept = false;
            reason = 1;
        }

        public override object InitializeLifetimeService()
        {
            return (null);
        }

        public ChargeConfirmation VerifyCharge(
            VerificationRequest cardInfo)
        {
            ChargeConfirmation returnValue =
                new ChargeConfirmation();

            if (accept == false)
            {
                returnValue.VerificationStatus =
                    ChargeConfirmation.Status.REJECTED;

                switch (reason)
```

Listing 10.4 The Verification Object

```
                {
                    case 1:
                        returnValue.ReasonForRejection =
                            ChargeConfirmation.Reason.EXPIRED;
                    break;

                    case 2:
                        returnValue.ReasonForRejection =
                            ChargeConfirmation.Reason.CANCELED;
                        break;

                    case 3:
                        returnValue.ReasonForRejection =
                            ChargeConfirmation.Reason.STOLEN;
                        break;

                    case 4:
                        returnValue.ReasonForRejection =
                            ChargeConfirmation.Reason.LOST;
                        break;

                    case 5:
                        returnValue.ReasonForRejection =
                            ChargeConfirmation.Reason.OVER_LIMIT;
                        break;

                    default:
                        reason = 1;
                        break;
                }
                accept = true;
                reason++;
            }
            else
            {
                returnValue.VerificationStatus =
                    ChargeConfirmation.Status.ACCEPTED;
                returnValue.ReasonForRejection =
                    ChargeConfirmation.Reason.NONE;
                accept = false;
            }

            return (returnValue);
        }
    }
}
```

Listing 10.4 The Verification Object *(continued)*

The FasterChargeVerifier class defines a fairly simple object that simulates a credit card charge verification service. It has two private data members that keep its state. The first determines whether the next charge will be accepted or rejected. The second specifies the rejection reason, if the charge is rejected. In the FasterChargeVerifier class's constructor, these two private data members are set to initial values.

This object will be offered as a singleton. We want it to keep its state information, so the FasterChargeVerifier class overrides the InitializeLifetimeService() method on lines 19-22. This method simply returns null, which means that the object's lease never expires.

On lines 24-79, the FasterChargeVerifier class provides its VerifyCharge() method. When a client calls this method, it declares a variable of type ChargeConfirmation called returnValue. If the private data member accept is currently false, the charge is rejected. The VerifyCharge() method stores that fact into the variable returnValue. It uses the switch statement on lines 34-65 to store the rejection reason into returnValue. Each time the charge is rejected, the private data member reason is incremented on line 67. As a result, each successive rejection will be for the next reason in the list. When a reason is incremented beyond its maximum allowed value, the default statement on line 62 sets it back to the first reason in the list.

Each time a charge is rejected, the private data member accept is set to true, indicating that the next charge will be accepted. When a charge is accepted, the VerifyCharge() method executes the else statement on lines 69-76. The else statement sets the verification status of the variable returnValue to ACCEPTED and the reason to NONE. It also sets the private data member accept to false so that the next charge will be rejected. At the end of the method, VerifyCharge() returns the variable returnValue.

The server program that publishes the FasterChargeVerifier object is no different than the console server programs in previous chapters. By now, you probably don't even need me to list the code. However, because it's so short, I'll go ahead and provide it here.

```
using System;
using System.Runtime.Remoting;
using System.Runtime.Remoting.Channels;
using System.Runtime.Remoting.Channels.Http;
using ChargeVerifier;

namespace Server
{
    class ServerAppClass
    {
        [STAThread]
        static void Main(string[] args)
        {
            RemotingConfiguration.Configure("Server.exe.config");
            System.Console.WriteLine(
                "Press Enter to end the server.");
            System.Console.Read();
        }
    }
}
```

Listing 10.5 The Server Program

This server program does most of its work by loading a configuration file. The server object in a distributed system resides on a server computer controlled by the company that publishes it. As a result, you don't have the kind of concerns and tradeoffs with using server configuration files that you do when using client configuration files. Therefore, systems designers usually find that it's best to use a configuration file on the server. The configuration file for the server program is given in Listing 10.6.

```
<configuration>
    <system.runtime.remoting>
        <application>
            <channels>
```

Listing 10.6 The Server's Configuration File *(continues)*

```
                <channel ref="http" port="8080"/>
            </channels>
            <service>
                <wellknown
                    mode="Singleton"
                    type="ChargeVerifier.FasterChargeVerifier, Server"
                    objectUri = "ChargeVerifier.soap" />
            </service>
        </application>
    </system.runtime.remoting>
</configuration>
```

Listing 10.6 The Server's Configuration File *(continued)*

By now, the statements in this little configuration file are very familiar. They state that the `FasterChargeVerifier` object is a singleton being published on an HTTP channel on port 8080. Its endpoint name is ChargeVerifier.soap.

We're now ready to look at the client program. I wrote this client as a Windows Forms program using Visual Studio.NET. When you write a WinForms program, Visual Studio generates *a lot* of code. Most of it does not pertain to the topic of remote objects. Therefore, I've omitted large sections of Listing 10.7. When you download the code for this book, all of the code I've omitted here is provided in the files you receive. For instructions on how to download the code, please see **Obtaining the Source Code** in the **Introduction** at the beginning of this book.

```
using System;
using System.Drawing;
using System.Collections;
using System.ComponentModel;
using System.Windows.Forms;
using System.Data;
using System.Runtime.Remoting;
using ChargeVerifier;

namespace Client
{
    /// <summary>
    /// Summary description for Form1.
```

Listing 10.7 The Client Program

```
    /// </summary>
    public class Form1 : System.Windows.Forms.Form
    {
        private System.Windows.Forms.GroupBox groupBox1;
        private System.Windows.Forms.Label label1;
        private System.Windows.Forms.TextBox cardNumberBox;
        private System.Windows.Forms.Label label2;
        private System.Windows.Forms.TextBox nameOnCardBox;
        private System.Windows.Forms.Label label3;
        private System.Windows.Forms.TextBox monthBox;
        private System.Windows.Forms.Label label4;
        private System.Windows.Forms.Label label5;
        private System.Windows.Forms.TextBox yearBox;
        private System.Windows.Forms.Button verifyButton;
        /// <summary>
        /// Required designer variable.
        /// </summary>
        private System.ComponentModel.Container components = null;
        private System.Windows.Forms.Label label6;
        private System.Windows.Forms.TextBox amountBox;
        private System.Windows.Forms.Button exitButton;

        private IFasterChargeVerifier chargeVerifier;

        public Form1()
        {
            //
            // Required for Windows Form Designer support
            //
            InitializeComponent();

            chargeVerifier =
                (IFasterChargeVerifier)Activator.GetObject(
                    typeof(IFasterChargeVerifier),
                    "http://localhost:8080/ChargeVerifier.soap");
        }

        /// <summary>
        /// Clean up any resources being used.
        /// </summary>
        protected override void Dispose( bool disposing )
        {
            // Code generated on lines 57-64 was removed.
            // Download this file to obtain the deleted code.
        }

        #region Windows Form Designer generated code
        /// <summary>
```

Listing 10.7 The Client Program *(continues)*

```
        /// Required method for Designer support - do not modify
        /// the contents of this method with the code editor.
        /// </summary>
        private void InitializeComponent()
        {
            // Code generated on lines 76-229 was removed.
            // Download this file to obtain the deleted code.
        }
        #endregion

        /// <summary>
        /// The main entry point for the application.
        /// </summary>
        [STAThread]
        static void Main()
        {
            Application.Run(new Form1());
        }

        private void exitButton_Click(object sender,
                                      System.EventArgs e)
        {
            this.Close();
        }

        private void verifyButton_Click(object sender,
                                        System.EventArgs e)
        {
            VerificationRequest request = new VerificationRequest();

            // Get the card number and convert it to an int.
            request.CardIDNumber =
                Convert.ToInt64(cardNumberBox.Text);

            // If the card number is invalid...
            if (request.CardIDNumber <= 0)
            {
                // Display an error message.
                MessageBox.Show(
                    "The card number is not valid",
                    "Error");
            }

            // If there is a name...
            if (nameOnCardBox.Text.Length > 0)
            {
                // Put it into the verification request.
```

Listing 10.7 The Client Program

```
                request.CardHolderName = nameOnCardBox.Text;
            }
            // Else the name is not valid...
            else
            {
                // Display an error message.
                MessageBox.Show(
                    "The name is not valid",
                    "Error");
            }

            // Get the month.
            DateTime expirationDate = new DateTime(
                Convert.ToInt32(yearBox.Text),
                Convert.ToInt32(monthBox.Text),
                1);

            // If the date is valid...
            if ((expirationDate.Month > 0) &&
                (expirationDate.Month <= 12) &&
                (expirationDate.Year > 0) &&
                (expirationDate.Year < 3000))
            {
                // Put it into the verification request.
                request.CardExpirationDate = expirationDate;
            }
            // Else the date is not valid...
            else
            {
                // Display an error message.
                MessageBox.Show(
                    "The expiration date is not valid",
                    "Error");
            }

            // Get the amount.
            request.ChargeAmount =
                Convert.ToDouble(amountBox.Text);
            // If the amount is not valid...
            if (request.ChargeAmount <= 0)
            {
                // Display an error message.
                MessageBox.Show(
                    "The charge amount is not valid",
                    "Error");
            }

            // Verify the charge.
```

Listing 10.7 The Client Program *(continues)*

```
                ChargeConfirmation confirmation =
                    chargeVerifier.VerifyCharge(request);

                // If the charge was verified...
                if (confirmation.VerificationStatus ==
                    ChargeConfirmation.Status.ACCEPTED)
                {
                    // Display a message
                    MessageBox.Show(
                        "The charge is verified.",
                        "Confirmation Status");
                }
                // Else the charge was not verified...
                else
                {
                    // Display an error message.
                    MessageBox.Show(
                        "The charge is rejected " +
                        "for the following reason:\n" +
                        confirmation.RejectionMessage,
                        "Confirmation Status");
                }
            }
        }
    }
```

Listing 10.7 The Client Program *(continued)*

When you run the program in Listing 10.7, it displays the form shown in Figure 10.2.

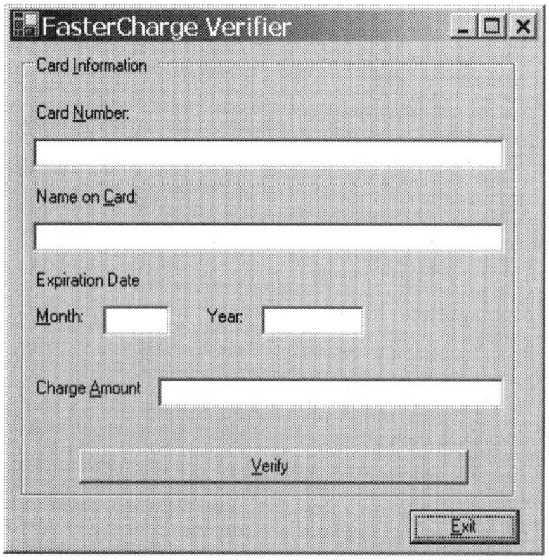

Figure 10.2 The Client Program

This is a very simple interface for the user, but a lot's going on here behind the scenes. Running the program instantiates an instance of the `Form1` type. The definition of this type begins on line 15 of Listing 10.7. It first declares variables for the edit boxes, labels, group box, and buttons that the form displays. The class's constructor is given on lines 38-49. One of the tasks the constructor performs is to create a reference for the remote object (lines 45-48). It saves the reference in a private data member called `chargeVerifier`. The class declares the `chargeVerifier` member back on line 36.

WARNING

For clarity, I've omitted the error checking that should occur in the constructor. Your client programs should not try to obtain a reference to a remote object without checking the reference (in this case, `chargeVerifier != null`). It should also enclose the call to `Activator.GetObject()` in a `try-catch` statement to catch any exceptions that might be thrown.

After obtaining a reference to the server object, the client is ready to accept input from the user. If you fill in the fields, as shown in Figure 10.3, and click the **Verify** button, the program executes the `verify-Button_Click()` method beginning on line 249. This method creates a variable of type `VerificationRequest` called `request`. It uses this variable to store the information it sends to the remote object.

On lines 255-256, the `verifyButton_Click()` method gets the card number from the appropriate edit box on the form. It converts the card number from a string to a 64-bit integer and stores the result in the `requestvariable's` `CardIDNumber` property. The only error checking

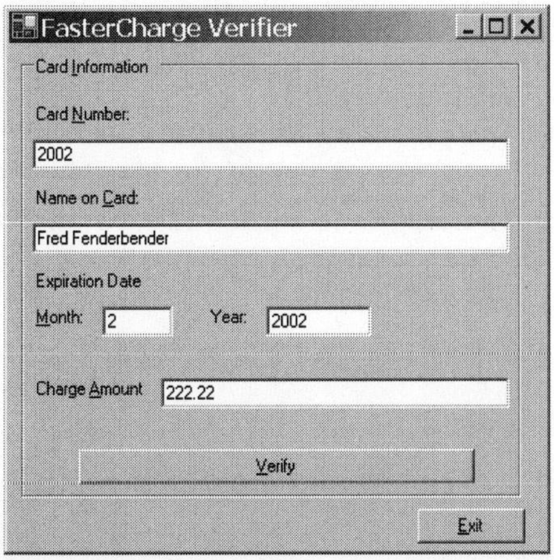

Figure 10.3 Entering Information into the Client Program

that the verifyButton_Click() method does on the card number is to ensure that it is greater than zero. If not, it pops up a message box to print an error message.

The verifyButton_Click() method next checks the edit box on the form that contains the name of the card holder. If the length of the name is greater than zero, it stores the name into the request variable's CardHolderName property. If the name string is empty, the verifyButton_Click() method displays an error message on lines 277-279.

Before it can store the card's expiration date into the variable request, the verifyButton_Click() method must convert the strings in the month and year edit boxes into a date. To do so, it allocates a variable of type DateTime. It converts the year and month into integers and passes those integers to the constructor for the DateTime class. On lines 289-292, it checks to ensure that the month and year are valid[1]. If they are, the verifyButton_Click() method stores the expiration date in the request variable's CardExpirationDate property. If the date is invalid, the verifyButton_Click() method displays an error message.

To complete the request, the verifyButton_Click() method converts the amount of the charge to a double (lines 307-308) and validates that the amount of the charge is greater than zero (line 310). If it is not, the verifyButton_Click() method pops up an error string in a message box.

As noted previously, sharing serializable objects in the manner shown in this program enables you to use the objects' methods and properties. Those methods and properties can and should provide the majority of the error checking on information that gets sent across the network. Because the VerificationRequest class does not perform the error checking it should, the client program must do it. If the FasterCharge company also distributed client programs for point of sale terminals, that client would need to perform the same error checking. This causes the code to be repeated in multiple clients. It's far better to perform the error checking in the VerificationRequest class so that the error-checking code needs to be written only once.

[1] Note the potential Y3K problem on line 292.

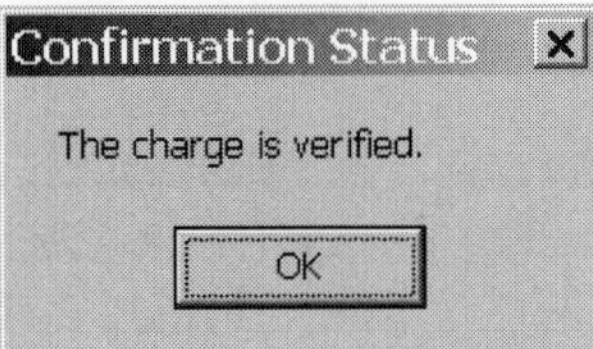

Figure 10.4 The Charge is Accepted

The `verifyButton_Click()` method is ready to send the information in the variable request to the remote server object for validation. It uses the `Form1` class's private data member `chargeVerifier` to call the `VerifyCharge()` method and passes the variable request as the parameter. The `FasterChargeVerifier` on the server either accepts or rejects the charge. If it accepts the charge, the `verifyButton_Click()` method displays a message box stating that fact, as shown in Figure 10.4. Otherwise, it shows a message box stating that the charge was rejected. It uses the `ChargeConfirmation` class's `RejectionMessage()` method to state the reason why. This is shown in Figure 10.5.

Deploying the FasterCharge Web Service

In the preceding section, the FasterCharge Web Service was developed and deployed as a Windows console program. In a real software production environment, it would, undoubtedly, be deployed as a Windows Service or in IIS.

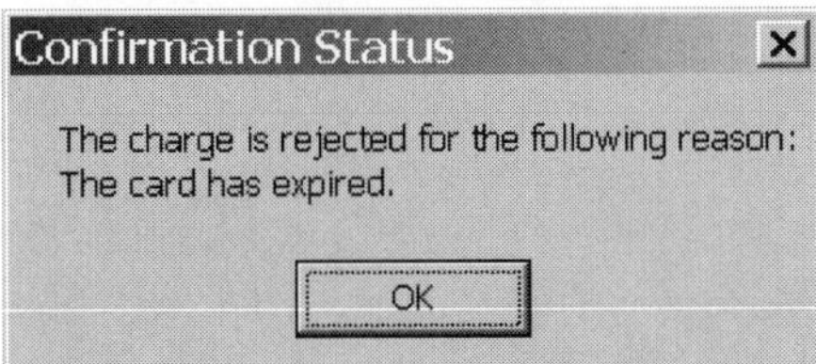

Figure 10.5 The Charge is Rejected

Deploying FasterCharge as a Windows Service

To deploy the FasterCharge Web Service as a Windows Service, changes need to be made to the server program and to its configuration file. No changes are needed in the remote object, the file that defines the `IFasterChargeVerifier` interface, or inthe client program. Listing 10.8 presents the code for the FasterCharge Web Service as a Windows Service.

```
using System;
using System.Collections;
using System.ComponentModel;
using System.Data;
using System.Diagnostics;
using System.ServiceProcess;
using System.Runtime.Remoting;
using ChargeVerifier;

namespace ChargeVerifierService
{
    public class ServerAppClass :
            System.ServiceProcess.ServiceBase
    {
        /// <summary>
        /// Required designer variable.
        /// </summary>
        private System.ComponentModel.Container components = null;

        public ServerAppClass()
        {
            InitializeComponent();
        }

        // The main entry point for the process
        static void Main()
        {
            System.ServiceProcess.ServiceBase[] ServicesToRun;

            ServicesToRun =
                new System.ServiceProcess.ServiceBase[]
                {
                    new ServerAppClass()
                };
```

Listing 10.8 The FasterCharge Server Program as a Windows Service

```

            System.ServiceProcess.ServiceBase.Run(
                ServicesToRun);
        }

        private void InitializeComponent()
        {
            components =
                new System.ComponentModel.Container();
            this.ServiceName = "FasterCharge Verifier";
        }

        protected override void Dispose(
            bool disposing)
        {
            if( disposing )
            {
                if (components != null)
                {
                    components.Dispose();
                }
            }
            base.Dispose( disposing );
        }

        protected override void OnStart(string[] args)
        {
             RemotingConfiguration.Configure(
                 "FasterChargeService.exe.config");
        }

        /// <summary>
        /// Stop this service.
        /// </summary>
        protected override void OnStop()
        {
        }
    }
}
```

Listing 10.8 The FasterCharge Server Program as a Windows Service *(continued)*

Most of this code is generated for us by Visual Studio when we create a Windows Service project. As developers, we need to pay attention to the statement in `InitializeComponent()` that sets the name of the service. In Listing 10.8, this statement appears on line 44. The statement must be set to the name of the Windows Service we're creating.

We also need to write code for the `OnStart()` method. This method must use the server's configuration file to set up the `FasterChargeVerifier` object. The statement on lines 62-63 do exactly that.

If you use a Windows Service to publish remote objects, you may need to perform cleanup tasks when the remote object shuts down. The cleanup code should go in the `OnStop()` method. In this example program, there is no cleanup that needs to be done, so the `OnStop()` method is empty.

Note that line 63 shows that the name of the configuration that the FasterCharge Windows Service program loads is now FasterChargeService.exe.config. The configuration file appears in Listing 10.9.

```
1     <configuration>
2         <system.runtime.remoting>
3             <application>
4                 <channels>
5                     <channel ref="http" port="8080"/>
6                 </channels>
7                 <service>
8                     <wellknown
9                         mode="Singleton"
10    type="ChargeVerifier.FasterChargeVerifier, ChargeVerifierService"
11                        objectUri = "ChargeVerifier.soap" />
12                </service>
13            </application>
14        </system.runtime.remoting>
15    </configuration>
```

Listing 10.9 The Server Configuration File for the Hosting the Charge Verifier as a Windows Service

I had to use odd indentation on line 10 of Listing 10.9 to get the entire string on one line of this printed page. In the version of the configuration file that you download, you'll see that the text for line 10 is aligned with the text on the lines above and below it.

The only real change from the previous version is the name of the program from which the .NET Remoting loads the remote object. It is now ChargeVerifierService (recall that we do not need to put on the .exe extension).

Before you compile the server program as a Windows Service, remember to add an installer to the project and set its properties as explained in Chapter 9.

In addition, you'll need to use the INSTALLUTIL program to install ChargeVerifierService.exe as a Windows Service. Alternatively, you can write an install program for ChargeVerifierService.exe. On large installations with multiple servers, writing an install program is probably the best approach.

Deploying FasterCharge in IIS

To deploy the FasterCharge Web Service in IIS, you do not need to change the DLL that contains the `IFasterChargeVerifier` interface. You do not need to write a server program. However, the remote object needs to be compiled into its own DLL. You'll use the name of that DLL in the web.config file that IIS requires.

Recall that IIS handles the port assignments itself. As a result, you won't need to put the server object's port number into the web.config file. You also need to remove it from the client program's source code and recompile the client. However, that's the only change you need to make to the client.

Listing 10.10 gives the web.config file that IIS needs for the FasterCharge Web Service.

```
<configuration>
    <system.runtime.remoting>
        <application>
            <channels>
                <channel ref="http"/>
            </channels>
            <service>
```

Listing 10.10 The web.config File for the Hosting the Charge Verifier in IIS *(continues)*

```
8                    <wellknown
9                        mode="Singleton"
10   type="ChargeVerifier.FasterChargeVerifier, ChargeVerifier"
11                       objectUri = "ChargeVerifier.soap" />
12                </service>
13            </application>
14        </system.runtime.remoting>
15    </configuration>
```

Listing 10.10 The web.config File for the Hosting the Charge Verifier in IIS *(continued)*

Again, because of the limitations of the printed page, I had to use odd indentation on line 10 of the configuration file.

I compiled the `FasterChargeVerifier` object into an assembly called ChargeVerifier.DLL. The name of its DLL appears on line 10. I also deleted the port number from the configuration file.

REMINDER

The specification of the HTTP channel on lines 4-6 of the web.config file in Listing 10.10 can be omitted. It is the default.

To deploy the `FasterChargeVerifier` object under IIS, you'll need to put it into a directory and make that directory an IIS virtual directory. Put the web.config file in Listing 10.10 into the virtual directory. It should also have a subdirectory called bin. The assembly ChargeVerifier.DLL goes into the bin directory.

Summary

You must know the context into which your application will be deployed. If you want your Web Service widely used, you must publish it in the most public manner possible. This means acquiring an understanding of the discovery mechanisms used for Web Services. Industry groups have defined several standards for these mechanisms. Among them are UDDI, DISCO, and WSDL. These standards enable users and programs to search for and discover the functionality of your Web Service.

You can see in the implementation of this application that building a Web Service requires more than just writing code. It necessitates an entire series of decisions about the pros and cons of particular implementations. You must decide before you do any coding how the application's remote objects are to be published. You also need to choose what type of error checking is performed and where it is performed. Should it be done by the client program, the application's serializable object, or on the remote server objects?

The client program (or programs) that use your Web Service may or may not be written by you. If you want to ensure that particular data validation is performed on the client, you have to provide a way to make that happen. One way to accomplish this is to provide serializable objects that clients can transmit to your service. The methods and properties of the serializable objects can perform data validation and throw exceptions when an error occurs. This forces developers of the client programs to catch the exception and handle the error.

If you are providing the client program, you need to decide whether it will use a configuration file or not. Configuration files provide flexibility and can decrease the need to update your client when the remote object's URL changes. However, on some operating systems, users can easily edit or corrupt configuration files.

PART THREE

Advanced Topics in Remoting

In some respects, the subject of .NET Remoting is somewhat like an onion. As you get into its workings, you peel away its layers. When you do, you find more layers underneath. .NET Remoting is a subject that can get about as complex as you want it to. Maybe even more.

Fortunately, you don't have to know all of the inner workings of .NET Remoting to use it and use it well. However, there are some advanced topics that developers must have expertise in before they can release a professional distributed application into a real-world environment. Part Three explains and demonstrates those topics.

In particular, it shows how to make asynchronous calls to methods on remote objects and how to receive asynchronous replies. It also introduces the most important concepts related to keeping your applications secure. This is a vital importance in today's distributed computing environment.

Lastly, Part Three shows are you can extend the .NET Remoting system and fundamentally change how it operates. The .NET Remoting system is built with extreme extensibility in mind. You'll see how you can add just about any sort of functionality to the .NET Remoting system that you need.

CHAPTER 11

Asynchronous Remoting

.NET Remoting enables you to treat remote method calls very much as if they were local calls. However, in spite of the fact that they *look*like local calls, remote method calls involve sending information over a network and receiving a response. This process introduces latencies and delays in response times into applications.

One technique for decreasing latencies and delays is to use asynchronous remote method calls. When a client application uses an asynchronous remote method call, it initiates the method call and continues executing without waiting for response. The remote call completes its task and sends a response when it can. The client does not wait for the method to return a value before continuing program execution.

This chapter introduces common techniques for calling remote methods asynchronously from client programs. It also shows how to receive an asynchronous response. In addition, it explains how to set up asynchronous calls that do not expect a response. Lastly, this chapter demonstrates how clients and servers can resynchronize themselves after an asynchronous call, if necessary.

Asynchronous Calls on Remote Objects

The .NET Framework uses a special type of object called a **delegate** to facilitate asynchronous calls. Delegates can be used for both local asynchronous calls and remote asynchronous calls.

NOTE

Calls made through delegates do not *have* to be asynchronous. Your program can also use them for synchronous calls.

A delegate is a reference type that defines a signature for method calls. A method's signature consists of its name, return type, and parameter list. Delegates define generic names for functions with particular return types and parameter lists.

When a client program defines a delegate, the Visual C# compiler uses the delegate to generate an object. The delegate object can accept and execute methods that match its method signature. Therefore, delegates fill a role in C# that is similar to function pointers in C and C++.

To get a good idea of how they work, we'll write an example program that uses a delegate for some synchronous calls. The example program we'll write will call different sorting functions through a delegate. Listing 11.1 gives the code for this sample program.

```
using System;

namespace Sorting
{
    class SortingAppClass
    {
        [STAThread]
        static void Main(string[] args)
        {
            int [] dataArray1 = new int [10];
            int i;

            for (i=0; i<10; i++)
            {
                dataArray1[i] = 10-i;
            }

```

Listing 11.1 Calling Multiple Functions through a Delegate

```
            Sorter.SortDelegate ascendSort =
                new Sorter.SortDelegate(AscendingSort);

            Sorter.SortDelegate descendSort =
                new Sorter.SortDelegate(DescendingSort);

            Sorter theSorter = new Sorter();

            theSorter.ArrayLength = 10;
            theSorter.DataArray = dataArray1;
            theSorter.Sort(ascendSort);

            for (i=0; i<10; i++)
            {
                System.Console.WriteLine(
                    dataArray1[i]);
            }

            System.Console.WriteLine("\n");

            int [] dataArray2 = new int [20];
            for (i=0; i<20; i++)
            {
                dataArray2[i] = i;
            }

            theSorter.ArrayLength = 20;
            theSorter.DataArray = dataArray2;
            theSorter.Sort(descendSort);

            for (i=0; i<20; i++)
            {
                System.Console.WriteLine(
                    dataArray2[i]);
            }

            System.Console.WriteLine(
                "Paused. Press Enter to continue...");
            System.Console.Read();
        }

        public static void AscendingSort(
            int [] dataArray,
            int arrayLength)
        {
            for (int i=1; i<arrayLength; i++)
            {
                for (int j=0;j<i;j++)
```

Listing 11.1 Calling Multiple Functions through a Delegate *(continues)*

```
            {
                if (dataArray[i] < dataArray[j])
                {
                    int temp = dataArray[i];
                    dataArray[i] = dataArray[j];
                    dataArray[j] = temp;
                }
            }
        }
    }

    public static void DescendingSort(
        int [] dataArray,
        int arrayLength)
    {
        for (int i=1; i<arrayLength; i++)
        {
            for (int j=0;j<i;j++)
            {
                if (dataArray[i] > dataArray[j])
                {
                    int temp = dataArray[i];
                    dataArray[i] = dataArray[j];
                    dataArray[j] = temp;
                }
            }
        }
    }
}

public class Sorter
{
    private int [] theData;
    private int numberOfArrayItems;

    public delegate void SortDelegate(
        int [] dataArray, int arrayLength);

    public void Sort(SortDelegate sortMethod)
    {
        sortMethod(theData,numberOfArrayItems);
    }

    public int [] DataArray
    {
        get
        {
            return (theData);
```

Listing 11.1 Calling Multiple Functions through a Delegate *(continued)*

```
114                 }
115                 set
116                 {
117                     theData = value;
118                 }
119             }
120 
121             public int ArrayLength
122             {
123                 get
124                 {
125                     return (numberOfArrayItems);
126                 }
127                 set
128                 {
129                     numberOfArrayItems = value;
130                 }
131             }
132         }
133 
134     }
```

Listing 11.1 Calling Multiple Functions through a Delegate *(continued)*

The program in Listing 11.1 defines two sorting methods. The first is called `AscendingSort()` and the second is called `DescendingSort()`. Other than their names, both of these methods have identical signatures. Both methods are members of the program's application class. They use simple Bubble Sorts to sort arrays of integers into ascending and descending order, respectively.

The `AscendingSort()` and `DescendingSort()` methods are called through a delegate defined in the `Sorter` class, which begins on line 96. The `Sorter` class has two private data members. The first is a reference to an array of integers. The second, called `numberOfArrayItems`, specifies the number of integers in the array. The program sets these two data members using a pair of property accessor methods that appear on lines 109-131. On lines 101-102, the `Sorter` class declares a delegate that specifies the signature of the sorting methods. The `AscendingSort()`,and `DescendingSort()` methods match that signature.

When the program starts, it allocates an array of 10 integers. On lines 13-16, it enters a loop that initializes the integers in the array. Next, the program uses a `new` statement to create a delegate. Because the delegate looks like a method signature, it may seem odd to use the `new` statement to create it. Recall, however, that Visual C# creates an object for the delegate. Therefore, the `new` statement allocates the delegate object. Notice that the parameter to the delegate object's constructor is a reference to the method that the delegate calls.

On lines 21-22, the program declares another delegate and passes a reference to the `DescendingSort()` method into the delegate's constructor. The program then allocates an object of type `Sorter`. It sets the array length on line 26. Next, the program sets the `DataArray` property equal to the `dataArray1` variable. On line 28, the program calls the `Sorter` class's `Sort()` method and passes in the delegate for the `AscendingSort()` method.

The `Sort()` method, which begins on line 104, has one parameter of type `SortDelegate`. When the example program calls the `Sort()` method and passes in the delegate, the `Sort()` method calls the method with which the delegate is associated. In this case, it is the delegate for the `AscendingSort()` method. Therefore, the program calls the `AscendingSort()` method, and the data array is sorted in ascending order.

After the `AscendingSort()` method finishes, program execution jumps back to the `Sort()` method. From there, it returns to line 28. The program demonstrates that it sorted the array by entering a for loop and printing the array' s contents.

The program then declares another array. This array, called `dataArray2`, contains 20 integers. As with the previous array, the program uses a `for` loop to initialize the contents of `dataArray2`. The program stores the array length and the array into the `Sorter` object. On line 46, it calls the `Sort()` method and passes the delegate for the descending sort as the parameter. As before, the `Sort()` method calls the method associated with its parameter's delegate. This time, the `DescendingSort()` method gets called. To prove that it sorted the array into descending order, the program uses a `for` loop to print the contents of the second array.

Although this program is fairly simple, it demonstrates the basics of using delegates to call other functions. Now let's take a look at how delegates can be used asynchronously.

Using Delegates for Local Asynchronous Calls

Whenever a program makes an asynchronous method call with a delegate, the classes in the .NET Framework automatically create a thread for the asynchronous method call. This saves you and me a lot of work. We don't have to worry about creating threads, synchronizing them, communicating with them, or cleaning them up when they're finished.

Under the .NET Framework, delegates provide the `BeginInvoke()` and `EndInvoke()` methods. These two methods begin and end asynchronous calls.

NOTE

The Visual C# compiler generates the BeginInvoke() and EndInvoke() methods automatically when you compile. As a result, it will not display any IntelliSense information for these two methods.

Let's write a program to demonstrate how they're used. In this program (see Listing 11.2), we'll use a delegate's `BeginInvoke()` and `EndInvoke()` methods to asynchronously call a local method.

```
using System;

namespace AsyncLocal
{

    class AppClass
    {
        [STAThread]
        static void Main(string[] args)
        {
            System.Console.WriteLine(
                "Please enter the string to repeat: ");
            string repeatString = System.Console.ReadLine();

            System.Console.WriteLine(
                "Please enter the number of repetitions: ");
            string repetitionsString =
                System.Console.ReadLine();

            int repetitions = Convert.ToInt16(
                repetitionsString);

            AsyncLocalCaller asyncCaller =
                new AsyncLocalCaller();

            AsyncLocalCaller.AsyncLocalCallerDelegate theDelegate
=
                new AsyncLocalCaller.AsyncLocalCallerDelegate(
                    asyncCaller.AsyncRepeatString);
```

Listing 11.2 Calling a Local Method Asynchronously *(continues)*

```

                IAsyncResult asyncResult =
                    theDelegate.BeginInvoke(
                        repeatString,
                        repetitions,
                        null,null);

                for (int i=0; i < repetitions/2; i++)
                {
                    System.Console.WriteLine(
                        "The Main() method is doing something else");
                }

                asyncResult.AsyncWaitHandle.WaitOne();
                if (asyncResult.IsCompleted)
                {
                    theDelegate.EndInvoke(asyncResult);
                }

                System.Console.WriteLine(
                    "End of Main(). Press Enter to continue...");
                System.Console.ReadLine();
            }
        }

        class AsyncLocalCaller
        {
            public delegate void AsyncLocalCallerDelegate(
                string outputString,
                int repetitions);

            public void AsyncRepeatString(
                string outputString,
                int repetitions)
            {
                for (int i=0; i<repetitions; i++)
                {
                    System.Console.WriteLine(outputString);
                }
            }
        }
    }
```

Listing 11.2 Calling a Local Method Asynchronously *(continued)*

The application in Listing 11.2 is a console program that prompts the user for a string to print repeatedly. It also asks the user how many times to repeat the string. The number of repetitions is read in as a string. On line 20-21, the example program converts the number of repetitions to an integer.

Next, the program allocates an object of type `AsyncLocalCaller`. The `AsyncLocalCaller` class is declared on lines 54- 69. It defines a delegate for an asynchronous method on lines 56-58. The asynchronous method itself appears on lines 60-68. It is a simple method that uses a `for` loop to repeatedly print a string to the console.

After the program allocates an object of type `AsyncLocalCaller`, it allocates a delegate object on lines 26-28. Notice that the parameter to the constructor for the delegate object is a reference to the asynchronous method.

With the delegate allocated, the program can call the `BeginInvoke()` method to start executing the asynchronous method. The `BeginInvoke()` method takes a variable number of parameters. All of its parameters except the last two are passed as parameters to the asynchronous method. In this sample program, the values that `BeginInvoke()` passes to the remote method are the values that the program got from the user. The last two parameters to the BeginInvoke() method are used for callback methods. We'll look at callback methods later in this chapter. For now, we'll just use values of `null` for the last two parameters.

Next, the `Main()` method enters a for loop to demonstrate that it is doing something while the asynchronous method is executing. When you run this program, you'll see the output of the asynchronous method interspersed with the output of the `Main()` method. This will be easier to see if you enter a large number for the repetitions. I recommend that you use a value of at least 1000.

The `for` loop on lines 36-40, is designed to finish before the asynchronous method ends. In such cases, delegates provide a way for programs to wait for asynchronous methods. Notice on line the 30 that the delegate's `BeginInvoke()` method returns an object that implements the `IAsyncResult` interface. The `IAsyncResult` interface has a member called `AsyncWaitHandle`. Your program can use the `AsyncWaitHandle` member to invoke the `WaitOne()` method, which causes the program to go to sleep until the asynchronous method completes. The call to the `WaitOne()` method appears on line 42.

In addition, the `IAsyncResult` interface has a property called `IsCompleted`. If this property evaluates to `true`, the asynchronous method has finished executing. Programs can use the `IsCompleted` property at any time after calling the `BeginInvoke()` method to determine whether the asynchronous method has finished executing.

After the asynchronous method completes, programs should use the `EndInvoke()` method to perform the necessary cleanup. Failing to do so may cause unexpected results.

To summarize, the program in Listing 11.2 called a method asynchronously using the following steps:

1. It defined an object to contain the delegate and the asynchronous method.
2. It defined the delegate.
3. It defined the asynchronous method.
4. Prior to calling the asynchronous method, the program allocated the object in which the asynchronous method was defined.
5. Next, it allocated the delegate and associated the asynchronous method with the delegate.
6. It used the delegate's `BeginInvoke()` method to call the asynchronous method.
7. When it determined that the asynchronous method had completed, the program used the `EndInvoke()` method to perform the cleanup associated with the asynchronous call.

All programs can use these general steps to invoke local methods asynchronously.

Using Delegates for Remote Asynchronous Calls

Calling methods on remote objects asynchronously is not substantially different than calling methods on local objects asynchronously. One difference is caused by the fact that the client and the server object are in two different programs. In the program in Listing 11.2, the delegate and the asynchronous method were defined in the same class. When using remote objects, this isn't possible. The method that will be invoked asynchronously is a member of the remote object's class. The definition of the delegate must be available on the client. It is not needed on the server. Therefore, the delegate's definition usually appears in the client program's application class.

Remote methods do not have to "know" that they're going to be called asynchronously. No special coding on the server side is required for asynchronous calls. However, the client must use the following steps to execute an asynchronous call on a remote method.

1. Define the delegate.
2. Obtain a reference to the remote object.
3. Allocate the delegate object and associate the remote method with the delegate object.
4. Use the delegate's `BeginInvoke()` method to call the remote method.
5. Call the `EndInvoke()` method to perform the cleanup associated with the asynchronous call when the asynchronous method is done.

Listing 11.3 shows the source code for an object whose method will be called asynchronously.

```
using System;

namespace Repeater
{
    public class StringRepeater
    {
        public StringRepeater()
        {
        }

        public void RepeatString(
            string outputString,
            int repetitions)
        {
            for (int i=0; i<repetitions; i++)
            {
                System.Console.WriteLine(outputString);
            }
        }
    }
}
```

Listing 11.3 The Remote Object for the Asynchronous Remoting Program

The server for this object is very much as you would expect. It requires no special code for asynchronous calls. Listing 11.4 gives its code. Listing 11.5 shows the server's configuration file.

```
using System;
using System.Runtime.Remoting;
using Repeater;

namespace AsyncRemoteServer
{
    class ServerAppClass
    {
        [STAThread]
        static void Main(string[] args)
        {
            RemotingConfiguration.Configure("Server.exe.config");
            System.Console.WriteLine(
                "Press Enter to end the server program.");
            System.Console.Read();
        }
    }
}
```

Listing 11.4 The Server for the Asynchronous Remoting Program

```
<configuration>
    <system.runtime.remoting>
        <application>
            <channels>
                <channel ref="http" port="8085"/>
            </channels>
            <service>
                <wellknown
                    mode="Singleton"
                    type="InfoMan.InformationManager, InfoMan"
                    objectUri = "InfoMan.soap" />
            </service>
        </application>
    </system.runtime.remoting>
</configuration>
```

Listing 11.5 The Server's Configuration File

Like most of the client programs presented so far, the client program for the asynchronous Remoting application uses a configuration file. The contents of the configuration file are shown in Listing 11.6.

```
<configuration>
    <system.runtime.remoting>
        <application>
            <client>
                <wellknown
                    type="InfoMan.InformationManager, Client"
                    url="http://localhost:8085/InfoMan.soap" />
            </client>
        </application>
    </system.runtime.remoting>
</configuration>
```

Listing 11.6 The Configuration File for the Asynchronous Remoting Client

The code for the client program is presented in Listing 11.7.

```
using System;
using System.Runtime.Remoting;
using System.Runtime.Remoting.Channels;
using System.Runtime.Remoting.Channels.Http;
using Repeater;

namespace Client
{
    class ClientAppClass
    {
        public delegate void AsyncRemoteCallerDelegate(
            string outputString,
            int repetitions);

        [STAThread]
        static void Main(string[] args)
        {
            RemotingConfiguration.Configure("client.exe.config");

            StringRepeater theRepeater =
                new StringRepeater();

            if (theRepeater != null)
            {
                System.Console.WriteLine(
                    "Please enter the string to repeat: ");
                string repeatString = System.Console.ReadLine();
```

Listing 11.7 The Client for the Asynchronous Remoting Program *(continues)*

```
                System.Console.WriteLine(
                    "Please enter the number of repetitions: ");
                string repetitionsString =
                    System.Console.ReadLine();

                int repetitions = Convert.ToInt16(
                    repetitionsString);

                AsyncRemoteCallerDelegate repeaterDelegate =
                    new AsyncRemoteCallerDelegate(
                        theRepeater.RepeatString);

                IAsyncResult asyncResult =
                    repeaterDelegate.BeginInvoke(
                        repeatString,
                        repetitions,
                        null,null);

                for (int i=0; i < repetitions/2; i++)
                {
                    System.Console.WriteLine(
                        "The client is still executing");
                }

                System.Console.WriteLine(
                    "The client is done. Time to sleep.");

                asyncResult.AsyncWaitHandle.WaitOne();
                if (asyncResult.IsCompleted)
                {
                    repeaterDelegate.EndInvoke(asyncResult);
                    System.Console.WriteLine(
                        "The remote method is done.");
                }
            }
            else
            {
                ServerAccessError(
                    "Remote object could not be activated");
            }

            System.Console.WriteLine(
                "\nPaused. Press Enter to continue...");
            System.Console.Read();
        }

        static void ServerAccessError(string errorMessage)
```

Listing 11.7 The Client for the Asynchronous Remoting Program *(continued)*

```
76             {
77                 System.Console.WriteLine(
78                     "{0}",
79                     errorMessage);
80             }
81         }
82     }
```

Listing 11.7 The Client for the Asynchronous Remoting Program *(continued)*

WARNING

You cannot use metadata when you compile this client program. Add a reference to the remote object into the client's project file. The reasons why this is necessary, and some possible workarounds, are discussed in The Gotchas of Asynchronous Calls, which is presented later in this chapter.

After loading its configuration file on line 18, the client program creates a proxy for the remote object on lines 20-21. Next, it prompts the user for a string to repeat and the number of repetitions. It converts the number of repetitions from a string to an integer on lines 34-35. The client program then creates the delegate object on lines 37-39 and associates the delegate with the remote method `RepeatString()`. On lines 41-45, the program calls the delegate's `BeginInvoke()` method to call `RepeatString()`. It saves the result of `BeginInvoke()` into the variable `asyncResult`. The client demonstrates that it is still running while the remote method is executing by entering a `for` loop and printing output to the console.

The client program in Listing 11.7 is designed to finish the `for` loop before the remote method is done executing. It uses the `WaitOne()` method to sleep until the remote method completes. After the remote method ends, the client program calls the `EndInvoke()` method on line 59.

This client program demonstrated the process of calling a remote method asynchronously by obtaining a reference to the remote object, allocating a delegate, associating the delegate with one of the remote object's methods, calling the delegate's `BeginInvoke()` method to invoke the remote method, and calling the `EndInvoke()` method when the asynchronous remote method finished.

Delegates and Callback Functions

Delegates enable client programs to make asynchronous method calls. They also enable clients to receive asynchronous replies. Clients do this through the use of **callback functions**. Callback functions are invoked when a delegate's asynchronous method finishes execution. The callback function is part of the client program and executes in the client's application space.

It's important to note that the callback function is called by the .NET Remoting system on the server when a remote method that was called asynchronously finishes execution. This means that the callback function is being called *from the server*. By using a callback function, client programs become servers and server programs become clients. A callback function is a remote method from the server object's point of view, and the server is the callback function's client. To use callback functions, your client program must qualify as a server to the server program. Generally, this is not a problem. However, it is possible for network administrators to prevent the execution of remote methods on their networks. If a client is on such a network, the client cannot use callback functions.

NOTE

One way that network administrators prevent the execution of remote methods from outside their networks is by filtering all incoming SOAP messages. They use programs that watch for method invocation messages coming from the Internet. These programs automatically delete the method invocation messages, preventing the execution of your callback function. The asynchronous method will execute properly and attempt to invoke the callback function. However, on this type of network, the callback function will never be invoked.

To use a callback function, you need to write a method in your client program that can be executed remotely. When your client program calls a delegate's `BeginInvoke()` method, it passes a reference to the callback function to `BeginInvoke()`. The server side of the application requires no special coding.

Listing 11.8 demonstrates the use of callback functions. It presents a variation on the client program used in Listing 11.7. The client program in Listing 11.8 uses the same remote object, server program, server configuration file, and client configuration file presented for the previous example. You'll find these in Listings 11.3 through 11.6.

```
using System;
using System.Runtime.Remoting;
using System.Runtime.Remoting.Channels;
using System.Runtime.Remoting.Channels.Http;
using System.Threading;
using Repeater;

namespace Client
{
    class ClientAppClass
    {
        [STAThread]
        static void Main(string[] args)
        {
            RemotingConfiguration.Configure("client.exe.config");

            StringRepeater theRepeater =
                new StringRepeater();

            if (theRepeater != null)
            {
                System.Console.WriteLine(
                    "Please enter the string to repeat: ");
                string repeatString = System.Console.ReadLine();

                System.Console.WriteLine(
                    "Please enter the number of repetitions: ");
                string repetitionsString =
                    System.Console.ReadLine();

                int repetitions = Convert.ToInt16(
                    repetitionsString);

                AsyncCaller asyncCaller = new AsyncCaller();

                AsyncCallback theCallback =
                    new AsyncCallback(
                        asyncCaller.AsyncCallbackMethod);

                AsyncCaller.AsyncDelegate repeaterDelegate =
                    new AsyncCaller.AsyncDelegate(
                        theRepeater.RepeatString);

                IAsyncResult asyncResult =
                    repeaterDelegate.BeginInvoke(
                        repeatString,
                        repetitions,
```

Listing 11.8 An Asynchronous Remoting Client Program that Uses a Callback Function *(continues)*

```
                        theCallback,null);

                for (int i=0; i < repetitions/2; i++)
                {
                    System.Console.WriteLine(
                        "The client is still executing");
                }

                System.Console.WriteLine(
                    "The client is done. Time to sleep.");

                asyncResult.AsyncWaitHandle.WaitOne();
                if (asyncResult.IsCompleted)
                {
                    // Make sure the callback completes.
                    Thread.Sleep(1000);

                    repeaterDelegate.EndInvoke(asyncResult);
                    System.Console.WriteLine(
                        "The remote method is done.");
                }
            }
            else
            {
                ServerAccessError(
                    "Remote object could not be activated");
            }

            System.Console.WriteLine(
                "\nPaused. Press Enter to continue...");
            System.Console.Read();
        }

        static void ServerAccessError(string errorMessage)
        {
            System.Console.WriteLine(
                "{0}",
                errorMessage);
        }
    }

    class AsyncCaller : MarshalByRefObject
    {
        public delegate void AsyncDelegate(
            string outputString,
            int repetitions);

```

Listing 11.8 An Asynchronous Remoting Client Program that Uses a Callback Function *(continued)*

```
95            public void AsyncCallbackMethod(IAsyncResult theResult)
96            {
97                System.Console.WriteLine(
98                    "***********Entered Callback***********");
99            }
100       }
101   }
```

Listing 11.8 An Asynchronous Remoting Client Program that Uses a Callback Function *(continued)*

Like the client program in Listing 11.7, the program in Listing 11.8 begins by loading its configuration file. It allocates a proxy for the `StringRepeater` object on lines 17-18. After getting the necessary input from the user, this version of the client program allocates an object of type `AsyncCaller` on line 34.

The definition of the `AsyncCaller` object begins on line 89. The `AsyncCaller` object is an MBR object that contains the definition of the asynchronous delegate. The callback method is also a member of the `AsyncCaller` object. When the server program for this application invokes the callback method, it becomes a client to the `AsyncCaller` object.

On lines 36-38, the client program allocates an object of type `AsyncCallback`. The `AsyncCallback` type is defined by the .NET Remoting system. It specifies that the callback function must have a return type of `void`. It must also take one parameter of type `IAsyncResult`.

When a program allocates an object of type `AsyncCallback`, it must pass a reference to the callback method to the `AsyncCallback` constructor. What the program is doing here is creating a delegate. The server invokes the callback function asynchronously. This requires the use of a delegate. However, to prevent the need for any special coding on the server, the client program creates the delegate. Passing a reference to the callback function to the `AsyncCallback` constructor associates the callback function with its delegate.

On lines 40-42, the client program allocates a delegate. This delegate is for the server program's remote method that the client calls asynchronously. The client program passes a reference to the server's remote method into the constructor for the asynchronous delegate.

The client then calls the delegate's `BeginInvoke()` method on lines 44-48. As with the previous version of the client program, the first two parameters to the `BeginInvoke()` method are the parameters that the client passes to the remote method on the server. The third parameter to the `BeginInvoke()` method is not null as it was in the previous version of the program. This time, it is a reference to the callback function's delegate. The final parameter is still `null`. This parameter is for passing state information to an asynchronously invoked method. It is not used in this example.

The program enters a `for` loop and does some processing, and then goes to sleep on line 59. While the client program is asleep, the server program finishes the asynchronously invoked remote method. As soon as the server's method ends, the client wakes back up. At essentially the same time, the server invokes the callback method. To be sure that the callback method completes before the client does anything else, the client goes to sleep on line 63. This is a rather poor way to synchronize the client and the server. It's much better to use one of the synchronization primitives provided by the .NET Framework's threading namespace. These primitives are discussed later in this chapter.

The method call on line 63 puts the client program to sleep for one second. This is enough time for the callback function to finish. The client then calls the `EndInvoke()` method on line 65 to perform the necessary cleanup. Because the callback function takes a parameter of type `IAsyncResult`, which is also needed by the `EndInvoke()` method, the call to `EndInvoke()` can be moved into the callback function. This is a good way to handle the cleanup tasks for an asynchronous method call. It frees you from the need to use the .NET Framework's synchronization primitives to wait for the callback to complete before calling the `EndInvoke()` method.

This program demonstrates that callback functions are fairly easy to add to asynchronous method invocations. They can perform virtually any processing that you need them to, use synchronization primitives to synchronize themselves to the client program, and even perform the cleanup for the asynchronous method call.

One-Way Method Calls

If your client asynchronously calls a remote method and does not need to receive a reply, it can use a one-way method call. For one-way asynchronous method calls, the server's remote method must be decorated with the `[OneWay]` attribute. The code on the client is identical to an asynchronous method call that receives a reply.

JARGON

Programmers often call one-way asynchronous remote method calls "fire-and-forget" calls.

You can turn the remote application given in Listings 11.3 through 11.7 into an application that uses a one-way call by adding the `[OneWay]` attribute on line 10 of Listing 11.3. Recompile the `StringRepeater` object, the server program, and the client program. Run the server, and then run the client. When you do, you'll notice that it behaves differently than before. Like the previous version, the output of the client program is interspersed with the output of the remote method in the client's console window. However unlike the previous version, the client does not wait for the remote method to finish. In Listing 11.7, the client calls the `WaitOne()` method on line 56. Instead of causing the client to wait, this call returns immediately. Using a one-way asynchronous remote call means that the client does not need to wait for the server's method to complete. Therefore, the `WaitOne()` method essentially does nothing. Also, the property `asyncResult.IsComplete` is always seen as true after the asynchronous remote method call has been made.

Because the `WaitOne()` method does not cause the client to wait on a one-way call and the `asyncResult.IsComplete` property is always seen as true, the client will go ahead and execute the `EndInvoke()` method. This causes the output of the client program to be different than the previous version. Before the remote method finishes printing its output in the client window, the client will print the string "The remote method is done." After it prints this string, the client program prints a prompt and pauses to wait for user input. However, the remote method continues to print its output.

NOTE

When a client executes a one-way asynchronous method, it actually does receive a reply. However, it completely ignores the reply.

The Gotchas of Asynchronous Calls

In this chapter, all of the example programs required you to put a reference to the remote object into the client's project file. Earlier chapters in this book stated that this technique is not generally a good idea in programs that you release. The reason I used it in this chapter was to avoid what I call one of the "gotchas" of asynchronous remote method calls. If you generate metadata for the remote objects presented in this chapter and link the metadata into the client programs, you'll find that the clients don't work. So here is gotcha No. 1.

GOTCHA 1

Metadata and asynchronous calls do not go together.

The reason for this is that the .NET Framework tries to load the remote type according to the `SoapType` attribute's `XmlTypeNamespace` property. The `SoapType` attribute and its `XmlTypeNamespace` property are generated automatically for your remote type by the SOAPSUDS utility.

A rather unsatisfying workaround for this problem is to generate an unwrapped proxy using the SOAPSUDS utility's -gc command-line option. This generates the metadata as source code. You can manually remove the `SoapType` attribute and compile the metadata's source code into the client. However, this only works for SAOs. Clients for CAOs cannot be compiled this way.

A better technique is to use interfaces or abstract base classes to share information about your remote objects. Alternatively, you can create a method on the client that serves as a wrapper for the asynchronous call. This is demonstrated in the code fragment in Listing 11.9.

```
public static void AsyncCallWrapper(
     StringRepeater theRepeater,
     string repeatString,
     int repetitions)
{
     theRepeater.RepeatString(repeatString,repetitions);
}
```

Listing 11.9 A Wrapper Method for an Asynchronous Call

The method in Listing 11.9 can be used with the client program in listing 11.7. This method would be a member of the `ClientAppClass` class. When the `Main()` method needs to asynchronously call the remote method `RepeatString()`, it calls the `AsyncCallWrapper()` method instead. The technique for doing this is shown in the program fragment in Listing 11.10.

```
37                  AsyncRemoteCallerDelegate repeaterDelegate =
38                      new AsyncRemoteCallerDelegate(
39                          this.AsyncCallWrapper);
40
41                  IAsyncResult asyncResult =
42                      repeaterDelegate.BeginInvoke(
43                          repeatString,
44                          repetitions,
45                          null,null);
```

Listing 11.10 Calling the Wrapper Method

The program fragment in Listing 11.10 is a segment of Listing 11.7. Therefore, it uses the same line numbers and indentation that were used in Listing 11.7. On line 39, the program associates the `AsyncCallWrapper()` method with the delegate. Instead of calling the remote method asynchronously, it calls the wrapper asynchronously. As a result, the asynchronous call is made locally. The remote call is synchronous with respect to the wrapper method and asynchronous with respect to the `Main()` method.

With this technique you can share information about the remote object with the client using metadata. However, it's really not a very clean solution because it litters your client application class with extra wrapper methods.

Another feature of asynchronous remote method calls that can sometimes be a gotcha is the fact that exceptions thrown by one-way methods are not propagated to the client.

GOTCHA 2

If a one-way method throws an exception, the .NET Remoting system does not propagate the exception to the client program.

Under many circumstances, this is not a problem. However, if your client needs to perform error handling when the remote method throws an exception, do not use a one-way method. Use a regular asynchronous call and ignore the return value.

The last gotcha of asynchronous remote method calls also occurs with one-way calls. You can see this gotcha by writing a remote application that performs a one-way call. Run the client, but do not run the server program. You'll see that the client executes as if the asynchronous method completed successfully. It does not throw an exception even though it cannot communicate with the server.

GOTCHA 3

Client programs that use one-way calls do not throw exceptions if they cannot communicate with the server program.

Asynchronous calls that do not use the `[OneWay]` attribute do not have this problem.

Synchronization Techniques

When you use asynchronous method calls and callback functions, it is often the case that you need to resynchronize the methods that your client program is executing. Invoking asynchronous methods and callback functions automatically creates multiple **threads** in a program. A thread is a block of code to which the operating system allocates microprocessor time. All programs have at least one thread. Just as operating systems can execute more than one program at a time, programs can execute more than one thread at a time. Each thread can be performing a different task. Synchronization primitives enable the various threads in multithreaded programs to notify each other when they reach certain spots in the code.

The .NET Framework supplies a collection of objects that programs use for synchronization. These objects, called synchronization primitives, enable asynchronous methods and callback functions to pass synchronization signals to each other and to other parts of a program. The .NET Framework's synchronization primitives are defined in the namespace System.Threading. Table 11.1 lists some of the primitives that the System.Threading namespace contains. The objects shown in the table are not the only synchronization primitives this namespace provides. However, these are the primitives that are most likely to be used in a distributed application.

Table 11.1 Synchronization Primitives Commonly Used in Distributed Applications

PRIMITIVE	DESCRIPTION
WaitHandle	A wrapper for Win32 synchronization handles. Can be used to represent all synchronization primitives.
Mutex	An object whose state is set to signal when a thread takes ownership.
ManualResetEvent	Enables threads to send signals to each other. The signal remains set until it is cleared by the program.
AutoResetEvent	Enables threads to send signals to each other. The signal is cleared automatically after it is received.
Interlocked	Lets multiple threads safely share a single variable.

WaitHandle

A `WaitHandle` is a generic representation of all synchronization primitives. Variables of type `WaitHandle` can be assigned a reference of any type of synchronization primitive. The `WaitHandle` type is actually just a wrapper for Win32 synchronization handles.

We've already used the `WaitHandle` type in some of the programs in this chapter. Objects that implement the `IAsyncResult` interface contain a member of type `WaitHandle`.

Mutex

Mutex objects are extremely useful for putting callback functions to sleep while they wait for something to happen in a client program. The name "mutex" is short for "mutually exclusive." Only one thread can own the mutex at a time. All other threads that use the mutex can go to sleep until ownership of the mutex is released.

If your client program's application class declares a mutex as a static data member, that mutex is available to your callback functions. The declaration of such a mutex would look like this:

```
static Mutex callbackMutex = new Mutex(true);
```

This mutex can be used in a callback function as shown in Listing 11.11.

```
public void AsyncCallbackMethod(IAsyncResult theResult)
{
    // Do any processing needed.
    callbackMutex.WaitOne();
    // Do any other processing needed.
}
```

Listing 11.11 A Callback Function that Uses a Mutex

Because the client program passed the value `true` to the `Mutex` constructor, the program's main thread owns the mutex. The callback function can do any processing that you need until it gets to the point where you need the callback function and the client program to be synchronized. At that point, the callback function calls the `WaitOne()` method. This causes the callback function to go to sleep until the client program's main thread releases ownership of the mutex.

The client program releases ownership of the mutex by calling the mutex's `ReleaseMutex()` method, like this

```
callbackMutex.ReleaseMutex();
```

This call would appear in the client program's main thread at the point where the client program and callback method must synchronize themselves.

ManualResetEvent

Another way to synchronize client programs and callback functions is to use the `ManualResetEvent` object. A thread can use this object to go to sleep until another thread sends it a signal.

Like a mutex, your client program can declare a `ManualResetEvent` object in its application class so that the program's main thread can share the `ManualResetEvent` object with its callback function. The declaration would look similar to the following:

```
static ManualResetEvent callbackEvent = new ManualResetEvent(false);
```

This declaration creates the `ManualResetEvent` object and sets its initial state to unsignaled. At the point where the client program's main thread needs to wait for the callback function to finish, it can call the `ManualResetEvent` object's `WaitOne()` method. This would put it to sleep until it received a signal from the callback function.

The callback function performs any processing that it needs to, and then sends a signal to the client program's main thread by calling the `ManualResetEvent` object's Set() method. This is demonstrated in the program fragment in Listing 11.12.

```
        public void AsyncCallbackMethod(IAsyncResult theResult)
        {
            // Do any processing needed, then send a signal to
            // tell the main thread that the callback is done.
            callbackManualResetEvent.Set();
        }
```

Listing 11.12 A Callback Function that Uses a ManualResetEvent

The `ManualResetEvent` object stays in the signaled state until it is manually reset. To reset it, one of the threads in the program calls the `Reset()` method.

AutoResetEvent

The `AutoResetEvent` works in nearly the same manner as the `ManualResetEvent` object. The difference is that the `AutoResetEvent` object automatically clears itself after its signal has been received.

Interlocked

When sharing variables between threads, it is possible for one thread to interrupt another thread at a critical time. For example, suppose two threads share an integer variable called `sharedVar`. Imagine further that the first thread has just incremented `sharedVar`, and it is about to test `sharedVar` with an if statement. If another thread is granted microprocessor time at this point, it could possibly decrement `sharedVar`. When control is given back to the first thread, the `if` statement will yield unexpected results.

The methods of the `Interlocked` object enable different threads to safely share variables. This is extremely useful if the main thread of a client program and a callback function need access to the same set of variables. Typically, the shared variables would be declared as data members of the client's application class.

The `Interlocked` object has four methods. They each perform operations that cannot be interrupted. These operations are guaranteed to complete before microprocessor time is given to another thread.

With the `CompareExchange()` method, your program can compare two values to see whether they are equal. If the two values are equal, the `CompareExchange()` method can replace one of them. If you want to perform an uninterruptible swap of the values in two variables, call the `Exchange()` method. To perform an uninterruptible decrement or increment on a variable, use the `Decrement()` or `Increment()` method.

Summary

Calls on remote methods can be made synchronously or asynchronously. Asynchronous calls are made through delegates. A delegate is a reference type that defines a signature for method calls. Your program can associate local methods or remote methods with a delegate. Either way, your program can invoke the method associated with a delegate asynchronously by calling the `BeginInvoke()` and `EndInvoke()` methods.

If your program associates a remote method with a delegate and uses the delegate to call the remote method asynchronously, it can receive an asynchronous reply from the server through a callback function. Client programs that use callback functions become servers themselves. The delegate for the callback function is a remote object from the point of view of the server program. Therefore, a client program that uses callback functions must be running on a computer that qualifies as a server for the remote object.

Client programs that asynchronously call remote methods and do not need a reply can use one-way method calls. To be called as a one-way asynchronous method, the source code of the remote method must be decorated with the `[OneWay]` attribute.

Using asynchronous calls and metadata together is not always straightforward. There are some workarounds. However, none are particularly satisfactory. You can either share information about remote objects with interfaces or abstract base classes, or you can write a wrapper for the asynchronous call.

Using asynchronous method calls and callback functions sometimes makes it necessary for you to synchronize the main thread of the client program and a callback function. You can do this with the synchronization primitives defined in the .NET Framework's System.Threading namespace.

CHAPTER 12

Security

At one time, personal computers were pretty much islands unto themselves. Viruses, hack attacks, and other security problems were not a concern for PC users. With increasing interconnectedness came increasing difficulty in keeping applications and information secure. In today's environment of highly distributed applications, security is of paramount importance.

Secure application use in a distributed environment involves the efforts of many different types of professionals. Someone must manage the physical facilities of the computing environment. That person must ensure that equipment is not stolen or vandalized. He or she must also prevent malicious attackers from planting devices on computers that enable them to monitor a user's activity. Others must monitor the company's network to keep out attackers and data thieves.

However, the efforts of these professionals alone will not ensure secure application use. Developers must design security into their applications. The techniques that developers employ help ensure that authorized users are accessing servers using authorized client code through authorized channels. Developers can also build applications such that data is protected as it travels over the network.

Building security into a distributed application can be a daunting task. It requires knowledge of many different tools and techniques. This chapter introduces the basics of security for developers of .NET Remoting applications.

Secure Code

As they build applications for release, developers should do what they can to ensure that users are accessing the distributed application with authorized code. Server code is usually kept on computers at a secure location. However, client programs are more widely distributed. They may be given to end users who access the server over the Internet. They may be used by employees at a branch office. That branch office may or may not communicate with servers over a secure network. Deployment scenarios such as these require that server programs validate the identity of the code used in client programs.

The .NET Runtime's CLR automatically provides a minimal form of checking to ensure that none of the program's assemblies have been altered or replaced. It utilizes a technique called hashing to generate an identifier for each assembly based on the assembly's contents. Every assembly generates a unique hash. Visual Studio stores the hash in a hash file and incorporates the hash file into each assembly. When the CLR loads an assembly, it rehashes the assembly and compares the results against the hash stored in the assembly. If they do not match, the CLR will not load the assembly.

Although this automatic check can help identify assemblies that have been tampered with, it is not sufficient to ensure the identity of an assembly. Developers must take advantage of the additional tools provided by the .NET Framework to validate the identity of released code.

Starting with Strong Names

The most fundamental tool that all developers should use for code identification is strong-named assemblies. Chapter 9 gave an overview of strong names and how to generate them for your code. Every single program and assembly that you release should have a strong name. A malicious attacker can replace any code that lacks a strong name. This can cause a serious breach of security.

Generate a strong name for every program and assembly that you release.

Strong names, which are stored in an assembly's manifest, ensure that a given module of code is globally unique. This helps the .NET Framework prevent **spoofing** on a network. In this form of attack, a malicious user makes a program or assembly written by the attacker look like an authorized program or assembly on the network. This is essentially a type of identity theft. The unauthorized program or assembly steals the identity of an authorized program or assembly and acts in its place.

Signcode Signatures

It is important to understand that strong names are only a *beginning* to your quest for secure computing in a distributed environment. Strong names help ensure the integrity of code. However, there are no trust levels built-in to strong names. Network administrators use trust levels to control what code can and cannot do on a network or a computer. For secure computing, network administrators need the cooperation of developers.

You can enable network administrators to assign trust levels to your assemblies by signing them with the Signcode tool. SIGNCODE.EXE is included with Visual Studio. It generates a unique signature for an assembly and stores the signature in the assembly's portable execution (PE) file that contains the manifest.

You can use strong assembly names without Signcode signatures. You can use Signcode signatures without strong assembly names. However, I highly recommend that you use both together. It adds only minor amounts of time to the release process, but it adds major amounts of security to your application.

If you assign a strong assembly name and a Signcode signature to your assembly, you must generates a strong assembly name first.

Authenticode Signatures

Strong names and Signcode signatures identify your code to the .NET Framework's CLR. You should also identify your code to your users.

A bit of contemplation shows the reasons for this. If your company's branch office receives a CD in the mail containing an update to a client program, how do they know that the CD was actually shipped from the company's headquarters? Alternatively, if your users download client programs from your Web site, how can they be sure they are truly connected to your Web page?[1]

One way to resolve these difficulties is to sign your code with the digital signature that users can verify independently. Microsoft uses its Authenticode technology for this purpose. Authenticode uses a third-party certificate authority (CA), such as VeriSign, to verify credentials supplied by software publishers. The credentials include, among other things, the company's name, address, and a public encryption key. You generate the public encryption key as one of a pair of encryption keys. The other key in the pair is private. Only the people in your company who actually release the software should have access to the public key/private key pair.

The certificate authority verifies the identity of the software publisher and uses the information the publisher supplies to generate a unique digital signature. The digital signature is called a Software Publisher Certificate (SPC), and it conforms to an industry standard for SPCs. The certificate identifies the publisher and contains the publisher's public key.

When you publish software, you sign it with your private key. You also incorporate your SPC into the software. This enables end users to validate that the software they receive actually comes from you.

Microsoft provides a number of tools for creating and managing Authenticode signatures. These are summarized in Table 12.1.

Table 12.1 Tools for Creating and Managing Authenticode Signatures

NAME	DESCRIPTION
MakeCert	Creates a test certificate.
Cert2SPC	Generates a test SCP from a certificate.
SignCode	Signs a file using the private key and the SPC.
MakeCTL	Builds a certificate trust list.
CertMgr	Manages certificates and trust lists.
SetReg	Sets registry entries that control the process of verifying certificates.

[1] It is possible for attackers to the make requests for your Web pages to resolve to pages on their server. This technique is called page-jacking. If your users are the victims of page-jacking, they may download client programs written by attackers.

If your remote object is a CAO, you can write it such that it will do nothing until the client program provides its Authenticode signature. The client program can get its signature information by calling the `Module.GetSignerCertificate()` method. It can then pass the signature information to the CAO.

You can handle this process in a couple of different ways. The first is to have the client call a remote method on the CAO that passes the digital signature to the CAO. The advantage of this is that it's very simple code to write. The disadvantage is that this approach will not work with SAOs. It can only work if the remote object keeps its state and if there is one remote object per client. Only CAOs fit this description.

If you're a bit braver, you can write a custom channel sink that provides the Authenticode information each time your client sends a message to the server. This approach is much more flexible because it allows you to use both CAOs and SAOs. However, custom channel sinks are not for the faint of heart. They're not easy to write or debug. Custom channel sinks are presented in Chapter 13.

TIP

If you decide that you need a custom channel sink, I advise you to check for available code before you try and write one. I've seen high quality C# source code for some very handy custom channel sinks in the public domain. Some companies have announced their intentions to make custom channel sinks commercially available.

Authenticode signatures are also valuable if your client includes downloadable add-on modules. This is common with online multiplayer games. The downloadable modules are typically called expansion packs. If your client does this, it should check the Authenticode signature of each downloadable module to ensure that the code was actually published by you.

In addition, Authenticode signatures can help you to securely automate the process of updating client programs. This is of vital importance to large corporations that deploy hundreds, or even thousands, of client programs each time they update. This scenario assumes that an automated update program is installed on all users' computers by a trusted individual and that all of the client computers are in secure locations. If these conditions are met, the automated update program can periodically check server computers for updates to the client program. When it downloads a new client, it can check the Authenticode signature.

To enable your company to take advantage of any of these precautions, you must become familiar with Authenticode, or equivalent technology, and use it to sign all of the programs assemblies.

Custom Certificates

If you don't want to use Authenticode, Microsoft also supplies a tool called Certificate Server. With Certificate Server, you can issue certificates that you can incorporate into your client programs. The certificates issued by the Certificate Server program perform much the same function as certificates issued by entities such as VeriSign. However, you have complete control over how many are issued and how they are used.

The disadvantage of this approach is that the certificates cannot be validated by a third party. The certificates enable your client code to identify itself to servers. You cannot use them to identify your code to your users. In large corporate deployments where code is installed by trusted personnel, identifying code to users may not be particularly important. It may be more important to ensure that every program that appears to be an authorized client is, in fact, an authorized client. In this case, Microsoft's Certificate Server tool, or equivalent technology, may be enough for your needs.

Secure Application Use

All of the information presented in this chapter so far does nothing more than ensure that you have an authorized server program communicating with an authorized client program. It does not protect the privacy or integrity of data that may move across the communication channel. It also does not ensure that your application is being used by an authorized individual. If you want your application to include these aspects of security you must build them in.

Secure Channels

Anyone who has a computer on a network can install software on that computer that enables him to monitor network traffic. Information that traverses the Internet passes through many computers owned by many different individuals and companies. Virtually anyone whose computer your information passes through can monitor the network traffic and view the information. These are not ideal situations for communicating sensitive business, government, or personal information between two computers.

When sensitive information must be exchanged across one or more networks, some means of secure communications must be employed. Modern operating systems such as UNIX, Linux, Windows XP, Windows 2000, and Windows NT provided secure network communication channels. To make communication channels secure, operating systems encrypt packets of information before they send the packets over the network. When they reach their destination, the operating system decrypts the packets.

IPSec

Most major operating systems provide a communication channel called IP Security Protocol (IPSec). The IPSec standard specifies a method of secure TCP/IP-based communication. IPSec is by far the most secure type of channel. However, it is connection-oriented. As a result, it maintains a constant connection between the client and the server until one of them disconnects. In that respect, it's very much like a telephone conversation between two people. No one else can use that particular telephone line until someone hangs up. In the same way, clients and servers that communicate with IPSec maintain a channel until the connection is closed.

Selecting the IPSec channel is done by configuring the operating system. You don't add anything to your source code to select it. This task is not usually handled by a company's developers. Typically, network administrators take care of it. However, deciding whether or not to use the IPSec channel is typically a decision made by developers. Developers must be aware that there are limitations to IPSec. The connection-oriented nature of IPSec causes problems when you attempt to scale your distributed application to large deployment. Maintaining connections to large numbers of clients can put a serious strain on network resources. IPSec is a very good type of secure channel to use if your application will be deployed to a limited number of clients. It keeps your data secure as the data traverses the network.

NOTE

Just how limited your IPSec-based deployment must be depends on your network hardware. For most corporate networks, you will not generally have problems with hundreds of users communicating through IPSec channels. However, as the number of users gets into the thousands or tens of thousands, your network is very likely to bog down.

PPTP

If users must access your remote objects over the Internet and you want the high level of security provided by IPSec, you can deploy your application over a **virtual private network** (VPN). VPNs give users access to all of the network resources they would have access to if they were on site and connected directly to the company's network backbone. Even though the connection is made across the Internet, VPN traffic is secure. You can use IPSec across a VPN to further protect sensitive data in the same way you use it across your company's internal network.

VPNs employ a protocol called point to point tunneling protocol (PPTP). PPTP wraps TCP/IP packets in HTTP packets. In addition to being wrapped, the TCP/IP packet is also encrypted. An offsite computer can send the HTTP packet across the Internet to a PPTP server. The PPTP server unwraps the packet and decrypts it. Next, the server sends the TCP/IP packet across the corporate network just as if the packet had originated on a computer connected to the network backbone.

Computers on the TCP/IP network can also send packets to the offsite computer. The PPTP server intercepts these packets, encrypts them, wraps them in HTTP packets, and transmits them across the Internet. When the offsite computer receives packets, it unwraps and decrypts them. It can then use the TCP/IP packets exactly as it would use packets from a network to which it was directly connected. Because VPNs establish a private TCP/IP connection, you can develop remote applications that communicate through IPSec channels.

VPNs suffer from the same disadvantages as IPSec connections. Being connection-oriented, they impose limits on the size of your deployment. Your network hardware must manage a constant connection for each user. In addition, transporting encrypted TCP/IP packets in HTTP packets takes time. A VPN is roughly half as fast as the underlying HTTP channel. So if your user dials up to the Internet with a 56K modem and then connects to your corporate network with a PPTP connection, his VPN connection will run at about 28K. For most remote applications other than simple email and small file transfers, this is not satisfactory. Users really need a broadband connection to make PPTP connections worthwhile.

NOTE

I have several years' experience connecting to corporate networks through VPN/PPTP connections. I do not recommend that you incorporate them into your deployment. I've found that, as the load on the PPTP server increases, the ability of users to connect and stay connected degrades quite rapidly. They sometimes say you are connected when you are not. I have had many problems accessing network resources through PPTP connections. Also, their slow speed sometimes had me pulling my hair out.

Secure HTTP

IPSec and PPTP will not work for large-scale deployments to the Internet. You must use another means to secure applications on the Internet. This is typically done by sending HTTP communications over a secure socket layer (SSL). This type of channel is called secure HTTP or HTTPS. If your servers run Windows NT, Windows 2000, or Windows XP, you can use HTTPS for your application by hosting the remote objects in IIS. Your network administrator must then configure IIS on your servers to communicate through HTTPS.

NOTE

If you use HTTPS in your distributed application, the URLs must contain the string `"https"` **rather than** `"http"`**.**

The problem with HTTPS is that it's not completely secure. Messages that you send to remote objects and the return values that you receive from remote objects are encrypted before they traverse the network. However, if your application uses callback functions, be careful. Callback functions do not use HTTPS. They use HTTP. Therefore, all data that the server sends to the client's callback function is not encrypted. Messages sent from the server to invoke the callback function are in plaintext XML. Anyone can intercept and read the data that the message contains.

Knowing this shortcoming of HTTPS in advance can enable you to design around it. Most of the time, you'll find that you can simply write your application in such a way that no sensitive information passes to or from a callback function. However, that is not always an option. In cases where you must have secure communications with callback functions over HTTPS, you must provide a means of securing the data yourself. This usually means that your application must programmatically encrypt the data that passes between the server and the callback function. A technique for doing this is presented later in this chapter.

WARNING

Callback functions over HTTPS are not secure. Invocation messages and return value messages for callback functions from the server to the client are sent via HTTP, not HTTPS. Anyone can intercept these messages and read the data they contain.

Encryption

As stated previously, secure channels encrypt data before it is sent over the network. However, the limitations of IPSec and HTTPS might make you consider a custom security solution. The .NET Remoting system is extremely extensible, although some methods of extending it are easier than others.

Encryption Essentials

Encryption is essentially a mathematical transformation of data to make the data unreadable to unauthorized parties. Modern encryption is based on the use of one or more keys. Common encryption methods also use an initialization vector. Encryption algorithms use keys and initialization vectors to create unique output. Two people using the same algorithm and the same data will generate different encrypted output if they use different keys and initialization vectors.

There are two approaches to encryption, symmetric and asymmetric.

Symmetric Encryption

Distributed applications perform **symmetric encryption** when both the client and the server use the same encryption key. To keep the data secure, the encryption key must be kept private. No one should have access to the encryption key except the sender and the recipient of the data. The initialization vector does not have to be private. However, it increases the application's security if it is. Because the key is private, symmetric encryption is also called **private key encryption**. Symmetric encryption algorithms are most appropriate when both the client and the server programs are kept in secure locations but must communicate across insecure channels.

Private key algorithms are fast. They perform their transformations on blocks of data. For this reason, they can be referred to as **block ciphers**. The .NET Framework provides several different types of private key encryption algorithms including RC2, DES, TrippleDES, and Rijndael.

TIP

I recommend that you get information on security that presents overviews of these encryption algorithms. Even though you don't need to know all of the details of these algorithms to use them, a familiarity with how they work helps you select the most appropriate algorithm for your application.

All of the block cipher algorithms provided in the .NET Framework use a chaining mode called cipher block chaining (CBC). CBC algorithms use both keys and initialization vectors. This ensures that two identical blocks of plaintext in the input stream do not produce identical blocks of encrypted text in the output stream. This makes it harder for attackers to decipher the encrypted text by looking for patterns in the output.

Asymmetric Encryption

Asymmetric encryption, the other primary approach to encrypting data, also involves a pair of keys. One of the keys is kept private. The other can be made publicly available. The two keys are linked mathematically. Asymmetric encryption works by enabling any sender to use the public key to encrypt messages sent to a particular recipient. However, only the recipient can decrypt them using the private key. If the recipient needs to respond to the sender in a secure way, the sender and the recipient switch roles.

For instance, suppose client program A must send encrypted data to remote object B. Further, imagine that both program A and object B have a private key/public key pair associated with them. A uses B's public key to perform the encryption. B's public key can be kept in A's configuration file. Or A can request B's public key through a method call before it sends data to B. B decrypts the data it receives from A using its own private key. To send data back to A in its reply, B encrypts the data with A's public key.

The public key/private key pair can also be used to identify data sent from the holder of the private key. This is because the private key can be used to digitally sign data. The signature can be verified with the public key. The public key will only validate data signed with the private key.

Public key algorithms are slower than private key algorithms. In general, it is not wise for your application to use public key/private key pairs to encrypt all traffic between them. Instead, clients or servers can use public key/private key pairs to exchange a private key that they can use for the remainder of the communication session. This enables your application to generate a different private key for every session. In fact, you can write your applications such that the private key expires after a set amount of time. The client and the server would then need to use a public key/private key pair once again to exchange a new private key.

Custom Encryption in Distributed Applications

To add custom encryption, you essentially have two choices. First, you can encrypt some objects and not others. Second, you can encrypt all data that flows across a channel.

Encryption Through Custom Serialization

It's not uncommon for branch offices to need to communicate with the main headquarters of their comapanies across the Internet. However, it may be that very little of the information that traverses between a company's headquarters and its branch offices needs to be encrypted. You may not need the overhead of a fully secure channel. Alternatively, your application might be using HTTPS, and you want to secure information that servers send to callback functions. In these situations, it might be advisable to encrypt certain objects and not others.

You can perform encryption on an object-by-object basis by adding custom encryption to any serializable object. To do custom serialization, objects must implement the `ISerializable` interface. Let's demonstrate how this is done by creating a new version of the credit card verification service we built in Chapter 10. This version of the program encrypts the credit card data that gets sent to the server. Encrypting data involves using the Cryptography API that is built into Windows (or an equivalent technology). You can access it through the .NET Framework's cryptography classes.

We'll build this application in two stages. In the first, we'll create the application and build a basic serialization system. The basic serialization system demonstrates a simple form of custom serialization. In the second stage, we'll actually add encryption into the serialization system.

Stage 1

To demonstrate custom serialization, we'll write a new version of the charge verifier program that appeared in previous chapters. The client program is shown in Listing 12.1.

```
1    using System;
2    using System.Drawing;
3    using System.Collections;
4    using System.ComponentModel;
5    using System.Windows.Forms;
6    using System.Data;
7    using System.Runtime.Remoting;
8    using ChargeVerifier;
9
10   namespace Client
11   {
12       /// <summary>
13       /// Summary description for Form1.
14       /// </summary>
15       public class Form1 : System.Windows.Forms.Form
16       {
17           Lines 17-34 omitted to save space.
35
36           private IFasterChargeVerifier chargeVerifier;
37
38           public Form1()
39           {
40               //
41               // Required for Windows Form Designer support
42               //
43               InitializeComponent();
44
45               chargeVerifier =
46                   (IFasterChargeVerifier)Activator.GetObject(
47                       typeof(IFasterChargeVerifier),
48                       "http://localhost:8080/ChargeVerifier.soap");
49           }
50
51           Lines 51-232 omitted to save space.
233          [STAThread]
234          static void Main()
```

Listing 12.1 The Client Program *(continues)*

```
        {
            Application.Run(new Form1());
        }

        private void exitButton_Click(
            object sender,
            System.EventArgs e)
        {
            this.Close();
        }

        private void verifyButton_Click(
            object sender,
            System.EventArgs e)
        {
            VerificationRequest request = new VerificationRe-
            quest();

            // Get the card number and convert it to an int.
            request.CardIDNumber =
                Convert.ToInt64(cardNumberBox.Text);

            // If the card number is invalid...
            if (request.CardIDNumber <= 0)
            {
                // Display an error message.
                MessageBox.Show(
                    "The card number is not valid",
                    "Error");
            }

            // If there is a name...
            if (nameOnCardBox.Text.Length > 0)
            {
                // Put it into the verification request.
                request.CardHolderName = nameOnCardBox.Text;
            }
            // Else the name is not valid...
            else
            {
                // Display an error message.
                MessageBox.Show(
                    "The name is not valid",
                    "Error");
            }

            // Get the month.
            DateTime expirationDate = new DateTime(
```

Listing 12.1 The Client Program *(continued)*

```
                Convert.ToInt32(yearBox.Text),
                Convert.ToInt32(monthBox.Text),
                1);

            // If the date is valid...
            if ((expirationDate.Month > 0) &&
                (expirationDate.Month <= 12) &&
                (expirationDate.Year > 0) &&
                (expirationDate.Year < 3000))
            {
                // Put it into the verification request.
                request.CardExpirationDate = expirationDate;
            }
            // Else the date is not valid...
            else
            {
                // Display an error message.
                MessageBox.Show(
                    "The expiration date is not valid",
                    "Error");
            }

            // Get the amount.
            request.ChargeAmount =
                Convert.ToDouble(amountBox.Text);
            // If the amount is not valid...
            if (request.ChargeAmount <= 0)
            {
                // Display an error message.
                MessageBox.Show(
                    "The charge amount is not valid",
                    "Error");
            }

            // Verify the charge.
            ChargeConfirmation confirmation =
                chargeVerifier.VerifyCharge(request);

            // If the charge was verified...
            if (confirmation.VerificationStatus ==
                ChargeConfirmation.Status.ACCEPTED)
            {
                // Display a message
                MessageBox.Show(
                    "The charge is verified.",
                    "Confirmation Status");
            }
            // Else the charge was not verified...
```

Listing 12.1 The Client Program *(continues)*

```
330                 else
331                 {
332                     // Display an error message.
333                     MessageBox.Show(
334                         "The charge is rejected " +
335                         "for the following reason:\n" +
336                         confirmation.RejectionMessage,
337                         "Confirmation Status");
338                 }
339             }
340         }
341     }
```

Listing 12.1 The Client Program *(continued)*

To save space, I've omitted the code generated by Visual Studio. As with previous versions, the client program for this application is a Windows Forms program. It does not require the configuration file because it establishes its connection to the server object programmatically on lines 45-48. When you input credit card information and click the **Verify** button, the program calls the `verifyButton_Click()` method, which begins on line 246. The `verifyButton_Click()` method creates a verification request on line 250 and stores the credit card information into the verification request on lines 252-314.

On lines 317-318, the `verifyButton_Click()` method calls the remote server object's `VerifyCharge()` method. The `VerifyCharge()` method transmits the charge verification request to the remote server object. As you'll see shortly, the charge verification request object performs its own custom serialization. However, the `verifyButton_Click()` method demonstrates that the client doesn't need to know that the charge verification request object performs custom serialization. No special coding is needed in methods that use objects that do custom serialization.

The server program and its configuration file for the custom serialization application are very much like most of those presented so far. They are shown in Listing 12.2 and 12.3.

```
using System;
using System.Runtime.Remoting;
using System.Runtime.Remoting.Channels;
```

Listing 12.2 The Server Program

```
using System.Runtime.Remoting.Channels.Http;

namespace Server
{
    class ServerAppClass
    {
        [STAThread]
        static void Main(string[] args)
        {
            RemotingConfiguration.Configure("Server.exe.config");
            System.Console.WriteLine(
                "Press Enter to end the server.");
            System.Console.Read();
        }
    }
}
```

Listing 12.2 The Server Program *(continued)*

```
<configuration>
    <system.runtime.remoting>
        <application>
            <channels>
                <channel ref="http" port="8080"/>
            </channels>
            <service>
                <wellknown
                    mode="Singleton"
                    type="ChargeVerifier.FasterChargeVerifier,
                    Server"
                    objectUri = "ChargeVerifier.soap" />
            </service>
        </application>
    </system.runtime.remoting>
</configuration>
```

Listing 12.3 The Server Program's Configuration File

In addition to the file in Listing 12.2, the Visual Studio project file for the server program should also hold the name of the file containing the source code for the `FasterChargeVerifier` object. This source code is presented in Listing 12.4.

```
using System;

namespace ChargeVerifier
{
    public class FasterChargeVerifier :
        MarshalByRefObject,
        IFasterChargeVerifier
    {
        private bool accept;
        private int reason;


        public FasterChargeVerifier()
        {
            accept = false;
            reason = 1;
        }

        public override object InitializeLifetimeService()
        {
            return (null);
        }

        public ChargeConfirmation VerifyCharge(
            VerificationRequest cardInfo)
        {
            ChargeConfirmation returnValue =
                new ChargeConfirmation();

            if (accept == false)
            {
                returnValue.VerificationStatus =
                    ChargeConfirmation.Status.REJECTED;

                switch (reason)
                {
                    case 1:
                        returnValue.ReasonForRejection =
                            ChargeConfirmation.Reason.EXPIRED;
                    break;

                    case 2:
                        returnValue.ReasonForRejection =
                            ChargeConfirmation.Reason.CANCELED;
                        break;

                    case 3:
                        returnValue.ReasonForRejection =
```

Listing 12.4 The `FasterChargeVerifier` Object

```
                            ChargeConfirmation.Reason.STOLEN;
                        break;

                    case 4:
                        returnValue.ReasonForRejection =
                            ChargeConfirmation.Reason.LOST;
                        break;

                    case 5:
                        returnValue.ReasonForRejection =
                            ChargeConfirmation.Reason.OVER_LIMIT;
                        break;

                    default:
                        reason = 1;
                        break;
                }
                accept = true;
                reason++;
            }
            else
            {
                returnValue.VerificationStatus =
                    ChargeConfirmation.Status.ACCEPTED;
                returnValue.ReasonForRejection =
                    ChargeConfirmation.Reason.NONE;
                accept = false;
            }

            return (returnValue);
        }
    }
}
```

Listing 12.4 The `FasterChargeVerifier` Object *(continued)*

Information about the `FasterChargeVerifier` object is shared between the client and the server by creating an interface called `IFasterChargeVerifier`. This interface is compiled into its own assembly and a reference to the assembly should appear in the project files for both the client and the server.

The file that contains the `IFasterChargeVerifier` interface also holds the definition of the charge verification request object. Therefore, this file is where the code that performs the custom serialization appears. It is given in Listing 12.5.

```
using System;
using System.Runtime.Serialization;


namespace ChargeVerifier
{
    [Serializable()]
    public class VerificationRequest : ISerializable
    {
        private long cardNumber;
        private string nameOnCard;
        private DateTime expirationDate;
        private double amount;

        public VerificationRequest()
        {
            cardNumber = 0;
            nameOnCard = null;
            amount = 0.0;
        }

        protected VerificationRequest(
            SerializationInfo info,
            StreamingContext context)
        {
            cardNumber =
                info.GetInt64("cardNumber");
            nameOnCard =
                info.GetString("nameOnCard");
            expirationDate =
                Convert.ToDateTime(
                    info.GetString("expirationDate"));
            amount = info.GetDouble("amount");
        }

        public virtual void GetObjectData(
            SerializationInfo info,
            StreamingContext context)
        {
            info.AddValue("cardNumber", cardNumber);
            info.AddValue("nameOnCard", nameOnCard);
            info.AddValue(
                "expirationDate",
                expirationDate.ToString());
            info.AddValue("amount",amount);
        }

        public VerificationRequest(
```

Listing 12.5 The `IFasterChargeVerifier` Interface and Its Associated Objects

```
            int cardIDNumber,
            string cardHolderName,
            DateTime cardExpirationDate,
            double amount)
        {
            cardNumber = cardIDNumber;
            nameOnCard = cardHolderName;
            expirationDate = cardExpirationDate;
        }

        public long CardIDNumber
        {
            get
            {
                return (cardNumber);
            }
            set
            {
                cardNumber = value;
            }
        }

        public string CardHolderName
        {
            get
            {
                return (nameOnCard);
            }
            set
            {
                nameOnCard = value;
            }
        }

        public DateTime CardExpirationDate
        {
            get
            {
                return (expirationDate);
            }
            set
            {
                expirationDate = value;
            }
        }

        public double ChargeAmount
        {
```

Listing 12.5 The `IFasterChargeVerifier` Interface and Its Associated Objects *(continues)*

```
            get
            {
                return amount;
            }
            set
            {
                amount = value;
            }
        }
    }

    [Serializable()]
    public class ChargeConfirmation
    {
        private Status confirmationStatus;
        private Reason rejectionReason;

        public enum Status
        {
            ACCEPTED,
            REJECTED
        }

        public enum Reason
        {
            NONE,
            EXPIRED,
            CANCELED,
            STOLEN,
            LOST,
            OVER_LIMIT
        }

        public ChargeConfirmation()
        {
            confirmationStatus = Status.REJECTED;
            rejectionReason = Reason.NONE;
        }

        public ChargeConfirmation(
            Status status,
            Reason reasonForRejection)
        {
            confirmationStatus = status;
            rejectionReason = reasonForRejection;
        }

        public Status VerificationStatus
```

Listing 12.5 The `IFasterChargeVerifier` Interface and Its Associated Objects *(continued)*

```
        {
            get
            {
                return (confirmationStatus);
            }
            set
            {
                confirmationStatus = value;
            }
        }

        public Reason ReasonForRejection
        {
            get
            {
                return (rejectionReason);
            }
            set
            {
                rejectionReason = value;
            }
        }

        public string RejectionMessage
        {
            get
            {
                string theMessage = null;

                switch (rejectionReason)
                {
                   case Reason.NONE:
                        theMessage = "No reason.";
                    break;

                    case Reason.EXPIRED:
                        theMessage = "The card has expired.";
                    break;

                    case Reason.CANCELED:
                        theMessage = "The card was canceled.";
                    break;

                    case Reason.STOLEN:
                        theMessage = "The card is stolen.";
                    break;

                    case Reason.LOST:
```

Listing 12.5 The `IFasterChargeVerifier` Interface and Its Associated Objects *(continues)*

```
193                     theMessage = "The card was lost.";
194                 break;
195
196                 case Reason.OVER_LIMIT:
197                     theMessage =
198                         "The spending limit has been exceeded.";
199                 break;
200             }
201             return (theMessage);
202         }
203     }
204 }
205
206 public interface IFasterChargeVerifier
207 {
208     ChargeConfirmation VerifyCharge(
209         VerificationRequest cardInfo);
210 }
211 }
```

Listing 12.5 The `IFasterChargeVerifier` Interface and Its Associated Objects *(continued)*

In Listing 12.5, the `VerificationRequest` object is of particular interest. It begins on line 7. Notice that it is marked with the `Serializable` attribute. It also implements the `ISerializable` interface. Both of these are required for objects that do custom serialization.

The serialization is performed in a method called `GetObjectData()`. This method appears on lines 36-46. Its first parameter, which is of type SerializationInfo, is where the `GetObjectData()` method stores the serialized data. The `GetObjectData()` method stores each data item by calling the SerializationInfo.`AddValue()` method and passing it a string and a value. The string identifies the value. Therefore, it must be unique within the SerializationInfo object. The `GetObjectData()` method in Listing 12.5 uses the names of the individual data items as the strings for the first parameter in the calls to the `AddValue()` method. Although this makes it easy to identify the individual pieces of serialized information, you do not have to do this. The strings can be anything you want them to be as long as there are no duplicates.

To deserialize the information in a `VerificationRequest` object, the .NET Remoting Framework calls the `VerificationRequest()` constructor that appears on lines 22-34. Like the `GetObjectData()`

method, the first parameter to this constructor is of type `SerializationInfo`. This parameter contains the data that was serialized by the `GetObjectData()` method.

The constructor loads the data from the `SerializationInfo` object by calling some of the "get" methods that the `SerializationInfo` object provides. These "get" methods all take a string identifier as their only parameter. The string identifiers must match the strings used in the `GetObjectData()` method. Not only do the `SerializationInfo` class's "get" methods retrieve the serialized data, they also cast it to a particular type. The names of the "get" methods indicate the type to which the data is cast. The `VerificationRequest()` constructor on lines 22-34 uses the `GetInt64()` and the `GetString()` methods to retrieve the serialized data and cast it to an integer and a string, respectively. In addition, it uses the `Convert.ToDateTime()` method to convert the string to a date.

All that it takes to make an object do custom serialization is writing the `GetObjectData()` method and a two-argument constructor that has the parameters shown on lines 23-24. With these methods implemented, we're now ready to build a version of the verification request object that encrypts its data.

Stage 2

To build a version of the charge verification program that automatically encrypts the credit card information before transmitting at across the network, the only file that we must change is the one in Listing 12.5. The new version of the application will reuse the files in Listings 12.1-12.4. Listing 12.6 gives the new version of the file containing the `IFasterChargeVerifier` interface and the serializable objects.

```
using Syste.m;
using System.Runtime.Serialization;
using System.IO;
using System.Security.Cryptography;


namespace ChargeVerifier
{
    [Serializable()]
    public class VerificationRequest : ISerializable
    {
```

Listing 12.6 A Version of The `IFasterChargeVerifier` Interface and Its Associated Objects with Encryption Added *(continues)*

```
        private long cardNumber;
        private string nameOnCard;
        private DateTime expirationDate;
        private double amount;

        [Serializable()]
        private class EncryptedData
        {
            private int length;
            byte [] dataBuffer;

            public EncryptedData(int bufferLength)
            {
                length = bufferLength;
                dataBuffer = new byte [length];
            }

            public EncryptedData(
                int bufferLength,
                byte [] buffer)
            {
                length = bufferLength;
                dataBuffer = buffer;
            }

            public int Length
            {
                get
                {
                    return (length);
                }
            }

            public byte [] DataBuffer
            {
                get
                {
                    return (dataBuffer);
                }
            }

            public byte DataByte(int arrayIndex)
            {
                byte returnValue = 0;

                if (arrayIndex<length)
                {
```

Listing 12.6 A Version of The `IFasterChargeVerifier` Interface and Its Associated Objects with Encryption Added *(continued)*

```
                returnValue = dataBuffer[arrayIndex];
            }
            else
            {
                throw new Exception(
                    "Array index out of range");
            }

            return (returnValue);
        }

        public void DataByte(int arrayIndex,byte byteValue)
        {
            if (arrayIndex<length)
            {
                dataBuffer[arrayIndex] = byteValue;
            }
            else
            {
                throw new Exception(
                    "Array index out of range");
            }
        }
    }

    public VerificationRequest()
    {
        cardNumber = 0;
        nameOnCard = null;
        amount = 0.0;
    }

    protected VerificationRequest(
        SerializationInfo info,
        StreamingContext context)
    {
        EncryptedData encryptedDataObject =
            (EncryptedData)info.GetValue(
                "dataBuffer",
                typeof(EncryptedData));

        byte [] encryptedBuffer =
            encryptedDataObject.DataBuffer;

        MemoryStream streamInMemory =
            new MemoryStream(encryptedBuffer);
        RijndaelManaged cryptographer =
```

Listing 12.6 A Version of The `IFasterChargeVerifier` Interface and Its Associated Objects with Encryption Added *(continues)*

```
            new RijndaelManaged();

        // Do not use this key in your application!
        byte[] cryptoKey =
            {
                0x01, 0x02, 0x03, 0x04, 0x05, 0x06, 0x07,
                0x08, 0x09, 0x10, 0x11, 0x12, 0x13, 0x14,
                0x15, 0x16
            };

        // Do not use this init vector in your application!
        byte[] initializationVector =
            {
                0x01, 0x02, 0x03, 0x04, 0x05, 0x06, 0x07,
                0x08, 0x09, 0x10, 0x11, 0x12, 0x13, 0x14,
                0x15, 0x16
            };

        CryptoStream decryptionStream =
            new CryptoStream(
                streamInMemory,
                cryptographer.CreateDecryptor(
                    cryptoKey,
                    initializationVector),
                CryptoStreamMode.Read);

        byte [] decryptedData =
            new byte [encryptedDataObject.Length];

        decryptionStream.Read(
            decryptedData,
            0,
            encryptedDataObject.Length);

        string dataString = null;
        for (int i=0; i<decryptedData.Length; i++)
        {
            dataString += (char)decryptedData[i];
        }

        string tempString =
            TokenizeString(dataString,0,'|');
        if (tempString.Length > 0)
        {
            cardNumber = Convert.ToInt64(tempString);
        }
        else
```

Listing 12.6 A Version of The `IFasterChargeVerifier` Interface and Its Associated Objects with Encryption Added *(continued)*

```
            {
                throw new Exception("Cannot parse card data");
            }

            int start = tempString.Length+1;
            tempString =
                TokenizeString(dataString,start,'|');
            if (tempString.Length > 0)
            {
                nameOnCard = tempString;
            }
            else
            {
                throw new Exception("Cannot parse card data");
            }

            start += tempString.Length+1;
            tempString =
                TokenizeString(dataString,start,'|');
            if (tempString.Length > 0)
            {
                expirationDate = Convert.ToDateTime(tempString);
            }
            else
            {
                throw new Exception("Cannot parse card data");
            }

            start += tempString.Length+1;
            tempString =
                TokenizeString(dataString,start,'|');
            if (tempString.Length > 0)
            {
                amount = Convert.ToDouble(tempString);
            }
            else
            {
                throw new Exception("Cannot parse card data");
            }

            decryptionStream.Close();
            streamInMemory.Close();
        }

        public virtual void GetObjectData(
            SerializationInfo info,
            StreamingContext context)
```

Listing 12.6 A Version of The `IFasterChargeVerifier` Interface and Its Associated Objects with Encryption Added *(continues)*

```
        {
            string tempString = cardNumber.ToString();
            tempString += '|' + nameOnCard;
            tempString += '|' + expirationDate.ToString();
            tempString += '|' + amount.ToString();

            // Do not use this key in your application!
            byte[] cryptoKey =
                {
                    0x01, 0x02, 0x03, 0x04, 0x05, 0x06, 0x07,
                    0x08, 0x09, 0x10, 0x11, 0x12, 0x13, 0x14,
                    0x15, 0x16
                };

            // Do not use this init vector in your application!
            byte[] initializationVector =
                {
                    0x01, 0x02, 0x03, 0x04, 0x05, 0x06, 0x07,
                    0x08, 0x09, 0x10, 0x11, 0x12, 0x13, 0x14,
                    0x15, 0x16
                };

            MemoryStream streamInMemory = new MemoryStream();
            RijndaelManaged cryptographer = new RijndaelManaged();

            CryptoStream encryptedStream =
                new CryptoStream(
                    streamInMemory,
                    cryptographer.CreateEncryptor(
                        cryptoKey,
                        initializationVector),
                    CryptoStreamMode.Write);

            byte [] tempBuffer =
                StringToByteArray(tempString);

            encryptedStream.Write(
                tempBuffer,
                0,
                tempBuffer.Length);

            byte [] dataBuffer =
                streamInMemory.GetBuffer();

            EncryptedData dataObject =
                new EncryptedData(
                    dataBuffer.Length,
```

Listing 12.6 A Version of The `IFasterChargeVerifier` Interface and Its Associated Objects with Encryption Added *(continued)*

```
                    dataBuffer);

                info.AddValue(
                    "dataBuffer",
                    dataObject,
                    typeof(EncryptedData));

                encryptedStream.Close();
                streamInMemory.Close();
            }

            public VerificationRequest(
                int cardIDNumber,
                string cardHolderName,
                DateTime cardExpirationDate,
                double amount)
            {
                cardNumber = cardIDNumber;
                nameOnCard = cardHolderName;
                expirationDate = cardExpirationDate;
            }

            public long CardIDNumber
            {
                get
                {
                    return (cardNumber);
                }
                set
                {
                    cardNumber = value;
                }
            }

            public string CardHolderName
            {
                get
                {
                    return (nameOnCard);
                }
                set
                {
                    nameOnCard = value;
                }
            }

            public DateTime CardExpirationDate
```

Listing 12.6 A Version of The `IFasterChargeVerifier` Interface and Its Associated Objects with Encryption Added *(continues)*

```
        {
            get
            {
                return (expirationDate);
            }
            set
            {
                expirationDate = value;
            }
        }

        public double ChargeAmount
        {
            get
            {
                return amount;
            }
            set
            {
                amount = value;
            }
        }

        private byte [] StringToByteArray(string inputString)
        {
            int length = inputString.Length;
            byte [] tempArray =
                new byte [length+1];

            for (int i=0; i<inputString.Length; i++)
            {
                tempArray[i] = (byte)inputString[i];
            }
            tempArray[length] = 0;

            return (tempArray);
        }

        private string TokenizeString(
            string sourceString,
            int start,
            char separator)
        {
            int length = sourceString.Length;
            string tempString = null;

            for (int i=start;
```

Listing 12.6 A Version of The `IFasterChargeVerifier` Interface and Its Associated Objects with Encryption Added *(continued)*

```
341                     (i<length) && (sourceString[i]!=separator);
342                     i++)
343                 {
344                     tempString+=sourceString[i];
345                 }
346 
347                 return (tempString);
348             }
349         }
350 
351         Lines 351- omitted to save space.
```

Listing 12.6 A Version of The `IFasterChargeVerifier` Interface and Its Associated Objects with Encryption Added *(continued)*

The code for the `ChargeConfirmation` object and the `IFaster-Charge-` Verifier interface are unchanged from Listing 12.5. Therefore, I have omitted the code for them from Listing 12.6.

The Microsoft .NET Framework provides an API that performs cryptography. This API is defined in the `System.Security.Cryptography` namespace. When you use the cryptography API, be sure to put a `using` statement specifying the `System.Security.Cryptography` namespace into your program as shown on line 4 of Listing 12.6.

The new version of the `VerificationRequest` object differs considerably from the version in Listing 12.5. In particular, the `VerificationRequest` object contains a private class called `EncryptedData`. The `EncryptedData` object has two private members. The first is an integer indicating the length of the data buffer. The second is the data buffer itself. When the `EncryptedData` object encrypts and serializes the data from the `VerificationRequest` object, it stores the encrypted data in a `dataBuffer`. It then transmits the `EncryptedData` object across the network.

Using the style implementation has two advantages. First, it simplifies the process of encrypting and decrypting the data. Second, it hides the structure of the data as the data is transmitted across the network. Because the `EncryptedData` object gets transmitted across the network instead of the `VerificationRequest` object, the structure of the `VerificationRequest` object is known only by the client and the server programs. Anyone who is able to intercept the encrypted verification request only sees an object that contains a buffer of encrypted data and the buffer's length. There's nothing that indicates the names or types of the encrypted data.

The `EncryptedData` class contains two constructors followed by a property accessor methods called `Length()` that returns the length of the data buffer. On lines 45-51, it provides a property accessor method for getting the data buffer. In addition, it provides access to individual bytes of data through a pair of methods called `DataByte()`.

The methods for the `VerificationRequest` class begin on line 84. If we look at line 197, we'll see the beginning of the `GetObjectData()` method. Recall that this is where the `VerificationRequest` object performs its custom serialization. The `GetObjectData`() method begins by concatenating all of its data into a single string on lines 201-204. It then defines two byte arrays. The first holds encryption key and the second contains the initialization vector. These are required to encrypt data.

WARNING

As the comments on lines 206 and 214 indicate, you should not use the encryption key and initialization vector shown in this example in your programs.

Microsoft's cryptography API classes operate on data streams. Often, data streams read information from or write information to files on disks. In this case, however, we want to store the encrypted information in a data buffer. Therefore, the `GetObjectData()` method creates a `MemoryStream` object and connects the MemoryStream object to the data buffer. When the `GetObjectData()` method writes encrypted information to the MemoryStream object, the `MemoryStream` object stores that information in the data buffer. The `GetObjectData()` method creates the `MemoryStream` object on line 222.

One line 223, the `GetObjectData()` method allocates an object that implements an encryption algorithm. The cryptography API contains several such objects, and any of them could have been used in the place of the `RijndaelManaged` object shown here.

On lines 225-231, the `GetObjectData()` method uses the `Memory Stream` object and the encryption object to create an encryption stream. It converts the string containing the unencrypted data into an array of bytes on lines 233-234. It then writes that array of bytes to the encryption stream on lines 236-239. The encryption stream encrypts the data and writes it to the `MemoryStream`. The `MemoryStream`, in turn, stores the data into a data buffer. On lines 241-242, the GetObjectData()

method retrieves the data buffer from the `MemoryStream` object. It creates an `EncryptedData` object on lines 244-247. When it does, it passes the data buffer and the data buffer's length to the `EncryptedData` constructor. The `GetObjectData()` method then calls the `AddValue()` method to serialize the `EncryptedData` object. It finishes by closing the streams it used.

When a `VerificationRequest` object is deserialized, the .NET Remoting Framework calls the constructor that begins on line 91. The tasks that the constructor must perform occur in essentially the reverse order of those in the `GetObjectData()` method. It must first deserialize the encrypted information. Next, the constructor has to decrypt the data and store it into a `VerificationRequest` object.

The `VerificationRequest` constructor deserializes the encrypted data on lines 95-98. On lines 100-101, it stores the encrypted information into a buffer of bytes. The constructor connects the buffer of bytes to a `MemoryStream` object on lines 103-104. It then creates an object from the cryptography API that implements the same algorithm that was used to encrypt data.

To decrypt the data, the constructor requires the same encryption key and initialization vector that were used to encrypt the data. These appear on lines 109-122. On lines 124-130, the constructor creates an input stream that it can use to decrypt the data. It allocates a buffer for the decrypted data on lines 132-133.

The constructor decrypts the data by simply reading from the decryption stream on lines 135-138. It converts the decrypted data to a string on lines 140-144. On lines 146-147, the constructor calls the `TokenizeString()` method. The `TokenizeString()` method is a private member of the `VerificationRequest` class. Its source code begins on line 332.

The `TokenizeString()` method parses a string by searching for the character specified in its `separator` parameter. When it finds the separator character, it extracts all of the characters from the starting point indicated by the `start` parameter up to the separator character. It stores these characters in a string and returns the string to the calling method.

When the `VerificationRequest` constructor calls the `TokenizeString()` method on lines 146-147, it searches for the first occurrence of the `'|'` character. This character was inserted between each data item at the beginning of the `GetObjectData()` method. If it is able to extract the first data item, the constructor converts that string into a 64-bit integer and stores the results in the `VerificationRequest` class's `cardNumber` data member. It follows the same procedure to parse the remaining data items. Before it ends, the constructor closes the streams it uses on lines 193-194.

Encryption Through Custom Channel Sinks

Another way to perform custom encryption is to create channel sink that uses the Cryptography API to encrypt all information exchanged between clients and servers. Custom channel sinks are presented in Chapter 13. Usually, you do not have to write this kind of channel sink yourself. You can obtain source code for encryption sinks on the Internet. If these do not meet your needs, you can purchase encryption sinks commercially.

A custom encryption sink, if it is well-written, can provide you with security levels comparable to IPSec. Applications can use them over HTTP. Data sent to and from callback functions is secure because the callbacks use the channel that includes the encryption sink.

User Authentication and Authorization

Using tools such as strong assembly names, Authenticode signatures, and so forth, helps to secure your distributed application by running authorized code. Using secure communication channels or encrypting data provides additional security by protecting the privacy of data. However, these measures alone do not make applications secure. You must also ensure that your application is being run by an authorized user in an authorized manner. Doing so involves two key security concepts, **authentication** and **authorization**.

When software performs authentication, it validates the user's identity. Ideally, it ensures that no unauthorized user can access the software. Authorization, on the other hand, defines the tasks an authenticated user can perform on a computer or network.

Fortunately (at least for developers), the task of authorization falls primarily to system administrators. Network administrators follow company policy in authorizing what users can and cannot do on a network. This aspect of authorization seldom requires coding on your part.

NOTE

Sometimes the code in a remote object must run with the credentials of the user to keep the applications secure. In such case, your object might have to use impersonation. When a remote object impersonates the credentials of the user, it runs code and accesses resources as if it were the user. Impersonation in this context is not a bad thing. In fact, it helps you prevent users from gaining unauthorized access to code and resources by executing remote objects that have a higher authorization level than the level assigned to the users' accounts.

User authentication can be performed by the operating system. Your application can also require a user logon so that it can perform authentication. In addition, your application can use a method of third-party authentication.

System-Level Authentication

Operating systems performs system-level authentication every time a user logs on. Your application can also take advantage of several different levels of user authentication if your remote objects are hosted in IIS.

The simplest and least secure method of user authentication is called basic authentication. It transmits a user's name and password as an encoded string in plaintext. It's important to emphasize here that the string is encoded and not encrypted. Applications that use basic authentication should not be considered secure.

To achieve greater security, applications can use basic authentication over SSL. This form of authentication transmits user names and passwords over a secure socket layer connection. This means that user names and passwords are encrypted before they are sent over the network. Although basic authentication over SSL requires more system overhead than does basic authentication, it is generally overhead that is well spent.

When deploying your distributed application to the Internet, it is wise to consider using digest authentication. Digest authentication transmits user credentials in a hashed form. Because the user credentials are transmitted as text, this form of authentication works well through proxy servers and firewalls. Currently, digest authentication is not widely supported on operating systems other than Windows. If you use it, you may be limiting your deployment to computers running Windows.

There are also security providers built directly into Microsoft Windows. You can use the security providers to perform user authentication. The most common security providers are NTLM and Kerberos. You do not need to add code to applications to take advantage of integrated Windows security providers. It's done by configuring IIS on the servers hosting your remote objects.

Application-Level Authentication

Applications sometimes perform their own user authentication. This can be handled a number of ways. First, your application can require the user to provide a user name and password before it will connect to remote objects. The client should encrypt the login information before it sends the information across the network. Once the distributed application has authorized user, it can allow the client to connect to and invoke methods on remote objects.

In a more secure scenario, the server can issue a session identifier that both the client and server include in the messages they send to each other. To improve security even further, the session key should be encrypted before it is transmitted over the network. Using this technique, the client is authenticated until the user logs off.

Security can be improved even further by attaching an expiration time to the session identifier. The session identifier and its expiration time together are referred to as a session key. When the session key expires, the server can send a message to the client asking it to resend the user's credentials. When the server validates the user's credentials, it transmits a new session key. Typically, this transaction is handled in an asynchronous callback function or in a custom channel sink.

Third-Party Authentication

Your application can rely on certain trusted third parties to validate your users' identities. For example, you can require them to have certificates that they obtain from agencies such as VeriSign. In this scenario, the users' certificates would probably be stored on a configuration file on their computers. Your client program would read the configuration file and transmit the user's certificate before being allowed to connect to remote objects.

Unfortunately, obtaining certificates can be a big hassle for users. A simpler method of third-party authentication can be achieved through the use of smartcards. A smartcard is a plastic card the size and shape of a credit card. It has a microchip embedded inside it that contains the user's identification information. When the user starts your client program, the client can insist that the user insert a smartcard into a reader attached to the computer. If the information from the smartcard is not provided, the application will not run.

Because the expense involved, third-party authentication is generally only used by large organizations. However, third-party authentication can be a very effective means for large organizations to keep distributed applications secure. This is especially true if the organization uses smartcards.

CAVEAT

There are only two provisos that need to be observed when using smartcards. First, the cards must be issued by a trusted entity. It does not matter whether the entity is inside or outside the company as long as it is trusted. Second, the cards must be passed to the user in a secure way. This generally means that they should not be sent through the regular mail. At the very least, they should be sent by registered mail. Preferably, they should be handed to the user by the trusted entity's representative after the representative has seen the user's photo ID.

Summary

Security is a complex topic that involves many aspects of development and deployment. To have a secure distributed application, you generally must secure the physical environment of the server. You may also need to secure the client's environment. You must ensure that the application is running authorized code and performing authorized tasks by authenticated and authorized users.

There are number of tools available to help ensure the identity of your distributed application's code. Among these are strong assembly names, Signcode signatures, Authenticode signatures, and custom certificates.

Secure application use often involves communicating through secure channels, encrypting data sent over unsecured channels, and performing user authentication and authorization.

The most common secure channels are IPSec and HTTPS. In small deployments, you can also use virtual private networks over PPTP. However, after many years of experience with this technique, I recommend against it. For Internet deployments, HTTPS is by far the best choice of secure channels.

If your application must communicate over unsecure channels, it is wise to encrypt sensitive information sent between clients and servers. You can do this on an object-by-object basis using custom serialization. To encrypt all traffic passed between a client and a server, consider using a custom channel sink.

The two main categories of encryption are symmetric and asymmetric encryption. Under symmetric encryption, both the client and server use the same encryption key. The encryption key must be kept private. With asymmetric encryption, clients and servers use a public key to encrypt messages that they transmit. They use a private key to decrypt messages that they receive.

To ensure that applications are being run by authorized users, distributed applications should employ some means of user authentication and authorization. Authorization is typically done by system administrators. Authentication can be performed by the operating system, by the application itself, or by a trusted third party.

CHAPTER 13

Message Sinks and Message Chains

The chapters thus far have demonstrated how to use .NET Remoting without delving too much into the underlying mechanics of how it works. That's one of the nice features of .NET Remoting. You can do a lot with it without having to dive down into the "guts" of the system, so to speak.

If, however, you want to be able to extend .NET Remoting, you need a thorough understanding of the underlying components and how they work together. There are several reasons why you might want to be able to extend .NET Remoting or modify its default behavior. Among them are:

- **Security**. The extensibility of .NET Remoting enables you to implement your own security measures, such as encrypting all traffic between the client and the server. You can also create channels that negotiate security providers (KERBEROS, NTLM, and so forth) before transmitting messages between clients and servers.
- **Data compression**. With an understanding of the underlying components of .NET Remoting, you can add special components that compress data that gets sent over slow communications links, such as phone lines.

- **Debugging**. Extending .NET Remoting can enable you to add debugging code to your application that logs all traffic between clients and servers.
- **Custom transports**. You are not limited to using the HTTP and TCP channels. If you need to, you can add other types of channels to .NET Remoting. These can include POP3, MSMQ, and SMTP.
- **Out-of-band data.** Your channels can add additional data to messages. For example, they can send custom security identifiers and credentials, transmit the priority of the client's process so the server object can be executed at the same priority level, and so forth.

This chapter examines some of the internals of .NET Remoting and explains how it can be customized. In particular, it presents a more detailed view of the process of calling remote objects' methods and passing data to them. It also demonstrates ways you and I can customize the channels that clients and servers use to communicate.

Proxies, Messages, and Message Sinks

To understand the internals of .NET Remoting, let's begin on the client with proxies. Whenever your client program calls a method on a remote object, the program really invokes a method in a proxy. The proxy translates that call, and any data that goes with it, into a message. A message is an object that implements the `IMesage` interface. The .Net Framework provides several different types of message objects. These include the `MessageCall`, `MessageResponse`, and `ConstructionCall` classes, among others. They are all found in the `System.Runtime.Remoting.Messaging` namespace.

The proxy sends the message to one or more **message sinks**. Message sinks are objects that receive messages and perform processing on them. A message sink implements either the `IClientChannelSink` or IServerChannelSink interface. Message sinks can be connected together into chains. Each sink in the chain performs its own unique processing on the message and passes the message to the next sink in the chain. Message **sink chains** provide a lot of the power of the .Net Remoting. In fact, channels are actually implemented as message sink chains.

A client channel creates its message sinks when the client acquires a reference to the remote object. The server channel, on the other hand, creates its sinks as soon as the channel itself is registered.

A Detailed Look at Channels

Figure 13.1 shows that when a method in the client process invokes a remote object's method, the proxy translates the call into a call message. The call message is then forwarded to the channel. Back in Chapter 2, Figure 2.7 showed, for simplicity, that the message was forwarded to a formatter and then into a channel. In actuality, a channel is an abstract concept that represents a complex sequence of processing. The formatter itself is part of the channel.

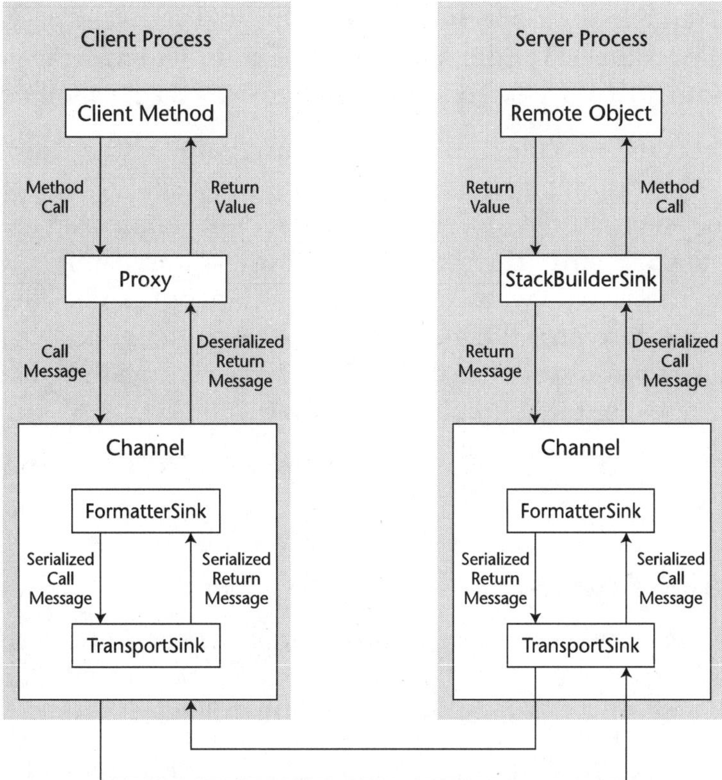

Figure 13.1 Calling a Remote Method

When a message arrives at the client channel, the .Net Remoting system sends the message to the formatter. Because the formatter is a type of message sink, it is called a **formatter sink**. The .Net Remoting system passes the message to the formatter sink by calling the `IMessageSink.SyncProcessMessage()` method (for synchronous calls) or the `IMessageSink.AyncProcessMessage()` method (for asynchronous calls). The formatter sink serializes the message using the specified channel format type. As explained in previous chapters, the Microsoft .NET Remoting system currently provides SOAP and binary formatter sinks.

The message is then sent to a special type of sink called a **transport sink**. Transport sinks send messages across the network to remote server objects. The channel that the remote object listens to is also a message sink chain. The first sink in its chain is the remote server object's transport sink. The server object's transport sink receives the message and sends it to the formatter sink. The formatter sink deserializes the message and sends it to a special type of sink that appears only on the server, called a **StackBuilder** sink. The StackBuilder sink translates the message into an invocation of one of the remote object's methods.

After the method executes, it sends its return value to the StackBuilder sink. The StackBuilder sink packages the return value as a message and sends it to the formatter sink. The formatter sink serializes it and sends it to the transport sink. The server's transport sink transmits the return message across the network to the client's transport sink. The client's transport sink forwards the message to the formatter sink, which deserializes it and passes it to the proxy. The proxy returns the value to the method in the client that invoked the remote method.

The entire collection of sinks in a channel is called the **channel sink chain.**

Customizing Sink Chains

There are two spots in the channel sink chain where you can add your own custom message sinks. The first is before the formatter sink. The second is between the formatter sink and the transport sink.

Custom message sinks that you add before the formatter sink are also called formatter sinks because they implement the `IClientFormatterSink` interface. The `IClientFormatterSink` interface is a combination of the `IMessageSink` and the `IClientChannelSink` interfaces. The binary formatter and the SOAP formatter both implement the `IClientFormatterSink` interface.

WARNING

Message sinks must not throw exceptions. Therefore, most of your sinks' code should be placed in `try-catch` blocks. The catch blocks can set error status variables, but they should not allow the exception to be propagated beyond the class that implements the sink.

Custom formatter sinks can process messages in virtually any way that you see fit. In fact, it is possible for a custom formatter sink to transmit several messages of its own before it forwards the message it received from the chain. Your custom formatter sink might use this technique if you want it to negotiate the server's security provider. After the negotiations are complete, your custom formatter sink forwards the original message and then becomes inactive.

NOTE

What you are essentially doing when you create your own formatter sink is fooling the .NET Remoting system into thinking that your custom formatter sink is the default formatter sink provided by the system.

Your custom formatter sink must perform its processing, and then use the `IClientFormatterSink` interface's `NextSink` property to get the next sink in the chain and invoke its message processing method. Typically, the last formatter sink in the chain is either the binary formatter sink or the SOAP the formatter sink. These sinks serialize the message after your custom formatter sinks perform their processing.

The last formatter sink on the client also translates the method call into a serialized message, which is just an object that implements the `IMessage` interface. The serialized message is also called a stream. The stream is passed to the transport sink, and the transport sink sends it across the network.

If you insert one or more custom sinks between the formatter sink and the transport sink, the stream goes to your chain of custom sinks instead of the transport sink. Channel sinks between the formatter sink and the transport sink can read from the stream but cannot write to it. However, they can replace it with a stream that they create. This enables them to perform virtually any processing on the stream.

Channel sinks that you insert between the formatter and the transport sinks must implement the `IClientChannelSink` or `IServerChannelSink` interface. Microsoft provides an abstract base class in the .NET Framework called `BaseChannelSinkWithProperties`. You can use this base class to more easily implement your custom channel sinks.

On the client, the transport sink is last in the channel's sink chain. However, on the server side, the transport sink is first. The transport sink on the server calls the `SyncProcessMessage()` or `AsyncProcessMessage()` method on the next sink in the chain. When it does, it passes a parameter of type `ServerChannelSinkStack`. This parameter is the server's stack builder sink. All custom sinks that you insert occur between the transport sink and the formatter sink. Each of your custom channel sinks must push itself onto the stack builder sink chain before calling the `SyncProcessMessage()` or `AsyncProcessMessage()` method on the next sink in the chain. When it does call the `SyncProcessMessage()` or `AsyncProcessMessage()` method, it must pass the server's stack builder sink chain to the next sink in the chain.

The server uses its stack builder sink as its mechanism for handling both synchronous and asynchronous calls. All custom sinks that push themselves on to the server's stack builder sink will be called to process the incoming message. This may occur right away, in the case of a synchronous call, but may occur later in the case of an asynchronous call.

Sink Providers

Applications do not instantiate channel sinks. Instead, they pass channel sink providers to the .NET Remoting system. The .NET Remoting system uses the sink providers to create the individual channel sinks. You can think of channel sink providers as factory objects that create channel sinks. If you make custom channel sinks, you must also write providers for your sinks. All channel sink providers must implement the `IClientChannelSinkProvider`, `IClientFormatterSinkProvider`, or `IServerChannelSinkProvider` interface. The channel sinks must link themselves into a chain. The providers themselves must also be in a chain.

When a remote object is first activated, the object's channel calls the `IClientChannelSinkProvider.CreateSink()` method on the first sink provider in the chain of sink providers. The first channel sink provider creates its channel sink, and then calls `CreateSink()` on the next channel sink provider in the chain. Each successive provider must repeat this process until the end of the chain is reached. Every channel sink provider must ensure that its channel sink is linked to the next sink. The provider must also return its sink as the return value of the CreateSink() method.

WARNING

If, for any reason, the sink provider cannot create its sink, the provider should return null as the return value of the `CreateSink()` method. This causes sink creation to be terminated and an exception to be thrown by the .NET Remoting system.

As stated previously, the transport sink must be the final sink in the client channel's sink chain. The .NET Remoting system creates the transport sink and passes it as a parameter to the first sink provider in the chain. Each subsequent sink provider must pass the transport sink to the next provider in the chain until the last provider is reached. After the final provider creates its channel sink, it must link the transport sink as the final sink in the chain.

This is not necessary on the server. The transport sink is the first sink in the server channel's chain. All channel sinks are linked in after the transport sink. Therefore, the CreateSink() method on the server has one less parameter than the CreateSink() method on the client.

Custom Message Sinks

Implementing custom message sinks can be a daunting task when you first approach it. It does not help that the Microsoft documentation is sometimes vague and not always accurate on this subject. In addition, custom message sinks are not easy to debug. To develop a complex message sink, you will occasionally have to delve down into the undocumented portions of the .NET Remoting system to find out what's wrong. Good luck.

The process of creating custom message sinks is slightly different on the client than it is on the server. So let's first see how it's done in the client. After we have that up and working, we'll implement a custom sink on the server.

Client-Side Sinks

Creating a channel sink on the client requires that you write both the sink and its provider. To get your client to use the sink, you must add information about it into the client's configuration file. The configuration file should contain the `<clientProviders>` element inside its `<channel>` element. The `<clientProviders>` element, in turn, contains the `<provider>` and `<formatter>` elements. Listing 13.1 shows a sample configuration file for a client that uses a custom sink.

```
1      <configuration>
2          <system.runtime.remoting>
3              <application>
4                  <channels>
5                      <channel ref="http" port="0">
6                          <clientProviders>
7                              <provider
8                  type="NamespaceName.SinkProviderName, DLLorProgName"/>
9                              <formatter ref="soap" />
10                         </clientProviders>
11                     </channel>
12                 </channels>
13             </application>
14         </system.runtime.remoting>
15     </configuration>
```

Listing 13.1 A Generic Configuration File for Using a Client Channel Sink

The configuration file in Listing 13.1 specifies the custom sink's provider on lines 7-8. As in some of the examples in previous chapters, I had to use odd indentation on line 8 because of the width limitations of the printed page. The `<clientProviders>` element can contain one or more `<provider>` elements. There should be one `<provider>` element for each custom sink provider your program adds to the chain. As the sample configuration file demonstrates, the `<provider>` element specifies the name of the channel sink provider through its type attribute. If the provider is not specified, the .NET Framework will not instantiate it.

WARNING

Despite what the Microsoft documentation says, order *does* matter in configuration files when you are creating custom message sinks. Specifically, the `<formatter>` element must come *after* `<provider>` element. If it does not, the .NET Framework will not call the sink provider's `Next()` method properly. It will never call `CreateSink()`.

Note that the generic configuration file in Listing 13.1 specifies an HTTP channel with the SOAP formatter. However, you can also use the TCP channel or a binary formatter (Listing 13.2).

```
1     <configuration>
2         <system.runtime.remoting>
3             <application>
4                 <channels>
5                     <channel ref="http" port="0">
6                         <clientProviders>
7                             <provider
8     type="MessageCountChannelSink.MessageCountSinkProvider, Client"/>
9                             <formatter ref="soap" />
10                        </clientProviders>
11                    </channel>
12                </channels>
13                <client>
14                    <wellknown
15     type="InfoMan.InformationManager, InfoManMetaData"
16                        url="http://localhost:8080/InfoMan.soap" />
17                </client>
18            </application>
19        </system.runtime.remoting>
20    </configuration>
```

Listing 13.2 The Client Configuration File for the Custom Channel Sink Application

For the sample program, we'll create an information manager object like those in examples in previous chapters. The client's configuration file tells the .NET Remoting system this on lines 14-16. Lines 7-8 tell it to instantiate an instance of the sink provider for the custom sink. The provider, in turn, creates the custom sink.

Listing 13.3 repeats the information manager's source code here for your convenience.

```
using System;

namespace InfoMan
{
    public class InformationManager : MarshalByRefObject
    {
        private const int ARRAY_SIZE = 20;
```

Listing 13.3 The Information Manager Object *(continues)*

```
        private string [] theData = new string [ARRAY_SIZE];

        public InformationManager()
        {
            // Initialize the array.
            theData[0] = "`Oh, THIS,' began Filby, `is all--'";
            theData[1] =  "`Why not?' said the Time Traveller.";
            theData[2] = "`It's against reason,' said Filby.";
            theData[3] = "`What reason?' said the Time Traveller.";
            theData[4] = "`You can show black is white ";
            theData[5] = "by argument,' said Filby, `but you ";
            theData[6] = "will never convince me.'";
            theData[7] = "`Possibly not,' said the Time Traveller.";
            theData[8] = "`But now you begin to see the object ";
            theData[9] = "of my investigations into the geometry ";
            theData[10] = "of Four Dimensions.  Long ago I had a";
            theData[11] = "vague inkling of a machine--'";
            theData[12] = "`To travel through Time!' exclaimed ";
            theData[13] = "the Very Young Man.";
            theData[14] = "`That shall travel indifferently in any";
            theData[15] = "`direction of Space and Time, as ";
            theData[16] = "the driver determines.'";
            theData[17] = "Filby contented himself with laughter.";
            theData[18] = "`But I have experimental verification,'";
             theData[19] = "said the Time Traveller.";
        }

        public string DataItem(int whichItem)
        {
            string theItem = null;

            // If the item number is valid...
            if ((whichItem >= 0) && (whichItem < ARRAY_SIZE))
            {
                // Get the item.
                theItem = theData[whichItem];
            }

            // Return the item to the client.
            return (theItem);
        }

        public void DataItem(
            int whichItem,
            string newValue)
```

Listing 13.3 The Information Manager Object

```
        {
            // If the item number is valid...
            if ((whichItem >= 0) && (whichItem < ARRAY_SIZE))
            {
                // Set the item.
                theData[whichItem] = newValue;
            }
        }

        public int DataCollectionLength()
        {
            return (ARRAY_SIZE);
        }
    }
}
```

Listing 13.3 The Information Manager Object *(continued)*

This listing demonstrates that programs that use custom channel sinks do not have to alter the remote objects they provide. The channel sinks are independent of the application's objects. The server program and its configuration file are also unchanged from examples in previous chapters. Listing 13.4 and 13.5 show the server program and its configuration file, respectively.

```
using System;
using System.Runtime.Remoting;
using System.Runtime.Remoting.Channels;
using System.Runtime.Remoting.Channels.Http;
using InfoMan;

namespace Server
{
    class ServerAppClass
    {
        [STAThread]
        static void Main(string[] args)
        {
            RemotingConfiguration.Configure("Server.exe.config");
```

Listing 13.4 The Server Program for the Custom Channel Sink Application *(continues)*

```
                System.Console.WriteLine(
                    "Press Enter to end the InformationManager.");
                System.Console.Read();
            }
        }
    }
```

Listing 13.4 The Server Program for the Custom Channel Sink Application *(continued)*

```
<configuration>
    <system.runtime.remoting>
        <application>
            <channels>
                <channel ref="http" port="8080"/>
            </channels>
            <service>
                <wellknown
                    mode="Singleton"
                    type="InfoMan.InformationManager, InfoMan"
                    objectUri = "InfoMan.soap" />
            </service>
        </application>
    </system.runtime.remoting>
</configuration>
```

Listing 13.5 The Server's Configuration File

A client program that uses custom channel sinks does require some changes. However, these changes do not have to occur in the client's application class. You can put them into a separate namespace in a different file. In fact, I recommend that you do so. This helps you if you are creating custom sinks for both the client and the server. It's a good idea to put the custom sinks, with their providers, in a single file that you compile into an assembly. The project files for the client and the server both reference this assembly. We'll use this style of file organization for the examples in this chapter. Therefore, the unchanged client application class occurs in a file by itself. This file is shown in Listing 13.6.

```
using System;
using System.Runtime.Remoting;
using System.Runtime.Remoting.Channels;
using System.Runtime.Remoting.Channels.Http;
using InfoMan;

namespace Client
{
    class ClientAppClass
    {
        [STAThread]
        static void Main(string[] args)
        {
            RemotingConfiguration.Configure("client.exe.config");

            InformationManager infoManager =
                new InformationManager();

            // If the remote object was activated...
            if (infoManager != null)
            {
                string tempString;
                int dataCollectionLength;

                try
                {
                    dataCollectionLength =
                        infoManager.DataCollectionLength();

                    // Print the data.
                    for (int i=0; i<dataCollectionLength; i++)
                    {
                        tempString = null;

                        // Get the item.
                        tempString = infoManager.DataItem(i);

                        // Print it to the console.
                        System.Console.WriteLine(tempString);
                    }
                }
                catch (Exception theException)
                {
                    ServerAccessError(theException.ToString());
                }
            }
```

Listing 13.6 The Client Program's Application Class *(continues)*

```
                // Else the remote object was not activated...
            else
            {
                // Print an error message.
                ServerAccessError(
                    "Remote object could not be activated");
            }

            System.Console.WriteLine(
                "\nPaused. Press Enter to continue...");
            System.Console.Read();
        }

        static void ServerAccessError(string errorMessage)
        {
            System.Console.WriteLine(
                "{0}",
                errorMessage);
        }
    }
}
```

Listing 13.6 The Client Program's Application Class *(continued)*

The file in Listing 13.6 can be complied into a program. However, the program's Visual Studio project file must contain a reference to the assembly that holds the implementation of the custom channel sink and its provider. Listing 13.7 gives their source code.

```
using System;
using System.Runtime.Remoting;
using System.Runtime.Remoting.Channels;
using System.Runtime.Remoting.Messaging;
using System.IO;
using System.Collections;


namespace MessageCountChannelSink
{
    class ClientMessageCountChannelSink :
        BaseChannelSinkWithProperties,
        IMessageSink,
```

Listing 13.7 The Client's Custom Channel Sink and Its Provider

```
        IClientChannelSink
    {
        private IClientChannelSink nextSink;
        private IMessageSink nextMessageSink;

        int totalMessages=0;


        public ClientMessageCountChannelSink(
            object nextSinkInChain)
        {
            nextSink =
                nextSinkInChain as IClientChannelSink;
            nextMessageSink =
                nextSinkInChain as IMessageSink;
        }

        public IMessageSink NextSink
        {
            get
            {
                return (nextMessageSink);
            }
        }

        public IMessageCtrl AsyncProcessMessage(
            IMessage theMessage,
            IMessageSink replySink)
        {
            this.CountMessage();

            return (nextMessageSink.AsyncProcessMessage(
                        theMessage,replySink));
        }

        public IMessage SyncProcessMessage(
            IMessage theMessage)
        {
            this.CountMessage();

            return (
                nextMessageSink.SyncProcessMessage(theMessage));
        }

        public IClientChannelSink NextChannelSink
        {
            get
            {
```

Listing 13.7 The Client's Custom Channel Sink and Its Provider *(continues)*

```
                return (nextSink);
            }
        }

        public void AsyncProcessRequest(
            IClientChannelSinkStack sinkStack,
            IMessage msg,
            ITransportHeaders headers,
            Stream stream)
        {
            sinkStack.Push(this,null);
            nextSink.AsyncProcessRequest(
                sinkStack,
                msg,
                headers,
                stream);
        }

        public void AsyncProcessResponse(
            IClientResponseChannelSinkStack sinkStack,
            object state,
            ITransportHeaders headers,
            Stream stream)
        {
            sinkStack.AsyncProcessResponse(
                headers,stream);
        }

        public Stream GetRequestStream(
            IMessage msg,
            ITransportHeaders headers)
        {
            return (nextSink.GetRequestStream(
                msg,headers));
        }

        public void ProcessMessage(
            IMessage msg,
            ITransportHeaders requestHeaders,
            Stream requestStream,
            out ITransportHeaders responseHeaders,
            out Stream responseStream)
        {
            this.CountMessage();

            nextSink.ProcessMessage(
                msg,
                requestHeaders,
```

Listing 13.7 The Client's Custom Channel Sink and Its Provider

```
                requestStream,
                out responseHeaders,
                out responseStream);
        }

        public void CountMessage()
        {
            try
            {
                System.Console.WriteLine(++totalMessages);
            }
            catch (Exception)
            {
            }
        }
    }

    class MessageCountSinkProvider :
        IClientChannelSinkProvider
    {
        private IClientChannelSinkProvider nextProvider = null;

        // Although this constructor currently does nothing,
        // it is required by the remoting system if you use
        // a configuration file to instantiate your channel
        // sink provider and channel sink.
        public MessageCountSinkProvider(
            IDictionary properties,
            ICollection providerData)
        {
        }

        public IClientChannelSinkProvider Next
        {
            get
            {
                return (nextProvider);
            }
            set
            {
                nextProvider = value;
            }
        }

        public IClientChannelSink CreateSink(
            IChannelSender channel,
            string url,
            object remoteChannelData)
```

Listing 13.7 The Client's Custom Channel Sink and Its Provider *(continues)*

```
158         {
159             ClientMessageCountChannelSink messageCountSink = null;
160 
161             IClientChannelSink sinkChain =
162                 nextProvider.CreateSink(
163                 channel,
164                 url,
165                 remoteChannelData);
166             try
167             {
168                 messageCountSink =
169                     new ClientMessageCountChannelSink(sinkChain);
170             }
171             catch (Exception)
172             {
173             }
174 
175             return (messageCountSink);
176         }
177     }
178 }
```

Listing 13.7 The Client's Custom Channel Sink and Its Provider *(continued)*

The custom channel sink in Listing 13.7 counts the messages the client sends. After specifying the namespaces it uses, the file defines the `MessageCountChannelSink` namespace to hold the channel sink and its provider.

The `ClientMessageCountChannelSink` class begins on line 11. It inherits from the `BaseChannelSinkWithProperties` class. As mentioned previously, Microsoft provides the `BaseChannelSinkWithProperties` class to help make implementing custom channel sinks easier. The `ClientMessageCountChannelSink` class also implements the `IMessageSink` and `IClientChannelSink` interfaces. All custom channel sinks in the client program must implement `IClientChannelSink`. If a custom sink occurs first in the chain, it must also implement `IMessageSink`.

To easily access the sink chain in the formats it needs, the ClientMessageCountChannelSink class declares two private data members. The first stores the sink chain as a reference to an IClientChannelSink interface. The second stores it as a reference to an IMessageSink interface. In addition, the class declares a private data member used to count the messages sent through the channel.

The constructor for the `ClientMessageCountChannelSink` class has one parameter. The parameter is a reference to the next sink in the chain. It uses the C# `as` keyword to cast the parameter as a reference to an `IClientChannelSink` interface on lines 25-26. On lines 27-28, the constructor casts the parameter as a reference to an `IMessageSink` interface.

NOTE

For those new to C#, the `as` keyword in this context performs essentially the same function as a type cast in C or C++.

To implement the `IMessageSink` interface, the `ClientMessageCountChannelSink` class defines the `NextSink()` method. This method uses the private data member `nextMessageSink` to return the sink chain as a reference to an `IMessage` interface.

On lines 39-47, the `ClientMessageCountChannelSink` class provides an implementation of the `AsyncProcessMessage()` method. This method gets called when the channel sink processes an asynchronous message. It uses a method from the `ClientMessageCountChannelSink` class called `CountMessage()` to count the message. It then calls `AsyncProcessMessage()` on the next sink in the chain and returns the result.

The ClientMessageCountChannelSink class implements the `SyncProcessMessage()` method to process synchronous messages. Like `AsyncProcessMessage()`, the `SyncProcessMessage()` method counts the message. Next, it calls the `SyncProcessMessage()` method for the next sink in the chain and returns the result.

As part of the implementation of the `IClientChannelSink` interface, the `ClientMessageCountChannelSink` class contains an implementation of the `NextChannelSink()` method. This method uses the private data member nextSink to return the sink chain as a reference to an `IClientChannelSink` interface. The `IClientChannelSink` interface also requires the `ClientMessageCountChannelSink` class to implement a method called `AsyncProcessRequest()`. You can put custom asynchronous processing here, but I've found it easier to put it in `AsyncProcessMessage()`. If it does nothing else, `AsyncProcessRequest()` should push the request onto the sink stack and call `AsyncProcessRequest()` for the next sink in the chain.

The AsyncProcessResponse() method appears on lines 80-88 of Listing 13.7. It is a short method that just calls AsyncProcessResponse() for the next sink in the chain. If you want to add custom processing to this method, you can. However, you will have to use a different configuration file than will be shown in this chapter. The code for the custom processing should go before invoking `AsyncProcessResponse()` for the next sink in the chain.

The `ClientMessageCountChannelSink` class also needs to implement the `GetRequestStream()` method, which is shown on lines 90-96. If you wish to replace the stream with a stream of your own, this is where you do it. If that's not the case, this method can just call `GetRequestStream()` on the next sink in the chain and return the result.

In this sample program, the real workhorse of the `ClientMessageCountChannelSink` class is the `ProcessMessage()` method. In fact, the configuration used in this program results in all invocations of the `CountMessage()` method originating from the `ProcessMessage()` method. You may justifiably wonder why we bothered to implement other methods such as `SyncProcessMessage()` and `AsyncProcessMessage()`. The answer is that these methods are called in different configurations. If your channel sink is very widely used, the programmers using your channel sink are likely to use a wide variety of configurations. As much as possible, your channel sink should handle them all. That's why the custom processing is done in the `CountMessage()` method. `CountMessage()` can be called from any of the message processing methods in the `ClientMessageCountChannelSink` class.

The `CountMessage()` method appears on lines 115-124. It increments the private data member `totalMessages` and writes the result to the console. Note that it does so in a `try-catch` block to prevent any exceptions from being propagated outside of the `ClientMessageCountChannelSink` class.

The provider that creates an instance of the `ClientMessageCountChannelSink` class is called `MessageCountSinkProvider`. It begins on line 127. The `MessageCountSinkProvider` class must implement the `IClientChannelSinkProvider` interface.

To be usable with configuration file, the `MessageCountSinkProvider` class must have the constructor on lines 136-140. Even though the constructor does nothing, it must be present or the .NET Remoting system cannot instantiate it as a result of a `<provider>` statement in a configuration file.

Because it implements the `IClientChannelSinkProvider` interface, the `MessageCountSinkProvider` class must provide a method called `Next()` that gets and sets the next provider in the chain. The `MessageCountSinkProvider` class defines this method on lines 142-152.

WARNING

If the .NET Framework calls the provider's `Next()` method to get the next provider in the chain before it calls `Next()` to set the next provider in the chain, your configuration file contains an error. Make sure that the `<provider>` element occurs before the `<formatter>` element.

Lines 154-176 contain the CreateSink() method. This is the method that instantiates your custom channel sink. It sets the local variable messageCountSink to null. If the provider cannot instantiate the sink, CreateSink() returns the null value to the .NET Framework.

On lines 161-165, `CreateSink()` calls `CreateSink()` on the next sink in the chain. The next provider does the same, and so forth until the end of the chain is reached. At that point, the `CreateSink()` methods for each provider create the chain from last to first. The `MessageCountSinkProvider` is the first one in the chain. After the rest of the chain is created, it instantiates an object of type `ClientMessageCountChannelSink` and passes the sink chain to the `ClientMessageCountChannelSink` constructor. The channel sink uses that parameter to link itself as the first sink in the chain.

To build this application, compile the `InformationManager` object in Listing 13.3 into an assembly. Add a reference to the assembly into the project file for the server program in Listing 13.4. After you compile the server program, be sure to copy the configuration file in Listing 13.5 into the directory that contains the server program's EXE file.

Next, generate metadata for the `InformationManager` object using the SOAPSUDS tool. Compile the channel sink and sink provider in Listing 13.7 into an assembly. Add references to the metadata and the assembly you generated from Listing 13.7 into the client program's project file. Finally, compile the client program in Listing 13.6. Remember to copy the configuration file in Listing 13.2 into the directory containing the EXE for the client program.

Server-Side Sinks

Adding custom sinks to the server side of an application is similar to adding them to the client side of an application. To demonstrate the differences, we'll add message counting to the server side of the application we already created for this chapter. We'll use the client configuration file, information manager object, server application class, and client program that are shown in Listings 13.2, 13.3, 13.4, and 13.6.

The first thing to do is create a custom sink, along with its sink provider, for the server program. We'll store it in the same file as the client sink and client sink provider. Listing 13.8 shows the new version of that file.

```
1     using System;
2     using System.Runtime.Remoting;
3     using System.Runtime.Remoting.Channels;
4     using System.Runtime.Remoting.Messaging;
5     using System.IO;
6     using System.Collections;
7
8
9     namespace MessageCountChannelSink
10    {
Lines 11 through 177 have been omitted to save space. They contain
the source code for the custom client sink and sink provider. They are
unchanged from Listing 13.7.
183
184       // Server sink.
185       public class ServerMessageCountChannelSink :
186           BaseChannelObjectWithProperties,
187           IServerChannelSink,
188           IChannelSinkBase
189       {
190           private IServerChannelSink nextSink;
191
192           int totalMessages=0;
193
194
195           public ServerMessageCountChannelSink(
196               IServerChannelSink sinkChain)
197           {
198               nextSink = sinkChain;
199           }
200
201           public void AsyncProcessResponse(
```

Listing 13.8 Adding a Custom Sink to a Server Program

```
            IServerResponseChannelSinkStack sinkStack,
            object state,
            IMessage message,
            ITransportHeaders headers,
            Stream stream )
        {
            this.CountMessage();

            sinkStack.AsyncProcessResponse(
                message,
                headers,
                stream);
        }

        public Stream GetResponseStream(
            IServerResponseChannelSinkStack sinkStack,
            object state,
            IMessage msg,
            ITransportHeaders headers )
        {
            return (null);
        }

        public ServerProcessing ProcessMessage(
            IServerChannelSinkStack sinkStack,
            IMessage requestMsg,
            ITransportHeaders requestHeaders,
            Stream requestStream,
            out Runtime.Remoting.Messaging.IMessage responseMsg,
            out ITransportHeaders responseHeaders,
            out Stream responseStream)
        {
            this.CountMessage();

            if (nextSink != null)
            {
                ServerProcessing serverProcessing
                    =  nextSink.ProcessMessage(
                        sinkStack,
                        requestMsg,
                        requestHeaders,
                        requestStream,
                        out responseMsg,
                        out responseHeaders,
                        out responseStream);

                return (serverProcessing);
```

Listing 13.8 Adding a Custom Sink to a Server Program *(continues)*

```
            }
            else
            {
                responseMsg = null;
                responseHeaders = null;
                responseStream = null;
                return (new ServerProcessing());
            }
        }

        public IServerChannelSink NextChannelSink
        {
            get
            {
                return nextSink;
            }
            set
            {
                nextSink = value;
            }
        }

        public void CountMessage()
        {
            try
            {
                ++totalMessages;
                System.Console.WriteLine(
                    "Server Message:" +
                    totalMessages.ToString());
            }
            catch (Exception)
            {
            }
        }
    }

    // Server sink provider.
    public class MessageCountServerSinkProvider :
        IServerChannelSinkProvider
    {
        private IServerChannelSinkProvider nextProvider = null;

        public MessageCountServerSinkProvider()
        {
        }

        public MessageCountServerSinkProvider(
```

Listing 13.8 Adding a Custom Sink to a Server Program

```
                IDictionary properties,
                ICollection providerData)
            {
            }

            public void GetChannelData(
                IChannelDataStore channelData)
            {
            }

            public IServerChannelSink CreateSink(
                IChannelReceiver channel)
            {
                IServerChannelSink nextSink = null;

                if (nextProvider != null)
                {
                    nextSink = nextProvider.CreateSink(channel);
                }

                return (new ServerMessageCountChannelSink(
                             nextSink));
            }

            public IServerChannelSinkProvider Next
            {
                get
                {
                    return nextProvider;
                }
                set
                {
                    nextProvider = value;
                }
            }
        }
    }

```

Listing 13.8 Adding a Custom Sink to a Server Program *(continued)*

This version of the file contains custom sinks for both the client and the server. To keep the listing to a reasonable length, I've omitted the code for the client sink and client sink provider. It is the same as the code shown in Listing 13.7.

Like the client sink, the server sink inherits from the `BaseChannel ObjectWithProperties` class. As noted previously, `BaseChannelObjectWithProperties` comes with the .NET Framework. Lines 187-188 show that the server sink implements the `IServerChannelSink` and `IChannelSinkBase` interfaces.

The ServerMessageCountChannelSink class declares two private data members. The first is declared on line 190 and the class uses it to store the sink chain. The second, which is shown on line 192, is used to count messages.

The class's constructor is given on lines 195-199. The constructor for the client sink took a reference to the client's sink chain as its parameter. The constructor for the `ServerMessageCountChannelSink` class follows the same pattern. It requires a reference to the server-side shink chain as its parameter.

As with the client sink, the server sink implements the `AsyncProcess Response()` method. It also contains a method called `GetResponse Stream()`. This method builds and returns the stream to serialized. If you want to substitute your own stream for the one that the channel sink received, the `GetResponseStream()` method return is a good place to do it. However, in this implementation it just returns the value null. Returning `null` tells the .NET Remoting system to build the stream itself.

On lines 225-257, the `ServerMessageCountChannelSink` class declares the `ProcessMessage()` method. This method calls the `CountMessage()` method. If this is not the last sink in the chain, the `ProcessMessage()` method calls the `ProcessMessage()` method for the next sink in the chain. It then returns the value it receives from the next sink in the chain.

If this sink is the last one in the chain, the `ProcessMessage()` method sets its `out` parameters to `null`. This tells the.NET Remoting runtime system that it has reached the end of the chain.

To implement the `IServerChannelSink` interface, the `ServerMessageCountChannelSink` class declares the `NextChannelSink()` method. `NextChannelSink()` gets or sets the value of the private data member nextSink. Lastly, `ServerMessageCountChannelSink` class implements the same `CountMessage()` method we saw in the client sink.

The server sink's provider begins on line 287 of Listing 13.8. It contains one private data member that stores the provider sink chain. The `MessageCountServerSinkProvider` class implements two constructors. Although they don't do anything, they are required. Likewise, the `GetChannelData()` method is also required in order to implement the `IServerChannelSinkProvider` interface. The `GetChannelData()` method enables you to store custom data into the channel. If you're not doing that, this method should do nothing.

Lines 307-319 show the source code for the `CreateSink()` method. As you might expect, this method creates the channel sink. If there are other sink providers in the chain, this method creates the sinks by calling the `CreateSink()` method on the next provider in the chain. It ends by creating its own sink on lines 317 and 318. Notice that the `CreateSink()` method passes the next sink in the sink chain to the `ServerMessageCountChannelSink` constructor. This enables the constructor to link the sink into the sink chain.

Finally, Listing 13.8 gives the code for the `Next()` property accessor method, which gets and sets the value of the private data member `nextProvider`.

The server program's application class needs no changes to accommodate custom sinks. However, the server program's Visual Studio project file must have a reference to the assembly that you generate from the file in Listing 13.8. In addition, the server program's configuration file requires statements specifically for custom channel sinks. In particular, you must add the `<serverProviders>`, `<provider>`, and `<formatter>` elements. Listing 13.9 shows their use.

```
<configuration>
    <system.runtime.remoting>
        <application>
            <channels>
                <channel ref="http" port="8080">
                    <serverProviders>
                        <provider
                            type =
```

Listing 13.9 Adding a Custom Sink to the Server's Configuration File *(continues)*

```
    "MessageCountChannelSink.MessageCountServerSinkProvider, Chan-
nelSink"
                            />
                            <formatter ref = "soap" />
                        </serverProviders>
                    </channel>
                </channels>
                <service>
                    <wellknown
                        mode="Singleton"
                        type="InfoMan.InformationManager, InfoMan"
                        objectUri = "InfoMan.soap" />
                </service>
            </application>
        </system.runtime.remoting>
    </configuration>
```

Listing 13.9 Adding a Custom Sink to the Server's Configuration File *(continued)*

The server's configuration file specifies the custom sink provider in the `<serverProviders>` element. The `<serverProviders>` element contains the `<provider>` and `<formatter>` elements. As with the client, the order of these elements *does* matter. The `<provider>` element must appear before the `<formatter>` element. The type property in the `<provider>` element specifies the custom channel sink provider and the assembly where the provider can be found. The `<formatter>` element selects the formatter to use with the channel.

Configuration Options for Channel Sinks

At this point, it's necessary to revisit the topic of configuration files. This chapter has demonstrated that configuration files contain statements that are specifically for using custom channel sinks. In particular, `<provider>` element, which appears in the `<serverProviders>` element, selects the sink provider for your custom sink.

Even if you do not use a custom channel sink, there are still some configuration options your program can use to customize communication channels. You can use configuration files to select non-default formatters for your channels. You can also produce communication channels with custom properties by creating channel templates.

Selecting Non-Default Formatters

The .NET Remoting system does not force you to use specific formatters with specific channels. In your programs' configuration files, you can select any formatter that is available. For example, an HTTP channel uses a SOAP formatter by default. However, your program can select a binary formatter instead. To do so, it uses the `<formatter>` element. Listing 13.10 demonstrates how.

```
1    <configuration>
2       <system.runtime.remoting>
3          <application>
4             <channels>
5                <channel ref="http">
6                   <clientProviders>
7                      <formatter ref="binary"/>
8                   </clientProviders>
9                </channel>
10            </channels>
11            <client>
12               <wellknown
13                  url="http://localhost:8080/SomeRemoteType.soap"
14                  type="NameSpace.SomeRemoteType, Assemblyname"
15               />
16            </client>
17         </application>
18      </system.runtime.remoting>
19   </configuration>
```

Listing 13.10 Selecting the Binary Formatter for an HTTP Channel

The statement on line 5 of Listing 13.10 tells the program to use an HTTP channel. The `<formatter>` statement overrides the default selection of the SOAP formatter. Instead, it chooses the binary formatter. The advantage of this is that the data is more compressed in a binary formatter than it is in SOAP format. The disadvantage of using a binary formatter over an HTTP channel is that it limits the types of clients that the server can use. Because SOAP is an industry-standard data format, servers can use it to communicate with clients written in virtually any language on virtually any operating system. Using a binary formatter typically means that the clients are programs written with .NET Remoting.

In addition to using a binary formatter with HTTP channels, your application can use the <formatter> statement to select a SOAP formatter for a TCP channel. This isn't often done. Generally, developers only use a SOAP formatter over a TCP channel if their servers communicate with clients that only understand SOAP.

Creating Channel Templates for Custom Channels

If you use a channel with customized properties often, you can define that channel in a template and give it a name. Because .NET Remoting enables you to load multiple configuration files for any given program, you can define your channel template in its own configuration file. Prior to loading any other configuration files it needs, your program would load the configuration file containing the channel template. The other configuration files can then reference the channel template by name.

Most of the configuration file elements presented so far appear within the <application> element. However, the definitions of channel templates do not appear in the <application> element. Listing 13.11 demonstrates how to declare a channel template.

```
    <configuration>
        <system.runtime.remoting>
            <channels>
                <channel
    type="System.Runtime.Remoting.Channels.Http.HttpChannel,
    System.Runtime.Remoting"
                    id="httpbinary" >
                    <clientProviders>
                        <formatter
type="System.Runtime.Remoting.Channels.BinaryClientFormatterSinkProvider,
System.Runtime.Remoting,"
                        />
                    </clientProviders>
                </channel>
            </channels>
            <application>
                <channels>
                    <channel ref="httpbinary"/>
                </channels>
                <client>
```

Listing 13.11 Defining and Using a Channel Template

```
21                <wellknown
22                    url="http://localhost:8080/SomeRemoteType"
23                    type="SomeRemoteType, AssemblyName"
24                />
25            </client>
26        </application>
27    </system.runtime.remoting>
28 </configuration>
```

Listing 13.11 Defining and Using a Channel Template *(continued)*

Configuration files define channel templates with the `<channels>` element. The individual channel templates appear in `<channel>` elements. Only one `<channels>` element should appear in the configuration file outside the `<application>` element. The `<channels>` element can contain multiple `<channel>` elements.

Each individual channel template must have its own unique name. The name of the channel template in Listing 13.11, `httpbinary`, appears on line 7. The channel template must also specify the complete name of the channel's implementation and the assembly that contains it. This specification appears on lines 5 and 6 of Listing 13.11.

WARNING

Recall from earlier chapters that you must specify complete information in a type attribute for assemblies in the global assembly cache. This includes version and culture information, as well as the assembly's strong name. Channels and formatters included with the .NET Remoting Framework are stored in the global assembly cache. Therefore, in order for the configuration file in Listing 13.11 to work, you would need to add complete information to the type statements on lines 5-6 and 10-11. The information is omitted in Listing 13.11 for brevity.

The `<formatter>` element, which begins on line 9, specifies the use of the binary formatter with the HTTP channel. It does this in the `type` attribute, which appears on lines 10 and 11.

The statements specific to this program appear within the `<application>` element. In particular, notice that it contains a `<channel>` element that references the channel template by name. When it does, it also selects all the properties specified in the channel template. Therefore, the program that uses the configuration file in Listing 13.11 communicates over an HTTP channel using a binary formatter.

Summary

Most of the work performed by a communication channel is done by a series, or chain, of channel sinks. The .NET Remoting system enables you to add custom extensions by writing your own channel sinks and including them in your application's communication channel. A channel sink, also called a message sink, is an object that implements the `IClientChannelSink` or `IServerChannelSink` interface. It receives a message, performs processing on the message, and forwards the message to the next sink in the chain.

On the client side, the object proxy sends messages to the channel sink chain. The first sink in the chain is the formatter sink. The formatter sink serializes the message for the specific type of channel. The last sink is the transport sink. It sends the message across the network. Your custom client channel sinks generally appear between the formatter sink in the transport sink. However, is possible to create your own custom formatter sinks and insert them before the formatter default sink.

The communication channel on the server side is almost a mirror image of the client communication channel. The first sink in the server's chain is the transport sink. The last is the formatter sink. Instead of communicating with a proxy, the server's formatter sink communicates with a StackBuilder sink. The StackBuilder sink translates the message into a remote method call.

Applications do not instantiate custom channel sinks directly. Instead, they use sink providers, which you can think of as object factories for custom channel sinks. .NET Remoting applications store their sink providers in the chain. Each provider in the chain instantiates its channel sink when its `CreateSink()` method is called. If it cannot create the sink, the `CreateSink()` method should return null.

To instantiate custom sink providers, applications use the `<provider>` element in their configuration files. The `<provider>` element should appear before the `<formatter>` element in the configuration file for the application to work correctly.

With the `<formatter>` element, programs can use the configuration files to select non-default formatters for their communication channels. In addition, they can define channel templates for channels with customized properties that they use repeatedly.

Obtaining the Source Code

All of the source code for this book is available on the Web at www.wiley.com/compbooks/conger. Select Source Code for the Sample Programs to see a listing of the chapters that offer sample programs. Clicking a link displays a list of programs available for the particular chapter. Choose the program you want and click its link. Most Web browsers will ask you whether you want to open the file or save it to your hard drive. Choose to save the file and then select a location to which the file will be downloaded. After you do, the sample program is downloaded as a ZIP file. You can then extract it for your use.

GLOSSARY

Application Space The memory in which a program runs.

Assembly A .NET component containing one or more objects.

Authentication The process of validating a user's identity.

Authorization Verifying the user or a client program is authorized to perform a particular task on a computer or network.

Black Box Code Highly reusable code that does not require a knowledge of its internal workings to be used.

Block Cipher See **Symmetric Encryption**.

Callback Function A method called by delegate when the delegate's asynchronous method completes.

Channel Sink Chain The entire collection of message sinks, including any custom sinks, in a channel.

Common Language Runtime (CLR) The Virtual Machine (VM) on which CLS-compatible programs execute.

Common Language Specification(CLS) A specification produced by Microsoft that defines Intermediate Language.

Delegate A special type of object provided by the .NET Framework that facilitates asynchronous method calls.

Formatter Sink A special type of message sink that serializes messages for transmission across a network.

Garbage Collection The process of collecting and freeing blocks of memory that were allocated by a program but are no longer in use.

Global Assembly Cache A collection of directories that contains objects visible to all programs on the computer.

Globally Unique Identifiers (GUIDs) A unique identifier used to establish the identity of individual objects on a network.

Intermediate Language (IL) A binary language similar to traditional object code or Java's byte code. IL is compiled by the JIT and runs on the CLR.

Intranet A company's internal network.

Lease A counter that specifies an MBR object's lifetime.

Lifetime The length of time that a remote object is in memory.

Managed Code Code that is executed by the CLR.

Marshaling The process of packaging data for transmission across a network.

Message Sink An object in the .NET Remoting system that receives messages and performs processing on them.

Private Key Encryption See **Symmetric Encryption**.

Program Context The current state of a program in memory, including the program's code, variables, and data it allocates from the heap.

Reference Object A remote object that is passed by reference between the client and the server.

Remoting Message A special type of message derived from the IMessage interface that the CLR uses to execute remote methods.

Request Message A message defined by HTTP that is transmitted from a client to a server.

Response Message A message defined by HTTP that is transmitted from a server to a client.

Serializable Data Data that can be packaged sequentially into a data stream and sent over the network.

Sink Chain A series of message sinks, each of which performs its own processing on a message, one after the other.

Sponsor An object that implements the ISponsor interface and is called periodically to renew a remote object's lease.

Spoofing A technique for breaking into applications that involves making an unauthorized assembly or program appear as if it is an authorized assembly or program. The unauthorized assembly or program spoofs the identity of the authorized assembly or program.

StackBuilder Sink A special type of sink used on servers that translates method call messages into invocations of methods on remote server objects.

Strong Name A unique identifier for assemblies that contains a digital signature for security purposes.

Symmetric Encryption A method of encryption in which both the sender and the recipient use the same encryption key.

Thread A basic unit of code to which the operating system allocates microprocessor time.

Transport Sink A special type of message sink that sends messages across a network.

Unmanaged Code Code that is not executed by the CLR.

Unmarshaling The process of unpackaging data received from across a network.

Unsafe Code Code that performs its own memory management.

Virtual Machine (VM) A computer that doesn't really exist. It is simulated in software.

Virtual Private Network (VPN) A private network formed by connecting computers over the Internet using a secure connection. Secure connections often employ PPTP for their underlying transport.

Web Service A Web site that exposes some or all of the functionality of a company's multitiered application. External developers can use this functionality in their own Web applications.

Well-Known Object A remote object that always uses a particular port number.

Well-Known Service A remote service that always uses a particular port number. The remote service may or may not be a remote object.

A

abstract base class, sharing between servers and clients, 119–129
Account property, Service ProcessInstaller, 213–214
Action menu, Services Control Manager command, 212
<activated> element
 <client> element, 184
 <service> element, 182
activation
 client-activated objects (CAOs), 33–34
 remote object, 67–70
 server-activated objects (SAOs), 32–33
Activator class, 52
Activator.GetObject( ) method, 53, 70, 143, 259
Active Server Pages, 235
ActiveX, .NET Remoting compared, 4
Add command, 72–73
Add Existing Item command, 72–73
Add Installer command, 211
Add New Project dialog box, 72
Add Reference command, 43, 44
AddValue( ) method, 324, 335
administration, centralized, 29
Administrative Tools options, 204, 218
algorithm, encryption, 311
alias, virtual directory, 218
app.config file, 178
<application> element
 channel templates in, 370–371
 description, 180
 name attribute, 220
ApplicationName property, 48
applications
 improving
  client program, 61–65
  server program, 57–61
 using, 56
 writing
  basic steps, 41–42
  client program, 42, 51–56
  server program, 41–42, 44–50
 See also distributed applications
application space
 definition, 23, 375
 location of, 23
<appname> element, 216
Ariba, 231

AscendingSort( ) method, 275–276
ASP.NET, 215, 235–236
.aspx files, 235
assembly
 datatypes
  assembly manifest, 15
  metadata, 15
  program code in Intermediate Language (IL), 15
  resources, 15
 definition, 375
 description, 14
 hashing and, 302
 identifiers for, 71
 keys, 200–201
 multiple versions of, 222
 strong name, 16, 199, 200–202, 302–303
 trust, 200
 wrapped proxy generation from, 131
AssemblyInfo.cs file, 201–202
AssemblyKeyFile class, 202
AssemblyKeyName class, 202
assembly manifest
 description, 15
 versioning and, 221
assembly name, 184
asymmetric encryption, 311–312
AsyncCaller object, 289
AsyncCallWrapper( ) method, 292–293
asynchronous calls
 advantages, 271
 callback functions, 286–290
 configuration file for, 281, 282, 283
 delegate use
  for local asynchronous calls, 276–280
  for remote asynchronous calls, 280–285
 description, 344, 346, 359–360, 366
 exceptions, non-propagation of, 293
 fire-and-forget calls, 291
 gotchas, 291–294
 metadata, incompatibility, 292
 one-way method calls, 290–291
 repetitions, setting number of, 279, 285
 synchronization primitives
  AutoResetEvent, 297
  description, 293, 294
  Interlocked, 297–298
  ManualResetEvent, 296–297
  mutex, 295–296
  table of, 295
  Wait Handle, 295
AsyncLocalCaller class, 279
AsyncProcessMessage( ) method, 344, 346, 359–360
AsyncProcessRequest( ) method, 359
AsyncProcessResponse( ) method, 359–360, 366
asyncResult.IsComplete property, 291
AsyncWaitHandle member, 279

AttributeCount property, Xml-TextReader object, 107
attributes
 node, 102
 tag, 100–101
Authenticated users group, 213
authentication
 application-level, 338
 in ASP.NET, 215
 basic, 337
 definition, 375
 description, 336
 digest, 337
 Internet Information Services (IIS) and, 337
 over SSL, 337
 security providers, 338
 smartcards, 339
 system-level, 337–338
 third party, 338–339
Authenticode signature
 certificate authority use by, 304
 client-activated objects (CAOs) and, 305
 downloadable modules and, 305
 tools for creating and managing, 304
 trusted assemblies and, 200
 uses, 305
authorization
 administrators of, 336
 definition, 375
AutoLog property, 206
AutoResetEvent object, 297

B

BaseChannelObjectWithProperties class, 366
BaseChannelSinkWithProperties class, 346, 358
base class, adding functionality to objects, 9
BeginInvoke( ) method, 277, 279–281, 285-286, 290
Bell Labs, 16–17
Berners-Lee, Tim, 98
binary formatter, 222
<binding> element, WSDL, 232
<bindingTemplate> element, 234
bin directory, 216, 219–220
black box code
 definition, 375
 description, 11
block cipher, 311, 375
blocking, 49
<Body> element, 113, 114
boolean parameters, 115
Browse button, 219
Bubble Sort, 124, 150, 275
buffer, data, 334–335
BuildWidget( ) method, 140–141, 143, 160–161, 163
<businessEntity> element, 234
business logic tier, 24
<businessService> element, 234

C

C#
 C++ compared, 17
 description, 16–17

destructors, role of, 7
Intermediate Language compatibility, 4
C++
C compared, 17
C# compared, 17
description, 6
syntax, 17
CA. *See* certificate authority
calendar control, 235
callback functions
definition, 375
description, 286
examples of use, 286–290
over HTTPS, 309–310
synchronization primitives, 294–298
calls
asynchronous
advantages, 271
callback functions, 286–290
configuration file for, 281, 282, 283
delegate use for local asynchronous calls, 276–280
delegate use for remote asynchronous calls, 280–285
description, 344, 346, 359–360, 366
exceptions, non-propagation of, 293
fire-and-forget calls, 291
gotchas, 291–294
metadata, incompatibility, 292
one-way method calls, 290–291
repetitions, setting number of, 279, 285
synchronization primitives, 293–298
fire-and-forget, 291
one-way, 290–291
synchronous
delegate use, 272–276
description, 344, 346, 359–360
CAOs. *See* client-activated objects
CardExpirationDate property, 240, 260
CardHolderName property, 240, 260
CardIDNumber property, 240, 259
cardNumber data member, 248, 336
catch blocks. *See* try-catch statements
centralized administration, 29
Cert2SPC tool, 304
certificate authority (CA), Authenticode use of, 304
certificates, third-party authentication, 338–339
Certificate Server, 306
CertMgr tool, 304
<channel> element
in <channels> element, 348
<clientProviders> element, 348
port specification, lack of, 217
channels
accessing, 47–48
call messages, 343
creating, 48, 51

formatters and, 343
HTTP channel
<channels> elements, 185–186
client source code for, 75–76
configuration file installation and, 177
firewalls and, 73
Internet Information Services (IIS) and, 216
servers, communication between, 126
server source code for, 74–75
SOAP formatter, 222, 349, 369
TCP channel compared, 74
virtual private networks and, 308
message sink
for Authenticode information, 305
chains, 342, 344–346, 347, 375
client creation of, 343
client-side sinks, 347–361
configuration options, 368–371
definition, 342, 376
difficulties in implementing, 347
encryption through, 336
formatters, selecting non-default, 369–370
formatter sink, 344
publicly available, 305
server creation of, 343
server-side sinks, 362–368
sink providers, 346–347
StackBuilder sink, 344
transport sink, 344, 345–346, 347
MSMQ, 342
out-of-band data, adding to messages, 342
POP3, 342
registering, 48, 51–52
secure channels
IP Security Protocol (IPSec), 307–308
point-to-point tunneling protocol (PPTP), 308–309
secure HTTP, 309–310
SMTP, 342
storage in global assembly cache, 371
TCP channel
accessing, 47–48
binary formatter, 222
configuration file installation and, 177
creating, 48, 51
HTTP channel compared, 74
using, 47–48
templates, 370–371
using, 47–48
<channels> element, 180, 185
ChannelServices class, 48
channel sink chain, 342, 344–346, 347, 375
ChargeAmount property, 240
ChargeConfirmation class, 249, 261, 333
chargeVerifier data member, 259, 261

ChargeVerifier.DLL, 266
ChargeVerifier namespace, 248
ChargeVerifierService.exe, 265
chunky calls, 78
cipher block chaining, 311
Class Library command
Class view, 19
client-activated objects (CAOs)
- <activated> element for publishing, 182, 184
- <lifetime> element, 187
- Authenticode signature, 305
- client-side sponsors, 173–174
- configuration files for, 194–197
- creation, 68
- description, 33–34
- Internet Information Services (IIS) and, 215
- lease, 146
- lifetime, 34
- recycling, 34
- sample code, 68–70
- version information and, 225

ClientAppClass class, 292
<client> element
- <activated> element, 184
- description, 180
- number of occurrences, 180
- <wellknown> element, 183–184

ClientMessageCountChannel Sink class, 358, 359, 360, 361
client program
- for asynchronous remoting program, 283–285
- callback functions, 286
- compiling remote objects into, 117–118
- configuration file for server-activated objects (SAOs), 191–193
- configuration file use in, 242
- for custom channel sink application, 352–361
- describing objects with metadata, 129–138
- enhancing, 61–65
- error detection by, 64
- example source code, 91–92
- FasterCharge program, 254–258
- HTTP channel use, 75–76
- lease renewal, 147–151
- pinging, 146
- proxies, 342
- for remote object with a managed lease, 162–164
- sharing abstract base classes between client and server, 119–129
- sharing interface between client and server, 118–119
- for two-server application, 126–129
- wrapped proxy program, 134–135
- writing
  - activating remote object, 52–53
  - basic steps, 42
  - connecting to server, 51–52
  - example source code, 53–56

identifying remote server object to client, 51
procedure, 51–56
using remote object, 53
<clientProviders> element, 186–187, 348
client/server communication channels
description, 34–35
HTTP channel, 36
multiple instances of programs and, 35
port selection, 34–35
TCP channel, 35–36
client-side sponsors, 173–174
CLR. *See* Common Language Runtime
CLS. *See* Common Language Specification
Cobol, 7
code
black box, 11, 375
Hamming, 88
managed, 7, 376
reuse, 11
secure code
Authenticode signatures, 303–306
certificates, 306
hashing, 302
Signcode signatures, 303
strong names, 200, 302–303
source code
location of, 44, 71
obtaining, 373
sharing object, 117–118
unmanaged, 7–8, 10, 377
unsafe, 7, 377
COM. *See* Component Object Model; Distributed Component Object Model
COM+, .NET Remoting and, 14–15
COM Interop, 15
command window, Visual Studio, 201
Common Language Runtime (CLR)
client-activated object (CAO) creation, 68
debugging program, 11
definition, 375
destructors, role of, 7
garbage collection, 7
Just in Time (JIT) compiler, 5
managed code, 7
memory management, 7
object lifetime, control of, 32–33
unmanaged code, 7–8
Virtual Machine (VM), 4
Common Language Specification (CLS)
definition, 375
.NET Framework and, 4
portability, 4
communication channels
HTTP channel, 73–76
<channels> elements, 185–186
client source code for, 75–76
configuration file installation and, 177

firewalls and, 73
Internet Information Services (IIS) and, 216
servers, communication between, 126
server source code for, 74–75
SOAP formatter, 222, 349, 369
TCP channel compared, 74
virtual private networks and, 308
TCP channel
accessing, 47–48
binary formatter, 222
configuration file installation and, 177
creating, 48, 51
HTTP channel compared, 74
using, 47–48
CompareExchange( ) method, 298
compilers
CLR-compatible, 5
IL-compatible, 4, 6–7
Just in Time (JIT), 5
compiling
procedure for compiling remote application properly, 72–73
remote objects into client programs, 117–118
source code for the remote object into the client, 51
Component Name list, 43–44
Component Object Model (COM)
GUIDs, 200
interoperability, 12
.NET Remoting and, 4, 14–15
SOAP use, 111
standard, 12
components, definition, 11–12
compression of data, extending .NET Remoting for, 341
Config File Hell, 179
<configuration> element, 179
configuration files
advantages of, 177
app.config file, 178
<application> element, 180
arcane arts of, 191
<channel> element, 180, 185–187
for client-activated objects (CAOs), 193–197
<client> element
<activated> element, 184
description, 180
number of occurrences, 180
<wellknown> element, 183–184
<configuration> element, 179
for controlling object lifetimes, 197–198
<lifetime> element
attributes, 187–188
description, 180
number of occurrences, 180
loading, 190
machine.config file, 178
naming, 178, 179
number of, 178, 179
pitfalls of, 179
protecting, 242

referencing channel templates, 370–371
for server-activated objects (SAOs), 188–193
<service> element
<activated> element, 182
description, 180
number of occurrences, 180
<wellknown> element, 181–182
standardized templates, 179
uses of, 177
Configure( ) method, 190, 209
connection, waiting for, 49
connection oriented protocol, 35
Console Application command, 43, 72–73
console applications, Windows, 203
ConstructionCall class, 342
constructor
AsyncCallback, 289
ClientMessageCount-ChannelSink class, 359
delegate, 276, 279
EncryptedData, 335
mutex, 296
non-default, 129, 137, 138, 157
VerificationRequest object, 240, 324–325, 335
ControlledLeaseMBRObject class, 157–158, 161
Control Panel, 204
Convert.ToDateTime( ) method, 325
CORDBG.EXE, source code, 11
counter, reference, 145
CountMessage( ) method, 359, 360, 366
CreateSink( ) method, 346–348, 361, 367
Cryptographic Service Provider (CSP), 202
cryptography API, 312, 333–335
currentGameState object, 81
CurrentLeaseTime property, 153, 154, 1500
CurrentState property, 85, 156

D

DataArray property, 276
database tier, scalability of, 25
data buffer, 334–335
DataByte( ) method, 334
data collection, size of, 47
DataCollectionLength( ) method, 58, 60, 137
data compression, extending .NET Remoting for, 341
DataItem( ) method, 47, 53, 58, 60, 132
Data Members attribute, 94
dataSource parameter, 124
data structures, defining in XML, 98–101
data tier, 24
data types, SOAP, 114–115
DateTime class, 248, 260
DCOM. *See* Distributed Component Object Model
Debug command

debugging
debugger, 11
extending .NET Remoting for, 342
Decrement( ) method, 298
decryption stream, 335
Default Web Site option, 219
<definitions> element, WSDL, 232
delegate
callback functions, 286–290
constructor, 276, 279
definition, 272, 375
function of, 272
for local asynchronous calls, 276–280
method signatures and, 272, 275–276
new statement allocation of object, 276
for remote asynchronous calls, 280–285
for synchronous calls, 272–276
Delegates attribute, 94
deployment
installing distributed application, 202–203
in Internet Information Services (IIS), 214–221
planning, 199
strong-named assemblies, 199, 200–202
upgrades, 226
versioning applications, 221–226
as Windows console application, 203
as Windows Forms application, 203
as Windows Service, 203–214
DescendingSort( ) method, 275–276
DES encryption algorithm, 311
deserialization, 324, 335
Deserialize( ) method, 88
designer, 19
destructor functions, 7
DHCP server, Windows Service implementation of, 203
digest authentication, 337
direct remoting, 138–144, 161
.disco extension, 231
DISCO file, 232
DisconnectWidget( ) method, 143
Discovery Protocol, 231, 232, 233
displayName attribute
<client> element, 183
<wellknown> element, 181, 183
DisplayOutput( ) method, 107
Dispose( ) method, 209
distributed applications
building
basic steps, 41–42
client program, 42, 51–56
server program, 41–42, 44–50
deployment
installing distributed application, 202–203
in Internet Information Services (IIS), 214–221
planning, 199

strong-named assemblies, 199, 200–202
versioning applications, 221–226
as Windows console application, 203
as Windows Forms application, 203
as Windows Service, 203–214
encryption, 312–317
improving
client program, 61–65
server program, 57–61
installing, 202–203
using, 56
Distributed Component Object Model (DCOM)
Java compatibility, 10
Microsoft Transaction Server (MTS) and, 13
.NET Remoting compared, 4, 42
ping use, 146
reference counts, 145
.dll extension, 131
DLL Hell, 12–13
downloadable modules, 305
Dynamic Help
description, 19–20
icons, 20
Dynamic Link Libraries (DLLs)
assemblies compared, 14, 15
description, 12
DLL Hell, 12–13
wrapped proxy generation from, 130

E

edit windows, 18–19
Eiffel, 7
element
description, 100
nesting, 100
See also specific elements
EncryptedData class, 333–335
encryption
algorithms, 311
asymmetric, 311–312
cryptography API, 333–335
custom channel sinks and, 336
description, 310
in distributed applications, 312–317
initialization vector, 310–311
of login information, 338
passwords, 337
point-to-point tunneling protocol (PPTP), 308–309
private key, 311
secure HTTP, 309
serialization and, 312–317
symmetric, 310–311
encryption stream, 334–335
EndInvoke( ) method, 277, 280, 281, 285, 290, 291
<Envelope> tag, 113
Equals( ) method, 94
error detection, by client program, 64–65
error handling, in Win32 API, 8
error message, SOAP, 112
errorOccurred variable, 64
event log, 210

Event Service, 13
Everyone group, 213
exception, non-propagation of, 293
Exchange( ) method, 298
expansion packs, 305
extensibility, in multitiered applications, 25–26
Extensible Markup Language (XML). *See* XML
extensions, 75

F

FasterCharge.exe.config file, 264
FasterCharge program
  deploying
    in Internet Information Service, 265–266
    as Windows Service, 262–265
  design
    configuration files, 241–242
    metadata, 240–241
    security, 242
    serializable objects, 237–241
    validation, 243
    verification, 243
    VerificationRequest object, 240
  implementing
    client program, 254–258
    interface development, 244–247
    serializable objects, 244–247
    server program, 252–254
    validation, 248–249
    verification, 248–252, 259–261
FasterChargeVerifier class, 252, 266
fault message, SOAP, 112
<FileName>, 130
file transfer protocol (FTP), 229
fire-and-forget calls, 291
firewall
  authentication through, 337
  between database and browser, 28
  HTTP channels and, 73
  HTTP passage through, 36
  multiple, 28
for loop, 279
formatter
  binary, 222
  <channel> element and, 186
  as channel part, 343
  custom, 88
  selecting non-default, 369–370
  SOAP, 216, 222, 349, 369
  storage in global assembly cache, 371
<formatter> element
  <clientProviders> element, 186, 348, 361
  description, 369–370
  order of elements and, 368
  ref property, 186
formatter sink
  custom, 344–345
  definition, 375
  description, 344
  serialization by, 344
FTP (file transfer protocol), 229
functions. *See* callback functions; methods

G

GameState object, 79–81
garbage collection
 definition, 376
 description, 7
 single-call objects, 146
-gc option, 221, 292
GetAnInt( ) method, 92–93
GetChannelData( ) method, 367
GET command, 232
GetCustomerName( ) method, 113
GetGameState( ) method, 79–81, 84–85
GetInt64( ) method, 325
GetLifetimeService( ) method, 150, 165
GetObjectData( ) method, 324–325, 334–335
GetObject( ) method, 52, 53, 70, 143, 259
GetRequestStream( ) method, 360
GetResponseStream( ) method, 366
GetSignerCertificate( ) method, 305
GetString( ) method, 325
global assembly cache, 181–182, 221, 371, 376
globally unique identifiers (GUIDs), 12, 200, 234, 376
go-mon.com, 4
green pages, 234
GUIDs, 12, 200, 234, 376

H

Hamming codes, 88
hashing, 302
header
 SOAP message, 113
 XML file, 99
Hewlett-Packard UUDI registry, 231
HTML. *See* HyperText Markup Language
HTTP. *See* Hypertext Transfer Protocol
HTTP channel
 <channels> elements, 185–186
 client source code for, 75–76
 configuration file installation and, 177
 firewalls and, 73
 Internet Information Services (IIS) and, 216
 servers, communication between, 126
 server source code for, 74–75
 SOAP formatter, 222, 349, 369
 TCP channel compared, 74
 virtual private networks and, 308
HttpChannel class, 75–76
HyperText Markup Language (HTML)
 ASP.NET and, 235
 SGML and, 98
Hypertext Transfer Protocol (HTTP)
 description, 36
 HTTP channel, 36

request message, 36
response message, 36
secure HTTP, 309–310

I

-ia switch, 131
IAsyncResult interface, 279, 289–290, 295
IBM UUDI registry, 231
IChannelSinkBase interface
IClientChannelSink interface, 342, 344, 358–359
IClientChannelSinkProvider. CreateSink( ) method, 346
IClientChannelSinkProvider interface, 346, 360–361
IClientFormatterSink interface, 344–345
IClientFormatterSinkProvider interface, 346
icons, in Dynamic Help window, 20
IDE window, Visual Studio, 18, 19
IFasterChargeVerifier interface, 262, 265, 325–333
IInformationManager interface, 58, 60, 64
IIS. *See* Internet Information Services
IL. *See* Intermediate Language
ILease, 150
IMessage interface, 87, 342, 344-345, 358–359
IMessageSink.AsyncProcess Message( ) method, 344
IMessageSink.SyncProcess Message( ) method, 344
ImmortalMBRObject, 157
impersonation, 337
includeVersions attribute, 222
Increment( ) method, 298
index, Dynamic Help, 20
Inetpub directory, 218
InfoManBase, 128
InfoProcBase, 125, 128
InformationManager class, 44–47, 53, 58–64, 119–125
InformationManagerSponsor object, 169–170
InformationProcessor object, 119, 124–125
inheritance, 9
initialization vector, 310–311, 334, 335
InitializeComponent( ) method, 207, 209, 264
InitializeLifeTimeService( ) method, 151, 154–157, 161, 168, 252
InitialLeaseTime property, 156, 161
installing
distributed applications, 202–203
Windows Service, 211–214
INSTALLUTIL.EXE tool, 212, 214
IntelliSense, 277
interface, sharing between client and server, 58, 118–119
Interlocked object, 297–298

Intermediate Language (IL)
in assemblies, 15
compatible languages, 4
compiling source code into, 5
definition, 376
description, 4
International Organization for Standards (ISO), 97
Internet Information Services (IIS)
advantages of, 214–215
ASP.NET and, 236
bin directory creation, 216, 219–220
deploying FasterCharge in, 265
deploying server objects in, 214–221
disadvantages, 215–216
extensions supported, 218
hosting remote objects, 199
HTTP channel use, 216
multiple instances of an object, 217
port management, 217
steps in hosting a remote object, 216
user authentication, 215, 337
virtual directory, 215, 216, 218–220
web.config file use by, 220
Internet Services Manager, 218
intranet, 73, 376
IP Security Protocol (IPSec), 307–308
IRemotingFormatter interface, 88
IsCompleted property, 279
ISerializable interface, 53, 77, 312, 324
IServerChannelSink interface, 342
IServerChannelSinkProvider class, 367
IServerChannelSinkProvider interface, 346
ISO (International Organization for Standards), 97
ISponsor interface, 165

J

J#, 6
Java
DCOM compatibility, 10
invention of, 6
.NET compared, 9–10
for .NET platform, 7
SOAP use, 111
Virtual Machine, 6
WordPerfect porting to, 10
Just in Time (JIT) compiler, 5

K

Kerberos, 338
keys, in strong names, 200–201

L

lease
CurrentLeaseTime property, 150, 153, 154, 156
definition, 146, 376

increasing renewal time, 153–154
InitialLeaseTime property, 156, 161
<lifetime> element, 187–188
Register( ) method, 165, 168, 174
renewing, 147–151
RenewOnCall property, 168
RenewOnCallTime property, 153, 156, 161
setting initial time
sponsor
client-side, 173–174
description, 164–165
server-side, 165–173
SponsorshipTimeout property, 165
useDefaultLease member value, 161
lease manager, 146, 152–154
leaseManagerPollTime attribute, <lifetime> element, 188
LeaseManagerPollTime property, 152
LeaseState.Initial constant, 154
leaseTime attribute, <lifetime> element, 188
LeaseTime property, 153
Length( ) method, 334
lifetime
of client-activated objects, 34
customizing object
InitializeLifetimeService method, 154–156
LifetimeServices class, 151–154
definition, 32, 376
indefinite, 82
lease renewal, 147–151
querying, 150
of server-activated objects, 32
singleton object, 33, 82
sponsor, 166
See also lease
<lifetime> element
attributes, 187–188
description, 180
modifying, 197–198
number of occurrences, 180
LifetimeServices class, 151–154
linker, 5
Linux
SOAP use, 111
as threat to Windows, 6
Load Balancing Service, 14
localhost, 52
LocalSystem account, 213
login information, encryption of, 338
looping, 49, 85, 124, 150, 279

M

machine.config file, dangers of modifying, 178
Main( ) method, 209, 210, 279, 292–293
MakeCert tool, 304
MakeCTL tool, 304
managed code, 7, 376
manifest, assembly, 15
description, 15
versioning and, 221
ManualResetEvent object, 296–297

MarshalByRefObject class, 45, 47
MarshalByRefObject.InitializeLifetimeService( ) method, 154
marshaling
 definition, 32, 376
 marshal by reference
  description, 32, 85
  proxy objects and, 86–88
 marshal by value
  description, 32
  efficiency of, 77–78
  implementing objects, 78–85
  scalability limitations, 77
  serialization, 77
Marshal( ) method, 86, 140–141, 161
memory
 application space, 23
 management by .NET platform, 7
MemoryStream object, 334
MessageCall class, 342
MessageCountChannelSink namespace, 358
MessageCountServerSinkProvider class, 367
MessageCountSinkProvider class, 360–361
messageCountSink variable, 361
<message> element, WSDL, 232
MessageResponse class, 342
message sink
 for Authenticode information, 305
 chains, 342, 344–346, 347
 client creation of, 343
 configuration options, 368–371
 custom
  client-side sinks, 347–361
  difficulties in implementing, 347
  server-side sinks, 362–368
  sink chains, 344–346
 definition, 342, 376
 encryption through, 336
 formatters, selecting non-default, 369–370
 formatter sink, 344
 server creation of, 343
 sink providers, 346–347
 StackBuilder sink, 344
 transport sink, 344, 345–346, 347
metadata
 asynchronous calls, incompatibility of, 292
 description, 15, 16
 drawbacks of, 129
 for serializable object, 240–241
 SOAPSUDS generation of, 129–130
 unwrapped proxy, 137–138
 wrapped proxy, 130–137
method call message, 112
method calls
 asynchronous calls
  advantages, 271
  callback functions, 286–290
  configuration file for, 281, 282, 283
  delegate use for local asynchronous calls, 276–280

delegate use for remote asynchronous calls, 280–285
description, 344, 346, 359–360, 366
exceptions, non-propagation of, 293
fire-and-forget calls, 291
gotchas, 291–294
metadata, incompatibility, 292
one-way method calls, 290–291
repetitions, setting number of, 279, 285
synchronization primitives, 293–298
one-way, 290–291
synchronous calls
delegate use, 272–276
description, 344, 346, 359–360
method invocation messages, 286
methods
Activator.GetObject( ), 53, 70, 143, 259
AddValue( ), 324, 335
AscendingSort( ), 275–276
AsyncCallWrapper( ), 292–293
AsyncProcessMessage( ), 344, 346, 359–360
AsyncProcessRequest( ), 359
AsyncProcessResponse( ), 359–360, 366
BeginInvoke( ), 277, 279–281, 285-286, 290
BuildWidget( ), 140–141, 143, 160–161, 163
CompareExchange( ), 298
Configure( ), 190, 209
Convert.ToDateTime( ), 325
CountMessage( ), 359, 360, 366
CreateSink( ), 346–348, 361, 367
DataByte( ), 334
DataCollectionLength( ), 58, 60, 137
DataItem( ), 47, 53, 58, 60, 132
Decrement( ), 298
DescendingSort( ), 275–276
Deserialize( ), 88
DisconnectWidget( ), 143
DisplayOutput( ), 107
Dispose( ), 209
EndInvoke( ), 277, 280-281, 285, 290, 291
Equals( ), 94
Exchange( ), 298
GetAnInt( ), 92–93
GetChannelData( ), 367
GetCustomerName( ), 113
GetGameState( ), 79–81, 84–85
GetInt64( ), 325
GetLifetimeService( ), 150, 165
GetObject( ), 52, 53, 70, 143, 259
GetObjectData( ), 324–325, 334–335
GetRequestStream( ), 360
GetResponseStream( ), 366
GetSignerCertificate( ), 305
GetString( ), 325

IClientChannelSinkProvider.
CreateSink( ), 346
IMessageSink.AsyncProcess
Message( ), 344
IMessageSink.SyncProcess
Message( ), 344
Increment( ), 298
InitializeComponent( ), 207,
209, 264
InitializeLifeTimeService( ),
151, 156–157, 161, 168, 252
Length( ), 334
Main( ), 209, 210, 279, 292–293
Marshal( ), 86, 140–141, 161
MarshalByRefObject.
InitializeLifetimeService( ),
154
Module.GetSignerCertificate( ),
305
Next( ), 348, 361, 367
NextChannelSink( ), 359, 366
NextSink( ), 359
Object.Equals( ), 94
OnStart( ), 207, 209, 210, 264
OnStop( ), 207, 210, 264
ProcessFile( ), 106
ProcessMessage( ), 360, 366
Read( ), 49
ReasonForRejection( ), 249
Register( ), 165, 168, 174
RegisterActivatedClientType( ),
70
RegisterActivatedService
Type( ), 69
RegisterChannel( ), 48
RegisterWellKnownService
Type( ), 48, 67, 69
RejectionMessage( ), 261
ReleaseMutex( ), 296
RemotingConfiguration.
Configure( ), 190, 209
RemotingConfiguration.
RegisterActivated
ClientType( ), 70
RemotingConfiguration.
RegisterActivated
ServiceType( ), 69
RemotingConfiguration.
RegisterWellKnown
ServiceType( ), 67, 69
RemotingReference( ), 137
RemotingServices.
Disconnect( ), 143–144
RemotingServices.Get
LifetimeService( ), 150, 165
RemotingServices.Marshal( ),
86, 140–141, 161
Renew( ), 147
Renewal( ), 169
RepeatString( ), 285, 292
Reset( ), 297
SerializationInfo.AddValue( ),
324
Serialize( ), 88
ServerAccessError( ), 64
Set( ), 297
Sleep( ), 150
Sort( ), 276
SortData( ), 124, 128
StaticGetAnInt( ), 93

StaticSetAnInt( ), 93
SyncProcessMessage( ), 344, 346, 359–360
System.Console.Read( ), 49, 56
System.ServiceProcess. ServiceBase.Run( ), 209
Thread.Sleep( ), 85, 173
TokenizeString( ), 335
ToString( ), 94
TraverseTree( ), 110
verifyButton_Click, 259–261, 316
VerifyCharge( ), 250, 252, 261, 316
WaitOne( ), 279, 285, 291, 296, 297
XmlDocument.Save( ), 110
method signature, 272, 275–276
microprocessor, speed of, 10
Microsoft
Active Server Pages, 235
ASP.NET, 235–236
Authenticode technology, 200
Certificate Server, 306
COM, 12
COM+, 14
COM+ Services, 14
IL-compatible compilers, 4, 6
MS Message Queuing (MSMQ), 13
reasons for .NET development, 5–6
SN.EXE tool, 200, 202
UUDI registry, 231
Win32 API, 8
Microsoft Interface Definition Language (MIDL), 42
Microsoft Transaction Server (MTS), 13
Minutes property, 150
mode attribute, <wellknown> element, 181
Module.GetSignerCertificate( ) method, 305
modules, downloadable, 305
MS Message Queuing (MSMQ), 13
MSMQ channel, 342
MTS (Microsoft Transaction Server), 13
multiple instances
object, 217
program, 35
multitiered applications
description, 24
extensibility, 25–26
scalability of, 25
mutex, 295–296

N

name, strong. *See* strong name
name attribute, <application> element, 220
Name property, XmlTextReader object, 107
namespaces, class library partitioning into, 9
nesting elements, 100
.NET
architecture of, 5
Java compared, 9–10

memory management, 7
multilanguage integration, 6
reasons for, 5–9
.NET Framework
communication channel, 35
debugging support, 11
description, 4
Dispose( ) method, 209
portability, 4
synchronization primitives, 294
XML in, 101–102, 103
.NET Framework Class Library
description, 8–9
Java class libraries compared, 9
namespaces, 9
platform independence, 9
Win32 API access through, 8
NetGame( ) constructor, 80
NetGame object, 82
.NET Remoting
ASP.NET compared, 236
code reuse, 11
ease of use, 31
extending, 341–342
rules, 94
scope of publication, 94
versioning applications, 221–226
XML use, 101–102
Netscape Navigator, 6
NetworkService account, 213
network traffic, monitoring, 306–307
New command, 43, 72
new keyword, 129, 138
New Project command, 72
New Project dialog box, 72, 206
new statement, 276
NextChannelSink( ) method, 359, 366
nextMessageSink data member, 359
Next( ) method, 348, 361, 367
nextProvider data member, 367
NextSink( ) method, 359
NextSink property, 345
NodeType property, 106, 107
non-wrapped proxies, 138
NTLM, 338
null session, 213
numberOfArrayItems data member, 275

O

-oa switch, 130
object
inheritance, 8
multiple instances, 217
well-known, 48
object activation
client-activated objects (CAOs), 33–34
server-activated objects (SAOs), 32–33
Object.Equals( ) method, 94
object factories
definition, 138
example program, 139–144
uses for, 138
Object Linking and Embedding (OLE), 4

objectUri attribute, <well-known> element, 181, 183–184
objectURI property, 224
ObjRef object, 86–88, 222
OLE (Object Linking and Embedding), 4
[OneWay] attribute, 291, 294
one-way method calls, 290–291
OnStart( ) method, 207, 209, 210, 264
OnStop( ) method, 207, 210, 264
Open Source movement, 5
operating system, authentication by, 337–338
out-of-band data, adding to messages, 342
Output window, 20

P

parsing XML files, 102, 104–108
passing data
 communication channels, 73–76
 example sample code, 89–92
 formatters, 88
 marshal by reference, 85–88
 marshal by value, 77–85
password, 214, 337
PE (portable execution) file, 303
Perl, 7
ping, 34, 146
pointers
 delegates compared, 272
 usefulness, 7
point-to-point tunneling protocol (PPTP), 308–309
polling leases, 152
POP3 channel, 342
port
 channel assignment, 34–35
 Internet Information Services (IIS) management of, 217
 specifying number in configuration file, 48
portable execution (PE) file, 303
port attribute, <channel> element, 185
<portType> element, WSDL, 232
POST command, 232
PPTP (point-to-point tunneling protocol), 308–309
presentation tier
 description, 24
 Web site as, 25–26
primitives, synchronization
 asynchronous calls, 293
 AutoResetEvent, 297
 description, 290, 294
 Interlocked, 297–298
 ManualResetEvent, 296–297
 mutex, 295–296
 table of, 295
 Wait Handle, 295
private key encryption
 definition, 376
 description, 311
Private Methods attribute, 94
privileges, 213
ProcessFile( ) method, 106

ProcessMessage( ) method, 360, 366
program context, 23, 376
programmable Web concept, 230
Programs menu option, 218
project, definition, 20
Project command, 43
Project Types list, 43, 72–73
Properties attribute, 94
Properties window, 19
property accessor methods, 275, 334
<provider> element
  <clientProviders> element, 348, 360, 361
  order of elements and, 368
proxy
  call messages and, 343
  client-activated object (CAO), 33
  creation from WSDL document, 116
  description, 342
  ObjRef relationship to, 86
  real, 87–88
  remoting message creation by, 87
  simple, 130
  SOAPSUDS generation of, 135
  source code in wrapped proxy program, 136–137
  transparent, 87–88
  unwrapped, 137–138
  from URL, 130, 138
  wrapped, 130–137
publication scope, 94
public key encryption, 304, 312

R

RC2 encryption algorithm, 311
Read( ) method, 49
real proxy, 87–88
RealProxy class, 87
ReasonForRejection( ) method, 249
reference, marshaling by, 32, 85–88
reference counts, 145
reference object
  client-activated objects (CAOs), 32–33
  definition, 32, 376
  server-activated objects (SAOs), 32–33
ref property
  <channel> element, 185
  <formatter> element, 186
RegisterActivatedClientType( ) method, 70
RegisterActivatedServiceType( ) method, 69
RegisterChannel( ) method, 48
Register( ) method, 165, 168, 174
RegisterWellKnownServiceType( ) method, 48, 67, 69
Registry Hell, 13
RejectionMessage( ) method, 261
ReleaseMutex( ) method, 296
.rem extension, 75, 218

remote object
 activating, 52–53
 activation, 67–70
 source code location, 44
 writing a simple remotable object, 45–47
remote procedure call (RPC)
 .NET Remoting compared, 4, 42
 Windows Service implementation of, 203
remoting
 architecture, 31–32
 definition, 3
 reasons for use, 23–31
  centralized administration, 29
  ease of use, 31
  extensibility, 25–26
  multitiered applications, 24
  scalability, 25
  security, 27–29
  Web services, 29–30
RemotingConfiguration.ApplicationName, 69
RemotingConfiguration.Configure( ) method, 190, 209
RemotingConfiguration.RegisterActivatedClient-Type( ) method, 70
RemotingConfiguration.RegisterActivated ServiceType( ) method, 69
RemotingConfiguration.RegisterWellKnown ClientType( ), 143
RemotingConfiguration.RegisterWellKnownService Type( ) method, 67, 69
remoting message
 contents of, 87
 creation by proxy object, 87
 definition, 376
RemotingReference( ) method, 137
RemotingService class, 215
RemotingServices.Disconnect( ) method, 143–144
RemotingServices.GetLifetime-Service( ) method, 150, 165
RemotingServices.Marshal( ) method, 86, 140–141, 161
Renewal( ) method, 169
renewing leases, 147–151
Renew( ) method, 147
RenewOnCall property, 168
RenewOnCallTime property, 153, 156, 161, 188
RepeatString( ) method, 285, 292
request messages, 36, 376
Reset( ) method, 297
resources, assembly, 15
response message, 36, 376
returnValue variable, 252
Rijndael encryption algorithm, 311
RijndaelManaged object, 334
Ritchie, Dennis, 16
role-based security, 28
RPC. *See* remote procedure call

S

SAOs. *See* server-activated objects
scalability, in multitiered applications, 25
scope of publication, and .NET Remoting, 94
search engine, for Web Services, 230–231
Seconds property, 150
secure HTTP (HTTPS), 309–310
secure socket layer (SSL), 309, 337
security
  authentication
    application-level, 338
    in ASP.NET, 215
    basic, 337
    definition, 375
    description, 336
    digest, 337
    Internet Information Services (IIS) and, 337
    over SSL, 337
    security providers, 338
    smartcards, 339
    system-level, 337–338
    third party, 338–339
  authorization, 335, 336
  configuration files, 242
  encryption
    algorithms, 311
    asymmetric, 311–312
    cryptography API, 333–335
    custom channel sinks and, 336
    description, 310
    in distributed applications, 312–317
    initialization vector, 310–311
    of login information, 338
    passwords, 337
    point-to-point tunneling protocol (PPTP), 308–309
    private key, 311
    secure HTTP, 309
    serialization and, 312–317
    symmetric, 310–311
  extending .NET Remoting for, 341
  firewall, 337
  hashing, 302
  impersonation, 337
  passwords, 337
  professionals, efforts of, 301
  remoting and, 27–29
  role-based, 28
  secure channels
    IP Security Protocol (IPSec), 307–308
    point-to-point tunneling protocol (PPTP), 308–309
    secure HTTP, 309–310
  secure code
    Authenticode signatures, 303–306
    certificates, 306
    hashing, 302
    Signcode signatures, 303
    strong names, 200, 302–303

session identifier expiration, 338
smartcards, 339
spoofing, 303
unmanaged code as problem source, 8, 10
Windows Service, 204
security providers, 338
[Serializable] attribute, 53, 77–79
serializable object
definition, 376
for FasterCharge application, 237–241, 244–247
metadata for, 240–241
placement into source files, 240
serialization
encryption through, 312–317
formatters and, 88
by formatter sink, 344
SOAP and, 114
sponsors, 165
in VerificationRequest object, 324–325
SerializationInfo.AddValue( ) method, 324
SerializationInfo object, 324–325
Serialize( ) method, 88
ServerAccessError( ) method, 64
server-activated objects (SAOs)
app.config file description of, 181–182
configuration files for, 188–193
deployment, 201
description, 32–33
proxy object, 33
single-call object, 33
singleton object, 33
stateless object, 32–33
version information and, 222–225
<wellknown> element use, 181–182
ServerChannelSinkStack parameter, 346
ServerMessageCountChannel Sink class, 366, 367
<servername> element, 216
server object deployment
in Internet Information Services (IIS), 214–221
as Windows console application, 203
as Windows Forms application, 203
as Windows Service, 203–214
server program
adding custom sink, 362–368
for the asynchronous remoting program, 282
blocking, 49
callback functions, 286
configuration files for server-activated objects (SAOs), 188–191
console application modification to Windows Service, 204–208

for custom channel sink application, 351–352
enhancing, 57–61
example source code, 90–91
FasterCharge program, 252–254
HTTP channel use, 74–75
installers, 211–214
lease customization, 151–154
lease manager object, 146, 152–154
for Object Factory program, 141
sharing abstract base classes between client and server, 119–129
sharing interface between client and server, 118–119
sponsor use, 169–173
wrapped proxy program, 133
writing
basic steps, 41–42
channel creation, 47–48
example source code, 49–50
procedure, 44–50
registering service on a channel, 48–49
remote object, simple, 45–47
<serverProviders> element, 186–187, 368
server-side sponsors, 165–173
<service> element
<activated> element, 182
description, 180
Internet Information Services (IIS) and, 217–218
number of occurrences, 180
<wellknown> element, 181–182
WSDL, 232
ServiceProcessInstaller, 213
Services command, 204
Services Control Manager, 204, 212
ServicesToRun variable, 209
session identifier, 338
session key, 338
Set( ) method, 297
SetReg tool, 304
Settings menu option, 204
SGML (Standard Generalized Markup Language), 97–98
sharing
abstract base classes, 119–129
interfaces, 118–119
object source code, 117–118
signature
Authenticode
certificate authority use by, 304
client-activated objects (CAOs) and, 305
downloadable modules and, 305
tools for creating and managing, 304
trusted assemblies and, 200
uses, 305
method, 272, 275–276
Signcode, 303
Signcode signature, 303
SignCode tool, 304

Simple Object Access Protocol.
    See SOAP
single-call object
  description, 33
  garbage collection, 146
  <wellknown> element
    description of, 182
singleton object
  creating, 67
  default lifetime, 82
  description, 33
  FasterChargeVerifier example,
    254
  lease, 146
  lifetime, 33, 82
  recycling, 33
  <wellknown> element
    description of, 182
sink, message
  for Authenticode information,
    305
  chains, 342, 344–346, 347, 376
  client creation of, 343
  client-side sinks, 347–361
  configuration options, 368–371
  definition, 342, 376
  difficulties in implementing,
    347
  encryption through, 336
  formatters, selecting non-
    default, 369–370
  formatter sink, 344
  server creation of, 343
  server-side sinks, 362–368
  sink providers, 346–347
  StackBuilder sink, 344
  transport sink, 344, 345–346,
    347
slash (/), 100
sleep, 295
Sleep( ) method, 150
Smalltalk, 17
smartcards, 339
SMTP channel, 342
SN.EXE tool, 200, 202
SOAP
  data types, 114–115
  formatter, 216, 222, 349, 369
  interoperability of, 110–111
  limitations of, 111
  messages
    error messages, 112
    format, 112–114
    method calls, 112
    response messages, 112
  open source implementation,
    111
  strings, 36
  transport method, 111
  Web Services, 232
  WSDL and, 115–116
SOAP <Envelope> tag, 113
SOAP-ENV namespace, 113
.soap extension, 75, 218
SOAPSUDS utility
  accessing, 129
  proxy generation, 135
  using, 130

WSDL generation by, 232
XmlTypeNamespace property generation, 292
SoapType attribute, 292
Software Publisher Certificate (SPC), 304
solution, description, 20
Solution Explorer
contents displayed, 20
description, 19
SortData( ) method, 124, 128
SortDelegate parameter, 276
Sorter class, 275–276
Sort( ) method, 276
source code
location of, 44, 71
obtaining, 373
sharing object, 117–118
SPC (Software Publisher Certificate), 304
sponsor
client-side, 173–174
definition, 164, 376
function of, 164
ISponsor interface, 165
lifetime, 166
location of, 165
multiple, 164
for multiple remote objects, 165
registering, 165
serializable, 165
server-side, 165–173
SponsorshipTimeout property, 165, 188
spoofing
definition, 377
description, 303
SQL queries, 27
SSL (secure socket layer), 309
StackBuilder sink
definition, 377
description, 87, 344
Standard Generalized Markup Language (SGML), 97–98
Start command, 130
Start New Instance command, 73
StartType property, 211, 212
startup directory, for Windows Service, 210
stateless objects, server-activated objects as, 32–33
Static Data Members attribute, 94
StaticGetAnInt( ) method, 93
Static Methods attribute, 94
StaticSetAnInt( ) method, 93
stream
decryption, 335
description, 345
encryption, 334–335
StringRepeater object, 289, 291
strong name
benefits of, 200
contents of, 200
creating, 201–202
definition, 377
description, 16

importance of, 302–303
security and, 200
Signcode signatures and, 303
storage, 302
versioning and, 221
Stroustrup, Bjarne, 16
Sun, Java invention by, 6
symmetric encryption
definition, 377
description, 310–311
synchronization primitives
asynchronous calls, 293
AutoResetEvent, 297
description, 294
Interlocked, 297–298
ManualResetEvent, 296–297
mutex, 295–296
table of, 295
Wait Handle, 295
synchronous calls
delegate use, 272–276
description, 344, 346, 359–360
SyncProcessMessage( ) method, 344, 346, 359–360
System.Console.Read( ) method, 49, 56
system-level authentication, 337–338
System namespace, 45
System.Reflection namespace, 202
System.Runtime.Remoting, 43–46, 125, 128
<system.runtime.remoting> element, 179–180
System.Runtime.Remoting. Lifetime namespace, 149–150, 156
System.Runtime.Remoting. Services.RemotingServices class, 215
System.SecurityCryptography namespace, 333
System.ServiceProcess.Service Base., 208
System.ServiceProcess.Service Base.Run( ) method, 209
System.Threading namespace, 294
System.Xml namespace, 106

T

tag
SGML, 97–98
SOAP, 113
XML
attributes, 100–101
closing, 100
elements, 100, 102
opening, 100
TCP channel
accessing, 47–48
binary formatter, 222
configuration file installation and, 177
creating, 48, 51
description, 35–36
HTTP channel compared, 74
using, 47–48
TcpChannel( ) constructor, 48, 52
template, channel, 370–371
Templates list, 43, 72–73
Thompson, Ken, 16
thread
creation, 276–277
definition, 294, 377

multiple, 294
synchronization primitives, 294–298
Threading.Sleep method, 150
Thread.Sleep( ) method, 85, 173
TimeSpan, 147, 150
<tModel> element, 234
TokenizeString( ) method, 335
ToString( ) method, 94
totalTimesCalled data member, 169
traffic, monitoring network, 306–307
Transmission Control Protocol/Internet Protocol (TCP/IP), 35
transparent proxy, 87–88
TransparentProxy class, 87
transport sink, 344, 345–346, 347
TraverseTree( ) method, 110
TripleDES encryption algorithm, 311
trusted entity, 339
try-catch statements, 64, 259, 345
type attribute
<activated> element, 182
<wellknown> element, 181, 183
TypeInfor property, ObjRef object, 222
Type Library Importer (TLBIMP.EXE), 14
<types> element, WSDL, 232

U

uniform resource identifier (URI)
GetObject parameter, 52
RegisterWellKnownServiceType parameter, 48
Universal Description, Discovery, and Integration (UDDI)
categories, 233–234
data structures, 234
description, 231
discovery document link, 231
public registries, 231
registries, 233–234
SDK, 233
Web site, 234
universally unique ID (UUID), 234
unmanaged code, 7–8, 10, 377
unmarshaling, 32, 377
unsafe code, 7, 377
unwrapped proxies, 137–138
updates, forcing, 226
URI. *See* uniform resource identifier
URI parameter, RemotingServices.Marshal( ) method, 140
url attribute, <client> element, 183–184
-url command-line switch, 130
<URL> element, 130
<URI.soap> element, 216
useDefaultLease member value, 161

User account, 213–214
user names, 337–338
UUID (universally unique ID), 234

V

validation request, 243
value, marshaling by, 32, 77–85
Value property, XmlTextReader object, 107
VB (Visual Basic), 4
verification request, 243
VerificationRequest class, 248–250, 259
VerificationRequest( ) constructor, 324–325, 335
VerificationRequest object, 240, 333–336
Verify button, 259, 316
verifyButton_Click method, 259–261, 316
VerifyCharge( ) method, 250, 252, 261, 316
VeriSign, 304, 306, 338
version information
  client-activated objects (CAOs) and, 225–226
  clients and, 222
  description, 221–222
  importance of, 221
  server-activated objects (SAOs) and, 222–225
virtual directory, 215, 216, 218–220
Virtual Directory Creation Wizard, 219
Virtual Machine (VM)
  Common Language Runtime (CLR), 4
  definition, 377
  Java, 6
virtual private network (VPN)
  definition, 377
  description, 308–309
Visual Basic (VB), 4
Visual C#. *See* C#
Visual C# Projects option, 43, 72–73
Visual Studio
  calendar control, 235
  Command Prompt, 212
  command window, 201
  Designer Interface, 206, 211
  INSTALLUTIL.EXE tool, 212, 214
  Windows Service creation, 206–208, 211–212
Visual Studio .NET
  Command Prompt option, 130
  components, 17–20
  edit windows, 18–19
  IDE window, 18–19
  opening screen, 17–18
  Solution Explorer, 19
  Tools command, 130
VM. *See* Virtual Machine
VPN (virtual private network), 308–309, 377

W

W3C (World Wide Web Consortium), 98
WAIS, 229

WaitHandle, 295
WaitOne( ) method, 279, 285, 291, 296, 297
web.config file, 215, 220
Web Forms, 236
Web Service Description Language (WSDL)
  description, 115–116
  file contents, 232
Web Services
  ASP.NET, 235–236
  benefits of, 230
  definition, 115, 230, 377
  deploying FasterCharge as, 262–265
  FasterCharge example, 30
    deploying as a Windows Service, 262–265
    deploying in Internet Information Service, 265–266
    designing, 237–243
    implementing, 244–261
  green pages information, 234
  requirements of, 230
  SOAP use by, 232
  technology models, 234
  UDDI registries, 231–234
  Web pages compared, 29–30
  white pages information, 233
  yellow pages information, 233
Web site, as presentation tier of multitiered application, 25–26
<wellknown> element
  <client> element, 183–184
  <service> element, 181–182
well-known object, 48, 377
WellKnownObjectMode. SingleCall value, 49
WellKnownObjectMode. Singleton value, 49
well-known service, 48, 377
white pages, 233
Win32 operating system application program interface (API)
  accessing through .NET Framework Class Library, 8
  description, 8
Windows DHCP server, Windows Service implementation of, 203
Windows Explorer, 56
Windows Forms (WinForm), deploying server objects as, 203
Windows Service
  adding Visual Studio components to, 208–209
  console application modification to, 204–208
  debugging, 210
  description, 203
  DHCP server implementation as, 203
  Dispose( ) method, 209
  InitializeComponent( ) method, 207, 209
  installing, 211–214
  Main( ) method, 209, 210
  OnStart( ) method, 207, 209, 210

OnStop( ) method, 207, 210
remote procedure call (RPC) implementation as, 203
security settings, 204
Services Control Manager, 204
starting and restarting, 204
startup directory, 210
Visual Studio use, 206–208, 211–212

WordPerfect, 10
World Wide Web Consortium (W3C), 98
wrapped proxies, 130–137, 140
WriteLine( ) method, 92–93
WSDL. *See* Web Service Description Language
wsdl.exe, 116

X

XCOPY command, 215
XML
advantages of, 98
defining data structures in, 98–101
discovery document, 231
HTTP channel use of, 36
in .NET Framework, 101–102, 103
reading and parsing files, 102, 104–108
Standard Generalized Markup Language (SGML), 97–98
tags, 100–101
version, 100
writing files, 108–110
WSDL, 232

XmlDocument class, 102, 108
XmlDocument.Save( ) method, 110
XmlNode class, 102
XML Schema, 114
XmlTextReader object, 102, 104, 106–107
XmlTypeNamespace property, 292
xsi:type attribute, 114

Y

yellow pages, 233